Exploring Blockchain Applications

Management Perspectives

Editors

Sezer Bozkus Kahyaoglu
Associate Professor
University of Johannesburg
College of Business & Economics
Department of Commercial Accounting
South Africa

Vahap Tecim
Professor
Management Information System Department
Dokuz Eylul University, Türkiye

CRC Press
Taylor & Francis Group
Boca Raton London New York

CRC Press is an imprint of the
Taylor & Francis Group, an **informa** business
A SCIENCE PUBLISHERS BOOK

First edition published 2024
by CRC Press
2385 NW Executive Center Drive, Suite 320, Boca Raton FL 33431

and by CRC Press
4 Park Square, Milton Park, Abingdon, Oxon, OX14 4RN

CRC Press is an imprint of Taylor & Francis Group, LLC

Library of Congress Cataloging-in-Publication Data (applied for)

ISBN: 978-1-032-48539-3 (hbk)
ISBN: 978-1-032-48541-6 (pbk)
ISBN: 978-1-003-38955-2 (ebk)

DOI: 10.1201/9781003389552

Typeset in Palatino Linotype
by Radiant Productions

Preface

The most important motivation for the emergence of this work has been to present a novel perspective on the issues discussed from the management perspective. From this point of view, it has been addressed in order to contribute to the use of the information revealed in business processes, especially for practical use. The progress brought about by technology every day, the effects of these developments on business processes, and the psychological pressure on the process owners cause the necessity to deal with the issues from an interdisciplinary perspective. It is examined in this work from an interdisciplinary perspective, which is stated about blockchain application in various sectors. Despite the speedy development process of the technological dimension of the blockchain, the handling of this technological development, especially in social sciences, lags behind. For example, while emphasizing the positive effects such as economic, social, and even individual opportunities and cost reductions, the adverse effects of blockchain applications are not emphasized. In this respect, it becomes essential to explain the said development by considering the risks arising from both practices and negative aspects.

By giving this information in the work, a study has emerged that will contribute to professionals from both academia and the business world. This work, which emerged with the authors contributing from different countries; is the result of an effort to be a reference source that will enable the emergence of new publications and new approaches in practice. In this context, we hope that it will be a source of new ideas and thoughts.

We sincerely thank our relatives and colleagues who supported us throughout this book production process. We express our appreciation for the efforts of our contributing chapter authors, and we sincerely congratulate all of them for participating in effective teamwork.

Sezer Bozkus Kahyaoglu

Vahap Tecim

Contents

Chapter 1
Introduction

Sezer Bozkus Kahyaoglu[1,*] and *Vahap Tecim*[2]

Blockchain is built upon a decentralized system of data management, and utilizes a peer-to-peer infrastructure (Marsal-Llacuna, 2018). It is a fact that blockchain applications have an enormous potential for industries and services as a basic and permanent solution for trust and transparency problems in the business world. Blockchain-based applications have revolutionized various industries worldwide. The features of transparency, security, and immutability offered by blockchain have made it suitable for fulfilling diverse requirements in different business fields and technological domains. This book aims to provide valuable insights to professionals and academics, as there is limited research available on Blockchain applications from a management perspective (Nesrene and Imene, 2022).

Blockchain is widely recognized as a "disruptive technology" capable of reshaping our social and economic systems. The key idea is that blockchain has the potential to transform the delivery of products and services, providing organizations with new perspectives to gain a competitive advantage and enhance their financial and operational performance. It is worth mentioning that blockchain technology serves not only organizational purposes but also holds strategic significance in facilitating peer-to-peer communication and securely storing a chronologically linked registry of transactions through cryptographic techniques (Kowalski et al., 2021).

[1] Assoc Prof of Finance, Kyrgyz Turkish Manas University, University of South Africa, University of Johannesburg.

[2] Professor of MIS, Dokuz Eylul University.

Email: vahap.tecim@deu.edu.tr

* Corresponding author: sezer.kahyaoglu@manas.edu.kg

Cryptocurrencies, especially bitcoin and generally accepted digital currencies are developing based on blockchain technology. While digital currencies and their applications are well-known for their usage and popularity, blockchain technology represents a "digital innovation" that introduces a trust-enhancing and transparent element in the digital era.

Blockchain has the potential to become the cornerstone and a "crucial tool for civil law" in the digital realm. It can serve as a new coordination mechanism that reduces transaction costs, expands trust, and enhances transparency in various practices. By enabling secure and reliable communication blockchain facilitates the establishment of mutual relationships in the digital age. Given its extensive range of applications, it is important to consider the broad-reaching and interconnected impact of blockchain across multiple sectors and sub-sectors, together with its widespread and far-reaching effects.

Blockchain is widely recognized as a "disruptive technology" that has the potential to reshape our social and economic systems. It is often referred to as the "new internet", "internet of trust" or "internet of value" to define blockchain applications. Some authors even argue that blockchain-based applications are the most transformative form of technology since the introduction of the "World Wide Web". However, this well-known technology is not well-understood by many people. For this reason, it is necessary to develop well-informed blockchain applications based on the managerial perspective of the technology and its probable foundational implications (Akgiray, 2019).

From this point of view, in this study, an attempt has been made to show and explain the applications of blockchain in different sectors as an example of the best practice. The link between the conceptual framework, which can form the basis of these explanations, and the studies dealing with the subject in the literature is also revealed together with the bibliometric analysis.

The chapters in the book have been prepared by a team of writers with both academic and professional work experience. Thus, practical examples are presented within the framework of ethical principles, emphasizing the conceptual framework and theoretical foundations of the subjects, as well as different needs in the business world. Blockchain applications are generally used in a wide variety of sectors within a financial and non-financial scope. In this respect, the book aims to explore different fields, including the private and public sectors from a management perspective. Accordingly, brief summaries of the chapters in the book are given as follows:

Chapter 2: Fundamentals of Blockchain: This chapter includes key definitions and technical concepts related to blockchain applications for the true understanding of the topics covered in the book and the creation of a common language for the readers.

Chapter 3: Bibliometrics Literature Review of Blockchain: The key works in the literature on blockchain applications are examined through bibliometric analysis. It has been attempted to provide a contribution including recommendations for new research topics. Future trends and potential research topics are presented with a systematic approach based on a critical literature review process together with major studies on blockchain best practices in the business world.

Chapter 4: Challenges of Blockchain Applications: While blockchain applications have many advantages for organizations, successfully implementing them is not easy. All aspects of the factors affecting the success of blockchain applications and emerging difficulties are discussed herein. The major challenges, problem areas, and emerging technology-based risks of blockchain applications in practice are introduced. This study was originally funded by Karabuk University Scientific Research Projects Coordination, Türkiye, with project number KBÜBAP-22-UIP-163.

Chapter 5: Security and Privacy on Blockchain Applications: Security is the basis of the advantages of blockchain technology. This chapter discusses all aspects of security and privacy issues and provides details to readers with a basic management perspective.

Chapter 6: Blockchain Applications in Healthcare: The key areas of change, opportunities, threats, weaknesses, and strengths that blockchain applications reveal in the healthcare sector are presented based on SWOT analysis.

Chapter 7: Blockchain Applications in Security: Technical information about the cryptographic algorithms and hash functions that are the basis of the blockchain and their security functions is presented.

Chapter 8: Blockchain Applications in Contract Management: This chapter describes the challenges, opportunities, and advantages of smart contract types for the use of smart contract models based on blockchain technology.

Chapter 9: Blockchain Applications in Marketing: Comprehensive explanations are presented within the framework of the innovations, opportunities, and risks that blockchain applications bring to the field of digital marketing.

Chapter 10: Blockchain Applications in Banking: The financial sector, particularly banking, has been the starting point where blockchain applications have made the most impact. This chapter explores the basic elements of the new banking approach based on blockchain technology and discusses and reveals future expectations.

Chapter 11: Block Chain Applications in Financial Markets: The main characteristic of blockchain technology is that it supports a decentralized structure. This structure has the potential to transform the functioning and future expectations of financial markets. However, there are risks as well as positive aspects of this transformation process. In this chapter, the scope, and effects of the change in financial markets are explored in all aspects based on blockchain applications with a management perspective.

Chapter 12: Blockchain Applications in Health Service: Data security and accuracy are important in healthcare services, which is one of the sectors where sensitive data is located and hence has the potential for being frequently abused. In this section, the background of the close relationship between the technologies used in the health sector and blockchain applications in the literature is investigated and the current situation is revealed through bibliometric analysis.

Chapter 13: Good Governance and Ethical Perspective of Blockchain Applications: The investigation of blockchain applications in terms of corporate governance and ethical standards is the subject of this chapter. In this context, there are two basic research questions. RQ 1: What are the ethical implications of applying blockchain applications? RQ 2: Are the users of blockchain applications applying good governance practices to mitigate ethical implications? For the analysis, QES, PRISMA, and CAPS techniques are applied. Policy recommendations are made based on the empirical findings.

Chapter 14: Blockchain Applications in Government: This chapter focuses on the utilization of blockchain technology in addressing the crisis of state legitimacy and its reproduction. This analysis involves an examination of state websites implementing blockchain as well as blockchain related documents from the Organization for Economic Co-operation and Development (OECD), and the European Union (EU). Policy recommendations based on blockchain applications are provided for governments in light of these findings.

Chapter 15: Blockchain Applications in the Public Sector: In this chapter, blockchain applications in government systems such as the electoral system, taxation, foreign aid and external debt, procurement, and property registration have been analyzed considering various countries' experiences. In addition to the positive aspects offered by the application in each implementation, an attempt has been made to assess the problems that have arisen and the potential threats. Policy recommendations are made for public services that could benefit from the implementation of blockchain technologies.

Chapter 16: Good Governance and Ethical Perspective of Block Chain Applications: In this chapter, the advantages, and disadvantages of blockchain applications within the framework of corporate governance and ethics are discussed. A conceptual framework is given about good governance, ethics, and blockchain applications based on the changing business model landscape.

Chapter 17: Accounting and Auditing Perspective of Block Chain Applications: One of the areas where blockchain applications are most affected is accounting and auditing. In this section, how accounting and auditing entered the process of change and transformation, the opportunities provided by the innovations that started with the blockchain applications, and the new risks that emerged are presented with examples.

An attempt has been made to reveal work that can guide future studies in the direction of providing information for blockchain applications within the managerial perspective. Please note that all the authors who contributed to the book are ready to cooperate and open to collaboration if requested.

References

Akgiray, V. (2019). The Potential for Blockchain Technology in Corporate Governance, OECD Corporate Governance Working Papers, No. 21, OECD Publishing, Paris, https://doi.org/10.1787/ef4eba4c-en.

Kowalski, M., Lee, Z. W. Y. and Chan, T. K. H. (2021). Blockchain technology and trust relationships in trade finance. Technological Forecasting & Social Change 166: 120641.

Marsal-Llacuna, M.-L. (2018). Future living framework: Is blockchain the next enabling network? Technological Forecasting and Social Change 128: 226–34. doi:10.1016/j.techfore. 2017.12.005.

Nesrine Ben Amor and Imène Ben Yahia. (2022). Investigating blockchain technology effects on online platforms transactions: Do Risk Aversion and Technophilia Matter? Journal of Internet Commerce 21(3): 271–296, DOI: 10.1080/15332861.2021.1961188.

Chapter 2
Fundamentals of Blockchain

Abdulkadir Tasdelen

2.1 Introduction

One of the most groundbreaking and revolutionary technologies to emerge in recent years is blockchain technology (Nakamoto, 2008). It's understandable that both organizations and consumers are keen to embrace this technology, considering its potential to transform a variety of industries, including finance, health, and supply chain management (Swan, 2015; Tapscott and Tapscott, 2016).

This chapter will delve into the fundamentals of blockchain technology, accompanied by numerous examples of its applications in various fields (Antonopoulos, 2014). There are vast blockchain applications, encompassing everything from cryptocurrencies (Nakamoto, 2008) to smart contracts (Gupta et al., 2020). Throughout this chapter, you will gain insights into the fundamental concepts essential to grasp before delving into blockchain technology. You will explore the exact definition of blockchain technology, its underlying structure or architecture, the different types of blockchains and consensus protocols employed. Furthermore you will discover crucial considerations for those intending to use blockchain technology when selecting a blockchain network type.

Department of Software Engineering, Ankara Yildirim Beyazit University, Ankara, Türkiye.
Email: abdulkadirtasdelen@aybu.edu.tr

2.2 Introductory Concepts

Prior to delving into blockchain technology, it would be beneficial to understand several fundamental concepts. These concepts include peer-to-peer (P2P) networks, cryptography, encryption and decryption, hash functions, hash chains, hash trees (Merkle trees), digital signatures, and timestamps (Bhutta et al., 2021).

The concept of a **P2P network** is closely associated with blockchain technology. In this peer-to-peer (P2P) network, a distributed network architecture is utilized to enable the sharing of resources, such as processing power and connectivity, among users. In such a network, each participating node or peer performs both server and client functions. Peer-A, can act as a client and directly request services or resources from Peer-B, who acts as a server, without the need for an intermediary. Similarly, when Peer-B operates as a client and requires content or services, peer A can assume the role of a server in that particular interaction (Bhutta et al., 2021).

The next concept is **cryptography**, which encompasses two types—symmetric key cryptography and asymmetric key cryptography. Cryptography is a mathematical technique employed to secure communication and protect data (Paar and Pelzl, 2010). Symmetric and asymmetric key cryptography utilize distinct keys for various cryptographic operations. This approach facilitates multiple functionalities to ensure confidentiality, integrity, authentication, and non-repudiation in secure communication (Bhutta et al., 2021).

The subsequent concept is **encryption**, which is utilized to guarantee the confidentiality of data within a security service. Encryption is the process of encoding plain text into ciphertext. **Decryption, on the other hand,** is the process of transforming ciphertext back into its plain text form. Both encryption and decryption operations can be performed using either symmetric or asymmetric cryptography (Bhutta et al., 2021; Stinson and Paterson, 2018).

A one-way mathematical function called a **hash** is used to protect the accuracy of data. It operates by calculating a fixed-size unique "hash value," for each input variable. As the hash function is unidirectional, it is impossible to retrieve the original data from a single output by reversing the process. A **hash chain** is formed by repeatedly executing the hash function on data. The data that the hash function is applied to in the current chain becomes the input of the following link. The data created by using the hash function in this case becomes the input of another ring of the chain. The same procedure is carried out repeatedly in this fashion until the chain is complete. Hash chains are widely used for preserving data integrity and are crucial to the blockchain (Bhutta et al., 2021).

Another concept is the **Merkle tree also known as a hash tree.** Merkle trees enable efficient and safe data verification by organizing data and associated hash values into a tree format. Each leaf node in the tree structure has a hash of several datasets labeled on it, and every non-leaf node has a hash of the nodes that comprise its child nodes (Bhutta et al., 2021; Merkle, 1988).

The final concepts are **digital signature** and **timestamp**. Digital signatures are used to verify the authorship of content in a similar way to physical signatures that are used every day. Public key cryptography is commonly used to implement digital signatures, where the signer signs a document with his private key, and the recipient verifies the signature with the signer's public key. Instead of the actual event's time, the timestamp indicates the time when the event was computer-recorded. It frequently keeps track of the day and time the incident happened and is precise to a fraction of a second. This timestamp's data is coherently re-encoded with the actual data to make it simple to compare two records and monitor development over time (Bhutta et al., 2021; Yi et al., 2022).

2.3 What is Blockchain Technology?

Blockchain technology is a distributed database that makes it possible to record and store data in a secure, decentralized manner. A blockchain is made up of several interconnected blocks, each of which contains a record of data. Cryptography is used to verify and encrypt the data in each block, ensuring that it cannot be changed or tampered with (Gupta et al., 2020; Nofer et al., 2017).

In comparison to conventional databases, blockchain technology has various benefits. In the first place, it is securer and less prone to hacking or attacks because it is dispersed throughout a network of computers. Second, once data is stored on the blockchain, it cannot be modified or erased since it is transparent and immutable. This makes utilizing blockchain to store private information like financial transactions or medical records desirable. Finally, blockchain makes it possible for multiple parties to share data in real-time without the use of an intermediary or centralized authority. Although it is still in its infancy, blockchain technology has the power to completely alter the way that data is stored and shared. Shortly, it will be possible for us to witness even more advanced applications for blockchain as more companies and organizations start using this technology (Gupta et al., 2020; Nofer et al., 2017).

2.4 Evolution of Blockchain Technology

Blockchain Technology was first conceptualized in 1991 by Stuart Haber and W. Scott Stornetta (Haber and Stornetta, 1991). Their initial project was developing a chain of blocks that was cryptographically secure such that document timestamps could not be altered. To improve efficiency and allow for the collection of extra documents on a single block, they modified their system in 1992 and added Merkle trees. The work of one individual or group by the name of Satoshi Nakamoto, however, is what gives blockchain history its first real relevance in 2008, as opposed to earlier years (Nakamoto, 2008).

The inventor of blockchain technology, Satoshi Nakamoto, is widely recognized. Nakamoto is assumed to be a person or group of persons that worked on Bitcoin, the first application of distributed ledger technology (DLT), however very little is known about them. In 2008, Nakamoto developed the first blockchain, which led to the development of the technology and its use in a variety of fields other than cryptocurrency. The initial whitepaper on the technology was released in 2009 by Satoshi Nakamoto. Given the decentralized feature, which ensured that no one would ever be in control of anything, he described in detail how the technology was perfectly suited to promote digital trust in the whitepaper (Nakamoto, 2008).

The DLT has advanced, giving rise to new applications that make up the history of the blockchain ever since Satoshi Nakamoto left the scene and gave control of Bitcoin development to other core developers.

When we look at the development of blockchain technology since 1991, we can divide this historical process into three phases: The first phase is the "Transaction" phase. The second phase is the "Contract" phase and the third is the "Application" phase (Bhutta et al., 2021; Cai et al., 2022).

2.4.1 *Phase 1 – Transactions*

Blockchain technology's initial phase, also called Blockchain 1.0 (Bhutta et al., 2021), concentrated on digital currency, particularly Bitcoin. As a decentralized digital currency that could be used for transactions without the aid of middlemen like banks, Bitcoin was developed in 2008. Without the need for a centralized authority, secure and transparent transactions were made possible by the blockchain technology that underpins Bitcoin (Nakamoto, 2008).

2.4.2 *Phase 2 – Contracts*

Smart contracts were the main topic of blockchain technology's second phase. Smart contracts enable the encoding of the specific terms and conditions of an agreement between a buyer and a seller directly into lines of code. These contracts self-execute. Without the use of intermediaries, they enable automated, secure, and transparent execution of agreements. The first blockchain platform to allow smart contracts was Ethereum (Buterin, 2014; Yi et al., 2022). This phase is called Blockchain 2.0 (Bhutta et al., 2021).

2.4.3 *Phase 3 - Applications*

The history and development of the blockchain go well beyond Ethereum and Bitcoin. Several initiatives that take advantage of the possibilities of blockchain technology have surfaced in recent years. Other initiatives have sought to remedy some of the limitations of Bitcoin and Ethereum in addition to creating new features using blockchain technology (Swan, 2015). A new phase known as Blockchain 3.0, therefore, started (Bhutta et al., 2021).

In this phase, Blockchain technology focuses on decentralized applications (dApps). These are blockchain-based applications that use smart contracts to execute code in a decentralized manner (Wood, 2018). Decentralized apps can be created for a range of use cases, including supply chain management, social media platforms, and decentralized finance (DeFi). Ethereum, EOS, and TRON are a few of the well-liked blockchain systems for dApps (Bhutta et al., 2021; Yi et al., 2022).

2.5 Types of Blockchain Technology

Blockchain technologies are of many different types. The most important difference between these types is the differentiation in access to the network and the authority in management. In this respect, blockchain consists of four different types. These are public, private, hybrid, and consortium (federated) blockchains (Swan, 2015). Although each type has its advantages and disadvantages, those who want to develop distributed applications using this technology should consider the differences (Bhutta et al., 2021).

2.5.1 *Public Blockchain*

The public blockchain comes first in this list. The most fundamental feature of a public blockchain network is that it is open to all users. Anyone can join the network on the public blockchain without needing any permission (Tapscott and Tapscott, 2016). This kind of blockchain verifies every transaction that is completed through it. Bitcoin and Ethereum are two examples of public blockchains (Buterin, 2014; Nakamoto, 2008).

2.5.2 *Private Blockchain*

Unlike the public blockchain, the private blockchain does not have a network structure that can be accessed by everyone. The process of joining the network is provided to any person by a certain blockchain authority. Therefore, unauthorized persons cannot be included in this network and cannot perform any transactions. Examples of private blockchains include Hyperledger Fabric and Corda (Brown et al., 2016; Cachin and Vukolic, 2017).

2.5.3 *Hybrid Blockchain*

Businesses that want the best of both worlds utilize a hybrid blockchain that combines the benefits of both private and public blockchains (Crosby et al., 2016). Businesses now have the option to build both a private, authorization system and a public, P2P system, enabling them to control access to their Blockchain data and determine which data is made public. On a hybrid blockchain, transactions and records are typically private, but access can be permitted through a smart contract if verification is necessary. Examples of hybrid blockchains include Dragonchain, Ardor, and Komodo (*Dragonchain*, n.d.; Vigna and Casey, 2015).

2.5.4 *Consortium Blockchain*

Similar to a hybrid blockchain, the Consortium blockchain (federated blockchain), contains both private and public blockchain functionalities. It varies, though, in that it makes use of numerous organizational members who operate together on a decentralized network (Biryukov et al., 2014). Consensus algorithms are under the control of predefined nodes in a consortium blockchain. The transaction initiation, retrieval, and validation are handled by a validation node. Transactions can be sent or received by member nodes. Examples of consortium blockchains include R3 Corda and Quorum (Brown et al., 2016).

The blockchain types, hybrid and consortium, are sometimes confused with one another. We can comprehend their main difference in terms of ownership. While consortium blockchains are owned and operated by a group of organizations, hybrid blockchains are owned by a single entity (Cachin and Vukolic, 2017).

Detailed information about the examples of different types of blockchains in this section is given under the heading "Popular Blockchain Frameworks".

2.6 How Blockchain works

Blockchain has a simple interface and operation. The P2P nature of the network necessitates that a user initiates a transaction. The said transaction is given a block once it is complete. All of the network's nodes receive the transaction block when it is broadcast to the network. After mining, the block is verified. Following a successful transaction, it is also included in the chain. Figure 2.1 shows the working processes of a blockchain (Rajasekaran et al., 2022).

Figure 2.1. The working processes of a Blockchain (Adapted from A Timeline and History of Blockchain Technology, n.d.).

2.7 The Architecture of Blockchain Technology

A basic blockchain architecture is made up of six major layers: the application, contract, incentive, consensus network, and data layers. Figure 2.2 depicts the architectural components of each layer. In the following sections, we will delve into these layers and their functions in detail (Xie et al., 2019).

The time-stamped data blocks are a component of the data layer. To handle the security of these blocks, a chain structure, Merkle (hash) tree, cryptography, and hash functions are used. Data propagation, verification, and distributed networking protocols are part of the network layer. For blockchain applications, the consensus layer offers a variety of consensus algorithms available. According to the processes outlined in the incentive layer, the nodes involved in administering applications receive incentives. The programming techniques for blockchain are displayed in the contact layer. The applications layer refers to blockchain-based business applications (Bhutta et al., 2021).

2.8 The Structure of a Block

The architecture of such a broadly defined blockchain system is depicted in Figure 2.3. Each P2P network member must independently store blockchain data while syncing every one of their blocks with those held by other peers using a consensus approach. In reality, the longest chain chosen by the majority of peer nodes serves as a representation of the consensus (Cai et al., 2018).

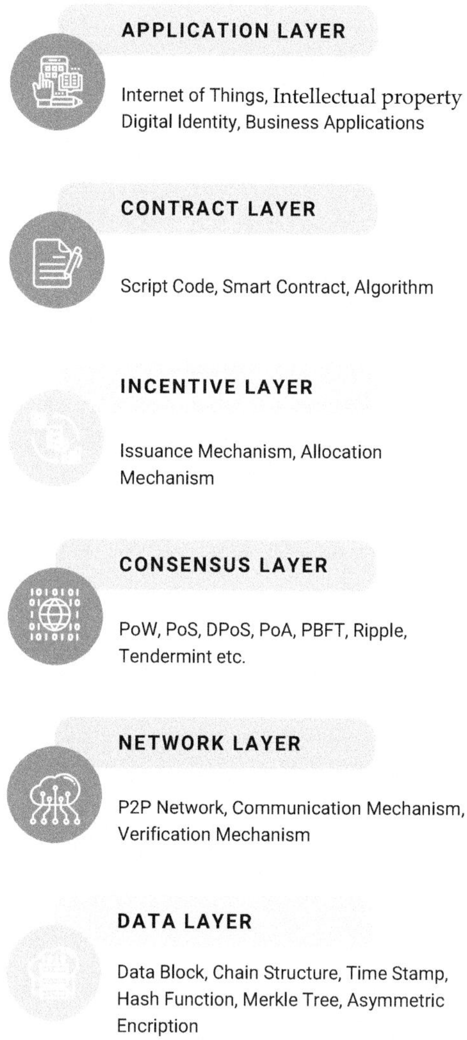

Figure 2.2. Layered architecture of Blockchain (Adapted from Xie et al., 2019).

The term "genesis block" refers to the initial block that is added to the blockchain (Nakamoto, 2008). A chain is formed when successive blocks are added chronologically and provide details about the preceding block. The information about Block #1 would be in Block #2, and the information about Block #2 would be in Block #3. This procedure keeps a permanent track of all network activity, creating an auditable record of events (Xie et al., 2019).

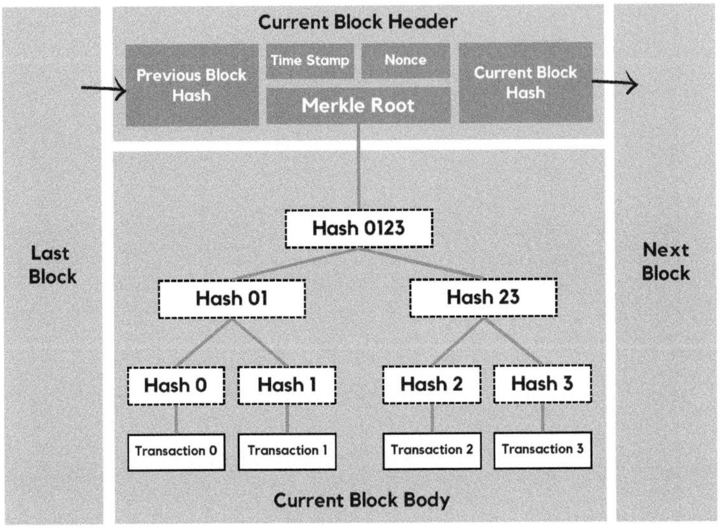

Figure 2.3. Simplified block structure (Adapted from Xie et al., 2019).

2.9 Basic Characteristics of Blockchain Technology

Blockchain technology has twelve key characteristics (Bhutta et al., 2021; Swan, 2015).

2.9.1 Decentralization

Blockchain technology operates without a central authority controlling the data or the network. This decentralized structure makes it more resistant to hacks and attacks.

2.9.2 Transparency

Blockchain technology allows for transparency in business transactions. This means that all parties involved in a transaction can see what is happening, ensuring that there is no room for corruption or fraud.

2.9.3 Autonomy

Due to the trust-based nature of blockchain technology, it can operate independently of third-party authorities. This attribute, particularly in the public blockchain, can be regarded to have a high degree of autonomy.

2.9.4 Security

Data can be stored securely and transparently. This means that businesses can avoid the risk of data breaches and cyberattacks.

2.9.5 *Immutability*

The blockchain's immutability means that the data it contains cannot be altered or manipulated.

2.9.6 *Traceability*

Traceability aims to keep track of the starting point, final destination, and order of numerous changes that the data goes through between nodes.

2.9.7 *Anonymity*

The preservation of anonymity is achieved by verifying transactions without disclosing any personal information regarding the individuals engaged in them. Nodal information is not required to be revealed or validated because data is sent between them using a predetermined mechanism that fosters confidence. As a result, data transfer can be carried out anonymously.

2.9.8 *Democratized*

In blockchain technology, all nodes are equally involved in the processes. The P2P structure of blockchain technology imbues the network with a democratic characteristic.

2.9.9 *Integrity*

Blockchain technology guarantees integrity with its decentralized structure and immutability. For this reason, any authority cannot make changes or updates contrary to the blockchain network's structure.

2.9.10 *Programmability*

Blockchain technology can be developed with many programming languages. For example, C++, Java, Python, Kotlin and Golang programming languages are just a few of them (Xie et al., 2019).

2.9.11 *Fault Tolerance*

Because blockchains are Byzantine Fault Tolerance (BFT) compliant, the network can still reach consensus even if some nodes are inactive or dysfunctional. The blockchain system's fault tolerance allows it to recover from Byzantine faults, where nodes start acting strangely owing to software bugs or malicious attacks, as well as failed interception errors, where some nodes are unable to join the consensus process for hardware or software reasons.

2.9.12 Automatic

The blockchain system's nodes can autonomously process and validate data using particular consensus methods.

2.10 Common Consensus Protocols

Each blockchain technology differs from the others. To make their platforms superior to one another, they all employ distinct consensus algorithms. They, therefore, play a crucial role in the network.

A blockchain consensus protocol is a collection of algorithms that controls how a blockchain network functions. These guidelines specify how new blocks are appended to the chain, how transactions are validated and stored, and what consensus procedures are employed to maintain the network's security (Tuan et al., 2017). The creation of new wallets or transmission transactions is only two examples of how users can communicate with the network according to blockchain protocols. Additionally, the main purpose of the protocols is to make sure that the right agreement is obtained and that no malicious nodes can persuade trustworthy nodes to approve invalid transactions (Bano et al., 2019).

The most commonly used protocols are Proof of Work (PoW), Proof of Stake (PoS), Delegated Proof of Stake (DPoS), Proof of Authority (PoA), Byzantine Fault Tolerance (BFT) (Bano et al., 2019; Kaur et al., 2021; Tuan et al., 2017).

2.10.1 Proof of Work (PoW)

PoW is a mechanism for confirming transactions independently on a blockchain network and avoiding double-spending. To create new blocks in a proof-of-work (PoW) system, network nodes compete to find solutions to a challenging mathematical puzzle called a hash function (Nakamoto, 2008). For malicious actors who could try to attack the network, this technique requires a significant amount of processing power and energy, which acts as a barrier to entrance.

When a node solves the hash function correctly, it broadcasts the outcome to the network so that other nodes may rapidly confirm it. The node that solves the problem first receives freshly minted money as compensation for its work (Nakamoto, 2008). Since it can be dominated by a small number of extremely large mining pools, PoW has attracted attention for both its high energy usage and potential for centralization. Despite this, it is still widely used as a common consensus mechanism in blockchain networks.

2.10.2 *Proof of Stake (PoS)*

PoS is another consensus process that is employed in various blockchain networks. In a PoS system, validators (also known as "forgers" or "minters") are chosen based on how much bitcoin they hold and "stake" in the network to add new blocks and approve transactions (King and Nadal, 2012).

In a PoS system validators are chosen based on their financial stake in the network, rather than competing to solve complex mathematical problems as in a PoW system (King and Nadal, 2012). The more cryptocurrency a validator possesses, the higher their likelihood of being chosen to generate a new block and receive transaction fees.

Since it does not require as much computer power or electricity, PoS is meant to be less energy-intensive than PoW (Buterin, 2014). As PoS is less dependent on large mining pools and does not favor those with the most computing power, it may minimize the possibility of centralization (Buterin, 2014).

Two possible downsides and challenges that PoS may present are the risk of "nothing-at-stake" attacks and the potential for centralization owing to the concentration of money among a limited number of powerful validators (King and Nadal, 2012).

2.10.3 *Delegated Proof of Stake (DPoS)*

DPoS protocol is a derived protocol from PoS. In this protocol, unlike PoS, witnesses are voted and they perform validation processes. DPoS is used in a variety of blockchain networks. Token holders in the network can vote to select a small number of nodes (known as "witnesses" or "delegates") who are in charge of creating new blocks and approving transactions in a DPoS system (Larimer, 2014).

In comparison to earlier consensus algorithms, DPoS is meant to be more effective and scalable since it allows for faster confirmation times for blocks and reduces the risk of centralization by limiting the number of validators. The chosen delegates are incentivized to act in the best interests of the network because they risk being voted out of office if they do not complete their tasks appropriately or act in a way that undermines the network (Larimer, 2014).

2.10.4 *Proof of Authority (PoA)*

PoA is the other consensus mechanism used in some blockchain networks that delegates the creation of new blocks and transaction validation to a group of known and trusted validators. In a PoA system, validators are frequently chosen based on their reputation or identification rather than their computing power or cryptocurrency holdings.

PoA is designed to be rapid and effective, with low energy usage and short transaction times. Yet, because the validators are known entities and there is less competition for block rewards, PoA foregoes some of the decentralization and security benefits of other consensus procedures such as PoW and PoS. PoA is frequently used in consortium or private blockchain networks with reputable and well-known members, such as in supply chain management and healthcare applications. The focus in these networks is on efficiency and privacy rather than the degree of decentralization present in public blockchain networks like Bitcoin or Ethereum.

2.10.5 Byzantine Fault Tolerance (BFT)

A consensus mechanism called **BFT** is used in distributed systems, including some blockchain networks, to guarantee that nodes can agree even in the presence of malicious or malfunctioning nodes. Nodes in a BFT system must agree on a common set of rules before new transactions can be validated and added to the blockchain. The nodes exchange messages and communicate with one another to reach a consensus. Each node then votes on the legitimacy of new transactions. The "Byzantine fault tolerance threshold" is the number of malicious or dysfunctional nodes that the system can tolerate before it becomes unreliable (Lamport et al., 1982).

2.11 Popular Blockchain Frameworks

2.11.1 Bitcoin

Blockchain-based P2P digital money systems were built on the foundational research work of Bitcoin. The primary contribution of Bitcoin research lies in the implementation of the concept of direct digital payments that do not rely on trusted third-party financial systems. By building a hashing chain, digital signatures combined with network timestamps exploit hash-based PoW. These connected blocks provide distributed databases with immutable records that can't be altered without performing another PoW. Nowadays, Bitcoin dominates the cryptocurrency market, but there are several alternative options (Nakamoto, 2008; Swan, 2015).

2.11.2 Ethereum

DApps have been developed using Ethereum as an open-source public Blockchain platform (*Ethereum Whitepaper | Ethereum.Org*, n.d.). Ethereum allows users to create rather complex apps with a variety of capabilities to carry out arbitrary actions, hence it can be used to create dApps other than cryptocurrency. dApps employ "smart contracts," a tiny, immutable software that is kept on the Ethereum network, to represent resources like money, real estate, and houses. This platform's main element is the Ethereum Virtual Machine (EVM), which is used to execute dApps for sophisticated algorithms. The contract-oriented programming language Solidity is used to create the code for dApps (*Solidity — Solidity 0.8.20 Documentation*, n.d.).

2.11.3 *Hyperledger Fabric*

A Private Blockchain distributed operating system called Hyperledger Fabric has been introduced by IBM. This is distinctive in that it is the first programmable Blockchain system that enables users to develop distributed applications independent from the use of native cryptocurrency (Androulaki et al., 2018). Sequential execution, nondeterministic code, and execution confidentiality were among the first order-execute design limitations to be recognized by the authors Androulaki et al. The blockchain community took a liking to this IBM suggestion. Moreover, there are some concerns with Hyperledger Fabric technologies. In the first place, they are unable to use permission-less blockchain, and in the second place, there aren't many programmers who can create applications that use this framework (Quasim et al., 2020).

2.11.4 *TRON*

Another open-source technology, called TRON, facilitates the development of a decentralized Internet and the necessary infrastructure for Blockchain applications (*TRON | Decentralize The Web*, n.d.). The TRON protocol offers significant benefits including high availability, scalability, and throughput to all dApps within the TRON ecosystem. Three layers comprise the TRON's architectural structure: the storage, core, and application layers. Since Google Protobuf is used, the TRON protocol is linguistically neutral. The core layer is composed of a variety of modules, including consensus, account management, and smart contracts. TRON possesses a streamlined set of instructions and an implementation of a virtual machine that operates based on a stack-based approach, resulting in enhanced efficiency. The computer language Solidity can be used to create dApps. For the TRON, a distributed storage protocol including block storage and state storage has been created (Bhutta et al., 2021; Francisco, 2018).

2.11.5 *MultiChain*

A platform called MultiChain is used to create and use private Blockchain applications. It facilitates the development and deployment of applications within a company or between companies in the financial sectors. It addresses the challenges of mining, privacy, and transparency as a private

Blockchain system by regulating user permissions globally. With complete control over transactions, only participants in MultiChain can view the activity on the Blockchain. Furthermore, mining reduces costs because no documentation effort is required. Using a simple API and command line interface, MultiChain is accessible on Windows, Linux, and Mac systems. Several blockchain applications place a high priority on scalability, which MultiChain addresses by regulating block size (*MultiChain*, n.d.).

2.11.6 OpenChain

OpenChain focuses on enabling compatibility with already-existing apps by supporting the development of highly scalable Blockchain applications. Interoperability fundamentally means that OpenChain offers a distinct, decentralized application gateway for pluggable integration with the backends of already-existing apps. This is a noteworthy technological accomplishment that has the potential to encourage the development and deployment of Blockchain applications on a large scale. With the help of the ORapid consensus algorithm and the OPEN Blockchain Load Balancing Protocol, OpenChain uses multi-threading and data parallelization to achieve great scalability. OpenChain utilizes a new technology called Scaffold to provide a payment schema for an application, which is subsequently translated into an OPEN state within the Blockchain application developed on OpenChain can be deployed on other Blockchain platforms that utilize their own unique consensus methods, thanks to OPEN cluster. OpenChain supports heterogeneous Blockchain platforms, enabling interoperability between different systems. The ORapid consensus approach can manage a sizable number of transactions at the beginning of OpenChain's transaction processing. The OPEN Blockchain Load Balancing Protocol is used by OpenChain to distribute transactions to other blockchains when the volume of transactions exceeds the capacity of the available approaches. This greatly expands the scope of data parallelization (*OpenChain 2.1 Is ISO/IEC 5230:2020, the International Standard for Open Source Compliance. – OpenChain*, n.d.).

2.11.7 Quorum

J.P. Morgan, one of the world's major financial firms, supports Quorum, an open-source permissioned Blockchain platform. Quorum, which is built on the Ethereum codebase and has J.P. Morgan's sponsorship, does indeed support blockchain technology. However, unlike Ethereum, Quorum provides a permissioned blockchain platform that offers enhanced contract privacy and facilitates the development of high-performance applications (Quorum: A Permissioned Implementation of Ethereum Supporting Data

Privacy, n.d). Although Quorum's fundamental functional model is very similar to Ethereum's, there are significant differences between the two in terms of performance, transaction and contract privacy, voting-based consensus mechanisms, management of network and peer permissions, and transaction and network security.

2.11.8 *IOTA*

IOTA is a blockchain platform that is open source and designed for the Internet of Things (IoT) to enable secure payment and communication. This is an IoT blockchain platform that uses DAG (Directed Acyclic Graph) (*IOTA | IOTA Wiki*, n.d.).

2.11.9 *Exonum*

Exonum is an open-source platform for building applications for heterogeneous domains, including the legal, financial, and governmental sectors. The framework was created in the Rust programming language using a service-oriented design, and it is intended for use with permissioned Blockchain applications in these fields. The Exonum architecture for permissioned blockchains makes it easier to construct application services with the Java Binding tool (Yanovich et al., 2018).

2.12 Potential Use Cases of the Blockchain

Blockchain technology can be used in diverse applications, such as banking and financial services, healthcare, supply chain management, e-voting, identity management, governance, energy resources and more. It is not equal to bitcoin but is one of the most successful applications of blockchain technology. Some visionaries predict that blockchain might influence the digital realm similarly to the internet. This section discusses some potential use cases of the blockchain (Monrat et al., 2019).

2.12.1 *Banking and Financial Services*

Blockchain technology may be used by banks to simplify operations and cut expenses. Banks, for instance, can utilize the blockchain to process payments more quickly and safely (Treleaven et al., 2017).

2.12.2 *Healthcare*

Health records for patients can be safely shared and stored using blockchain technology. This might help lower healthcare expenses while also enhancing care quality (Shahnaz et al., 2019).

2.12.3 *Supply Chain Management*

The supply chain can be followed using blockchain to track the flow of goods. This could support firms in ensuring that goods are delivered on schedule and by expectations (Álvarez-Díaz et al., 2017).

2.12.4 *Identity Management*

Blockchain can be used to authenticate individuals and make sure they are whom they claim to be. This might be used for things like document authentication (Imam et al., 2021) and online voting (Chaieb et al., 2019).

2.12.5 *Internet of Things*

Blockchain technology can be used to control how the connectedness of devices made possible by the IoT is handled. This could assist businesses in monitoring their IoT equipment and guarding against unauthorized access or manipulation (Christidis and Devetsikiotis, 2016).

2.13 Conclusion

In this section, the fundamentals of blockchain technology are covered. Several industries, including finance, supply chain management, healthcare, and others, might use blockchain technology. It has the potential to transform how we conduct business and trade value while also improving transparency, efficiency, and security in several industries. There are several consensus processes used to confirm transactions, including Proof of Work, Proof of Stake, Delegated Proof of Stake, Byzantine Fault Tolerance, and Proof of Authority. Blockchains come in a variety of forms, including public, private, hybrid, and consortium blockchains. To create and implement their blockchain networks, developers can make use of blockchain frameworks like Ethereum, Hyperledger Fabric, Corda, Quorum, and IOTA.

The fundamentals of blockchain technology are discussed in detail in this section. The next sections will go into great detail on current blockchain technology applications. Also, you will be able to discover the advantages and disadvantages, as well as the challenges and solutions of this technology.

References

A timeline and history of blockchain technology. (n.d.). Retrieved March 2, 2023, from https://www.techtarget.com/whatis/feature/A-timeline-and-history-of-blockchain-technology.

Álvarez-Díaz, N., Herrera-Joancomartì, J. and Caballero-Gil, P. (2017). Smart contracts based on blockchain for logistics management. ACM International Conference Proceeding Series. https://doi.org/10.1145/3109761.3158384.

Androulaki, E., Barger, A., Bortnikov, V., Muralidharan, S., Cachin, C. et al. (2018). Hyperledger fabric: a distributed operating system for permissioned blockchains. Proceedings of the 13th EuroSys Conference, EuroSys 2018, 2018-January. https://doi.org/10.1145/3190508.3190538.

Antonopoulos, A. M. (2014). Mastering Bitcoin: Unlocking Digital Cryptocurrencies. O'Reilly Media.

Bano, S., Sonnino, A., Al-Bassam, M., Azouvi, S., McCorry, P. et al. (2019). SoK: Consensus in the Age of Blockchains. pp. 183–198. *In*: AFT '19: Proceedings of the 1st ACM Conference on Advances in Financial Technologies. ACM: Association for Computing Machinery: New York, NY, USA. (2019). https://doi.org/10.1145/3318041.3355458.

Bhutta, M. N. M., Khwaja, A. A., Nadeem, A., Ahmad, H. F., Khan, M. K. et al. (2021). A survey on blockchain technology: evolution, architecture and security. IEEE Access 9: 61048–61073. https://doi.org/10.1109/ACCESS.2021.3072849.

Biryukov, A., Khovratovich, D. and Pustogarov, I. (2014). Deanonymisation of clients in bitcoin P2P network. Proceedings of the ACM Conference on Computer and Communications Security, 15–29. https://doi.org/10.1145/2660267.2660379.

Brown, R. G., Carlyle, J., Grigg, I. and Hearn, M. (2016). Corda: An Introduction.

Buterin, V. (2014). Ethereum: A Next-Generation Smart Contract and Decentralized Application Platform.

Cachin, C. and Vukolic, M. (2017). Blockchain Consensus Protocols in the Wild. ArXiv.

Cai, L., Li, Q. and Liang, X. (2022). Advanced Blockchain Technology. Advanced Blockchain Technology. https://doi.org/10.1007/978-981-19-3596-1.

Cai, W., Wang, Z., Ernst, J. B., Hong, Z., Feng, C. et al. (2018). Decentralized applications: the blockchain-empowered software system. IEEE Access 6: 53019–53033. https://doi.org/10.1109/ACCESS.2018.2870644.

Chaieb, M., Yousfi, S., Lafourcade, P. and Robbana, R. (2019). Verify-your-vote: A verifiable blockchain-based online voting protocol. Lecture Notes in Business Information Processing 341: 16–30. https://doi.org/10.1007/978-3-030-11395-7_2/COVER.

Christidis, K. and Devetsikiotis, M. (2016). Blockchains and smart contracts for the internet of things. IEEE Access 4: 2292–2303. https://doi.org/10.1109/access.2016.2566339.

Crosby M., Nachiappan, Pattanayak Pradan, Verma Sanjeev and Kalyanaraman Vignesh et al. (2016). BlockChain Technology: Beyond Bitcoin.

Dragonchain. (n.d.). Retrieved May 27, 2023, from https://dragonchain.com/.

Ethereum Whitepaper | ethereum.org. (n.d.). Retrieved March 14, 2023, from https://ethereum.org/en/whitepaper/.

Francisco, S. (2018). Advanced Decentralized Blockchain Platform Whitepaper Version: 2.0.

Gupta, S., Sinha, S. and Bhushan, B. (2020). Emergence of blockchain technology: fundamentals, working and its various implementations. SSRN Electronic Journal. https://doi.org/10.2139/SSRN.3569577.

Haber, S. and Stornetta, W. S. (1991). How to time-stamp a digital document. Journal of Cryptology 3(2): 99–111. https://doi.org/10.1007/BF00196791/METRICS.

IOTA | IOTA Wiki. (n.d.). Retrieved March 14, 2023, from https://wiki.iota.org/learn/about-iota/an-introduction-to-iota/.

Imam, I. T., Arafat, Y., Alam, K. S. and Aki, S. (2021). DOC-BLOCK: A blockchain based authentication system for digital documents. Proceedings of the 3rd International Conference on Intelligent Communication Technologies and Virtual Mobile Networks, ICICV 2021: 1262–1267. https://doi.org/10.1109/ICICV50876.2021.9388428.

Kaur, S., Chaturvedi, S., Sharma, A. and Kar, J. (2021). A research survey on applications of consensus protocols in blockchain. Security and Communication Networks, 2021. https://doi.org/10.1155/2021/6693731.

King, S. and Nadal, S. (2012). PPCoin: Peer-to-peer crypto-currency with proof-of-stake. https://www.peercoin.net/read/papers/peercoin-paper.pdf.

Lamport, L., Shostak, R. and Pease, M. (1982). The Byzantine Generals Problem. ACM Transactions on Programming Languages and Systems, 382–401. https://www.microsoft.com/en-us/research/publication/byzantine-generals-problem/.

Larimer D. (2014). Delegated Proof of Stake (DPOS). White Paper.

Merkle, R. C. (1988). A digital signature based on a conventional encryption function. Lecture Notes in Computer Science (Including Subseries Lecture Notes in Artificial Intelligence and Lecture Notes in Bioinformatics) 293 LNCS, 369–378. https://doi.org/10.1007/3-540-48184-2_32/COVER.

Monrat, A. A., Schelén, O. and Andersson, K. (2019). A survey of blockchain from the perspectives of applications, challenges, and opportunities. IEEE Access 7: 117134–117151. https://doi.org/10.1109/ACCESS.2019.2936094.

MultiChain. (n.d.). Retrieved March 14, 2023, from https://www.multichain.com/blog/.

Nakamoto, S. (2008). Bitcoin: A Peer-to-Peer Electronic Cash System. www.bitcoin.org.

Nofer, M., Gomber, P., Hinz, O. and Schiereck, D. (2017). Blockchain. Business and Information Systems Engineering 59(3): 183–187. https://doi.org/10.1007/S12599-017-0467-3.

OpenChain 2.1 is ISO/IEC 5230:2020, the International Standard for open source compliance. - OpenChain. (n.d.). Retrieved March 14, 2023, from https://www.openchainproject.org/featured/2020/12/15/openchain-2-1-is-iso5230.

Paar, C. and Pelzl, J. (2010). Understanding Cryptography: A Textbook for Students and Practitioners. Springer. https://doi.org/10.1007/978-3-642-04101-3.

Quasim, M. T., Khan, M. A., Algarni, F., Alharthy, A. and Alshmrani, G. M. M. et al. (2020). Blockchain Frameworks. Studies in Big Data 71: 75–89. https://doi.org/10.1007/978-3-030-38677-1_4/COVER.

Quorum: A permissioned implementation of Ethereum supporting data privacy. (n.d.). Retrieved March 14, 2023, from https://github.com/ConsenSys/quorum.

Rajasekaran, A. S., Azees, M. and Al-Turjman, F. (2022). A comprehensive survey on blockchain technology. Sustainable Energy Technologies and Assessments 52: 102039. https://doi.org/10.1016/J.SETA.2022.102039.

Shahnaz, A., Qamar, U. and Khalid, A. (2019). Using blockchain for electronic health records. IEEE Access 7: 147782–147795. https://doi.org/10.1109/ACCESS.2019.2946373.

Solidity — Solidity 0.8.20 documentation. (n.d.). Retrieved March 14, 2023, from https://docs.soliditylang.org/en/latest/.

Stinson, D. R. and Paterson, M. B. (2018). Cryptography Theory and Practice Fourth Edition. CRC Press.

Swan, M. (2015). Blockchain: Blueprint for a New Economy. O'Reilly.

Tapscott, D. and Tapscott, A. (2016). Blockchain revolution: how the technology behind bitcoin is changing money, business, and the world. 348.

Treleaven, P., Brown, R. G. and Yang, D. (2017). Blockchain technology in finance. Computer 50(9): 14–17. https://doi.org/10.1109/MC.2017.3571047.

TRON | Decentralize The Web. (n.d.). Retrieved March 14, 2023, from https://tron.network/about?lng=en.

Tuan, T., Dinh, A., Liu, R., Zhang, M., Chen, G. et al. (2017). Untangling Blockchain: A Data Processing View of Blockchain Systems. https://doi.org/10.1109/TKDE.2017.2781227.

Vigna, Paul and Casey, M. (2015). The age of cryptocurrency: how bitcoin and digital money are challenging the global economic order. 357. St. Martin's Publishing Group.

Wood, G. (2018). Ethereum: A secure decentralised generalised transaction ledger eip-150 revision.

Xie, J., Tang, H., Huang, T., Yu, F. R., Xie, R. et al. (2019). A survey of blockchain technology applied to smart cities: research issues and challenges. IEEE Communications Surveys and Tutorials 21(3): 2794–2830. https://doi.org/10.1109/COMST.2019.2899617.

Yanovich, Y., Ivashchenko, I., Ostrovsky, A., Shevchenko, A. and Sidorov, A. et al. (2018). Exonum: Byzantine fault tolerant protocol for blockchains. https://exonum.com/theme/public/img/downloads/wp_consensus_181227.pdf.

Yi, X., Yang, X., Kelarev, A., Lam, K. Y. and Tari, Z. et al. (2022). Blockchain Foundations and Applications. https://doi.org/10.1007/978-3-031-09670-9.

Chapter 3
The Systematic Review of Blockchain
A Bibliometric Analysis

Serhat Burmaoglu,[1,*] *Junus Ganiev*[2] and *Azamat Maksudunov*[2]

3.1 Introduction to Blockchain

First described in a 2008 white paper by an anonymous individual using the pseudonym Satoshi Nakamoto, blockchain is a technology that encompasses a digital ledger. The whitepaper proposed a decentralized electronic cash system, called Bitcoin, which used a novel technology called a blockchain to securely record transactions. Essentially, a blockchain is a distributed database that maintains a growing list of records, called blocks, linked, and secured using cryptography. Each block contains a cryptographic hash, timestamp, and transaction data. This structure creates an immutable and transparent ledger of transactions that can be maintained by a network of computers without requiring a central authority.

The first successful implementation of a blockchain was the Bitcoin network, which went live in 2009. Since then, the use of blockchain technology has expanded beyond digital currencies and is now applied in various industries, including finance, supply chain management and

[1] Izmir Katip Celebi University, Izmir, Turkiye; Kyrgyz-Turkish Manas University, Bishkek, Kyrgyzstan.

[2] Kyrgyz-Turkish Manas University.

Email: junus.ganiev@manas.edu.kg; azamat.maksudunov@manas.edu.kg

* Corresponding author: serhat.burmaoglu@ikcu.edu.tr; serhat.burmaoglu@manas.edu.kg

even voting systems. Blockchain is considered to be important because of its distributed ledger technology, which enables records to be kept in a secure and transparent manner. Blockchain's decentralized nature makes it tamper-proof, allowing digital assets to be transferred securely without intermediaries. The rise of blockchain has also led to the creation of numerous other cryptocurrencies, as well as the development of decentralized applications and platforms that run on top of blockchain technology. All in all, the invention of the blockchain has the potential to revolutionize a number of industries by providing a secure and transparent method for the transfer of value and information.

This chapter aims to provide an overview of publications on blockchain, with a view to visualizing a bigger picture of blockchain technology in this decade through scientific publications. Although there are many review studies on blockchain technology in the literature, it can be said that every review study has the potential to create new information, since the subject is seen as a popular topic by researchers, especially due to the sharp increase in the number of publications since 2000s. The study is outlined as follows; after introduction the evolutionary review of blockchain has been studied to understand literally the milestones and developments in blockchain technology. Then, in the third section, methodology has been demonstrated and findings have been presented in the fourth section. Finally, a discussion and the conclusion have been presented in the fifth section.

3.2 Literature Review and Background of Blockchain

It is widely accepted that the beginning of the blockchain technology (BCT) started with the paper published by Nakamoto in 2008 (Butijn et al., 2019; Konstantinidis et al., 2018; Ahmad et al., 2022). A new electronic payment system called BCT, based on cryptographic proof rather than trust, was introduced. This system allows any two interested parties to connect with one another directly without the involvement of a third party. The proposed system also requires minimal structure, allowing for easy scalability and flexibility in terms of node participation.

In broad terms, blockchain refers to a form of distributed ledger technology (DLT) that employs cryptographic techniques to store data in blocks and interconnect them. The primary objective of blockchain technology is to eliminate the requirement for intermediaries and substitute them with a decentralized network of online users who work together to validate transactions and uphold the integrity of the ledger (Andoni et al., 2019). This technology facilitates secure, transparent, and unalterable transactions among multiple parties without the involvement of a third-party intermediary. Each block contains information about previous blocks as well as new transaction data which are cryptographically secured to ensure their integrity. This makes it difficult to tamper with any part of the chain since all other parts would be affected by such changes (Guo et al., 2021; Iqbal and Matulevicius, 2019).

By contrast centralized BCT systems do not have a need for a trusted third party for all kinds of transactions and any two parties willing to do business can proceed directly with each other. In the BCT system, an electronic coin is defined as a series of digital signatures. The blockchain network is maintained by multiple computers (or nodes) connected to it that validate transactions on the network through consensus algorithms like Proof-of-Work or Proof-of-Stake before they can be added to a new block and stored permanently on the blockchain database (Andoni et al., 2019). In order to transfer ownership of a coin to a succeeding owner, the current owner must append the next owner's public key and a digitally signed hash of the preceding transaction to the end of the coin. The chain of ownership can be authenticated by the recipient of the payment through signature verification. However, this method does not provide the recipient with any assurance that the coin has not been used twice, as it is impossible to check whether the previous owner signed the previous transaction (Nakamoto, 2008; Butijn et al., 2019).

On the other hand, the conventional method calls for a single, centralized body to keep track of all transactions and modifications. It was to run and inject concurrency control across the database (Nakamoto, 2008; Singhal et al., 2018; Fuloria, 2020). A centralized transaction system is a traditional method of storing and sharing data where all the information is stored in one central location. This means that there are single points of failure which can be vulnerable to cyber-attacks or manipulation by malicious actors. It also requires trust between parties as they have no control over how their data is being used or shared with third parties (Andoni et al., 2019).

Blockchain-based solutions are becoming increasingly popular due to their enhanced security features which make them less vulnerable to malicious attacks than traditional systems (Iqbal and Matulevicius, 2019). In addition to finance and cryptocurrencies, there are ongoing initiatives to utilize blockchains for voting systems and identity verification processes. Blockchain technology is an innovative approach to securely store and distribute data, holding the potential to revolutionize various sectors such as energy supply companies, emerging businesses, financial institutions, and governmental bodies (Andoni et al., 2019). The implementation of blockchain technology is expected to revolutionize various industries in the coming years, albeit with a gradual and arduous process of adoption. The utilization of this technology is anticipated to enhance the financial and public service sectors in the foreseeable future (Javaid et al., 2021). The innovative technology of blockchain holds the potential to transform numerous industries by offering solutions for decentralization, trust, identity, data ownership, and data-driven decision-making, all of which are crucial in the contemporary digital landscape. Furthermore, blockchain technology can facilitate the creation of self-executing smart contracts that operate autonomously upon the fulfillment of predetermined conditions, without the need for any third-party intervention or influence. This helps reduce costs associated with traditional contract management processes while also providing greater security against fraud or malicious activities (Guo et al., 2021).

Besides its popularity and benefits, there are pitfalls and the most mentioned ones in literature are related to its complicated usability, legalization, wasted resources, and latency (Islam et al., 2020). Scalability is also a major challenge for blockchain technology. As more users join a network, it becomes increasingly difficult to process transactions in an efficient manner due to the limited computing power and storage capacity available on each node. Security poses another challenge as malicious actors may attempt to gain unauthorized access or manipulate data stored on blockchains, which could lead to financial losses for the parties involved. Regulatory uncertainty also poses a risk since governments are still trying to figure out how best to regulate this new technology while ensuring consumer protection at the same time. Finally, there is a lack of understanding among the general public regarding the exact functionality of blockchain which makes adoption slower than expected despite its potential benefits over traditional systems (Konstantinidis et al., 2018).

While blockchain diffuses to different sectors, BCT has also shifted too. According to the literature, Blockchain has four generations (AL-Ashmori et al., 2022; Colomo-Palacios et al., 2020). However, the primary era of blockchain answers (Blockchain 1.0) advanced into a number of systems such as IBM Blockchain, Hyperledger Sawtooth, Ethereum, Hyperledger Fabric, and Quorum and now taken into consideration in Blockchain 2.0. The focus on decentralized applications is further expanded by Blockchain 3.0, which fundamentally overhauls blockchain. Blockchain 3.0 aims to enhance the visibility of blockchain-based solutions by broadening the scope of traditional industries such as finance and goods transactions to encompass government, supply chain management, smart energy, health, market surveillance, and education. The next-generation platform gains additional capabilities thanks to these new applications. Important elements like platform connectivity and more sophisticated "smart contracts" are included in this. As a result, Blockchain 4.0, a new generation of solutions, is now being developed.

Another point of view is phase-based classification. With this perspective, blockchain research has been classified in three phases: (i) the emergence of terms like "bitcoin" and "cryptocurrencies" in the

1st stage (2008–2013); (ii) the growing expansion of the "bitcoin literature" in the 2nd stage (2014–2015); and (iii) the relevance of blockchain technology and "smart contracts" in the 3rd stage (2016 onwards) (Gupta and Dhawan, 2020). These findings are supported by other review studies on this topic (Miau and Yang, 2018; Dabbagh et al., 2019; Casino et al., 2019; AL-Ashmori et al., 2022).

Due to its popularity and diffusion int different sectors, there are various review studies in the literature especially after 2016 with an increasing trend. Reviewed papers have been listed and summarized in Table 3.1.

As can be seen in Table 3.1, the main part of the review studies consists of papers covering the period from the year 2007 onwards. Both scientific and grey literature were studied based on international databases such as WoS and Scopus and search engines such as Google Scholar. The number of articles ranges from 35 to 4629 with an average of approximately 1500 documents.

One of the earliest review studies on BCT was conducted based on a limited number of studies (35 papers) and concluded that BCT can be utilized to promote a decentralized and private-by-design internet of things (IoT). The authors identified eighteen use forms of this technology in the bibliography, four of which were specifically addressed to IoT applications, while several others were found to support data management with privacy as a primary goal. Issues related to integrity, anonymity, and adaptability have been identified by the research team during their review process; however, they also provided recommendations for future work towards addressing those issues effectively (Conoscenti et al., 2016). Another paper published in the same year aimed to carry out a mapping study with the objective of gathering all pertinent BCT research (41 publications), in order to comprehend the present research subjects, difficulties, and future directions. According to authors, the majority of research (80%) focuses on exposing and addressing Blockchain's privacy and security flaws, however many suggested fixes lack tangible evidence of their efficacy (Yli-Huumo et al., 2016).

Miau and Yang (2018) undertook a study utilizing 801 academic papers from the Scopus database to examine the expansion of literature and author productivity in the subject of Blockchain. The findings of their study revealed the existence of three distinct phases of Blockchain research. The first phase, spanning from 2008 to 2013, was characterized by topics pertaining to Bitcoin and cryptocurrencies. The second phase, occurring between 2014 and 2015, witnessed a significant surge in literature on Bitcoin. The third and final phase, commencing after 2016, saw a greater emphasis on techniques such as blockchain and smart contracts. Another study based both scientific (Scopus) and grey literature (Google Scholar)

Table 3.1. Overview of previous review studies on BCT.

Studies	Database	Time Span	Used Keywords	Doc.
Conoscenti et al., 2016	IEEE Xplore; ACM Digital Library; SpringerLink; ScienceDirect; Google	–2016	"blockchain"	35
Yli-Huumo et al., 2016	IEEE Xplore, ACM Digital Library, Springer Link, ScienceDirect, EBSCO, and PLOSOne	2012–2015	"blockchain"	41
Miau and Yang, 2018	Scopus	2008–2017	'Blockchain', 'bitcoin', 'ethereum', 'hyperledger', 'cryptocurrency' and 'smart contract'	801
Casino et al., 2019	Scopus/Google Scholar	2014–2018	"blockchain"	260
Dabbagh et al., 2019	Web of Science (WoS)	2013–2018	'Blockchain', 'bitcoin', 'cryptocurrency', 'ethereum', and 'smart contract	995
Firdaus et al., 2019	Scopus	2013–2018	"blockchain"	1119
Xu et al., 2019	Web of Science (WoS)	2015–2019	"blockchain"	756
Kamran et al., 2020	Web of Science (WoS)	2008–2019	"Blockchain & IoT", "Blockchain AND Internet of thing", "Blockchain AND Internet of things".	151
Colomo-Palacios et al., 2020	Google Scholar	2016–2020	"Blockchain" AND "Assessment Model."	400
Gupta and Dhawan, 2020	Scopus	2010–2018	"Blockchain" OR "Bitcoin" OR "Ethereum" OR "Hyperledger" OR "Cryptocurrency" OR "Smart contract".	4629
Guo et al., 2021	Web of Science (WoS)	2013–2020	"blockchain"	3826
Luo et al., 2021	Web of Science (WoS)	2014–2020	"BLOCKCHAIN" and "BLOCKCHAINS"	2993

Table 3.1 contd. ...

...Table 3.1 contd.

Studies	Database	Time Span	Used Keywords	Doc.
Nasir et al., 2021	Scopus, Web of Sciences, Emerald, Elsevier, Google	2015–2020	"Blockchain" OR "Bitcoin" OR "Cryptocurrency" OR "Digital Currency" OR "Technology"	1965
Prajapati and Singh, 2021	Scopus	2017–2021	TITLE (blockchain technology) AND PUBYEAR > 2016 AND PUBYEAR < 2022	2651
Wang et al., 2021	Web of Science (WoS)	2013–2019	"blockchain"	2451
Zhou et al., 2021	Web of Science (WoS)	2013–2018	"blockchain"	2870
Ahmad et al., 2022	Google Scholar	2017–2021	"Blockchain AND Survey OR Blockchain AND Review"	801
Kuzior and Sira, 2022	Scopus	2007–2021	"blockchain"	1842

conducted by Casino et al. (2019) for the period of 2014–2018. The authors have provided an all-encompassing categorization of diverse sectors that are facilitated by Blockchain Technology (BCT), which includes supply chain, business, healthcare, Internet of Things (IoT), privacy, and data management. The majority of the available applications are business-oriented, followed by governance, IoT, and data management applications for all years.

Dabbagh et al. (2019) analyzed papers (995) from WoS for the period of 2013 to 2018 in their bibliometric study. According to the results, 2016 was a turning point in terms of the number of publications on BCT. Authors revealed that in 2013 there were only two papers and while in 2017 and 2018, over 400 papers were published each year and the USA has been identified as the country with a high number of publications. Xu et al. (2019) also investigated scientific literature (756) from WoS for almost the same period (2015–2019) of time. The findings of this paper are very close to those of the Dabbagh et al. (2019) study. In the year 2016, there was a significant surge in the quantity of papers published on the topic of BCT. The three nations that produced the highest number of papers on this subject were identified as the United States, United Kingdom, and Germany.

In contrast to these two papers, Firdaus et al. (2019) focused on papers (1119) from Scopus for the same period. The USA, China and Germany are reported as the most productive countries and 2016 was the turning point. The authors have disclosed that the adoption of BCT has been motivated by various factors, including but not limited to safeguarding data privacy, facilitating digital storage, ensuring data security, managing big data, and utilizing distributed databases.

Kamran et al. (2020) analyzed papers (151) from Web of Science (WoS) for the period 2008 to 2019. In this study, China was found as the most productive country, followed by the USA and South Korea. Moreover, the study revealed that BCT has been the focus of academic studies in the last several years and the number of papers and citations has been growing rapidly since 2017. On the other hand, Gupta and Dhawan (2020) carried out a similar study on the same topic based on the Scopus papers (4629) in a 9-year period from 2010 to 2018. This study also confirmed the fact that the number of academic outputs increased from 2016 to 2017. The USA, China and the UK were found to be the top three countries to have contributed to BCT research. Another study was conducted by Colomo-Palacios et al. in 2020. The authors conducted a bibliometric study based on papers retrieved Google Scholar covering the period from 2016 to 2020. Through this study a total of 19 factors (14 technical and 5 business contexts) were identified.

Further studies were mainly based on papers from the Web of Science for the period 2013 to 2020. Guo et al. (2021) analyzed 3826 papers in 7 years from 2013 to 2020, Luo et al. (2021) included 2993 papers for the 2014 to 2020 period, Wang et al. (2021) conducted a research based on 2451 papers for the period 2013 to 2019 and Zhou et al. (2021) analyzed 2870 papers for the same period. According to Guo et al. (2021) after 2016, the quantity of publications related to BCT experienced a significant surge, escalating from 469 articles in 2017 to 1434 articles in 2018, and ultimately culminating in 1729 articles in 2019. Authors revealed that BCT research is concentrated on BCT applications such as finance, healthcare and supply chain management. This study also reported China, USA and UK the top contributors to the field. Luo et al. (2021) achieved similar results revealing that the number of scientific publications on BCT was very low until the year 2016, after which the number has demonstrated a sharp rise. Again, China was found to be the leader followed by USA and South Korea. The study has identified five distinct clusters, which include data security and personal privacy, novel algorithms, the characteristics and applications of blockchain, research on emerging technologies, and cloud technology. According to Wang et al. (2021) there has been a significant increase in the number of papers and contributing countries in the field of blockchain. In 2013 there were only 8 papers and 6 countries involved. However, by 2016, the numbers had risen to 176 papers and 48. Countries. In 2018, the figures further surged and 1148 and 94 in

2018 respectively. In 2018, the figures further surged to 1,148 papers and 94 countries. The top three countries in terms of research remain the same. USA holds the first position,followed by China and UK, in that order. In accordance with the results, the research priorities of the clusters are in a state of constant change. In the preceding cluster (cluster #1), the primary focus of researchers was on bitcoin and the bitcoin network. Subsequently, some researchers shifted their attention towards cryptocurrency in the context of blockchain research. In particular, in recent times, BCT and public ledgers are of particular interest to more scholars. Zhou et al. (2021) also support the findings of previous studies. 2016 is the turning point in the number of scientific publications on BCT. Authors identified 8 clusters, namely Bitcoin, Framework, Economy, Application, Fintech, Social governance, Data preservation and Income. On the other hand, Prajapati and Singh (2021) analyzed papers (2651) from Scopus and got similar results. Authors revealed that the quantity of academic outputs in BCT has been increasing since 2017. Nasir et al. (2021) published a paper based on several databases such as WoS, Scopus, Emerald, Elsevier and Google. According to results, USA, India and China were found to be the top three countries based on the country of origin of the corresponding authors. On the other hand based on citations USA holds the top position followed by China and Singapore in that order. The authors proposed that the subjects that would determine the future focus of the blockchain and cryptocurrency literature include fintech, the adoption of Islamic finance principles, cryptocurrency valuation techniques, and the structural growth of cryptocurrencies.

One of the latest review studies on BCT conducted by Ahmad et al. (2022) is based on 801 papers from Google Scholar from 2017 to 2021. The authors concluded that the number of survey papers has been rapidly increasing in the field of BCT since 2017. The total number of contributing countries is 74, and 27% of them have contributed only one paper. The major proportion of published papers belongs to India and China. Another study was carried out by Kuzior and Sira (2022) based on 1842 papers published in the period, 2007 to 2021, retrieved from Scopus. In terms of the number of published papers, this study found results similar to those of previous studies. The number has been increasing rapidly since 2018. 10 papers were published in 2016 which grew to 35 papers in 2017. Australia, Canada, and China were found to be the top three contributing countries.

According to the literature, the number of scientific publications on the topic mainly were concentrated in the period 2020 to 2022 and although different authors revealed different turning points in the evolution of BCT research, we can conclude that 2008 to 2016 is the first period and starting from 2017 a new stage started and the number of papers doubled and tripled year by year. Review studies used almost all international databases and search engines to identify related academic and grey literature on BCT. There is a need for review studies on this topic since the number of papers are sharply increasing and the state-of-the-art has been also changing very fast. Moreover, the latest review studies are based on databases other than WoS.

Overall, the study of blockchain has shown that it holds great promise for shaping the future of technology and commerce. It is imperative for scholars, decision-makers, and practitioners to persist in investigating and comprehending the capabilities and constraints of blockchain technology to fully unleash its potential.

3.3 Methodology

The methodology of the present study can be expressed in four stages as demonstrated in Figure 3.1.

As in Figure 3.1, the first step is selecting the appropriate database by comparing various databases. Then, in the second step, a lexical search query strategy is decided, and the documents are downloaded from the database. Various bibliometric studies on this subject and the keywords used in those studies are systematically presented in Table 3.1. Taking these into account, it was found appropriate to search for documents using the "blockchain" keyword within the "Topic" section. In the third stage, related visualizations are obtained by using Biblioshiny on R and VOSviewer software. In the last stage, the results of the analysis are interpreted and discussed.

The selection of lexical search queries is determined based on a review of the existing literature, and the criteria for choosing different keywords prioritize high inclusiveness. After downloading data from database, the analysis has been performed by using keyword co-occurrence analysis and time-based keyword evolutionary analysis by considering Cobo et al. (2012)'s science mapping approach. An important graph in this

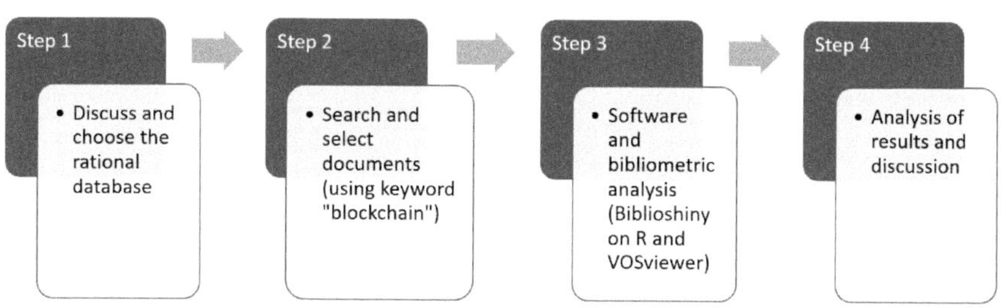

Figure 3.1. The developed methodology stages (Source: Prepared by authors).

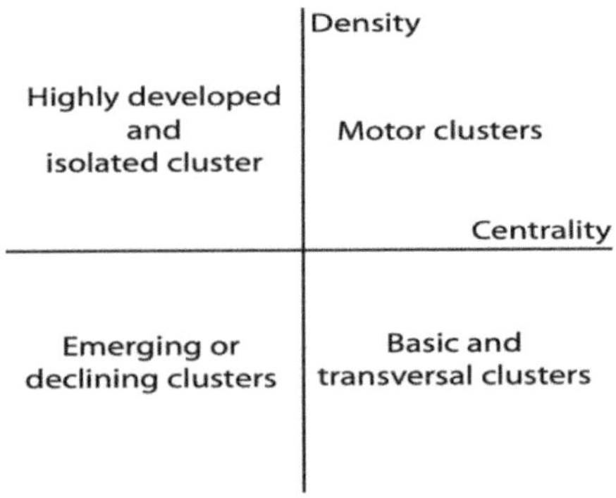

Figure 3.2. The strategic diagram (Source: prepared by authors based on Saritas et al., 2022).

science mapping approach is the strategic diagram which is demonstrated in Figure 3.2.

In the strategic diagrams, the clusters that have been identified and the scientific themes for each of these four time periods are the focus of attention. These are presented in a two-dimensional space: the density and the centrality (Cobo et al., 2011, 2012). The strategic diagram illustrates the 'local' and 'global' contexts of the research themes. Based on the calculated indices of density and centrality, it shows the clusters identified in each period of the quadrant. As the density value increases, the cluster's autonomy increases. Centrality measures a cluster's ability to interact with others (He, 1999) and the degree of network interaction, representing the importance of a topic in research development, while density counts the degree of internal network strength.

3.4 Data, Analysis, and Findings

Google Scholar, CSA Illumina, Scopus, and Web of Science (WoS) are the commonly used databases for the bibliometric analysis (Norris and Oppenheim, 2007). However, there are various arguments stated by the authors about database selection. For instance, Firdaus et al. (2019) preferred the Scopus database because it contains ranked articles indexed by both ISI and Scopus. Boyack et al. (2005) used the WoS to capture a large amount of technical and scientific literature. According to Norris and Oppenheim (2007), the main advantage of WoS over the other databases is that it includes social science literature, as the success of a bibliometric analysis depends mainly on the availability of an adequate number of studies in the area under study. WoS contains explicit information about each document and ensures comprehensive search outcomes as a detailed search engine (Luo et al., 2021). Dabbagh et al. (2019) systematically expressed the reasons for choosing WoS Core Collection as the database as follows: (a) WoS is considered the leading science citation index in the world; (b) it produces high quality and effective research publications through a rigorous selection process; (c) containing over 20,000 influential journals, conference proceedings and books, WoS is highly regarded by the academic community; (d) offers researchers some useful analytical possibilities. Due to such arguments and reasons, it was found appropriate to choose the WoS database in this study.

In order to cover as much literature on the subject as possible, the search field is chosen as "Topic", the search keyword is "blockchain", and the search time is January 17, 2023. All documents, such as articles, papers and books, with a time span of 2013–2023 are considered. According to statistics, the first article related to blockchain in the WoS database was published in the year 2013. So, the research period of this study begins from 2013.

In this study, a total of 24295 works (articles, books, etc.) published in 5622 sources between 2013–2023, obtained from the WoS database, were analyzed. Studies on this subject are increasing rapidly and the annual growth rate is above 58%. The average number of citations per document is equal to 12. The average document age is 2.69, which is a proof that the subject is new and up-to-date. The two main document types are articles (11955 or 49%) and proceedings papers (9213 or 38%). The first analysis is the co-word analysis and findings have been visualized by using co-occurrence network map. Considering the large number of documents, the threshold value has been determined as fifty. In order to make the analysis more understandable, these items are excluded: (a) "blockchain", "blockchains", "block chain" (because they are the various uses of the main keyword), and (b) internet of things (iot), smart contract, 5G mobile communication, smart grids, industry 4.0, distributed ledger technology (dlt), distributed ledger technologies (due to duplication of the words having the same meaning). Co-occurrence of keywords by clusters is shown in Figure 3.3.

Although the concept of blockchain was introduced with bitcoin, which is a type of cryptocurrency (Nakamoto, 2008), due to its wide usage areas and potential, the finance part of the subject today constitutes only one of the six big clusters (Figure 3.3). The main keywords of these clusters are as follows:

- Bitcoin, cryptocurrencies, trust, artificial intelligence, covid-19, sustainability (finance cluster),
- Security, machine learning, internet of things, fog computing, architecture, smart cities, 5G (technology cluster),
- Smart contracts, distributed ledger, decentralized, voting, data management (government cluster),

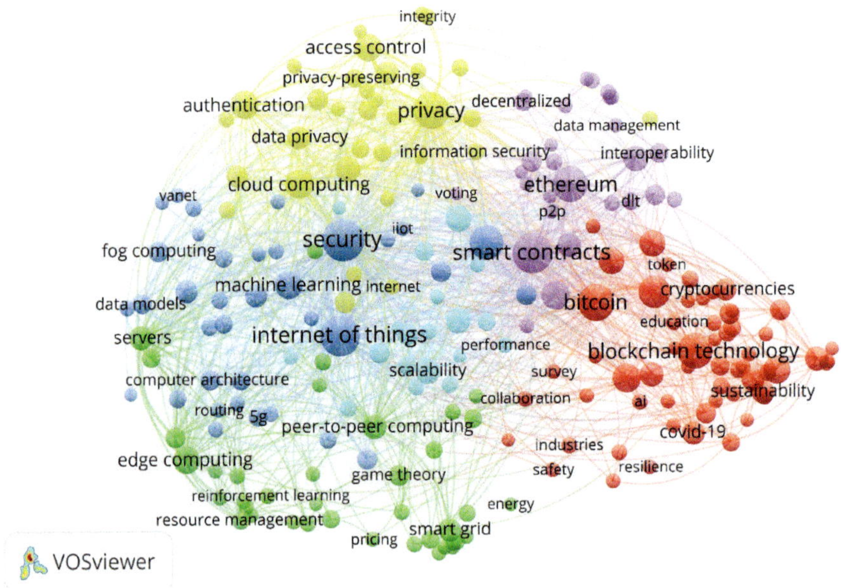

Figure 3.3. Co-occurrence of keywords (Source: Prepared by authors using VOSviewer).

- Edge computing, task analysis, servers, resource management, reinforcement learning, smart grid, energy, peer-to-peer computing (data management and smart technologies cluster),
- Privacy, cloud computing, data privacy, authentication, access control (cyber security cluster),
- Scalability, performance, consensus, distributed computing, performance evaluation (efficiency cluster).

In order to see the developments in the time span more clearly, the evolutionary development of the studies published in the WoS database on blockchain since 2013 has been examined and demonstrated in Figure 3.4.

As can be seen in Figure 3.4, concepts such as bitcoin, trust, and big data came to the fore in the period from 2013 to 2017, when the number of studies was comparatively low. In the one year period from 2018 to 2019, the concepts of management, innovation and privacy came to the fore, and discussions on different usage areas of the blockchain system started to increase. The frequent use of the concept of impact in the pandemic and post-pandemic period (2020 to 2023) shows that blockchain technology is now widely used, and therefore its effects have become the most discussed topics. It will be better to examine periods solely to understand

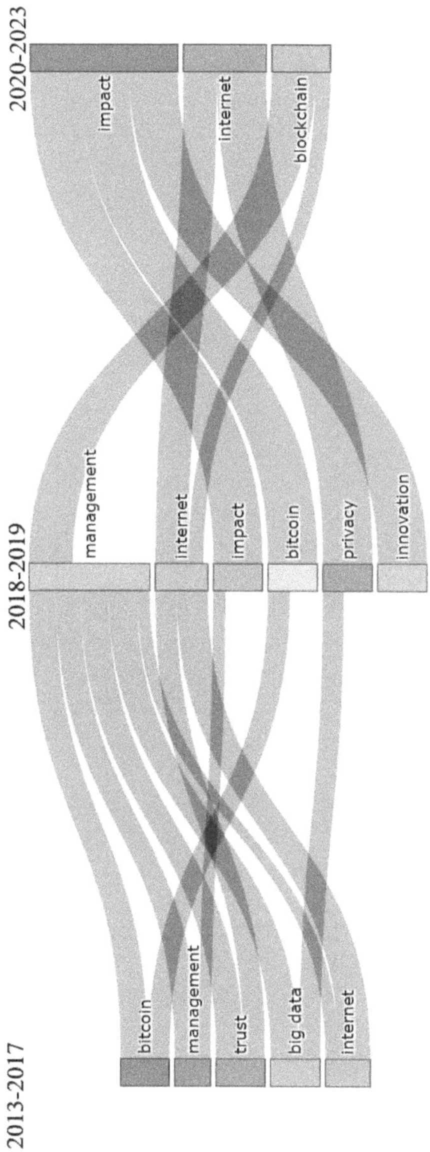

Figure 3.4. Evolution of keywords in the 2013–2023 period (Source: Prepared by authors using Biblioshiny on R).

the dynamics in these periods. The first period is from 2013 to 2017 and its strategic diagram is presented in Figure 3.5.

As can be seen in Figure 3.5, in the 2013 to 2017 time period, the concepts of "bitcoin", "trust" emerged as a basic theme, and the concepts of "internet", "things", "model" played the role of a motor theme. The concepts of "management", "power", "big data", "design science", "privacy" have started to turn into new topics of interest. This result is in line with similar studies conducted in this period. Conoscenti et al. (2016) states that there are very few studies on the Internet of Things and data management. According to another study (Yli-Huumo et al., 2016), more than 80% of studies focused on the bitcoin system, while less than 20% addressed other blockchain applications such as smart contracts and licensing. Especially after 2016, many researchers started to draw attention to Blockchain and smart contract techniques (Miau and Yang, 2018). The 2018 to 2019 period has been demonstrated in Figure 3.6.

When Figure 3.6 is examined, it can be seen that, in the 2018 to 2019 period, the concepts of "management", "technology", "security", "blockchain" took the role of basic themes, while the concepts of "privacy", "cloud", "scheme" turned into a motor theme. Now the focus of attention of the authors has started to shift towards the concepts of "innovation", "impact" and "performance". Specifically, security and fraud detection, insurance, record-keeping, IoT, smart contracts (Butijn et al., 2019), security and privacy (Dabbagh et al., 2019), data privacy, digital storage, big data, and distributed database (Firdaus et al., 2019) have come to the fore. According to Kamran et al. (2020) the IoT, is projected to reshape various sectors such as smart cities, smart agriculture, smart grids, smart transportation, smart homes and smart healthcare systems. Consequently the emergence of Blockchain in the realm of IoT, referred to as BIoT, is expected. BIoT signifies the adoption of Blockchain technology in the context of, IoT applications. Over time, blockchain applications have evolved from cryptocurrency and asset management to broader scopes (Colomo-Palacios et al., 2020). Finally, 2020–2023 period has been examined and visualized in Figure 3.7.

As can be seen in Figure 3.7, in the pandemic and post-pandemic (2020–2023) period, the concept of "challenges" has turned into a basic theme, as an indicator of the increase in risks and uncertainties, along with the concepts of "blockchain" and "management". On the other hand, the concepts of "internet", "security", "things" have become central topics. The concepts of "impact" and "performance" still remain as the potential research subjects. It can be expected that research studies will focus on these issues in the near future.

According to recent studies, the main concepts related to blockchain are as follows: direct payments, tempered data security, improved speed

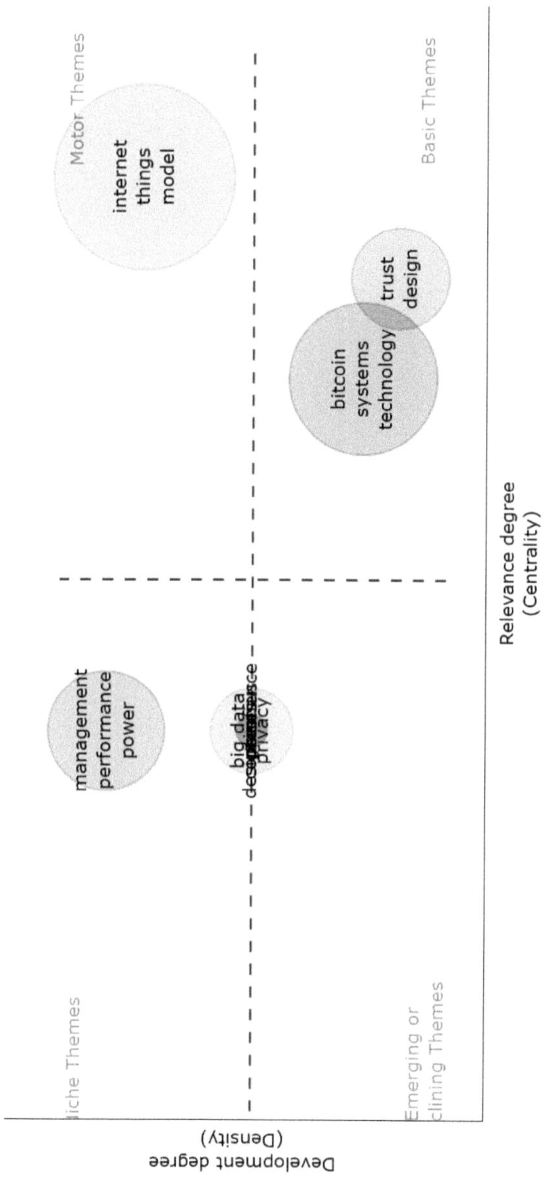

Figure 3.5. Strategic diagram for the 2013–2017 time period (Source: Prepared by authors using Biblioshiny on R).

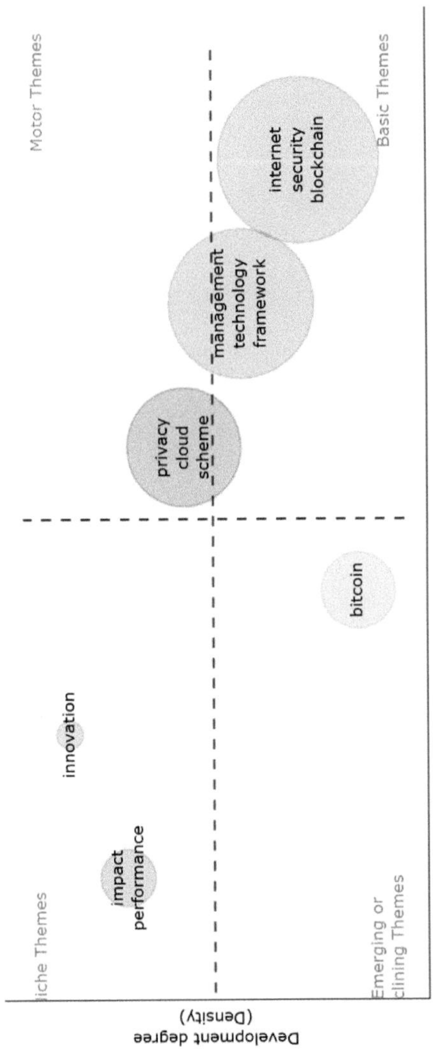

Figure 3.6. Strategic diagram for the 2018–2019 time period (Source: Prepared by authors using Biblioshiny on R).

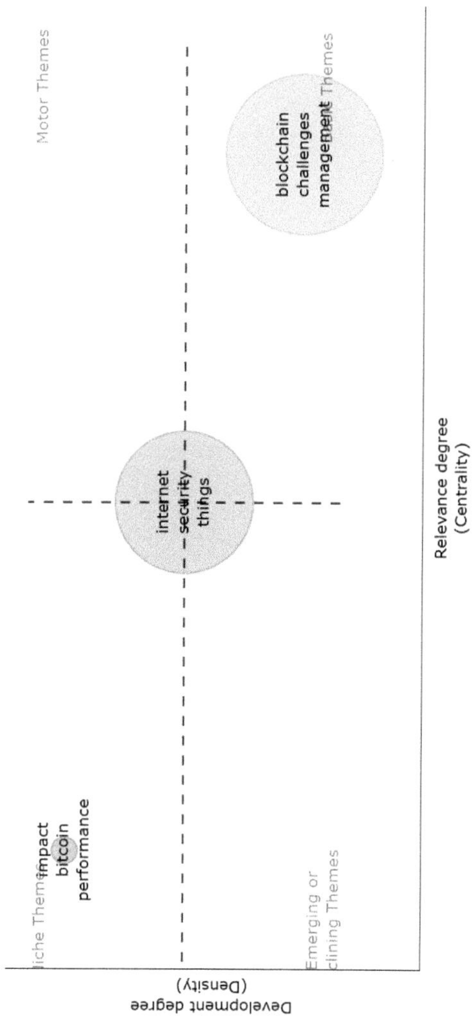

Figure 3.7. Strategic diagram for the 2020–2023 time period (Source: Prepared by authors using Biblioshiny on R).

of delivery (Gupta and Dhawan, 2020); cryptocurrency, sustainability, federated blockchain, industrial-web, scalability, public health, wireless communication, gaming, proof-of-work (Luo et al., 2021); consensus protocols, distributed ledger technology (Nasir et al., 2021); fog computing, internet of things, and artificial intelligence (Zhou et al., 2021); healthcare (Ahmad et al., 2022). On the other hand, we can expect to see an increase in discussions about opportunities and challenges, the efficiency (or inefficiency) of blockchain systems, and potential solutions to problems that arise (Wang et al., 2021; Kuzior and Sira, 2022).

3.5 Conclusion

In conclusion, due to its secure, decentralized, and transparent nature, the literature review on blockchain technology has highlighted its potential to transform various industries. Blockchain technology is being explored as a viable solution to a number of issues that traditional systems have struggled to address, across various sectors, including finance, healthcare, supply chain management ad governanace. Its ability to facilitate trust and eliminate intermediaries has the potential to increase the efficiency, cost-effectiveness, and reliability of processes.

Moreover, the literature review has also shed light on some of the challenges and limitations of blockchain. Issues such as scalability, interoperability, governance, and regulation pose significant obstacles to the widespread adoption of this technology. Furthermore, concerns around energy consumption, security, and privacy must be addressed to ensure that blockchain solutions are sustainable and safe. It can be asserted that, BCT is one of the hot topics in the technology literature during the last few years, which has been rapidly attracting attention of both scholars and practitioners around the world. As a technology blockchain is the proposed alternative for the traditional transactions in all fields and today it is being used in different fields including finance, healthcare, supply chain management, education, government, and others. Moreover, application areas of the BCT are also widening very fast. Although, in the first stage it was mainly limited to Bitcoin and cryptocurrency transactions. Advantages of BCT such as transparency, low cost and speed are making this technology more attractive. In conclusion, blockchain technology is a revolutionary force which has the capacity to bring about significant changes in various industries. The study of blockchain has revealed its advantages, such as increased security, transparency, and efficiency in transactions and data management. The technology is still in its infancy and further research is necessary to have a full understanding of its potential and limitations. Despite its potential, the adoption of blockchain technology is not without challenges, such as scalability issues, regulatory concerns, and the need for standardization. These challenges need to be addressed in order to ensure that blockchain can be effectively integrated into existing systems. The literature review also emphasizes the importance of interdisciplinary research and collaboration in order to realize the full potential of the blockchain. As blockchain technology evolves, it will require expertise from various fields, including computer science, economics, law, and policy. Collaboration between academia, industry, and government can help overcome some of the challenges and accelerate the development and adoption of blockchain solutions.

In summary, blockchain technology has the potential to disrupt a wide range of industries and create a world that is more transparent, secure, and efficient. While there are still challenges and limitations to overcome, the literature review has shown that the benefits of blockchain outweigh the risks. As more research is conducted and more use cases are explored, we can expect blockchain to become an increasingly important part of our digital lives.

References

Ahmad, H., Ahsan, M. A. and Mian, A. N. (2022). Trends in Publishing Blockchain Surveys: A Bibliometric Perspective (Preprint submitted to Elsevier). http://arxiv.org/abs/2109.09730.

AL-Ashmori, A., Basri, S. B., Dominic, P. D. D., Capretz, L. F., Muneer, A. et al. (2022). Classifications of sustainable factors in blockchain adoption: a literature review and bibliometric analysis. Sustainability 14(9): Article 9. https://doi.org/10.3390/su14095176.

Andoni, M., Robu, V., Flynn, D., Abram, S., Geach, D. et al. (2019). Blockchain technology in the energy sector: A systematic review of challenges and opportunities. Renewable and Sustainable Energy Reviews 100: 143–174. https://doi.org/10.1016/j.rser.2018.10.014.

Boyack, K., Klavans, R. and Börner, K. (2005). Mapping the backbone of science. Scientometrics 64: 351–374. https://doi.org/10.1007/s11192-005-0255-6.

Butijn, B.-J., Tamburri, D. A. and Heuvel, W.-J. V. D. (2019). Blockchains: A Systematic Multivocal Literature Review (arXiv:1911.11770). arXiv. http://arxiv.org/abs/1911.11770.

Casino, F., Dasaklis, T. K. and Patsakis, C. (2019). A systematic literature review of blockchain-based applications: Current status, classification and open issues. Telematics and Informatics 36: 55–81. https://doi.org/10.1016/j.tele.2018.11.006.

Cobo, M. j., López-Herrera, A. g., Herrera-Viedma, E. and Herrera, F et al. (2011). Science mapping software tools: Review, analysis, and cooperative study among tools. Journal of the American Society for Information Science and Technology 62(7): 1382–1402. https://doi.org/10.1002/asi.21525.

Cobo, M. j., López-Herrera, A. g., Herrera-Viedma, E., Herrera, F. et al. (2012). SciMAT: A new science mapping analysis software tool. Journal of the American Society for Information Science and Technology 63(8): 1609–1630. https://doi.org/10.1002/asi.22688.

Colomo-Palacios, R., Sánchez-Gordón, M. and Arias-Aranda, D. (2020). A critical review on blockchain assessment initiatives: A technology evolution viewpoint. Journal of Software: Evolution and Process 32(11): e2272. https://doi.org/10.1002/smr.2272.

Conoscenti, M., Vetro, A. and De Martin, J. C. (2016). Blockchain for the Internet of Things: A systematic literature review. 2016 IEEE/ACS 13th International Conference of Computer Systems and Applications (AICCSA), 1–6. https://doi.org/10.1109/AICCSA.2016.7945805.

Dabbagh, M., Sookhak, M. and Safa, N. S. (2019). The evolution of blockchain: a bibliometric study. IEEE Access 7: 19212–19221. https://doi.org/10.1109/ACCESS.2019.2895646.

Firdaus, A., Razak, M. F. A., Feizollah, A. and Hashem, I. A. T. (2019). The rise of "blockchain": Bibliometric analysis of blockchain study. Scientometrics 120(3): 1289–1331. https://doi.org/10.1007/s11192-019-03170-4.

Fuloria, S. (2020). Blockchain research: a bibliometric and text mining-based review of literature. International Journal of Business Forecasting and Marketing Intelligence 6(1): 50–62. doi:10.1504/ijbfmi.2020.109281.

Guo, Y.-M., Huang, Z.-L., Guo, J., Guo, X.-R., Li, H., Liu, M.-Y. et al. (2021). A bibliometric analysis and visualization of blockchain. Future Generation Computer Systems 116: 316–332. https://doi.org/10.1016/j.future.2020.10.023.

Gupta, B. M. and Dhawan, S. M. (2020). Blockchain research a scientometric assessment of global literature during 2010 to 2018. DESIDOC Journal of Library & Information Technology 40(01): 397–405. https://doi.org/10.14429/djlit.40.01.1472.

He, Q. (1999). Knowledge discovery through co-word analysis. Library Trends 48(1): 133–159.

Islam, I., Munim, K. Md., Oishwee, S. J., Islam, A. K. M. N., Islam, M. N. et al. (2020). A critical review of concepts, benefits, and pitfalls of blockchain technology using concept map. IEEE Access 8: 68333–68341. https://doi.org/10.1109/ACCESS.2020.2985647.

Iqbal, M. and Matulevicius, R. (2019). Blockchain-based application security risks: a systematic literature review. pp. 176–188. *In*: Proper, H. A. and Stirna, J. (eds.). Advanced Information Systems Engineering Workshops (caise 2019) (Vol. 349). Springer-Verlag Berlin. https://doi.org/10.1007/978-3-030-20948-3_16.

Javaid, M., Haleem, A., Pratap Singh, R., Khan, S., Suman, R. et al. (2021). Blockchain technology applications for Industry 4.0: A literature-based review. Blockchain: Research and Applications 2(4): 100027. https://doi.org/10.1016/j.bcra.2021.100027.

Kamran, M., Khan, H. U., Nisar, W., Farooq, M., Rehman, S.-U. et al. (2020). Blockchain and Internet of Things: A bibliometric study. Computers & Electrical Engineering 81: 106525. https://doi.org/10.1016/j.compeleceng.2019.106525.

Konstantinidis, I., Siaminos, G., Timplalexis, C., Zervas, P., Peristeras, V. et al. (2018). Blockchain for business applications: a systematic literature review. pp. 384–399. *In*: Abramowicz, W. and Paschke, A. (eds.). Business Information Systems. Springer International Publishing. https://doi.org/10.1007/978-3-319-93931-5_28.

Kuzior, A. and Sira, M. (2022). A bibliometric analysis of blockchain technology research using VOSviewer. Sustainability 14(13): Article 13. https://doi.org/10.3390/su14138206.

Luo, J., Hu, Y. and Bai, Y. (2021). Bibliometric analysis of the blockchain scientific evolution: 2014–2020. IEEE Access 9: 120227–120246. https://doi.org/10.1109/ACCESS.2021.3092192.

Miau, S. and Yang, J.-M. (2018). Bibliometrics-based evaluation of the Blockchain research trend: 2008–March 2017. Technology Analysis & Strategic Management 30(9): 1029–1045. https://doi.org/10.1080/09537325.2018.1434138.

Nakamoto, S. (2008). Bitcoin: A Peer-to-Peer Electronic Cash System. [online] Available: https://bitcoin.org/bitcoin.pdf.

Nasir, A., Shaukat, K., Khan, K. I., Hameed, I. A., Alam, T. M. et al. (2021). What is core and what future holds for blockchain technologies and cryptocurrencies: a bibliometric analysis. IEEE Access 9: 989–1004. https://doi.org/10.1109/ACCESS.2020.3046931.

Norris, M. and Oppenheim, C. (2007). Comparing alternatives to the Web of Science for coverage of the social sciences' literature. J. Informetr. 1(2): 161–169.

Prajapati, P. and Singh, D. M. P. (2021). Measuring the global research trends of blockchain technology: a bibliometric analysis. EPRA International Journal of Multidisciplinary Research (IJMR) 7(12): Article 12.

Saritas, O., Burmaoglu, S. and Ozdemir, D. (2022). The evolution of Foresight: What evidence is there in scientific publications? Futures 137: 102916. https://doi.org/10.1016/j.futures.2022.102916.

Singhal, B., Dhameja, G. and Panda, P. S. (2018). How Blockchain Works. pp. 31–148. *In*: Singhal, B., Dhameja, G. and Panda, P. S. (eds.). Beginning Blockchain. Apress. https://doi.org/10.1007/978-1-4842-3444-0_2.

Wang, G., Zhang, S., Yu, T. and Ning, Y. (2021). A systematic overview of blockchain research. Journal of Systems Science and Information 9(3): 205–238. https://doi.org/10.21078/JSSI-2021-205-34.

Xu, M., Chen, X. and Kou, G. (2019). A systematic review of blockchain. Financial Innovation 5(1): 27. https://doi.org/10.1186/s40854-019-0147-z.

Yli-Huumo, J., Ko, D., Choi, S., Park, S., Smolander, K. et al. (2016). Where is current research on blockchain technology?—a systematic review. PLOS ONE 11(10): e0163477. https://doi.org/10.1371/journal.pone.0163477.

Zhou, L., Zhang, L., Zhao, Y., Zheng, R., Song, K. et al. (2021). A scientometric review of blockchain research. Information Systems and E-Business Management 19(3): 757–787. https://doi.org/10.1007/s10257-020-00461-9.

Chapter 4
Challenges of Blockchain Applications

Elif Calik

4.1 Introduction

Blockchain technology, with its core attributes of decentralization, security, transparency, tanperproofing, and traceability is continuously advancing. While initially recognized for its association with virtual currencies, blockchain has expanded its spectrum of applications across various domains including the Internet of Things (IoT), healthcare, education, supply chain, and more. Notably advancements in consensus mechanisms and smart contracts have further enhanced the capabilities of blockchain technology. The pandemic process in recent years has caused a rapid shift in how technology is positioned in relation to people. Currently, there is a process in which almost everything that can be physically located in real life is tried to be created in the virtual world. Of course, in this process, the blessings of the revolutionary blockchain technology are also utilized in order to eliminate the problems that can be encountered by assets that can be transacted electronically. This makes it easier to identify the challenges that need to be considered. The underpinning of this chapter is the challenges that existing blockchain application examples have to deal with.

Karabuk University.
Email: elifcalik@karabuk.edu.tr

4.1.1 Blockchain

Bitcoin, an application of blockchain technology, was introduced in the article published under the pseudonym Satoshi Nakamoto (Nakamoto, 2008; Merkle, Protocols for public key cryptosystems, 1980; Szabo, Smart contracts: building blocks for digital markets, 1996). Although Bitcoin is the first successful application of Blockchain technology, other technical advancements that contributed to its development between 1980 and 2008 should not be forgotten (Narayanan and Clark, 2017). These can be listed as follows;

1979 Merkle Tree: The hierarchical tree structure model, called "tree signature", was developed by Ralph Merkle for validating large datasets. In addition, this model is used as a digital signature technique (Merkle, A Certified Digital Signature, 1979; Merkle, Protocols for public key cryptosystems, 1980). It is an improvement that has significantly contributed to the advancement of blockchain technology. The leaves of the Merkle tree represent the transaction data itself in the block. A leaf is a hash value or hash value of another piece of data contained in a transaction or block. Each leaf contributes the "root hash", which is the summary of all the block data. If any manipulation is done on an appended block, it will cause the root-hash value in the Merkle tree to change. Therefore, the root-hash of the block changes. This is very easily detected. In this way, the Merkle tree helps maintain the integrity of transactions on the blockchain (Monrat et al., 2019).

1982 A new cryptographic method: Two separate approaches are often used to handle economic processes. The first is to conduct economic transactions through a third party such as banks; the second is to conduct transactions using hard cash. Both approaches have benefits over the other. However, the discussed point in here summarizes the challenges of traditional methods that are the starting point of blockchain technology. The first is the challenge of completely documenting transactions performed through a third party and the loss of personal privacy because it can be traced by parties apart from the person herself or himself. The other issue is that due to the use of hard cash in economic activities there is a lack of transactional evidence, as well as difficulties in ensuring the security of hard cash as a personal asset. However, if the money is stolen from the real owner, the absence of a sanction restricting its spending or the lack of deterrence of the sanction is another difficulty. To overcome these difficulties, David Chaum introduced a new cryptographic method to the scientific world. This method has the characteristics that may allow an automatic payment system where the third party cannot see the information, providing proof of payment and identification of creditors when necessary, and preventing the payment instruments from double-spending in case of theft (Chaum, 1982). With DigiCash in 1989, he added to the creation of the concept of digital currencies (Chaum, 1982).

1991 Time-stamping: A paper on the timestamp of digital documents was created by Stuart Haber and W. Scott Stornetta. In this article, in order to prevent users from backward or forward-dating digital records, a solution is offered. The article provides an offer for a way to stop users from backward or forward-dating digital records. Its goal was to avoid the requirement for a timestamp service's record-keeping and to preserve total confidentiality of the document. Its purpose was to fully protect the document's privacy without a need for the timestamp service to record anything (Haber and Stornetta, 1991). Furthermore, Haber and Stornetta updated their designs to include the Merkle tree structure in their next article (Bayer et al., 1992).

1996 Smart Contracts: What's more, Szabo introduced Smart Contracts (SC), in 1996, another significant advancement that operates automatically on the blockchain and enables two parties to interact with each other without the use of intermediaries (Szabo, Smart contracts: building blocks for digital markets, 1996).

1997 Hashcash: To reduce spam, Adam Back developed hashcash in 1997. The hashcash mechanism is meant to stop spam. It necessitates the creation of a "postage stamp" by the email sender for each message delivered. Using this stamp requires solving a challenging math puzzle. So, it serves as a marker to validate that the email the receiver is supposed to receive actually is an email. In addition, Hashcash is used as the "proof of work" needed to add a new block to the blockchain. By resolving the mathematical conundrum, a miner must show that they have put in the minimum amount of proof-of-work necessary to build a new block (Back, Hashcash - A Denial of Service Counter-Measure, 2002; Back, Hash cash postage implementation, 1997).

1998 Bit-Gold: Bit-Gold is a project developed by Nick Szabo that contributes to the development of bitcoin. The term Bit-Gold was used to describe information objects that were mathematically provable and costly to create, which included models based on cryptographic system puzzles (Szabo, Bit-Gold, 1998).

1998 B-money: B-money is a digital currency idea that Wei Dai put out in 1998. It is intended for decentralized, safe, anonymous, and intermediary-free money transfers. The B-money system employs cryptographic methods for safe user-to-user money transfers. They authenticate other users using public-key encryption. In this way, money transfer security is ensured (Dai, 1998).

1990–1999 Peer-to-Peer network: Along with these, there have been further breakthroughs that have contributed to the development of blockchain technology. For example, peer-to-peer (P2P) technology originally gained popularity in 1999 with the spread of the file-sharing program Napster. It was used as a P2P network that allowed users to share music files. The company, which gained great popularity among Internet users, also allowed millions of people to download their music files for free. However, the company was sued by the music industry for allegedly "infringing on copyrights". As a result of the 2001 court case, Napster was terminated and compelled to pay legal damages (Saroiu et al., 2001).

2004 Reusable Proof of Work (RPOW): Afterward, in 2004, Hal Finney announced his IBM-funded research, a PoW variant entitled Reusable Proof of Work (RPOW). Instead of using RPOW for Bitcoin mining, PoW was the mathematical puzzle that emerged (Finney, 2004).

2008 Bitcoin: Bitcoin was introduced by Satoshi Nakamoto, and the first bitcoin was produced in late 2008 and early 2009. It went down in history as the first successful digital currency example of blockchain technology (Nakamoto, 2008).

Blockchain has a chain structure in which validated transactions are added in blocks as one-way input. Hence, once a transaction has been completed, it cannot be modified, destroyed, or erased. The blockchain system surpasses centralized solutions thanks to this characteristic. The most well-known blockchain platforms include Hyperledger, R3 Corda, Ripple, and Ethereum. All of them have solution strategies that are appropriate for the situation, although having characteristics diverse from one another. The blockchain, which is briefly defined as a decentralized distributed record list, is a structure that works by transforming transactions into blocks sequentially using timestamps and cryptographic hashes, and connecting the blocks in which each transaction takes place according to the transaction order. The hash of each block's transaction records is stored in the Merkle root hash. The timestamp contains the current time in seconds relative to the start of 1970 UTC. While being added to the end of the preceding block, each new block carries the hash of the previous block. The chain's first block, referred as Genesis, has a hash value of zero (Nakamoto, 2008; Merkle, Protocols for public key cryptosystems, 1980; Szabo, Smart contracts: building blocks for digital markets, 1996; Narayanan and Clark, 2017). The hash value connecting the blocks is created using a cryptographic one-way hash function known as SHA256. As a result, the block acquires the properties of anonymity, immutability, and compactness. Peer-to-peer (P2P) networks connect the peers, which are referred to as nodes in the blockchain. Digital signatures are one of the primary techniques for verifying the security and accuracy of the data stored on the blockchain. Each peer in the network has a public and private key pair for this purpose. If we consider the situation where Peer A wants to message Peer B as an example of how keys are used, key pairs are employed as follows; Peer A encrypts its message with its private key and sends the encrypted message and original data to peer B. Peer B authenticates the incoming message with the public key of peer A. In this way, peer B easily checks whether the data has been manipulated. One of the most well-known tracking techniques is the Elliptic Curve Digital Signature Algorithm (ECDSA).

In general, blockchain workflow steps are as follows. Firstly, the transaction requests are made by the peer; second, the transaction is broadcasted to all nodes; third, the transaction is approved by all nodes; lastly, the transaction is permanently added to the chain.

4.1.2 Blockchain Characteristics

The characteristics of Blockchain can be articulated as shown in Table 4.1 after reviewing the literature.

4.1.3 Blockchain Technological Advancement

Although the literature discusses advances in blockchain technology in three phases, several publications use alternative classifications (Bhutta et al., 2021; Wenhua et al., 2023). According to a study by Wenhua et al. (Wenhua et al., 2023), five stages have been identified to characterize the advancement of blockchain technology.

Blockchain 1.0, also known as the digital currency phase, is characterized by major developments in consensus algorithms and distributed ledgers. Bitcoin is an application example.

Blockchain 2.0 is also referred to as the digital economy. Smart contracts have been developed to manage financial processes such as bonds, promissory notes and bank contracts.

Blockchain 3.0 provides additional distributed storage space and scalability. While providing this, it does not compromise on security. For this, it makes use of decentralized applications (DApps). It also helps integrate data from various sources without compromising privacy. Hyperledger and quorum can be given as examples.

Blockchain 4.0 includes industry application examples. R chain and metaverse can be given as examples.

Blockchain 5.0 is also referred to as the digital society. It is the technological development stage of blockchain technology, which can be briefly summarized as an application example of the Internet of Everything (IoE). Relictum pro and decentralized web are good examples.

Table 4.1. Blockchain characteristics and their explanations.

	Characteristics of Blockchain	**Explanation**
1	Decentralization	It is the operation of a system with the equal participation of multiple nodes in a network, without relying on a single central management authority. This approach ensures that the network continues even in the case of failure or an attack on part of the system.
2	Anonymity	This is a technique that enables users to conduct transactions on the blockchain without specifying them in detail. A random address or digital identity (public key), which they use to conduct transactions, is produced in place of the individuals' actual identities. Despite the fact that these addresses are contained in the transaction records, this information does not reveal who the actual user is.
3	Immutability/ Persistance/ Tamperproof	This adresses the impossibility of changing data after it has been stored in a blockchain. This is possible by creating a chain of each block in the blockchain based on the previous block and combining the hash of each block with the hash of the previous block to ensure the accuracy of the blockchain.
4	Transparency	It indicates that any user of the blockchain can monitor all network transactions. All transactions on the blockchain are recorded openly and transparently, and all users can verify these transactions.
5	Accountability	This implies that the identities of every transaction on the blockchain may be confirmed. Every transaction in the blockchain is processed using the unique identifying code (address) that each user has.
6	Fault tolerance	Each node in a blockchain network maintains a ledger with the exact same blockchain data, and other nodes in the network can take over the failing node's responsibilities. This makes the blockchain network resilient to failure scenarios and enables it to function.
7	Security	Blockchain's decentralized structure, cryptography, consensus algorithm, and open source nature all contribute to its security features.
8	Traceability	Each block in its structure builds a chain by referring to the one before it. This makes the information contained in each block permanent, unchangeable, and traceable.
9	Integrity	It refers to the accurate and complete storage, processing, and transmission of data from the beginning to the end. Each block in a blockchain network builds a chain by referring to the one before it.

4.2 Application Domain

Blockchain technology, which started with the emergence of Bitcoin, is actually a virtual ledger that can record and verify large volumes of digital transactions. It is rapidly advancing towards becoming a preferred technology that can be encountered not only in the banking sector, but also in a wide range of application examples from automotive to art. Contrary to what is known, as seen in Table 4.2, it is possible to encounter application examples of blockchain technology in many areas apart from bitcoin, which is a digital currency (Sharma et al., 2022; Ma and Fang, 2020; Madaan et al., 2020; Madaan et al., 2020; Makridakis and Christodoulou, 2019; McGhin et al., 2019; Reyna et al., 2018; Siyal et al., 2019; Wang et al., 2022; Zheng et al., 2018).

Table 4.2. Blockchain application domains and their challenges.

	Application Domain	Example	Challenges
1	Finance	Bitcoin, Ethereum, Ripple, Tether	Scalability, security, regulation, energy consumption
2	Internet of Things	Filament, IOTA, Chronicled	High transaction costs, scalability, standardization
3	Supply chain	IBM Food Trust, Provenance, Everledger, VeChain, Modum, ShipChain	Data accuracy, scalability, interoperability and compatibility
4	Healthcare	MedRec, Medicalchain, Gem Health, SimplyVital Health, Mediledger	Confidentiality and security of data, legal compliance, integration, cooperation between other health sector stakeholders, adoption
5	Energy	Power Ledger, WePower, Grid +	Scalability, compatibility, high transaction costs, compatibility
6	Education	ODEM, Sony Global Education, Learning Machine	Scalability, high transaction costs, regulation, adoption, data security
7	Security and privacy	Monero, Zcash, Hyperledger Fabric, Enigma	Scalability, regulation, ease of use
8	Government	Estonya e-Residency, Dubai Blockchain Strategy, Sweden's Land Registry Blockchain pilot application, Singapore's trade finance blockchain network	Regulation, data security, ease of use

4.3 Challenges

The growth of blockchain application examples in recent years has aided in the experience of developers. The challenges and threats in the realm of applications have thus been made even more obvious in light of the benefits and advantages provided by blockchain technology. In this section, scalability, security and privacy, regulation and legislation, fairness and trustworthiness, and interoperability are going to be discussed.

4.3.1 Scalability

The basic approach of blockchain technology is to store data securely and transparently in a decentralized structure. However, scalability is a key challenge, as the blockchain retains all transaction data and historical transactions from each node participating in the network. Scalability challenges can often be listed as limitations of storage and block volume, number of peers, usage of energy, latency, weak cost-effectiveness, and more. Although the transaction volume with platforms such as Bitcoin and Ethereum is rising, a high transaction volume causes the system to become cumbersome and latent. Verifying the source of the transaction is one of the procedures used in public blockchains. This means that each node must store and verify each transaction. In public chains, verification and validation procedures are carried out through consensus mechanisms. Proof of Work (PoW), Proof of Stake (PoS), Delegated Proof of Stake (DPoS) Practical Byzantine Fault Tolerance (PBFT), Proof of Authority/Proof of Identity (PoA/PoID) are the consensus techniques that are most frequently utilized. Although being a secure and robust consensus technique, PoW has certain drawbacks. The most significant of these is the extensive computer infrastructure and high energy consumption needed to tackle the challenging mathematical puzzle. It is inefficient due to these challenges. When the literature is examined, it has been observed that energy usage estimates are regularly made for Bitcoin (Digiconomist, 2023). According to estimations by Digiconomist, changing the Bitcoin consensus mechanism from a PoW system to a PoS-, for example, could potentially reduce energy requirements by 99.95%.

The scalability challenge isn't just about the low number of transactions per second or the high cost of throughput. Traditional databases require a centralized structure and a third party even if they are capable of handling thousands of transactions per second. The real difficulty is how blockchains like Bitcoin, Ethereum, and others will compete with centralized databases' performance while retaining a high degree of decentralization. Performance and security requirements are provided with serious costs in decentralized structures. According to the literature, the proposed scalability solutions for a blockchain are; on-chain, off-chain, different architectural approaches and consensus mechanisms. In the Bitcoin network, solution proposals such as the Segregated Witness (SegWit) on-chain solution, the second layer solution called the Lightning Network, the Ripple solution with a different architecture that allows the storage of transaction data in a decentralized structure known as the XRP Ledger, and the PBFT consensus algorithm have been put forward to address challenges. At this point, consideration should be given to the fact that the proposed scalability solutions should help maintain or even develop other desired blockchain features while improving performance. For instance, bitcoin has a transaction volume of about 7 transactions per second (tps) and an average transaction confirmation time of 60 min while Ethereum has a higher transaction volume compared to Bitcoin, with an estimated capacity of about 25 tps and an average transaction confirmation time of around 6 minutes and Ripple has the highest transaction volume of 1500 tsp with an average confirmation time of 4s. It is vital to consider which and to what extent significant elements of the blockchain network, such as decentralization and security, were sacrificed in order for many blockchain applications with high TPS levels to achieve these performance figures (Khan et al., 2021; Alshahrani et al., 2023; Dutta et al., 2020).

4.3.2 *Security and Privacy*

Although blockchain technology has the potential to revolutionise numerous industries, it also poses security and privacy concerns. It is possible to summarize the arguments that contributed to this as follows (Bhutta et al., 2021; Gao et al., 2018; Lacity, 2018; Mohanta et al., 2019).

Smart Contracts: The self-executing code that is kept on a blockchain is referred to as a smart contract. Smart contracts are created by the software developer to automate operations and transactions. However, due to their being inherently immutable, they are vulnerable to attacks. To clarify, the smart contract cannot be undone once it has been generated and placed on the chain. Therefore, the software development stage of smart contracts is the most crucial component. A smart contract may experience unfavourable outcomes and suffer considerable losses if maliciously constructed or improperly coded. For instance, it should be recalled that the Decentralized Autonomous Organization (DAO) attack on the Ethereum blockchain in 2016 that aimed to invest and administer automatically resulted in significant financial losses owing to a vulnerability in the smart contract code.

Private Key: In blockchain technology, private keys are crucial in authorizing access to user accounts and validating transactions. However, if they are stolen or lost, the assets of users may be in danger. This can take place through malware or phishing attacks. As an instance, a cryptocurrency exchange in Japan suffered significant losses in 2018 as a result of a breach using inadequate private key management procedures.

Consensus Mechanisms: Transactions are endorsed and added to the blockchain via consensus procedures, thus it's critical to understand what they are, how they work, and their advantages and disadvantages. Nonetheless, some mechanisms might be weak to assaults like the 51% attack. This attack takes place when a single entity has 51 percent or more of the processing power in a blockchain network, which provides it the capability to alter transactions. An example is the 51% attack on the Bitcoin Gold network in 2018.

Privacy: Blockchain technology has to overcome its challenges to privacy while providing transparency. Transactions are visible to all participants in the network, which can lead to loss of privacy for individuals. Moreover, the privacy challenge becomes even more prominent as some blockchain applications, such as healthcare, education, and supply chain management, require the sharing of personal and sensitive information that could be abused. For instance, the Australian government's use of a blockchain-based infrastructure for online voting in 2019 was found to be vulnerable to anonymization assaults. A comprehensive approach that includes strong encryption, secure coding practices and effective governance models must be adopted to meet current challenges.

4.3.3 Interoperability

The capacity of various blockchain networks to communicate and exchange data with one another is known as interoperability. Due to a lack of standardization and the existence of several blockchain platforms with various goals, functions, and features, interoperability in the context of blockchain applications offers serious difficulty. The challenges with interoperability can be summed up as follows.

Incompatible blockchain protocols: Since different blockchain networks frequently utilize distinct protocols, this can cause problems with compatibility. For instance, Ethereum's Turing completeness feature enables more sophisticated smart contracts to be created using programming languages, in contrast to other blockchain platforms. As a result, it's possible that an Ethereum-based blockchain platform and a platform employing the Hyperledger Fabric protocol cannot connect with one another.

Consensus mechanisms: Blockchain networks use different consensus mechanisms to validate transactions, which can make it difficult to exchange information amongst them. For example, a PoW-based blockchain may not be able to communicate with a PoS-based blockchain.

Data privacy and security: Information sharing amongst blockchain networks may be challenging due to the varying levels of data security and privacy. For instance, it could be challenging to communicate data between private and public blockchains because of the stronger data protection standards of the former.

Smart contract interoperability: Many blockchain applications use smart contracts as a fundamental building block. However, differing smart contract languages might make interoperability difficult. For instance, a platform supporting the Go smart contract language may not be capable of decoding a smart contract written in Solidity.

To address these issues, several approaches have been put forth, such as the usage of blockchain bridges, cross-chain communication protocols, and interoperability protocols. For instance, the Polkadot network uses a uniform protocol that supports many blockchain platforms to facilitate interoperability between various blockchain networks (Wood, 2016). The Inter-Block Communication (IBC) protocol is used by the Cosmos network to enable communication between various blockchain networks (Cosmos, 2023). The Wanchain network facilitates asset transfers between several blockchain networks using an inter-chain communication mechanism (Wanchain, 2023).

The potential of blockchain technology must be unlocked, and a frictionless interchange of data and assets between various blockchain networks must be made possible, among other standardization measures, in order to solve the interoperability problem.

4.3.4 *Regulation and Legislation*

Technology needs regulation just like any other field does, and in this case there are laws, regulations, agreements, standards, and guidelines that must be followed at both the national and international levels. Of these, the European General Data Protection Regulation is the most well-known (GDPR). In order to comply with GDPR, blockchain applications must overcome several obstacles. For instance, users cannot modify or remove the data that is kept on immutable, public blockchains. Once added to a blockchain, any data which is stored in a transaction becomes accessible to all blockchain nodes. These nodes store the entire chain locally. Thus, the challenge faced by blockchain applications occurs when a person's identity or sensitive data is added to a blockchain. The system's nature—namely, its immutability, decentralization, and consensus protocols—protects the data tied to it against manipulation. An application for cryptography called Chameleon Hash Function (CHF), which was created at the transaction level, was said to have been used to build a solution for data alteration (Finck, 2019; Niya et al., 2022).

Another issue is the lack of clarity, which relates to ambiguity in the current rules and regulations. For instance, it appears that many countries are still unsure whether to classify cryptocurrencies as assets, stocks, or currencies. The fact that the legal framework of smart contracts in many jurisdictions has not yet been determined, paves the way for legal difficulties in case of conflict (Law, 2022).

Anti-Money Laundering (AML) and Know Your Customer (KYC) Compliance; Cryptocurrencies are frequently utilized in blockchain applications, yet they can be exploited for illegal purposes like money laundering. Due to the decentralized nature of the technology, AML and KYC compliance are necessary but can be difficult in the blockchain sector. For instance, the Securities and Exchange Commission (SEC) in the United States has taken legal action against multiple initial coin offerings (ICOs) for breaking securities regulations. ICOs and cryptocurrency trading are totally forbidden in China, according to the authorities. The General Data Protection Regulation (GDPR) in the European Union has control over blockchain applications that process personal data (Finck, 2019).

Regulators, policymakers, and industry participants must work together to build legal frameworks that can enable technical innovations and change while assuring consumer protection and safety in order to address the legislative and regulatory challenges in blockchain applications (Upadhyay, 2020).

4.3.5 Ethics

Ethics must be broad enough to apply to a number of choices in order to be helpful in solving practical problems. Moreover, they ought to be understandably straightforward. There are four fundamental ethical precepts mentioned. They are (1) respect for autonomy; (2) non-harm; (3) helpfulness; and (4) fairness. It covers a variety of topics, including fundamental ethical precepts like fairness, utility, and non-harm. Benefit, which includes the elements of not harming and benefiting, refers to maximizing the net benefit to humanity. Justice here is considered the "fair distribution model of benefits."

Respect for autonomy, on the other hand, argues that practices made as a result of independent (without coercion or interference) choices made by individuals tend to be correct as long as the choices do not harm others. Although this framework does not mean that these are the only principles and rules that may be relevant, these four core ethical principles provide an adequate framework for most practices. When the literature is examined, it has been seen that the issue is still in the intellectual stage, as it is insufficient in Blockchain-based developed applications (Tang et al., 2020).

4.4 Conclusion

In this section, the structure of the blockchain, its characteristics, application areas, difficulties and applications to overcome these difficulties were discussed. Although the decentralized and immutability core attributes of blockchain technology offer many advantages, it has been found that scalability, regulatory restrictions, privacy concerns, and ethical issues are among the most significant difficulties encountered. The scalability issues appear to be caused by the fact that blockchain technology is still in its infancy and performs less well than more established centralized database-based apps. Despite this, platforms like Polkadot, which have partially enabled blockchain interoperability, indicate that higher-level advancements may contribute as their future reflection. The existence of such platforms raises the idea that there may be platforms in the future where smart contracts that can communicate with each other and be shaped according to system needs can be designed. Examining the literature reveals that the legal framework surrounding digital currency is gradually coming into existence. However, the general framework's ambiguity still presents a problem. As a result, this section covered the scalability, legal restrictions, privacy, ethics, security, interoperability, and future problems of blockchain technology.

4.5 Acknowledgments

This study was funded by Karabuk University Scientific Research Projects Coordination, Türkiye, with project number KBÜBAP-22-UIP-163.

References

Alshahrani, H., Islam, N., Syed, D., Sulaiman, A., Al Reshan et al. (2023). Sustainability in blockchain: a systematic literature review on scalability and power consumption issues. Energies 16(3): 1510. doi:10.3390/en16031510.

Back, A. (1997, March 28). Hash cash postage implementation. Retrieved March 3, 2023, from http://www.hashcash.org/papers/announce.txt.

Back, A. (2002, August 1). Hashcash - A Denial of Service Counter-Measure. Retrieved March 3, 2023, from https://www.cs.miami.edu/home/burt/learning/csc597.231/docs/hashcash.pdf.

Bayer, D., Haber, S. and Stornetta, W. S. (1992, March). Improving the effciency and reliability of digital time-stamping. pp. 329–334. *In*: Capocelli, R., De Santis, A. and Vaccaro, U. (eds.). Methods in Communication, Security, and Computer Science. New York: Springer-Verlag. Retrieved from https://citeseerx.ist.psu.edu/document?repid=rep1&type=pdf&doi=1256bbc65fcc39ea3e797d179a907f69b96ad85f.

Bhutta, M. N., Khwaja, A. A., Nadeem, A., Ahmad, H. F., Khan et al. (2021). A survey on blockchain technology: evolution, architecture and security. IEEE Access 9: 61048–61073. doi:10.1109/ACCESS.2021.3072849.

Chaum, D. (1982). Blind Signatures For Untraceable Payments. Springer. Retrieved from http://www.hit.bme.hu/~buttyan/courses/BMEVIHIM219/2009/Chaum.BlindSigForPayment.1982.PDF.

Cosmos. (2023). Retrieved from Cosmos: https://cosmos.network/.

Dai, W. (1998). B-money. Retrieved March 3, 2023, from http://www.weidai.com/bmoney.txt.

Digiconomist. (2023). Retrieved from Bitcoin Energy Consumption Index: https://digiconomist.net/bitcoin-energy-consumption.

Dutta, P., Choi, T.-M., Somani, S. and Butala, R. (2020, October). Blockchain technology in supply chain operations: applications, challenges and research opportunities. Transportation Research Part E: Logistics and Transportation Review 142(102067): 1–33. doi:10.1016/j.tre.2020.102067.

Finck, M. (2019). Blockchain and the general data protection regulation: can distributed ledgers be squared with European data protection law? European Parliament, Directorate-General for Parliamentary Research Services. Publications Office of the European Union. doi:10.2861/535.

Finck, M. (2019). Blockchain and the general data protection regulation : can distributed ledgers be squared with European data protection law? (E. P.-G. Services, Ed.) Publications Office of the European Union. doi:10.2861/535.

Finney, H. (2004). Rpow-reusable proofs of work. Retrieved March 1, 2023, from http://web.archive.org/web/20071222072154/http://rpow.net/.

Gao, W., Hatcher, W. G. and Yu, W. (2018). A survey of blockchain: techniques, applications, and challenges. 2018 27th International Conference on Computer Communication and Networks (ICCCN) (pp. 1–11). Hangzhou, China: IEEE. doi:10.1109/ICCCN.2018.8487348.

Haber, S. and Stornetta, W. S. (1991). How to time-stamp a digital document. pp. 437–455. *In*: Menezes, A. J. and Vanstone, S. A. (eds.). Advances in Cryptology-CRYPTO' 90 (Vol. 537). Springer Berlin Heidelberg. doi:10.1007/3-540-38424-3_32.

Khan, D., Jung, L. T. and Hashmani, M. A. (2021, October). Systematic literature review of challenges in blockchain scalability. Applied Sciences 11(20): 9372. doi:10.3390/app11209372.

Lacity, M. C. (2018, Seotember). Addressing key challenges to making enterprise blockchain applications a reality. MIS Quarterly Executive 17(3): 201–222. Retrieved from https://aisel.aisnet.org/misqe/vol17/iss3/3.

Law, F. (ed.). (2022). Cryptocurrency and Blockchain. Retrieved March 2, 2023, from Freeman Law: https://freemanlaw.com/cryptocurrency/.

Ma, Y. and Fang, Y. (2020). Current status, issues, and challenges of blockchain applications in education. International Journal of Emerging Technologies in Learning 15(12): 20–31. doi:10.3991/ijet.v15i12.13797.

Madaan, L., Kumar, A. and Bhushan, B. (2020). Working principle, Application areas and Challenges for Blockchain Technology. 2020 IEEE 9th International Conference on Communication Systems and Network Technologies (CSNT) (pp. 254–259). Gwalior, India: IEEE. doi:10.1109/CSNT.2020.47.

Makridakis, S. and Christodoulou, K. (2019, December). Blockchain: Current challenges and future prospects/applications. Future Internet 11(12): 258. doi:10.3390/fi11120258.

McGhin, T., Choo, K.-K. R., Liu, C. Z. and He, D. (2019, June). Blockchain in healthcare applications: research challenges and opportunities. Journal of Network and Computer Applications 135: 62–75. doi:10.1016/j.jnca.2019.02.027.

Merkle, R. C. (1979, December 14). A Certified Digital Signature. CACM 1–43. Retrieved from http://www.ralphmerkle.com/papers/Certified1979.pdf.

Merkle, R. C. (1980). Protocols for public key cryptosystems. pp. 122–134. *In*: IEEE (ed.). Symposium on Security and Privacy. Retrieved from http://www.ralphmerkle.com/papers/Protocols.pdf.

Mohanta, B. K., Jena, D., Panda, S. S. and Sobhanayak, S. (2019, December). Blockchain technology: a survey on applications and security privacy challenges. Internet of Things 8(100107): 1–19. doi:10.1016/j.iot.2019.100107.

Monrat, A. A., Schelén, O. and Andersson, K. (2019, September). A survey of blockchain from the perspectives of applications, challenges, and opportunities. IEEE Access 7: 117134–117151. doi:10.1109/ACCESS.2019.2936094.

Nakamoto, S. (2008). Bitcoin: A Peer-to-Peer Electronic Cash System. 1–9. Retrieved from https://bitcoin.org/bitcoin.pdf.

Narayanan, A. and Clark, J. (2017, August 29). Bitcoin's academic pedigree. ACM Queue 15(4): 20–49. doi:10.1145/3134434.3136559.

Niya, S. R., Willems, J. and Stiller, B. (2022). A case study of a blockchain-GDPR adaptation. 2022 IEEE International Conference on Blockchain and Cryptocurrency (ICBC) (pp. 1–3). Shanghai, China. doi:10.1109/ICBC54727.2022.9805553.

Reyna, A., Martín, C., Chen, J., Soler, E., Díaz, M. et al. (2018, Novebmer). Manuel on blockchain and its integration with IoT. Challenges and Opportunities. Future Generation Computer Systems 88: 173–190. doi:10.1016/j.future.2018.05.046.

Saroiu, S., Gummadi, P. K. and Gribble, S. D. (2001). Measurement study of peer-to-peer file sharing systems. pp. 156–170. *In*: Kienzle, M. G. and Shenoy, P. J. (eds.). Multimedia Computing and Networking 2002 (Vol. 4673). SPIE. doi:10.1117/12.449977.

Sharma, P., Jindal, R. and Borah, M. D. (2022, March). A review of blockchain-based applications and challenges. Wireless Personal Communications 123: 1201–1243. doi:10.1007/s11277-021-09176-7.

Siyal, A. A., Junejo, A. Z., Zawish, M., Ahmed, K., Khalil, A. et al. (2019, January). Applications of blockchain technology in medicine and healthcare: challenges and future perspectives. Cryptography 3(1): 3. doi:10.3390/cryptography3010003.

Szabo, N. (1996). Smart contracts: building blocks for digital markets. EXTROPY: The Journal of Transhumanist Thought 16. Retrieved from https://www.fon.hum.uva.nl/rob/Courses/InformationInSpeech/CDROM/Literature/LOTwinterschool2006/szabo.best.vwh.net/smart_contracts_2.html.

Szabo, N. (1998). Bit-Gold. Retrieved March 2, 2023, from https://www.difotech.it/immagini_articolo/Nick-Szabo/Unenumerated_Bit_gold_inglese.pdf.

Tang, Y., Xiong, J., Becerril-Arreola, R. and Iyer, L. (2020, March 9). Ethics of blockchain: a framework of technology, applications, impacts and research directions. Information Technology & People 33(2): 602–632. doi:10.1108/ITP-10-2018-0491.

Upadhyay, N. (2020, October). Demystifying blockchain: a critical analysis of challenges, applications and opportunities. International Journal of Information Management 54(102120): 1–26. doi:10.1016/j.ijinfomgt.2020.102120.

Wanchain. (2023). Retrieved from wanchain: https://www.wanchain.org/.

Wang, T., Hua, H., Wei, Z. and Cao, J. (2022, February). Challenges of blockchain in new generation energy systems and future outlooks. International Journal of Electrical Power and Energy Systems 135(107499): 1–17. doi:10.1016/j.ijepes.2021.107499.

Wenhua, Z., Qamar, F., Abdali, T.-A. N., Hassan, R., Jafri, S. T et al. (2023). Blockchain technology: security issues, healthcare applications, challenges and future trends. Electronics 12: 246. doi:10.3390/electronics12030546.

Wood, G. (2016). Polkadot: Vision for a Heterogeneous Multi-Chain Framework Draft-1. WhitePaper. Retrieved Feb 20, 2023, from https://assets.polkadot.network/Polkadot-whitepaper.pdf.

Zheng, Z., Xie, S., Dai, H.-N., Chen, X., Wang, H. et al. (2018, October). Blockchain challenges and opportunities: a survey. International Journal of Web and Grid Services 14(4): 352–375. doi:10.1504/IJWGS.2018.10016848.

Chapter 5
Security and Privacy on Blockchain Applications

Hakan Aşan

5.1 Introduction

Blockchain is a technology in which data is kept in a decentralized database using various encryption methods, and it is almost impossible to change the recorded data (Juma et al., 2019).

It can be said that blockchain technology has revolutionized data management, sharing, and governance. It has been used in various applications due to its decentralized nature and transparency. Applications have been implemented in different sectors, from supply chain management to healthcare. The increasing number of blockchain applications has made privacy and security issues more important. As a new technology, its response to attacks is also a matter of curiosity.

In this section, the importance of security and privacy in blockchain applications is discussed. The blockchain structure, possible attacks on the blockchain system, and measures that can be taken are mentioned.

Security in Blockchain Applications

Security is an essential aspect of blockchain applications. Blockchain does not have a central control mechanism because it has a decentralized structure. In a decentralized system like blockchain, where everyone is a part of the network and has ownership, there can be potential threats

Dokuz Eylul University.
Email: hakan.asan@deu.edu.tr

that arise from various sources. Therefore, several measures are needed to ensure the security of the system.

Security in blockchain applications can be approached from many different angles. The most important ones are consensus algorithms and smart contract auditing. A robust consensus algorithm can prevent many attacks. The most important consensus applications are Proof-of-Work (PoW) and Proof-of-Stake (PoS). While PoW relies on computational power to verify transactions and prevent double spending, PoS uses a certain amount of cryptocurrency share or ownership to verify transactions. Both algorithms have their own pros and cons. Smart contracts are self-executing codes on the blockchain. They are used to automate transactions. Auditing smart contracts is crucial to identify and resolve network problems before they are distributed.

Privacy in Blockchain Applications

Blockchain applications are used in various sectors and deal with important and sensitive information. Because all transactions are visible to all participants in the blockchain structure, ensuring privacy becomes more difficult. There are various methods for ensuring privacy in the blockchain mechanism. One of the most commonly used methods is to encrypt the data before it is recorded on the blockchain. This is done through a hidden layer. Another method is to establish a decentralized identity system. Unlike traditional identity solutions, decentralized identity (DID) management in a blockchain allows authorized parties to access the data. DID use a public-private key pair for verification.

Threats to Blockchain Applications

Due to its decentralized database structure, it is extremely difficult to perform attacks on blockchain applications. However, there are many possible attack methods discussed in theory. Some of these attacks can come from outside the blockchain system, whereas others can come from within. External attacks are usually aimed at taking over the system, freezing it, or performing double-spending transactions. Internal attacks, on the other hand, can be carried out by someone who is a part of the system and may have goals such as taking over the system or making more profit. With the growing economy of blockchain applications, it is natural for old attack methods to increase and new attack methods to emerge.

5.2 Features of Blockchain

Blockchain technology has the characteristics of interoperability, decentralization, immutability, and anonymity. Thus, here we can merge all the features of blockchain as follows (Figure 5.1).

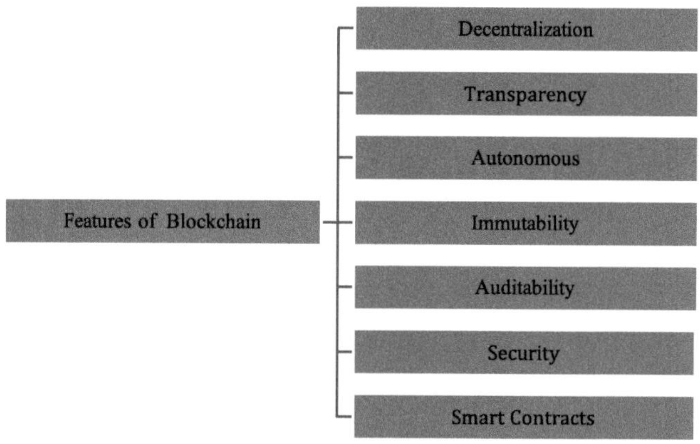

Figure 5.1. Features of Blockchain. Source: Krishnan et al., 2020; Subha, 2020.

5.2.1 Decentralization

Decentralization means that control is not centralized to a single point. In this structure (as shown in Figure 5.2), the system is completely peer-to-peer. It is different from the traditional client-server model where data is centralized. In the client-server model, each client communicates

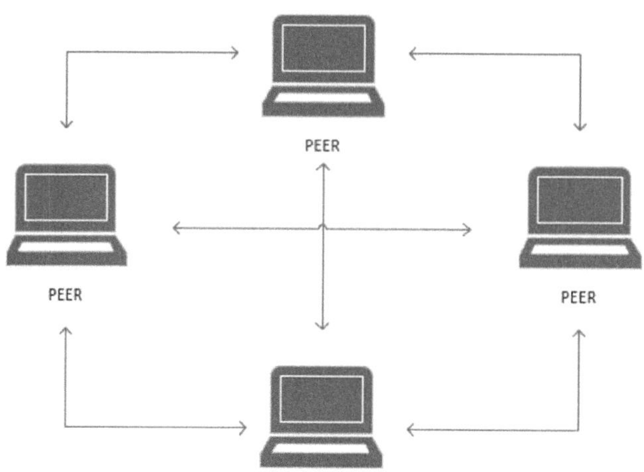

Figure 5.2. Peer to Peer. Source: Prepared by author.

with the central server to perform transactions. However, since each client holds all the information on the blockchain, there is no need for centralized control. This is advantageous since a problem with the server does not affect the entire system. Additionally, in the client-server model, an attack on the server would impact the entire system, whereas in a blockchain, this risk is mitigated. The workload is distributed among peers in the blockchain, while in the client-server model, the entire workload is distributed on the server. In the case of data corruption or unavailability on the server, the system shuts down completely. In blockchains, since the data is distributed among peers (as shown in Figure 5.2), accessing the data is possible. This feature provides transparency and security in Blockchain (Rudra, 2020).

5.2.2 *Transparency*

It is one of the most fundamental features of the blockchain. It is also called visibility (Rathee, 2020). All transactions made (updated or added) are visible to other nodes. All transactions are transparent. No confidential or unknown operation can be performed. The transparency of transactions allows nodes to trust the blockchain.

5.2.3 *Autonomous*

Each of the blockchain blocks can update or transfer its data without getting permission from a central structure (Zeba and Amjad, 2021). It performs this process with the agreement of most nodes in the network.

5.2.4 *Immutability*

The transactions conducted on the blockchain are immutable. Once the data is written to a block, it becomes immutable and protected (Zeba and Amjad, 2021; Rudra, 2020). For a transaction to change, all recipients to which the transaction is reported must be changed, as data is not retained at just one point. This process is not possible in theory. The block must be changed to change a transaction. Changing a block also affects all blocks due to the hash.

In summary, the data in the blockchain cannot be changed by an outside transaction.

5.2.5 *Auditability*

In blockchain technology, all peers keep a copy of the block. The transaction made in this block is timestamped and verified. Thus, the transactions are validated by all peers. Previous records can be easily traced and verified, providing transparency and traceability of the transactions (Sharma et al., 2020). Therefore, it is easy to verify and track transactions (Kaur et al., 2020).

5.2.6 Security

Blockchain technology is inherently secure, as each transaction on the network is cryptographically linked to the previous transaction. This creates a chain of records that is nearly impossible to tamper with, making the blockchain an ideal tool for storing sensitive data, such as financial records and personal identity information. Additionally, blockchain eliminates the need for intermediaries, reducing the risk of fraud and increasing the security of transactions.

5.2.7 Smart Contracts

Smart contracts are structures programmed for the automatic execution of transactions in a blockchain system. They are an essential feature of blockchain technology. Smart contracts enable the automation of transactions and the application of business rules without the need for intermediaries in the blockchain system. Since the smart contracts cannot be changed once they are distributed in the blockchain, they play an active role in ensuring the security of the system.

5.3 Classification of Blockchain

Designs of Blockchain applications vary depending on their usage purpose and the sector in which they are used. Some applications operate within a specific private area, while others are designed to be accessible to everyone. Blockchain applications can be classified into four different groups (Raman et al., 2021).

5.3.1 Public Blockchain

A permissionless and open network where anyone can join the blockchain network and access its content creates a public blockchain (Gencer et al., 2018). It is not under the control of any organization (Paul et al., 2014). Transactions made in the blockchain are transparent and can be discussed by anyone, and the details can be examined. The advantage of a public blockchain is its high reliability, while its disadvantages are the privacy and, energy requirements due to its large computational power.

Examples: Bitcoin, Ethereum, Dash, and Litecoin.

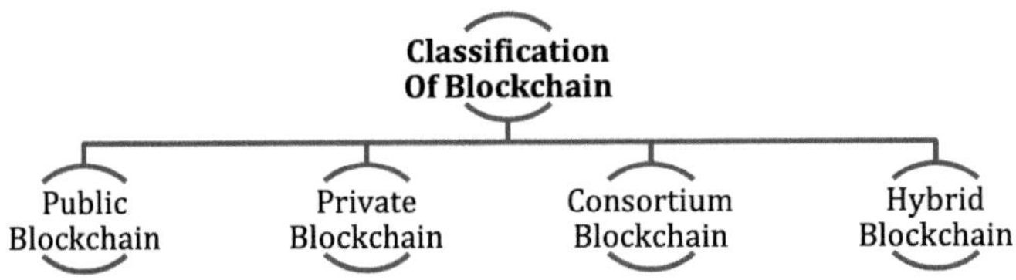

Figure 5.3. Blockchain classes comparison. Source: Prepared by author.

5.3.2 *Private Blockchain*

This type of blockchain requires a special invitation to join the network. They are closed systems and are only used by businesses, government agencies, or individuals (Dinh et al., 2017). In private blockchains, users can join or leave the system within their authority. It is a centralized network controlled by an organization.

Examples: Monox, MultiChain, Bankchain, and Ripple.

5.3.3 *Consortium Blockchain*

They are semi-open blockchains and can only be accessed with permission. Control is not in a single center. Multiple organizations manage the blockchain in a consortium. Limited to the participation of associate members. Only members in the organization can share information and resources (Dutta et al., 2020). It is partially decentralized.

Examples: Quorum, HyperLedger, R3CEV, and Corda.

5.3.4 *Hybrid Blockchain*

This type of blockchain is a combination of both private and public blockchains. It incorporates the advantages of private and public blockchains. In this network, some data is allowed to be public while the rest is private.

Example: Dragonchain.

Table 5.1 provides a comparison of the different features of public, private, and consortium blockchain applications.

The blockchain application to be created according to the needs should be designed on the basis of the features in Table 5.1.

Table 5.1. Public vs. private vs. consortium blockchain.

	Public	**Private**	**Consortium**
Network structure	Decentralized	Centralized	Partly decentralized
Participants	Permissionless Anonymous	Participants Known Participants	Permissionless Known Participants
Controlled by	All network participants	Trusted entity (blockchain owner)	Predefined and authorized network participants group
Efficiency Security	Low Higher due to distribution Consensus mechanism Proof of work/proof of stake	High Lower due to centralization Pre-approved Voting/multiparty consensus	Medium Average due to partial distribution Pre-approved Voting/multiparty consensus
Access	Anyone	Single Organization	Multiple Organizations
Privacy	Low (all transactions are transparent and traceable)	High (access to data is only by trusted entity)	Medium (access to data is controlled by a specific group of network participants)
Transaction Speed	Slow	Medium and Fast	Medium and Fast

Source: Kim and Deka, 2020; Maleh et al., 2020.

5.4 Security and Privacy Issues of Blockchain Technology

In this section, the possible types of attacks on blockchain technology are categorized under headings such as application areas and the individuals who perform the attack.

5.4.1 Network Vulnerabilities and Attacks

5.4.1.1 Distributed Denial-of-Service (DDos)

One of most frequent attacks observed in blockchain networks is DDoS. The main purpose of the attackers is to lock the system by making many requests to the processing resources. This crash prevents other users from doing business. Popular cryptocurrencies such as Ethereum and Bitcoin often encounter this attack. For example, 40 Bitcoin services were attacked by 142 DDos in 2 years. In addition, companies such as BitQuick and CoinWallet had to close after a while (Conti et al., 2018).

Countermeasures: Authentication, Proof-of-Activity (PoA) protocol (Biryukov et al., 2014).

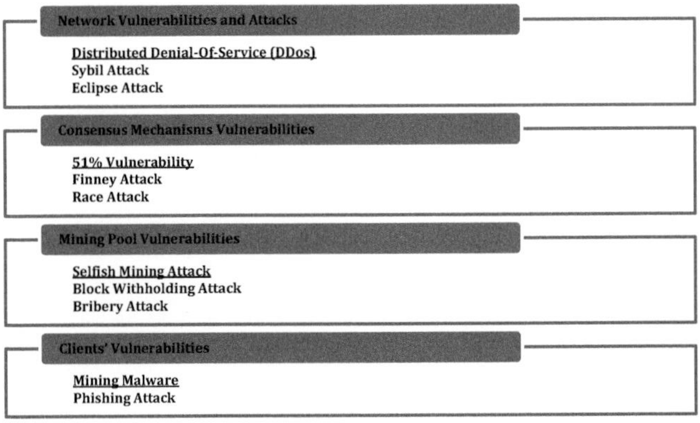

Figure 5.4. Blockchain security vulnerabilities. Source: Prepared by author.

5.4.1.2 *Sybil Attack*

The Sybil attack controls the blockchain by generating many fake nodes by the attacker. These nodes both unnecessarily occupy the network and prevent the movement of real nodes. In this way, the attacker manipulates the network. Blockchains use different "consensus algorithms" to protect themselves from the Sybil attack. If the Sybil attack is successful, it can render the consensus algorithm dysfunctional, causing a double-spend attack.

Countermeasures: Xim (a two-party mixing protocol) (Koshy et al., 2014).

5.4.1.3 *Eclipse Attack*

Eclipse attack is an attack on the network. The attack is aimed at communication between spouses. The attacked person is surrounded and isolated from the rest of the network. This form of attack lays the groundwork for the double-spending and selfish mining attack to occur.

Countermeasures: Using a whitelist (Heilman et al., 2015).

5.4.2 *Consensus Mechanisms Vulnerabilities*

5.4.2.1 *Vulnerability 51%*

Due to the blockchain structure, a pirate who seizes most of the computing capacity of systems, which is 51%, can manipulate transactions. It is theoretically the most well-known method. However, implementing it is extremely difficult. It is also known as the Goldfinger attack. It can do so once an attacker has seized most of the computing capacity within the blockchain. In July 2014, the mining pool "GHash.IO" held more than 51% of the hash rate in Bitcoin for one day (Bastiaan, 2015). The DAO attack that occurred in 2016 (Atzei et al., 2017), had put the entire

Ethereum ecosystem at risk. This attack can cause vulnerabilities such as double spending, excluding transactions, reverse transaction attacks, and changing transactions (Krishnan et al., 2020; Xu, 2016).

Countermeasures: Create double spend alert and add observers to the network (Karame, 2012).

5.4.2.2 Finney Attack

The attacker acquires a copy of a transaction that has already been executed by this type of attack. The attacker sends a version of this transaction to a user. It is important to know that, when the user accepts the transaction, the attacker broadcasts the block belonging to the first transaction to the blockchain system. This will render the transaction sent to the user invalid. The attacker would have somehow managed to perform the double-spend operation (Saad, 2019).

Countermeasures: Wait for multiple confirmations before committing.

5.4.2.3 Race Attack

This attack is carried out using the time between the creation of an attacker and the verification process. The attacker manages to obtain the results of the double-expensive processing process before investigating the verification process (Li et al., 2020).

5.4.3 Mining Pool Vulnerabilities

Mining pools are an important component of the cryptocurrency mining process because they enable individual miners to combine their computing power and work together to mine blocks more efficiently. However, these pools can also be vulnerable to a range of security threats, such as distributed denial-of-service (DDoS) attacks, pool hopping attacks, and selfish mining attacks. It is important to identify and address these vulnerabilities because as they cannot only compromise the security and stability of the mining pool, but also the entire blockchain network.

5.4.3.1 Selfish Mining Attack

Naturally, each attack has a different purpose. The attacker targets one or more blockchain miner whose main goal is to earn more profits. That's why it is called the Selfish Miner attack. It was first proposed by Eyal and Sirer (Eyal and Sirer, 2014). A selfish miner intentionally does not maliciously broadcast mined blocks to the network, aiming to mislead other miners to increase their reward. It is also known as a Block Withholding attack. It is a highly challenging attack to execute practice and easy to detect (Bonneau et al., 2015).

Countermeasures: Include working with trusted miners, ZeroBlock Technique (Solat and Potop-Butucaru, 2016), Heilman Defense Proposition (Heilman, 2014).

5.4.3.2 *Block Withholding Attack*

An attack is made with a different scenario. Here, the attacker joins the system to help block mining by infiltrating users. But it never publishes the blocks, resulting in reduced revenue or no revenue at all. No miner including the attacker, can earn any profit from this attack. That is why it is also called a sabotage attack (Rosenfeld, 2011). However, Courtois and colleagues claim that the attacker can still earn profits from this attack (Courtois and Bahack, 2014).

Countermeasures: Include working with trusted miners, monitoring and controlling revenue distribution.

5.4.3.3 *Bribery Attack*

This attack involves the miner incentivizing other miners by using blocks. The attacker can validate and propagate random transactions by paying dishonest nodes to validate them. The bribe attack can be performed through three different methods: out-of-band payments, negative-fee mining pool, and in-band payments.

For in-band payments, the attacker creates a fork that includes a bribe for any miner who validates it in an attempt to corrupt the blockchain. In the case of out-of-chain payments, the attacker directly compensates the owner of computing resources for mining their blocks. The attacker sets up a mining pool that operates with a negative fee, thereby providing an incentive for participants to earn higher profits.

Countermeasures: Improving the opportunities provided to miners; some rewards and increase in transaction fee.

5.4.4 *Clients' Vulnerabilities*

5.4.4.1 *Mining Malware*

An attacker installs malicious software on the victim's computer or mobile device in order to hijack its computing power and use it to mine cryptocurrency, which can consume significant amounts of electricity and potentially disrupt the target's system performance.

Countermeasures: Keeping software up-to-date, using antivirus software.

5.4.4.2 *Phishing Attack*

By creating phishing websites, the hacker can trick users into disclosing their login credentials, which the hacker can then use to gain unauthorized access to sensitive data on the network (Sopori, 2015). Phishing attacks are low cost and low risk. This is why they are often used by hackers. Hackers often perform this attack through a fake website. Sometimes they use a fake replica of a well-known website.

Countermeasures: Using platforms with known reliability, Not opening links from various platforms.

5.4.5 Privacy Concerns

While blockchain is designed to be secure, it is not inherently private. All transactions on the blockchain are public, meaning that anyone can view them. While this transparency is desirable in some situations, it can also compromise the privacy of individuals and organizations. Blockchain technology can expose sensitive information, such as personal identities and financial transactions.

Conclusion

The decentralized and transparent nature of blockchain technology has enabled its effective use in many industries. The increasing use of cryptocurrency markets worldwide has also increased interest in blockchain. With their increased usage, blockchain applications have become targets for attackers. Therefore, it is crucial to identify possible attacks and the measures to be taken against them. Additionally, privacy has become a significant concern in blockchain applications with the increasing number of applications. The confidentiality of sensitive information shared and stored within blockchain applications is essential, especially in areas such as healthcare and supply chain.

Considering all this information, security and privacy are critical concerns in blockchain applications. Due to the structure of blockchain systems, it is highly improbable that they will be attacked, or data loss will occur. It is also challenging for one person or group to take over the system. In contrast, in systems built around a centralized database, taking over the database means to take over the entire system. However, to take over the blockchain system, one must have at least 51% control of the system. Nonetheless, attacks that may cause interruptions, slowdowns, or double-spending in the system are possible. On the other hand, malicious users and miners who are part of the system can also engage in various actions.

Eliminating security and privacy concerns in blockchain applications is essential for the development of this technology. A trust environment needs to be established for individuals who will participate in the system, as it is not governed by a central authority. Smart contracts need to be monitored, and authorization controls should be implemented for privacy.

In summary, although blockchain technology has tremendous potential due to its structure, it is necessary to be aware of security and privacy concerns. Measures should be taken against possible attacks, and attention should be paid to various applications in terms of privacy. This section discusses blockchain technology in terms of security and privacy. It also addresses possible attacks and the measures to be taken against them. Lastly, it emphasizes what should be considered to produce more secure blockchain applications.

References

Atzei, N., Bartoletti, M. and Cimoli, T. (2017). A survey of attacks on ethereum smart contracts (SoK). *In*: Maffei, M. and Ryan, M. (eds.). Principles of Security and Trust. POST 2017. Lecture Notes in Computer Science, vol. 10204. Springer, Berlin, Heidelberg. https://doi.org/10.1007/978-3-662-54455-6_8.

Bastiaan, M. (2015). Preventing the 51%-attack: a stochastic analysis of two-phase proof of work in bitcoin. http://referaat. cs. utwente. nl/conference/22/paper/7473/preventingthe-51-attack-a-stochasticanalysis-oftwo-phase-proof-of-work-in-bitcoin. pdf (12.02.2023).

Biryukov, A., Khovratovich, D. and Pustogarov, I. (2014). Deanonymisation of clients in Bitcoin P2P network. Proceedings of the 2014 ACM SIGSAC Conference on Computer and Communications Security, ACM pp. 15–29.

Bonneau, J., Miller, A., Clark, J., Narayanan, A., Kroll, J. A. et al. (2015). Sok: Research perspectives and challenges for bitcoin and cryptocurrencies. pp. 104–121. *In*: 2015 IEEE Symposium on Security and Privacy. IEEE.

Conti, M., Sandeep Kumar, E., Lal, C. and Ruj, S. (2018). A survey on security and privacy issues of bitcoin. IEEE Communications Surveys Tutorials 20(4): 3416–3452.

Courtois, N.T. and Bahack, L. (2014). On subversive miner strategies and block withholding attack in bitcoin digital currency. arXiv preprint arXiv:1402.1718.

Dinh, T.T.A., Wang, J., Chen, G., Liu, R., Ooi, B.C. and Tan, K.-L. (2017). BLOCKBENCH: A framework for analyzing private blockchains. pp. 1085–1100. In Proceedings of the ACM SIGMOD International Conference on Management of Data, Part F127746.

Dutta, A., Kumar, S. and Basu, M. (2020). A gated recurrent unit approach to bitcoin price prediction. Journal of Risk and Financial Management 13(2): 23.

Ethereum. (2023). What Is Ethereum? https://ethereum.org/en/what-is-ethereum/ (02.01.2023).

Eyal, I. and Sirer, E. G. (2018). Majority is not enough: Bitcoin mining is vulnerable. Communications of the ACM 61(7): 95–102.

Gencer, A. E., Basu, S., Eyal, I., Van Renesse, R., Sirer, E. G. et al. (2018). Decentralization in bitcoin and ethereum networks. Lecture Notes in Computer Science 439–457. doi:10.1007/978-3-662-58387-6_24.

Heilman, E. (2014). One weird trick to stop selfish miners: Fresh bitcoins, a solution for the honest miner. pp. 161–162. In Financial Cryptography and Data Security: FC 2014 Workshops, BITCOIN and WAHC 2014, Christ Church, Barbados, March 7, 2014, Revised Selected Papers 18. Springer Berlin Heidelberg.

Heilman, E., Kendler, A., Zohar, A. and Goldberg, S. (2015). Eclipse attacks on Bitcoin's peer-to-peer network. pp. 129–144. *In*: Proc. 24th USENIX Conf. Security Symp. (SEC), Washington, DC, USA: USENIX Assoc.

Juma, H., Shaalan, K. and Kamel, I. (2019). A survey on using blockchain in trade supply chain solutions. IEEE Access 7: 184115–184132.

Karame, G. O., Androulaki, E. and Capkun, S. (2012). Double-spending fast payments in bitcoin. pp. 906–917. In Proceedings of the 2012 ACM Conference on Computer and Communications Security.

Kaur, A., Nayyar, A. and Singh, P. (2020). Blockchain: A path to the future. Cryptocurrencies and Blockchain Technology Applications 25–42.

Kim, S. and Deka, G. C. (2020). Advanced Applications of Blockchain Technology. Berlin/Heidelberg, Germany: Springer.

Koshy, P., Koshy, D. and McDaniel, P. (2014). An analysis of anonymity in bitcoin using p2p network traffic. pp. 469–485. In Financial Cryptography and Data Security: 18th International Conference, FC 2014, Christ Church, Barbados, March 3–7, 2014, Revised Selected Papers 18. Springer Berlin Heidelberg.

Krishnan, S., Balas, V. E., Golden, J., Robinson, Y. H., Balaji, S. et al. (2020). Handbook of Research on Blockchain Technology. Massachusetts: Academic Press.

Li, X., Jiang, P., Chen, T., Luo, X. and Wen, Q. (2020). A survey on the security of blockchain systems. Future Generation Computer Systems 107: 841–853.

LITECOIN. (2023). What Is Litecoin? https://litecoin.org (08.02.2023).

Maleh, Y., Shojafar, M., Alazab, M. and Romdhani, I. (2020). Blockchain for Cybersecurity and Privacy: Architectures, Challenges, and Applications. New York: CRC Press.

Paul, G., Sarkar, P. and Mukherjee, S. (2014). Towards a more democratic mining in bitcoins. International Conference on Information Systems Security 14(7): 120–123.

Raman, C. J., Kiruthika, S. U., Ali, L. J. and Raja, S. K. S. (2021). Blockchain technology for privacy and security issues and challenges in IOT-based systems. Blockchain for Information Security and Privacy 193–215.

Rathee, P. (2020). Introduction to blockchain and IoT. Advanced Applications of Blockchain Technology 1–14.

Rosenfeld, M. (2011). Analysis of bitcoin pooled mining reward systems, arXiv preprint: https://doi.org/10.48550/arXiv.1112.4980.

Rudra, B. (2020). Impact of blockchain for internet of things security. Cryptocurrencies and Blockchain Technology Applications 99–127.

Saad, M., Spaulding, J., Njilla, L., Kamhoua, C., Shetty, S. et al. (2019). Exploring the attack surface of blockchain: A systematic overview. arXiv preprint arXiv:1904.03487.

Sharma, D. K., Pant, S., Sharma, M. and Brahmachari, S. (2020). Cryptocurrency mechanisms for blockchains: models, characteristics, challenges, and applications. Handbook of Research on Blockchain Technology 323–348.

Solat, S. and Potop-Butucaru, M. (2016). Zeroblock: Preventing selfish mining in bitcoin. arXiv preprint arXiv:1605.02435.

Sopori, D., Pawar, T., Patil, M. and Ravindran, R. (2017). Internet of things: security threats. International Journal of Advanced Research in Computer Engineering & Technology (IJARCET) 6(3). March, ISSN: 2278–1323.

Subha, T. (2020). Assessing Security Features of Blockchain Technology. pp. 115–138. In Blockchain Technology and Applications. Auerbach Publications.

Xu, J.J. (2016). Are sblockchains immune to all malicious attacks? Financial Innovation 2(1): 25.

Zeba, S. and Amjad, M. (2021). Sustainable and Effective Blockchain-based Solutions for the Security and Privacy of Healthcare Data. pp. 159–176. In Blockchain for Healthcare Systems. CRC Press.

Chapter 6 Blockchain Applications in Healthcare

Onur Doğan

6.1 Introduction

Blockchain technologies have quickly penetrated and contributed to every field of Information and Communication Technology. Thanks to blockchain technology, operations could be performed between entities even in the absence of a trusted and authoritative third party. Blockchain technologies have found different application areas in every field, especially in digital payment systems.

Since its introduction in the field of finance, blockchain technologies have been found to have the potential to perform several jobs in wider areas. However, application areas and effective solution methods related to these areas have not been developed yet. Blockchain promises major changes in many industries beyond finance such as government, healthcare and supply chain (Casino et al., 2019). Perhaps the most important one among the various fields that blockchain technologies serve is the field of healthcare. Individual and social health are fundamental elements of the development of an organization, a company or even a state.

There are many stakeholders such as hospitals, doctors, insurance companies and patients, operating in the healthcare system. In the traditional model, health authorities can access patient information easily since this information is protected in data centres. On the other hand, the modern model consists of big data due to the diversity and volume of digital data collected from various sources (Shuaib et al., 2021).

Dokuz Eylul University, Izmir Vocational School, Management and Organization Department Izmir Turkiye.
Email: onur.dogan@deu.edu.tr

Patients, healthcare professionals, doctors and pharmacists produce a huge amount of health data in many different formats every day. This health data consists of data in many different forms such as texts (prescriptions), images (X-rays, MRIs), audio files (diagnosis, patient stories), and tables (medical device request forms).

Many platforms, software and communication technologies have made innovations for the safe storage of health information. The main idea behind these technologies is to improve the security of health records, track diseases and develop disease prevention strategies around the World (Sharma et al., 2021:2).

It is vital to process this big data, ensuring its transparency, security and reliability. Since, considering the basic characteristics of blockchain technologies; decentralisation, transparency and anonymization (Nakatomo, 2008), it seems appropriate to use it in healthcare, which is a very data-driven sector.

Reducing complexity and costs and improving security, transparency and regulation are considered as potential benefits and the main purpose of blockchains. However, health is characterized as a traditional industry and executing changes in this sector are harder than in others. Healthcare-related issues such as; privacy, quality of care, and

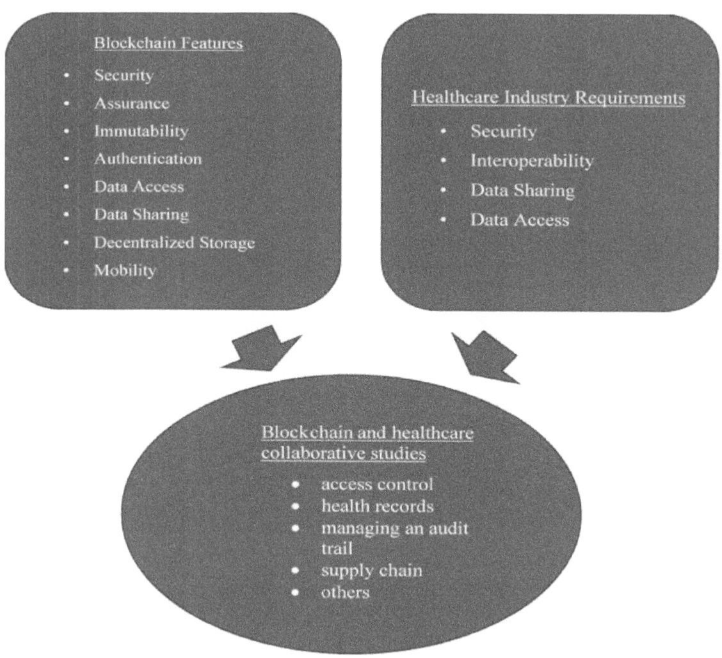

Figure 6.1. Blockchain and healthcare collaboration. Source: Retrieved and compiled from Hölbl et al. (2018) and McGhin et al. (2019).

information security have received worldwide attention in recent years. Blockchain technologies are increasingly recognized as a response to current information distribution problems (Prokofieva and Miah, 2019:1). Considering blockchain capabilities and features and healthcare industry requirements, blockchain Technologies could be useful for healthcare industry concerns. Hölbl et al. (2018), investigated many scientific papers using blockchain technologies in the healthcare industry and they indicated that blockchain can be used in several fields of healthcare such as data sharing, access control, electronic health records, electronic medical records, personal health records, managing audit trails, supply chain and others. The authors indicate that data sharing and health records are the main topics of the papers about blockchain applications in healthcare (Hölbl et al., 2018:9–12).

On the other hand, many studies have also mentioned concerns about using blockchain technologies in the field of healthcare. Misuse of patient information, data security, unrealistic commitments, and policy considerations (Sharma et al., 2021; Hasselgren et al., 2020; OECD, 2020) have been discussed in various studies.

While new technologies have the chance to create various advantages in terms of application areas, they naturally involve various risks and concerns. The main aim of this study is to reveal the current situation regarding the use of blockchain technologies in the field of health. Along with this, the risks, opportunities and challenges of the use of blockchain technology in healthcare will also be discussed.

6.2 Works and Applications

As noticed in the previous part, blockchain solutions and healthcare requirements are accordant fields due to their natures. Data privacy-driven approaches are good examples of blockchain applications in healthcare since blockchain ensures data privacy thanks to its distributed structure while privacy is a very crucial matter in the field of healthcare. Patients need privacy in terms of their health stories. Ensuring privacy for patients and satisfying them about privacy is a way of building trust between healthcare system stakeholders. Many studies have been made by researchers in terms of data privacy and blockchain collaborative usage. Some of them have been mentioned below.

Technological developments in the healthcare systems have increased security challenges, privacy problems, and the leakage of their integrity. Digitalization, wireless connectivity and open access increase the risks in terms of security. Security and privacy of the healthcare systems are important matters for all the stakeholders of the systems including hospitals, clinics and patients. Since healthcare systems have security and privacy problems, emerging and efficient blockchain technology may offer pervasive and sustainable solutions (Zeba and Amjad, 2022:160).

Liu et al. (2019) have highlighted these security and privacy concerns in healthcare systems and proposed a blockchain-based model in their works. According to their model, any data requester can make a query from a healthcare system and can find the relevant record on the EHR consortium blockchain after getting the data owner's authorization. Besides they indicated that the proposed protocol ensures security since it successfully passed the security analysis.

Johari et al. (2022) proposed a model named BLOSOM (Blockchain technology for Security Of Medical records) to keep patients' medical records. Researchers have developed a BlockChain framework (Medichain) which contains all the basic functionalities of a BlockChain to secure a patient's data. Their model also allows users to upload the file containing the list of records in a decisive, distributed and decentralized network.

Another blockchain technology usage in healthcare addresses data sharing since blockchain allows users to share data with related peers. Liu et al. (2019) proposed a model which enables users to share medical data. Thanks to the model, data sharing among physicians could be possible. The model also allows patients who suffer from the same disease to communicate with each other by matching their disease. Das et al. (2022) proposed a blockchain-based model ensuring the privacy and security of health data in terms of sharing and storing. Their main model could be visualized in Figure 6.2.

Blockchain Technologies are also useful in healthcare systems concerning medical supply chain management. Chauhan and Kaul (2022), summarized the process of the supply chain in blockchain as follows. When a new medicine is developed, a specific block which records all information containing the clinical trials and process details is generated. After that, when the clinical trials have been started and as soon as this process is accomplished the medical product receives a unique recognition. Another block is generated which is aggregated with the previous block. Hereafter the medicines are sent to the warehouse, for distribution. In this phase, the blockchain contains information such as barcode, manufacturing and expiration dates. In addition, transportation details could be covered and blockchain could execute a different transaction as well. Thanks to the blockchain supply chain, trustworthy, verifiable and transparent information is provided in all steps of the process.

Kushwa et al. (2023) indicated that current supply chains have problems and challenges such as traceability, lack of trust between stakeholders, lack of transparency, problems in data sharing, and compliance with national standards. Blockchain is seen as a new technology with the capacity to handle all these components in medical supply chains.

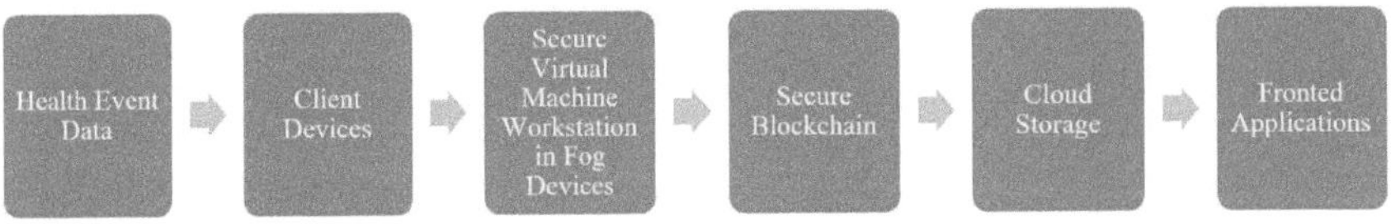

Figure 6.2. Secure medical record management and storage model (Das et al., 2022:34).

Electronic medical records are shared among peers such as clinics, hospitals and insurance companies. Since EMRs consist of sensitive and private health-related information and insurance companies are one of such organizations holding this kind of data it is important to manage health data (Hussein et al., 2018:1–2).

Patients should have health insurance and the health insurance companies are approved authoritities for providing insurance. Patients send the digitally signed confirmation request to the health insurance companies and health insurance companies verify the digitally signed attestation of the patient. In this phase, authentication could be provided by using blockchain technologies (Shuaib et al., 2021:4).

Akbar and Khan (2022) suggest that blockchain technologies can be used to modernize health insurance systems in their work.

Besides these issues which are subject to blockchain and healthcare interaction, Rather and Idrees (2022) remarked that blockchain technologies are also useful in health insurance claim settlement and authentication of digital identities of subjects.

Furthermore, many companies operating in the healthcare industry which are utilizing blockchain-based systems.

BurstIQ (bursitiq.com) is one of the companies which presents blockchain-based solutions in healthcare. BurstIQ's product named LifeGraph eases the development of intelligent solutions using personal health information. LifeGraph which is a web3-ready blockchain platform enhances the data collection, management, and control processes.

Medicalchain (medicalchain.com) is a platform recording electronic health data by using blockchain Technologies. Thanks to Medicalchain patients could share their health data with healthcare professionals.

Nebula Genomics (nebula.org) is a genomic project which manages data and protects genomic data privacy by using blockchain technologies.

Aetna (aetna.com), is a blockchain-based network improving transparency and interoperability in the healthcare industry which aims to create an inclusive blockchain network that could be useful for the healthcare ecosystem.

6.3 Challenges

As indicated in previous chapters, blockchain technology can answer many problems of shareholders of the healthcare ecosystem. In fact, blockchain technology has the potential to revolutionize the healthcare industry. However, several challenges need to be addressed before they can be widely adopted by healthcare institutions. The possible challenges are valid for all the components of the healthcare system; patients, healthcare institutions, doctors and even all healthcare workers.

The first and not the last challenge for individuals including both healthcare workers and patients, it is not about health directly but about digital capabilities. It is clear that new technologies are penetrating all areas and most of the time their usage is highly dependant on the technology skills of individuals. So, even if blockchain technologies respond to many healthcare problems, an individual's lack of knowledge can prevent their usage. Digital literacy is somehow one of the most important challenges of blockchain usage in healthcare applications in a sense. Patients or healthcare workers may not be familiar with blockchain technology and its potential benefits for healthcare applications. Therefore, there is a need to educate them about blockchain and how it can help improve the security, privacy, and sharing of health data.

Another challenge that patients should cope with is security concerns. Blockchain technology is known for its security features, but patients may still have concerns about the privacy and security of their health data. Ultimately, the underlying reason for using a blockchain is to allow people who did not know or trust each other before to share their data in a secure, tamper-proof manner. But even the security of the best-designed blockchain can fail in some scenarios (Boulos et al., 2018). In addition to this, issues such as, data access, updated data and ownership stand have to be dealt with by the patients. With blockchain-based systems, patients may have more control over their health data, including who can access it and how it is used. However, patients may also need to learn how to manage their data and ensure that it is accurate and up-to-date. Besides, it is possible that patients are not aware of regulatory requirements when using blockchain-based systems for healthcare applications.

Due to the lack of digital capabilities of individuals mentioned above patients, doctors and other healthcare workers could think that blockchain is just related to coins and a financial tool. So, they would not be aware of its capabilities.

Convincing experts and other healthcare professionals to switch from paper to technology can be difficult. Many people struggle to transition from paper-based prescriptions to electronic records and prescriptions. Such subjects pose efficiency problems for blockchain-based systems. However, for example, doctors rarely fill in unnecessary fields when filling out forms related to their daily work. The use of blockchain technologies can also raise concerns about data accuracy (Abiodun et al., 2022:14).

One of the challenges that health institutions face-off is the possible high cost of this kind of system. Yousuf et al. (2022) indicated that Blockchain technology is fundamentally computationally expensive. Besides such a system requires large bandwidth and this makes it cost-ineffective.

Hölbl et al. (2018) made a systematic review of the usage of blockchain technologies in healthcare. They found that most of the studies which focus on the use of blockchain in healthcare are based on proof-of-work (PoW). Thus they point out that PoW is a very slow and computationally demanding algorithm. So, this kind of blockchain usage would be impractical for hospitals.

Akbar and Khan (2022) handled this subject concerning the health insurance industry. Researchers defined the pros and cons of the use of blockchain in healthcare according to health insurance companies. They also highlighted cost of the systems. Even further, the researchers stated that the storage and form of local copies is an important challenge. Updating the information is also an issue that needs to be considered. In addition to these possible challenges, the researchers also specified that blockchain is a secure system but it would not able to stop hacking.

Agbo and Mahmoud (2020) indicated that there is a need for incentives to encourage healthcare stakeholders to adopt blockchain technologies while discussing the challenges of blockchain-based technology usage in healthcare in their paper.

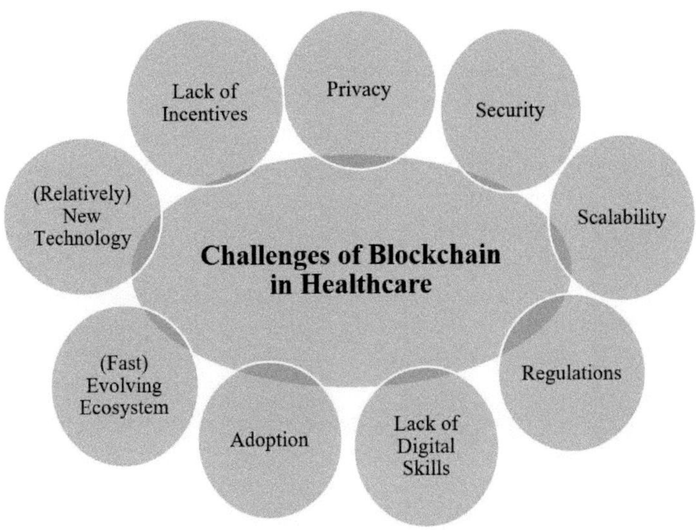

Figure 6.3. Challenges of blockchain in healthcare.

It should be accepted that blockchain is a new technology which is still evolving. Many projects are still starting and ending in a very short period. For example blockchain projects in healthcare such as Akiri, Secure Health Chain and HCX, etc. are non existant today. This situation also can be counted among challenges.

As can be seen, there are many challenges in the use of blockchains in healthcare in terms of individuals (doctors, patients, healthcare workers, etc.) and institutions (hospitals, health insurance companies, etc.). All these challenges in the literature can be visualized in Figure 6.3.

6.4 Opportunities and Future Direction

Blockchain technology has the potential to transform the healthcare industry in many ways and for all the stakeholders irreversibly. When the capabilities of blockchain-based technologies are taken into account, many opportunities for the healthcare ecosystem are created.

Agbo and Mahmood (2020) have defined five main opportunities for blockchain usage in healthcare; patient-centric electronic medical record management, pharmaceutical supply chain management, remote patient monitoring, health ınsurance claim processing, and health data analytics. In the sense of medical records, it has been implied that up-to-date and transparent medical records can be accessed by authorized individuals. Pharmaceutical supply chain management is particularly about drug production and distribution. Improved drug traceability could be possible thanks to blockchain methodologies. Remote patient monitoring covers medical data collection through various technological devices. Health insurance claim processing and health data analytics are the areas that can take advantage of blockchain features such as decentralization, immutability and high computational power.

In addition to these opportunities, Yaqoob et al. (2021) indicate some other opportunities such as clinical trials and precision medicine, maintaining consistent permissions, and protecting telehealth systems.

Hölbl et al. (2018) point out that future implementation of blockchain technology in healthcare should be prepared for collaboration with areas and techniques such as quantum computing, artificial intelligence, big data and the internet of things.

Blockchain technology has a chance to take all components of the healthcare ecosystem to the next level in the future thanks to its capabilities. The use of blockchains in healthcare would reduce transaction time and costs. In addition, with the effective use of blockchain technologies in the future, it will be possible to reduce possible individuals' medical story errors. In addition, thanks to the ability to monitor real-time data, doctors will have access to complete and accurate medical data. From the patients' perspective, due to the transparency of the data, patients will not have a need for a second opinion from another doctor. Keeping patient records on a blockchain network will allow people to know and connect with others who have similar health conditions. In this way, it may be possible for patients to have a feeling of belonging to a community and it will also strengthen the will of the patients to fight the disease (Siyal et al., 2019:13).

6.5 Results and Evolution

In this study, the relationship between blockchain technologies and healthcare has been examined from different aspects. The literature on the relationship between these two areas has been reviewed. Different blockchain methods and applications in healthcare are mentioned in this study. Furthermore, opportunities and challenges related to the use of blockchain technologies in healthcare have been revealed. In addition, a future direction has been presented about the use of blockchain technologies in healthcare.

Blockchain technologies promise a big change in the healthcare industry. Due to their characteristics, these technologies are likely to meet the needs of all components of the healthcare industry. On the other hand, this combination also has risks and weaknesses. Siyal et al. (2019) made a SWOT analysis on blockchains in healthcare. In this section, some other criteria were found while the literature review has been added to their results and the SWOT structure has been extended (Figure 6.4).

Eventually, according to all these literature reviews and after this detailed investigation, it could be said that blockchain usage in healthcare

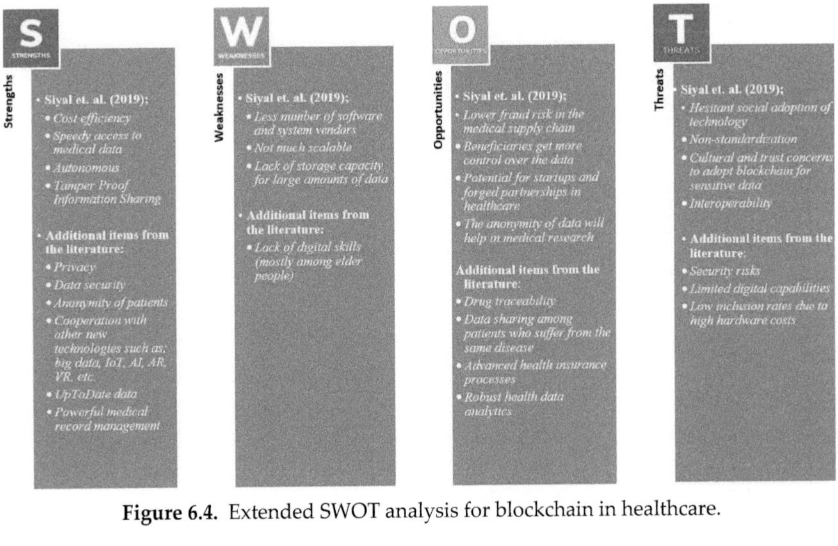

Figure 6.4. Extended SWOT analysis for blockchain in healthcare.

is promising but there are some concerns as well. Furthermore, it seems these technologies solve many problems but still have a long way to go.

References

Abiodun, K. M., Adeniyi, E. A., Awotunde, J. B., Chakraborty, C., Aremu, D. R. et al. (2022). Blockchain and internet of things in healthcare systems prospects, issues, and challenges. pp. 1–22. *In*: Chakraborty, C. (eds.). Digital Health Transformation with Blockchain and Artificial Intelligence. CRC Press, Taylor & Francis Group, Boca Raton, FL, USA.

Agbo, C. C. and Mahmoud, Q. H. (2020). Blockchain in healthcare opportunities, challenges, and possible solutions. International Journal of Healthcare Information Systems and Informatics 15(3): 82–97.

Akbar, A. and Khan, A. M. A. (2022). Modernizing the health insurance industry using blockchain and smart contracts. pp. 17–26. *In*: Idrees, S. M., Agarwal, P. and Alam, M. A. (eds.). Blockchain for Healthcare Systems Challenges, Privacy, and Securing of Data. CRC Press, Taylor & Francis Group, Boca Raton, FL, USA.

Boulos, M. N. K., Wilson, J. T. and Clauson, K. A. (2018). Geospatial blockchain: promises, challenges, and scenarios in health and healthcare. International Journal of Health Geographics 17(25): 1–10.

Casino, F., Dasaklis, T. K. and Patsakis, C. (2019). A systematic literature review of blockchain-based applications: Current status, classification and open issues. Telematics and Informatics 36: 55–81. https://doi.org/10.1016/j.tele.2018.11.006.

Chauhan, R. and Kaul, V. (2022). Blockchain technology: a panacea for medical distribution ailments. pp. 43–60. *In*: Idrees, S. M., Agarwal, P. and Alam, M. A. (eds.). Blockchain for Healthcare Systems Challenges, Privacy, and Securing of Data. CRC Press, Taylor & Francis Group, Boca Raton, FL, USA.

Das, S., Karmakar, S. and Saha, H. N. (2022). Secure digital health data management in internet of things using blockchain and machine learning. pp. 23–45. *In*: Chakraborty, C. (eds.). Digital Health Transformation with Blockchain and Artificial Intelligence. CRC Press, Taylor & Francis Group, Boca Raton, FL, USA.

Hasselgren, A., Kralevska, K., Gligoroski, D., Pedersen, S. A., Faxvaag, A. et al. (2020). Blockchain in healthcare and health sciences—A scoping review. International Journal of Medical Informatics 134: 1–10.

Hölbl, M., Kompara, M., Kamišalic, A. and Zlatolas, L. N. (2018). A systematic review of the use of blockchain in healthcare. Symmetry 470(10): 1–22.

Hussein, A. F., Arun Kumar, N., Ramirez-Gonzalez, G., Abdulhay E., Tavares, J. et al. (2018). A medical records managing and securing blockchain-based system supported by a Genetic Algorithm and Discrete Wavelet Transform. Cognitive Systems Research 52: 1–11.

https://bursitiq.com.

https://medicalchain.com/en/whitepaper/.

https://nebula.org/technology/.

Johari, R., Kumar, V., Gupta, K. and Vidyarthi, D. P. (2022). BLOSOM: BLOckchain technology for Security Of Medical records. ICT Express 8(1): 56–60, ISSN 2405-9595, https://doi.org/10.1016/j.icte.2021.06.002.

Kushwa, S. S., Bairwa, A., Joshi, S., Chaurasia, S., Hemrajani, P. et al. (2023). Blockchain in healthcare, supply-chain management, and government policies. pp. 145–156. *In*: Tanwar, S., Badotra, S. and Rana, A. (eds.). Machine Learning, Blockchain, and Cyber Security in Smart Environments. CRC Press, Taylor & Francis Group, Boca Raton, FL, USA.

Liu, X., Wang, Z., Jin, C., Li, F., Li, G. et al. (2019). A blockchain-based medical data sharing and protection scheme. In IEEE Access 7: 118943–118953, doi: 10.1109/ACCESS.2019.2937685.

McGhin, T., Choo, K. R., Liu, C. Z. and He, D. (2019). Blockchain in healthcare applications: Research challenges and opportunities. Journal of Network and Computer Applications 135: 62–75.

Nakamoto, S. (2008). Bitcoin: a Peer-to-Peer Electronic Cash System.

OECD. (2020). Blockchain Policy Series: Opportunities and Challenges of Blockchain Technologies in Health Care. https://www.oecd.org/daf/blockchain/.

Prokofieva, M. and Miah, S. J. (2019). Blockchain in healthcare. Australasian Journal of Information Systems 23: 1–22.

Rather, I. H. and Idrees, M. S. (2022). Blockchain technology and its applications in the healthcare sector. pp. 17–26. *In*: Idrees, S. M., Agarwal, P. and Alam, M. A. (eds.). Blockchain for Healthcare Systems Challenges, Privacy, and Securing of Data. CRC Press, Taylor & Francis Group, Boca Raton, FL, USA.

Sharma, P., Borah, M. D. and Namasudra, S. (2021). Improving security of medical big data by using Blockchain technology. Computers and Electrical Engineering 96: 1–14.

Shuaib, M., Alam, S., Alam, M. S. and Nasir, M. S. (2021). Self-sovereign identity for healthcare using blockchain. Materials Today: Proceedings. ISSN 2214-7853, https://doi.org/10.1016/j.matpr.2021.03.083.

Siyal, A. A., Junejo, A. Z., Zawish, M., Ahmed, K., Khaliland, A. et al. (2019). Applications of blockchain technology in medicine and healthcare: challenges and future perspectives. Cryptography 3(3): 1–16.

Yaqoob, I., Salah, K., Jayaraman, R. and Al-Hammadi, Y. (2021). Blockchain for healthcare data management: opportunities, challenges, and future recommendations. Neural Computing and Applications 34: 11475–11490.

Yousuf, R., Khan, D. A. and Jeelani, Z. (2022). Security and privacy concerns for blockchain while handling healthcare data. pp. 177–192. *In*: Idrees, S. M., Agarwal, P. and Alam M. A. (eds.). Blockchain for Healthcare Systems Challenges, Privacy, and Securing of Data. CRC Press, Taylor & Francis Group, Boca Raton, FL, USA.

Zeba, S. and Amjad, M. (2022). Sustainable and effective blockchain-based solutions for the security and privacy of healthcare data. pp. 159–176. *In*: Idrees, S. M., Agarwal, P. and Alam, M. A. (eds.). Blockchain for Healthcare Systems Challenges, Privacy, and Securing of Data. CRC Press, Taylor & Francis Group, Boca Raton, FL, USA.

Chapter 7
Blockchain Applications in Security

Rita Ismailova

7.1 Introduction

Blockchain is a relatively new technology that is growing in popularity thanks to its many benefits. The advantages of blockchain technology are due to security mechanisms that protect privacy while sharing data and creating tamper-proof records (Ali et al., 2021). As a result, blockchain is becoming increasingly important for businesses (Tijan et al., 2019; Garg et al., 2021) and governments (Walport, 2016; Ølnes and Jansen, 2017; Hjálmarsson et al., 2018) that need to protect their data and applications from making unauthorized alterations.

Blockchain technologies' security stems from their decentralization. That is, they function on a distributed network, which means that information is copied and these copies are stored among several nodes rather than in a single location. This network operates through consensus mechanisms, allowing multiple participants to validate and record transactions, and thus, eliminating the need for validation of transactions by a central authority. A decentralized approach enhances security, as it makes it more difficult for a single entity to manipulate or corrupt the data (Glaser and Bezzenberger, 2015). Additionally, it can also increase transparency and accountability, as the decentralized network provides a more open and transparent system for tracking transactions. In addition, since blockchain is decentralized, it is difficult for anyone to hack or corrupt the system. While blockchain was initially proposed as a means

Computer Engineering department, Kyrgyz-Turkish Manas University, Bishkek, Kyrgyzstan.
Email: rita.ismailova@manas.edu.kg

of virtual currency transactions (Nakamoto, 2008) and focused on the cryptocurrency sector, applications for this technology have expanded since 2016 as a reliable and secure technology that can be used in a variety of applications (Taylor et al., 2020).

Many applications were proposed to utilize the transparency and accountability properties of blockchain technologies. These applications would allow for increased trust and security within a collaborative environment, for example, in supply chain management—to track the origin and authenticity of products (Tseng et al., 2018; Abbas, 2020). These systems allow consumers to track the origin and journey of products, ensuring that product information is not tampered with. Another such application is a blockchain-based voting system. This system would allow for transparent and secure voting between stakeholders without the need for a third party. The system would also be tamper-proof, ensuring that votes cannot be manipulated. Thus, the usage of blockchain-supported systems allows providing a secure and transparent system for casting and counting votes, reducing the risk of fraud and manipulation (Singh and Chatterjee, 2018; Hjálmarsson et al., 2018).

Finally, blockchain-based land registry systems are used to address data privacy issues in digital identity management—to securely store and manage personal information, providing users with more control over their data (Zyskind and Nathan, 2015), and in healthcare systems—to securely store and manage medical records, reducing errors and improving patient privacy; the ability of blockchain technologies to verify the authenticity can find its applications in healthcare systems and real estate—to securely store and transfer property ownership records and reduce fraud, and in art and collectibles—to verify the authenticity and ownership of items, reducing the risk of fraud in the market.

Thus, besides cryptocurrencies, blockchain technology is being explored and used in various industries and applications. Its importance rises as many businesses and government services move to the internet; a large amount of personal data is to be stored and processed. Many services started utilizing blockchains in order to provide personalized services to users. For example, Zyskind and Nathan (2015) proposed a platform that aims to provide a secure and efficient way to manage access control using a combination of blockchain and off-chain storage solutions where the blockchain acknowledges consumers as the sole proprietors of their personal data.

However, with this variety of blockchain applications, there are many issues related to the security of records in a ledger. The main advantage of the technology—decentralization, can turn into its weakest point as it is vulnerable to hacking and theft of funds (Pilkington, 2016). Additionally, because the blockchain is a distributed system, records can be corrupted or lost in transmission. This could lead to incorrect or missing data in the ledger, which would be difficult to correct. Other security concerns in blockchain applications include regulatory compliance, scalability, and ensuring data privacy. In this study, we will briefly describe the underlying building blocks of blockchain and focus on regulatory compliance and privacy and their implications for blockchain applications.

7.2 Conceptual Background of Blockchain Technologies

Blockchain technology relies on the idea that if a digital ledger with transaction records is decentralized and distributed among many network nodes, its integrity cannot be compromised. All participating nodes keep a copy of the entire blockchain ledger, and when a new transaction is proposed, it is broadcast to the network, and each node independently validates the transaction according to a set of predefined rules. Thus, the security in blockchain technology can be attributed to the combination of (1) decentralization, (2) usage of cryptographic hash functions and digital signature algorithms, and (3) chaining of blocks. The decentralization of transaction details (or ledgers) reduces the chances for malicious parties to change the data stored in records since any single point of failure in the network is detected immediately due to its distributed feature—this ledger is maintained by a network of computers, and thus, tampering with or manipulating the recorded data is infeasible. Hash functions provide a secure way of encrypting data in each block and verifying its integrity. Chaining of blocks strengthens the security by ensuring that previous blocks are linked to each other, and tampering with one block would require tampering with all blocks, making it computationally infeasible. Each block in the chain is linked to the previous block as it contains an output of the cryptographic hash from the previous block, and the integrity of the entire chain can be verified by comparing the hashes. Additionally, since there is no central authority, it is difficult for a single malicious actor to compromise the system. This makes blockchains ideal for use in security applications such as cryptocurrency transactions, secure document storage, and secure voting systems.

1. *Cryptographic Primitives*

Cryptographic hash functions are mathematical algorithms that compress a string (a block of information or a sequence of bytes) of arbitrary length into a string of characters (bytes) of a specific, strictly fixed-length string of bits, referred to as a hash value or simply a hash. This hash value is unique to the original message and is used to ensure the integrity and authenticity of the data (Stinson, 2005). That is, cryptographic hash functions are algorithms that map bit strings of arbitrary finite lengths into strings of fixed lengths. This sequence is the hash code (or hash value) of the original information block. The primary purpose of hash functions is to protect the integrity of information.

The main property of cryptographic hash functions is that any change made to the original message, which serves as an input value of the hash function, will result in a completely different output string. This property, called the avalanche effect, is desirable in hash functions as it ensures that even minor modifications to the input data are reflected in the resulting hash value, making it easier to detect tampering or changes to the original data. The avalanche effect helps ensure data security and integrity is hashed using cryptographic hash functions. Thus, if (unauthorized) one modifies an electronic record whose integrity needs to be protected, recalculating the hash code will give a completely different result. As a result, any changes to the original document can be tracked (Ismailova, 2012).

Another important property is the impossibility of reverse transformation (Damgård, 1990). In other words, the original text from which this hashcode was calculated is impossible to restore. This security criterion of hash functions is called preimage resistance. Preimage resistance provides a level of security because it makes it difficult for an attacker to manipulate the input in a way that would result in the desired hash value. Therefore, preimage resistance is an essential property of cryptographic hash functions for ensuring the integrity and authenticity of digital data. Another crucial criterion is a second preimage resistance—a property of cryptographic hash functions that states it is computationally infeasible to find a message, different from the given one, that maps to the same hash output as a given message. Again, it refers to the property of hash functions that even a small change made in an input message should result in a completely different hash output, making it difficult to find two inputs that map to the same hash value (Rogaway and Shrimpton, 2004). Finally, a hash collision resistance property refers to the requirement that it must be computationally infeasible for a malicious actor to find two different messages that produce the same hash-output (Menezes et al., 2018). In other words, if two distinct inputs are hashed, the outputs should be completely different.

Another cryptographic primitive used in blockchain technologies is a public key algorithm. First proposed by Diffie and Hellman (1976), the development of digital signature technology has been a major breakthrough in the field of cryptography and had a significant impact on the security of electronic transactions and communications. The idea behind public key cryptography is the usage of a pair of keys, one of which is public and used for encryption, and the other part is kept secret and used for decryption. However, in public key cryptosystems, a message can be encrypted using a private key. In that case, the receiver can verify the sender's identity using the public key, and thus, the algorithm can be used to ensure non-repudiation (Rivest et al., 1978). This property is used in blockchain applications for the verification of transactions.

2. *Chaining Hash Values in a Blockchain*

The avalanche effect and security criteria of hashing functions made it possible to utilize them as building blocks in blockchain technologies. In blockchain technologies, a digital asset or information is verified and digitally signed by the sender using their private key. Once a transaction has been created, it is broadcast to the network of computers (known as nodes) that make up the blockchain. Each node verifies the transaction by checking its validity and ensuring that the sender has the necessary funds to complete the transaction. Valid transactions are then bundled together using a hash algorithm that combines transaction records in the block. Each block's hash-value includes the hash-output of the preceding block in the chain, forming a chronological and unbreakable chain of blocks linked to each other by two main principles, namely internal consistency and consensus on transactions (Dhillon et al., 2017). That is, the network can be considered a decentralized database.

If there is a need to add something to this document, the system must calculate the following hash code based on the previous one, and the next entry is added to the database. This process is repeated for every transaction that takes place on the blockchain, creating a constantly growing chain of blocks that form an unbreakable and tamper-proof record of all transactions on the network. That is, an already existing record is not changed. A change in the actual data in a block that was processed by the system results in a change in its hash value. Furthermore, since copies of this hash value are stored in other databases, it is impossible to hide modifications since the records will not match. Thus, all modification data can be tracked. In other words, the essential advantage of blockchain technologies is that transactions are transparent and publicly available, allowing for faster processing and information exchanges. Furthermore, utilizing public-key cryptographic algorithms allows the information within transactions to remain confidential while giving confirmation of each node's validity, providing proof of authenticity and preventing participants from denying their actions as the public key of node-holders is available to everyone in a network, while the private key is stored secret and known only by the key owner. This helps to guarantee that only authorized block-chain technology entities may access the network, which improves security and trust. Researchers also investigate the provision of pseudonymity or privacy inside a blockchain network by public key cryptography techniques within a blockchain when combined with other techniques. Participants can conceal their identities while establishing the legitimacy of their transactions or blocks by using cryptographic techniques such as zero-knowledge proof protocols (Jaoude and Saade, 2019).

7.3 Regulatory Compliance in Blockchain Applications

While considering the relationship between blockchain and regulatory compliance, we focus on three main areas: (1) the regulatory challenges of blockchain adoption, (2) the potential benefits of blockchain for regulatory compliance, and (3) the legal and ethical implications of blockchain technology.

The potential benefits include lower costs and more efficient business processes, higher data security and privacy levels, and an enhanced ability to integrate smart contracts into business processes at a lower cost due to decentralization. However, the decentralized nature of blockchain makes it difficult for regulators to determine who is responsible for ensuring compliance. Blockchain technology operates outside government regulation and is not governed by any central authority, making it difficult to monitor and enforce compliance with existing regulations (Lin et al., 2017). Thus, the need for more regulatory guidance on incorporating the technology into existing legal frameworks has become one of the primary obstacles to wider adoption of blockchain technologies. According to Sandner et al. (2022), neither the regulators nor the governments have the necessary understanding of technology for legal enforcement, nor are they able to provide adequate regulatory frameworks or adapt to the phenomenon.

Another issue is the question of jurisdiction. Because blockchain technology is decentralized, it can be difficult to determine which laws and regulations apply. It creates challenges for cross-border transactions, which may involve multiple legal jurisdictions. This issue was also raised in research by Fazi (2022); the author highlights vulnerabilities related to the lack of jurisdiction and scalability of blockchain transactions. Thus, to reduce risks and to make the use of blockchain more secure for the parties involved in transactions, regulations supporting the innovative potential of the blockchain should be developed since the untraceable nature of blockchain applications and agreements poses a significant challenge to its widespread adoption as a trusted means of trading.

Based on the number of researches conducted concerning legislation, the regulatory issues mostly arise in the adoption of blockchain in the financial sector. Yeoh (2017) examined laws related to blockchain usage in the financial sector in the European Union and the USA; as the author states, the "smart hands-off approach" to regulating blockchain technology usage is beneficial to the efficiency of their use, particularly for financial services.

Nevertheless, despite the challenges, there are several potential benefits of blockchain for regulatory compliance. The use of blockchain can increase transparency and reduce the potential for fraud and errors in the record-keeping process. Blockchain also has the potential to streamline regulatory reporting and improve the efficiency of compliance procedures.

Besides the regulatory compliance issues, there are studies on the usage of blockchain technologies in court systems as well. For example, a work by Bergquist (2021) focuses on the use of blockchain technology in the criminal law sector, specifically in the context of virtual hearings. The author then proposes the use of blockchain technology as a way to address challenges associated with virtual hearings in criminal law and limitations by providing a secure and decentralized platform. The idea is to use blockchain's immutability and transparency features to provide a secure and tamper-proof system for storing and sharing court records. This would help to prevent data tampering, ensure authenticity and increase the transparency and reliability of court proceedings, thus making it an attractive solution for the criminal law sector. The use of blockchain also helps to streamline processes, reduce the risk of errors, and make it easier to access court records in real-time. Despite its benefits, blockchain in the court system also has some challenges, including ensuring privacy and data security, maintaining a high level of scalability, and ensuring regulatory compliance.

Due to its potential to create secure and transparent systems for recording and verifying transactions, blockchain technology not only attracted attention among researchers, but also has led to its adoption in various industries, including the finance sector, supply chain management, and healthcare as well. However, as in the case of the criminal law sector, the regulatory implications of blockchain are still not fully understood. Another issue is that in such systems, there is always sensitive data stored. The regulatory environment surrounding blockchain and privacy protection may be unclear, inconsistent, or even hostile, which can create barriers to the implementation of privacy-preserving blockchain systems (Zyskind et al., 2015).

The adoption of blockchain raises several legal and ethical concerns, particularly around data confidentiality and security. Due to the decentralized nature of blockchain, personal data can also be distributed and thus, stored and processed in various places, making compliance with data protection requirements difficult (OECD, 2019). In addition, the use of blockchain for financial transactions raises questions about money laundering and terrorist financing.

As it can be seen, along with obvious advantages, blockchain technologies adoption is challenging. The lack of regulatory guidance and legal frameworks for a blockchain means that its implementation requires careful consideration of the legal and ethical implications. As applications of blockchain technologies continue to develop, it is essential that regulators and businesses take the time to understand its potential implications so that they can develop appropriate regulations and guidelines. In the meantime, businesses must continue to monitor developments in the blockchain space to ensure compliance with applicable laws (Snyder, 2019). Further research is needed to explore the potential benefits and challenges of blockchain for regulatory compliance in more detail.

7.4 Data Privacy and Integrity

One of the major issues with blockchain is that it is a public system, which means that data on the blockchain is exposed to anyone who has access to the network. This can potentially compromise the privacy of individuals, as their data can be accessed by other users. Moreover, data in blockchain cannot be modified or deleted, which makes it immutable. This could lead to data leakage, as malicious actors could take advantage of this feature to gain access to sensitive information (Zhang et al., 2019). Blockchain-based systems can address challenges such as data breaches, unauthorized access, and data manipulation (Zhang et al., 2022). However, despite the use of encryption, records in a blockchain technology are distributed among network nodes, and thus, personal and sensitive information stored on a blockchain may still be vulnerable to unauthorized access and hacking, which creates challenges for compliance with data protection laws, such as the General Data Protection Regulation (GDPR) adopted in the European Union (Manteghi, 2021). Since records are decentralized, it can be hard to identify the data controller, data processor, and data subjects. Furthermore, it can be challenging to ensure that processing of personal data is carried out in accordance with the relevant laws and regulations.

Thus, although from a message integrity point of view a decentralized, blockchain-based system could be used to store and manage sensitive information, such as personal data and financial transactions, in a secure and transparent manner compared to traditional centralized systems due to the usage of cryptographic algorithms, depending on the specific implementation and context, the challenges and limitations of implementing a blockchain-based privacy system maintain the need for further research in this field (Zyskind et al., 2015). In addition, the security of blockchain systems is a significant concern, as they can be vulnerable to attacks that compromise the privacy of users' personal data.

Some systems, such as those in finance, healthcare, or education, require better security as there is personal data involved. For example,

Zhang et al. (2022) explored the use of blockchain technology for the secure and privacy-preserving management of electronic health records (EHRs) that utilizes cryptographic techniques to protect patient privacy and secures the storage and sharing of medical records. By evaluating the performance and security of the proposed system, including the privacy-preserving properties of the cryptographic techniques used, it was shown that a blockchain-based EHR system provides a secure and privacy-friendly solution for the management of electronic health records by enabling patients to control and share their EHRs selectively with authorized parties, and by protecting EHRs from unauthorized access and data breaches. There are many other proposed implementations of the blockchain technologies in healthcare, such as SEMRES (Lee et al., 2022) and Agent Free Insurance System (Karmakar et al., 2023). Although proposed systems differ in teir specific design and evaluation, they reach similar findings on the potential benefits of employing blockchain technology for medical record management.

Studies on the usage of blockchain technologies in education primarily focus on three themes: standardized scholarship, behavioral patterns, and digital badging (Zhao et al., 2023). Blockchain helps to monitor progress, evaluate oneself, provide real-time communication between students and teachers, and shares digital resources. Moreover, it can help to maintain and validate digital identities of entities, track and trace student records, ensures privacy and security of online assessments, certification, and verification of credentials, secures storage and sharing of student records, and improvement of transparency and trust in the education system (Bhaskar et al., 2021). Current research on blockchain usage is mainly focused on secure online examination since, during the COVID-19 pandemic, the educational sector faced the challenge of an online assessment. In the study by Sattar et al. (2023), an analysis of the online test platform features was carried out. Based on the results, the authors proposed a blockchain-based secure online examination system for educational institutions that prevent students from cheating on exams. While, according to the authors, blockchain technology helps to ensure security in online exams and, thus, plays a vital role in the evolution of e-learning, improvements to the system need to be made in two main areas: question labeling and questionnaire automation.

On the other hand, while ensuring exam safety, the system leaks potential limitations, such as the need for permission to access the camera, microphone, and GYRO, as well as the need for a stable internet connection. Samanta et al. (2021) investigated blockchain usage from a different perspective and proposed a smart contract for a university examination system. The researchers categorized the current works into three distinct blocks. They attempted to enhance the security of the chains, resulting in decreased processing speed and reduced efficiency, assuming that "Even though there are different security measures for smart contracts, their transactions and data are always under the threat of cyber terrorism."

Although there are many benefits to implementing blockchain in online learning, tailored strategies are needed to bridge blockchain and online learning (Zhao et al., 2023). Although blockchain-based systems can provide secure storage and management of sensitive or personal data, they can still be vulnerable to unauthorized access or attacks due to potential limitations of blockchain technology, such as permission and stability requirements of the systems.

7.5 Conclusion

While blockchain technology offers enhanced data security and faster transactions due to its decentralized and distributed nature, it also poses privacy challenges. The transparency of the blockchain ledger means that all transactions are visible to all participants, which could potentially reveal sensitive information about the parties involved. Additionally, since the ledger is immutable, any data stored on it cannot be erased or modified, which can create challenges for compliance with data privacy regulations. As a result, companies must carefully evaluate the privacy implications of employing blockchain technology and implement appropriate measures to secure sensitive information. First, protecting blockchain users' personal data is an issue that most blockchain platforms struggle with. With a distributed database, anyone can view personal data stored on the blockchain, making it difficult to protect individual privacy (Shah et al., 2019). Most blockchains store all user data on their respective nodes, making them vulnerable to hacking and modification by third parties. Additionally, most blockchains have no built-in mechanisms for protecting user data from misuse by corporations or state agencies. There is also no legal way for users to control who has access to their data on the blockchain; this leaves everyone susceptible to unwanted third-party access. Therefore organizations must take steps to remain compliant and informed on the risks of using blockchain technology for personal data storage (Snyder, 2019). Data privacy is a significant concern in the digital world. Blockchain is a revolutionary technology that promises to provide an immutable ledger and secure transactions, making it an attractive option for businesses and individuals alike. However, it is important to recognize the potential data privacy risks associated with blockchain and take steps to mitigate these risks. This includes staying up to date on the most recent regulations, such as the EU General Data Protection Regulation, and implementing best practices for managing personal information on the blockchain (Walters and Coutu, 2022).

As a result of a systematic review of applications of blockchain technology, Mohanta et al. (2019) highlighted the limitations of blockchain technology, including scalability, interoperability, and the lack of standardization. Yet, while discussing the potential benefits of blockchain technology, e-government academics should focus on technically straightforward solutions with few organizational or institutional impediments (Ølnes and Jansen, 2017).

In conclusion, we can say that blockchain technology has the ability to significantly impact the way data is kept and transactions are carried out. Although blockchain technology holds great promise, there is still much work to be done to address the various security issues and challenges faced by blockchain systems (Lin et al., 2017). It is critical to identify and investigate the potential data privacy issues related to this technology, as well as take efforts to reduce them. By employing good data hygiene practices, utilizing multi-signature authentication, and making use of new technologies such as zero-knowledge proofs, businesses, and individuals can ensure that their data remains secure and private.

References

Abbas, K., Afaq, M., Ahmed Khan, T. and Song, W. C. (2020). A blockchain and machine learning-based drug supply chain management and recommendation system for smart pharmaceutical industry. Electronics 9(5): 852.

Abou Jaoude, J. and Saade, R. G. (2019). Blockchain applications–usage in different domains. IEEE Access 7: 45360–45381. DOI: 10.1109/ACCESS.2019.2902501.

Ali, O., Jaradat, A., Kulakli, A. and Abuhalimeh, A. (2021). A comparative study: Blockchain technology utilization benefits, challenges and functionalities. IEEE Access 9: 12730–12749.

Bergquist, C. (2021). Virtual hearings and blockchain technology solutions in criminal law. Mitchell Hamline Law Review 47(3): 10.

Bhaskar, P., Tiwari, C. K. and Joshi, A. (2021). Blockchain in education management: present and future applications. Interactive Technology and Smart Education 18(1): 1–17.

Damgård, I. (1990). A design principle for hash functions. pp. 416–427. In Crypto (Vol. 89).

Dhillon, V., Metcalf, D. and Hooper, M. (2017). Blockchain Enabled Applications. Berkeley, CA: Apress.

Diffie, W. and Hellman, M. (1976). New directions on cryptographic techniques. In Proceedings of the AFIPS National Computer Conference.

Fazi, M. A. (2022). A contextual study of regulatory framework for blockchain. pp. 40–51. In Regulatory Aspects of Artificial Intelligence on Blockchain. IGI Global.

Garg, P., Gupta, B., Chauhan, A. K., Sivarajah, U., Gupta, S. and Modgil, S. (2021). Measuring the perceived benefits of implementing blockchain technology in the banking sector. Technological Forecasting and Social Change 163: 120407.

Glaser, F. and Bezzenberger, L. (2015, March). Beyond cryptocurrencies—a taxonomy of decentralized consensus systems. In 23rd European Conference on Information Systems (ECIS), Münster, Germany.

Hjálmarsson, F. Þ., Hreiðarsson, G. K., Hamdaqa, M. and Hjálmtýsson, G. (2018, July). Blockchain-based e-voting system. pp. 983–986. In 2018 IEEE 11th International Conference on Cloud Computing (CLOUD). IEEE.

Ismailova, R. (2012). Analysis of three block cipher based hash functions: Whirpool, Grøstl and Grindahl [Ph.D. - Doctoral Program]. Middle East Technical University. OpenMETU https://open.metu.edu.tr/bitstream/handle/11511/22067/index.pdf?sequence=1.

Karmakar, A., Ghosh, P., Banerjee, P. S. and De, D. (2023). ChainSure: Agent Free Insurance System using Blockchain for Healthcare 4.0. Intelligent Systems with Applications, 200177.

Lee, Y. L., Lee, H. A., Hsu, C. Y., Kung, H. H. and Chiu, H. W. (2022). SEMRES—A triple security protected blockchain based medical record exchange structure. Computer Methods and Programs in Biomedicine 215: 106595.

Lin, I. C. and Liao, T. C. (2017). A survey of blockchain security issues and challenges. Int. J. Netw. Secur. 19(5): 653–659.

Manteghi, M. (2021). Blockchain and the European Union's General Data Protection Regulation: from Conflict to "Peaceful" Coexistence? Available at SSRN 3805647.

Menezes, A. J., Van Oorschot, P. C. and Vanstone, S. A. (2018). Handbook of Applied Cryptography. CRC Press.

Mohanta, B. K., Jena, D., Panda, S. S. and Sobhanayak, S. (2019). Blockchain technology: A survey on applications and security privacy challenges. Internet of Things 8: 100107.

Nakamoto, S. (2008). Bitcoin: A peer-to-peer electronic cash system. Decentralized Business Review 21260.

OECD. (2019). The Policy Environment for Blockchain Innovation and Adoption: 2019 OECD Global Blockchain Policy Forum Summary Report, OECD Blockchain Policy Series. www.oecd.org/finance/2019-OECD-Global-Blockchain-Policy-Forum-Summary-Report.pdf.

Ølnes, S. and Jansen, A. (2017). Blockchain technology as support infrastructure in e-government. pp. 215–227. In Electronic Government: 16th IFIP WG 8.5 International Conference, EGOV 2017, St. Petersburg, Russia, September 4–7, 2017, Proceedings 16. Springer International Publishing.

Pilkington, M. (2016). Blockchain technology: principles and applications. pp. 225–253. In Research Handbook on Digital Transformations. Edward Elgar Publishing.

Rivest, R. L., Shamir, A. and Adleman, L. (1978). A method for obtaining digital signatures and public-key cryptosystems. Communications of the ACM 21(2): 120–126.

Rogaway, P. and Shrimpton, T. (2004, February). Cryptographic hash-function basics: Definitions, implications, and separations for preimage resistance, second-preimage resistance, and collision resistance. pp. 371–388. In FSE (Vol. 3017).

Samanta, A. K., Sarkar, B. B. and Chaki, N. (2021). A blockchain-based smart contract towards developing secured university examination system. Journal of Data, Information and Management 3: 237–249.

Sandner, P. G., Ferreira, A. and Dunser, T. (2022). Crypto regulation and the case for Europe. pp. 661–693. In Handbook on Blockchain. Cham: Springer International Publishing.

Sattar, M. R. I., Efty, M. T. B. H., Rafa, T. S., Das, T., Samad, M. S., Pathak, A. and Ullah, M. H. (2023). An advanced and secure framework for conducting online examination using blockchain method. Cyber Security and Applications 1: 100005.

Shah, P., Forester, D., Berberich, M., Raspé, C. and Mueller, H. (2019). Blockchain Technology: Data Privacy Issues and Potential Mitigation Strategies. Practical Law.

Singh, A. and Chatterjee, K. (2018, September). Secevs: Secure electronic voting system using blockchain technology. pp. 863–867. In 2018 International Conference on Computing, Power and Communication Technologies (GUCON). IEEE.

Snyder, S. (2019, January 14). The Privacy Questions Raised by Blockchain. Law360. Retrieved February 12, 2023, from https://www.law360.com/banking/articles/1115579/the-privacy-questions-raised-by-blockchain.

Stinson, D. R. (2005). Cryptography: Theory and Practice. Chapman and Hall/CRC.

Taylor, P. J., Dargahi, T., Dehghantanha, A., Parizi, R. M. and Choo, K. K. R. (2020). A systematic literature review of blockchain cyber security. Digital Communications and Networks 6(2): 147–156.

Tijan, E., Aksentijević, S., Ivanić, K. and Jardas, M. (2019). Blockchain technology implementation in logistics. Sustainability 11(4): 1185.

Tseng, J. H., Liao, Y. C., Chong, B. and Liao, S. W. (2018). Governance on the drug supply chain via gcoin blockchain. International Journal of Environmental Research and Public Health 15(6): 1055.

Walport, M. (2016). Distributed ledger technology: beyond block chain. UK Government Office for Science, London. Haettu osoitteesta https://www. gov. uk/government/ publications/distributed-ledgertechnology-blackett-review.

Walters, N. and Coutu, S. (2022, June 9). The privacy paradox in blockchain: Best practices for data management in crypto. Retrieved February 9, 2023, from https://www. dentons.com/en/insights/articles/2022/june/9/the-privacy-paradox-in-blockchain-best-practices-for-data-management-in-crypto.

Yeoh, P. (2017). Regulatory issues in blockchain technology. Journal of Financial Regulation and Compliance.

Zhang, R., Xue, R. and Liu, L. (2019). Security and privacy on blockchain. ACM Computing Surveys (CSUR) 52(3): 1–34

Zhang, G., Yang, Z. and Liu, W. (2022). Blockchain-based privacy preserving e-health system for healthcare data in cloud. Computer Networks 203: 108586.

Zhao, M., Liu, W., Saif, A. N. M., Wang, B., Rupa, R. A., Islam, K. M. and Rahman, M. A. (2023). Blockchain in online learning: a systematic review and bibliographic visualization. Sustainability 15(2): 1470.

Zyskind, G. and Nathan, O. (2015). Decentralizing privacy: Using blockchain to protect personal data. pp. 180–184. In 2015 IEEE Security and Privacy Workshops. IEEE.

Zyskind, G., Nathan, O. and Pentland, A. (2015). Enigma: Decentralized computation platform with guaranteed privacy. arXiv preprint arXiv:1506.03471.

Chapter 8
Blockchain Applications in Contract Management

Mert Donercark

8.1 Introduction

Contracts, whether written or verbal, guide our behavior and define our boundaries in every aspect of life. The execution of contracts following established rules and guidelines, provides a framework for institutions and individuals to fulfill their obligations towards each other professionally, ensuring completeness and timeliness in business transactions.

Managers representing organizations have an obligation to structure all activities to be conducted with counterparties in a manner that safeguards the interests of the organization. However, organizations engage in various activities involving employees, suppliers, customers, governments, and investors. Despite the intensive labor involved, tracking all these activities with the limited resources of human personnel often results in inadequate protection of the organization's interests due to human errors. Nowadays, technological advancements offer new infrastructures and autonomous systems that make it easier to monitor, supervise and manage all activities carried out with counterparties. These solutions require significantly less labor while providing effective means to track and direct such activities.

Regardless of the legal systems in different countries, it is crucial for all parties involved to ensure that contract terms are not unilaterally changed after acceptance and that transactions are conducted in accordance with the contractual stages. Up until now, parties have shared their contracts

Consultant at MicroDestek Company.
Email: mertd@microdestek.com.tr

through means such as notaries, physical exchange of documents with wet signatures, or the exchange of electronic certificates, allowing for monitoring of the process. However, in cases where one party fails to fulfill the contract terms, obtaining the rights of the other party can involve a lengthy and expensive process.

Through blockchain technology, contract terms recorded immutably and retrospectively can distribute gains to parties automatically based on activities carried out during the contract process and can assist parties in minimizing disputes. Furthermore, conducting transactions in digital environments allows systems that form the digital memory of organizations to benefit from this structure (https://en.bitcoin.it/wiki/Contract, 2023).

In the subsequent sections of the article, the design of contracts in a digital environment, unlike traditional contracts, will be explained with an example design. In addition, infrastructure and programming methods that allow the execution of such contracts on the blockchain will be discussed.

From a management perspective, it is evident that the use of new-generation technologies that enable seamless monitoring of the entire contract lifecycle encompassing creation, agreement, approval, execution, and completion will significantly enhance managerial efficiency. These technologies allow managers who bear the responsibility for contracts, by virtue of their representative powers, to electronically or physically sign contracts with their wet signatures, thereby streamlining the management process.

8.2 Contract Management

Contracts are written or verbal agreements that express the mutual rules, responsibilities, and expectations of multiple parties involved in an activity. When creating these agreements, the parties express their needs, obligations, and expectations in line with their requirements and responsibilities.

Contracts can be broadly categorized into two main groups: standard-form contracts and non-standard (negotiated) contracts.

a) *Standard contracts*: are contract types where one of the parties to the contract signs a pre-determined standard text without negotiating all the terms with the other party. These types of contracts can generally be exemplified as subscription contracts, package product sales contracts, and so on.

b) *Non-standard contracts*: these contracts are agreements in which the parties negotiate and determine the conditions through mutual negotiation and sign the final text agreed upon. Contracts such as software development contracts, contractor agreements, consulting agreements, and service procurement agreements fall into this category.

In all types of contracts, using the steps known as the contract lifecycle systematically forms the basis of contract management. Although the number of steps may differ in type contracts and non-type contracts, they contain the same headings (Donercark and Selimoglu, 2022).

The contract lifecycle includes:

- Contract initiation request,
- Drafting and negotiation,
- Agreement and signature,
- Commencement of effectiveness and obligations,
- Tracking all documents, information, and deadlines in digital environments,
- Audit and management reports,
- Renewal and archiving process,
- Destruction and conversion steps.

Milestones, also known as contractual milestones, refer to predetermined steps in a contract that parties must meet in order to achieve their agreed-upon goals. Warning periods and control of milestones are important in terms of tracking parties' obligations specified in the contract.

From a management perspective, the creation, execution, monitoring, and management of contract processes involving different departments of the organization and counterparties directly affect not only legal, material, and immaterial losses but also the quality and expected attributes of the services provided or received. Although different departments may be responsible for monitoring contracts, high-level executives who have a brief understanding of the contract details may also sign the agreed text. Therefore, it is essential for all members of the management team to review the pre-designed processes and manage the contract process following the agreed plans. As you can see in the Figure 8.1.

Observations highlight that the technology used in accounting, finance, production, and customer management areas is not being fully leveraged in contract management processes, which serve as a crucial intersection point for multiple departments. Firstly, enhancing process efficiency can be achieved by identifying the contract flows among departments and managing contract management through processes derived from these flows.

The presentation of contracts, particularly those involving mutual negotiation, for review or approval by various departments within a

Figure 8.1. Contract management lifecycle. Photograph by the author.

company is crucial. This step ensures that the contract is aligned with the company's policies and plays a significant role in its structuring. Figure 8.2 depicts an example process highlighting the steps involved and demonstrating how the actions of different departments trigger subsequent actions based on their feedback, approval, or rejection of the contract. As you can see in Figure 8.2.

a) The field labeled "Process Number" indicates the number assigned to the process flow.
b) The "Step Name" field defines which task will be performed in which step.
c) The fields of "Approval Group" and "Approval Type" specify the individuals or groups responsible for carrying out the contract approval process and the manner in which it will be conducted. Depending on the organizational structure, the authorized individuals or groups assigned to review the contract may be designated as individuals or as a collective group.
d) The "Step Number" field records which step of the process is being taken.
e) The "If approved" and "If Declined" fields indicate which step will be taken if the step is approved or declined.
f) The "Approval seniority" field defines which users with certain seniority levels can participate in the process in the case of group or individual approvals.

The "Warning Day range" field signifies the number of days before reminders will be sent if there is no response to within the designated time frame. By identifying the primary types of contracts in contract

Process Number	Step Name	Approval group	Approval Type	Step Number	if approved	if declined	approval seniority	warning day range
4444406	The request for the contract has been added to the system.	Dynamic	Dynamic	1	2	1	5	2
4444406	Contract documents have been added to the system.	Dynamic	Dynamic	2	3	2	5	2
4444406	Contract cover approval completed.	SUPPLIER AUTHORIZED,	group approval	3	4	2	5	1
4444406	The responsible information technology officer was selected.	INFORMATION TECHNOLOGIES,	group approval	4	5	2	3	2
4444406	Responsible information technology approval has been completed.	Dynamic	Dynamic	5	6	2	5	2
4444406	Responsible lawyer was selected.	LAW DEPARTMENT,	group approval	6	7	2	3	2
4444406	Responsible attorney approval has been completed.	Dynamic	Dynamic	7	8	2	5	2
4444406	Supplier Representative contract control and legalization have been completed.	SUPPLIER AUTHORIZED,	group approval	8	9	2	5	10
4444406	The supplier legal team signature process has been completed.	SUPPLIER LAW,	group approval	9	10	8	3	2
4444406	Purchase confirmation completed.	PURCHASING DEPARTMENT,	group approval	10	11	8	5	2
4444406	Signed documents are uploaded to the system.	SIGNATORY,	group approval	11	12	10	3	2
4444406	The user who initiated the agreement addition request selected agreement cover approvals.	Dynamic	Dynamic	12	13	10	5	2
4444406	Stamp tax procedures have been completed.	ACCOUNTING,	group approval	13	0	12	5	14

Figure 8.2. Contract progress. Photograph by the author.

management and defining the relevant business units involved in these processes, management decisions can be effectively implemented. This approach ensures that the true stakeholders are actively engaged in the entire contract lifecycle.

8.3 Blockchain

This technology, referred to as the digital notary of today, can be briefly described as a distributed ledger. In this technology, transactions performed by all stakeholders within a blockchain network are encrypted and recorded in a sequential series of blocks. These blocks are accumulated in an immutable manner, along with timestamps, ensuring the integrity of the recorded information. All transactions executed by users on the blockchain network can be retrospectively verified in a transparent manner.

Data can be stored on relational databases and distributed databases in digital environments. The hardware that enables the recording of data in both data recording methods works with integrity and the execution is carried out using the resources of a service provider or institution. In blockchain technology, transactions are executed anonymously through servers that make up the hardware power of the system. In the blockchain infrastructure, no single server used for recording transactions can be trusted alone.

The data recorded within a distributed ledger system is simultaneously distributed to multiple servers. In the event of an external attempt to alter the integrity of the data it is expected to remain uncompromised as long as more than 51% of the computers that make up the entire system are not under attack (Anderson et al., 2016).

To be classified as a blockchain infrastructure certain criteria must be met. These include the ability to operate in a distributed manner to allow for transparent retrospective verification and immutability. The blockchain should also be able to facilitate independent and anonymous registration operations (Lin and Liao, 2017).

If a recording of activities with the parties involved is requested to be made by an independent source, blockchain technology stands out today with much lower costs, higher efficiency, and interoperability than traditional verification and registration mechanisms such as notaries, digital timestamped electronic certificates and physical verification organizations (Clack et al., 2016).

8.3.1 Types of Blockchain Infrastructure

Developing applications using blockchain or combining existing applications requires identifying your needs correctly and using a blockchain network that supports those needs properly. Blockchain networks can be grouped under four main headings.

- **Open blockchain** is a type of blockchain that anyone can participate in without the need for a central authority. Examples of this infrastructure include Ripple, Avalanche, Bitcoin, and Ethereum. Additionally, these infrastructures provide a programming language and infrastructure for developers to create and execute applications such as decentralized smart contracts on a decentralized network as can be seen in the Figure 8.3.
- **Private blockchains** are a type of blockchain that is not open to everyone and only allows authorized users to participate in the network. There is a need for an authority to identify authorized users and operate the system. The hardware used for recording transactions can be provided by a specific organization. Private blockchains can be designed as a much smaller and more restricted structure than open blockchains and can be used within a company or between companies (https://www.ibm.com/blockchain, 2023). For example, a holding company could create and use an internal blockchain to conduct and

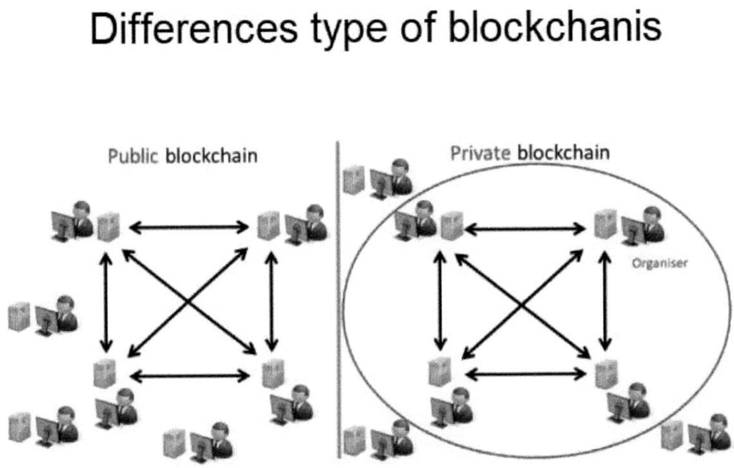

Figure 8.3. Differences in types of blockchains. Photograph by the author.

record controlled sales activities between its subsidiaries, rather than using a public blockchain can be seen in the Figure 8.3.

- **Hybrid blockchains** are blockchains that are structured to allow applications that work with open blockchains to also communicate and reach a consensus with specific conditions on private blockchains.
- **Consortium blockchains** are similar to hybrid blockchains in structure but differ from hybrid blockchains in that the consensus procedures are predefined and the authority is not a single entity but as many participants as there are in the consortium. This reduces the risks associated with having a single authority (Ünal and Uluyol, 2020).

The fact that blockchain applications have different use cases can sometimes lead to the use of different infrastructures with different features, either together or separately. It is important to investigate the possibilities and capabilities of the selected infrastructure, such as integration, consensus, and application development, and make choices based on the results in order to use the infrastructure efficiently.

8.3.2 Blockchain Smart Contract Application Development Language

Popular blockchain application development languages for smart contracts are exemplified below. Before developing a blockchain application, it is important to check which languages are supported by the intended blockchain infrastructure.

- **Solidity** is commonly used by Ethereum developers and has a syntax similar to JavaScript.
- **Simplicity** is an object-oriented programming language that supports the Bitcoin ecosystem.
- **C++** is a widely used programming language in various fields.
- **JavaScript** is an easy and fast programming language commonly preferred by developers due to its widespread resources.
- **Rust** is a platform that significantly reduces development times with its ready-made functions. It mainly supports protocols such as Polkadot, Elrond, Solana, and Near.
- **Vyper** is a structure that prioritizes security and is preferred in the creation and programming of Ethereum and compatible smart contracts, allowing developers to develop with fewer parameters than Solidity.
- **Python** is a popular programming language that can be used with its easy-to-use interface and widespread library support.

Solidity and Simplicity programming languages are preferred for designing smart contracts on blockchain infrastructure, especially due to their rich libraries and wide integration capabilities, which help to shorten development times and reduce labor costs (O'Connor, 2017).

8.3.3 A Sample Smart Contract Design that Operates on a Blockchain

The framework and conditions of the smart contract to be designed are determined and executed through a three-stage process, which is referred to as the Analysis, Design, and Implementation phases. As you can see in the Figure 8.4.

A smart contract management system that operates on a blockchain can include not only basic contract information, but also rules, runtime codes, and GPS data. Once the contract is processed and included in the blockchain ledger, it is shared with other validators who join the network. The rule engine inside the contract operates on an 'if/then' logic, checking the status of the current step with the defined rules and data sources.

The data sources can be obtained through GPS data, smart sensors, or information services integrated into the structure. If the current step of the contract meets the conditions to move to the next step, the code for the next step is executed and the necessary actions are initiated. If the status conditions do not meet the criteria for moving to the next step, a pre-defined notification is sent to the responsible parties as can be seen in Figure 8.5.

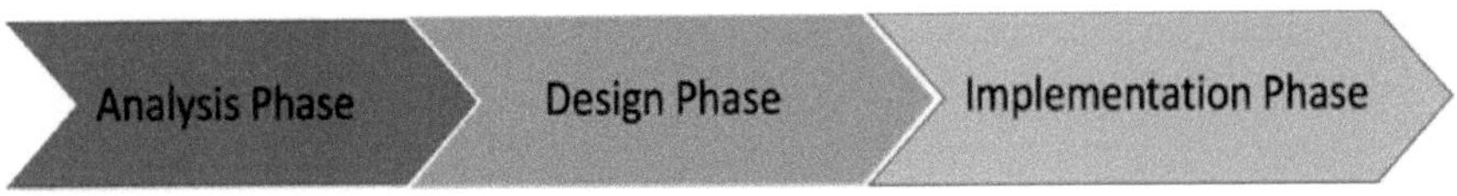

Figure 8.4. Three-stage process. Photograph by the author.

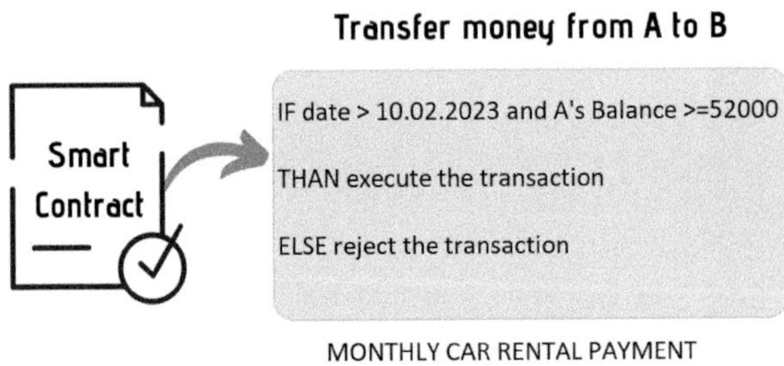

Figure 8.5. Car rental payment. Photograph by the author.

8.4 Contract Management via Blockchain Infrastructure

Contracts can be recorded transparently without the risk of being centralized or altered. However, recording the agreed-upon version of the contracts in one place without alteration does not eliminate all concerns of the parties involved. It is just as important to fulfill all agreed-upon activities in a timely and complete manner as it is to not change the conditions of the contract.

The concept of smart contracts enables the automatic monitoring of subsequent actions through software after each obligation is fulfilled by the parties involved. This technology allows for the automation of various steps, including payment transactions, service delivery control. By integrating and communicating with the parties' internal applications, smart contracts streamline and automate these processes (Delmolino et al., 2016). The concept of smart contracts was introduced by Nick Szabo in the mid-1990s, almost a decade before blockchain technology gained attention. In his article titled "Smart Contracts" published in 1994, he recorded a computer-supported transaction protocol based on the "If/Then" working logic that can fulfill the conditions of a contract based on information obtained over the internet.

To utilize blockchain infrastructure in contract management and automate contract processes, it is necessary to initially decide whether the contract management system will be managed exclusively within the organization or openly accessible to all parties involved (Clack et al., 2016). If it is to be utilized exclusively within the organization, a private blockchain infrastructure can be preferred. If management by counterparties and third parties via the system is involved, open, hybrid or consortium-type blockchain infrastructures can be preferred.

To record contracts mutually, reach an agreement, and ensure the fulfillment of obligations by parties, blockchain libraries shared on GitHub can be used for both financial flow and integration into institutional systems. OpenZeppelin, which operates on the Ethereum network, can be given as an example of these libraries.

Contract management applications that operate on the blockchain can often be used for controlling and managing contract processes and conditions. In this case, the contract management system leverages Internet of Things (IoT) devices, smart sensors and real-time data from external data systems. Compliance checks are conducted to verify the execution of predetermined smart contracts, and all subsequent processes, including financial payments, are executed if the incoming data satisfy the agreement's terms.

8.4.1 Management of Third Parties with Contracts Operating on Blockchain Infrastructure

Companies often choose to outsource certain tasks or entire operations third parties to enhance efficiency or lower expenses (Chu et al., 2022). However, effectively monitoring whether outsourced work is being executed according to agreed conditions can require significant labor. Inadequate monitoring may result in an inability to assess whether the work performed meets expectations.

Contract systems built developed on blockchain infrastructure can assign responsibilities to the involved parties with the completion criteria for these responsibilities can being specified in the contracts as contractual rules (Nair and Sebastian, 2017). Smart contracts can utilize the Internet of Things (IoT) or smart sensors to gather data, and if the data aligns with the contract's the criteria and conditions, it can trigger the remaining steps of the contract. Alternatively, if the criteria are not met, the parties can be notified through various scenarios.

For example, let's consider a food production company in the food industry that enters into a smart contract, utilizing blockchain, with a third-party company for the distribution of their products. In this process, smart sensors installed in the distributing vehicles can capture and validate temperature, distance, and time data, to check if the distribution conditions specified in the contract have been fulfilled. If the conditions are met, the payment process can be automatically executed. This scenario exemplifies how contract systems built on blockchain technologies can enhance the management and efficiency of business processes.

8.5 Are Blockchain Applications in Contract Management a Waste of Time or a Revolution?

First, it is necessary to highlight the pros and cons of contract management applications operating on the blockchain.

When it comes to listing the advantages of contract management applications on the blockchain, they can be summarized as follows:

- Transparent tracking of contract information by all the involved parties,
- Irreversibility and immutability,
- Autonomous execution of processes,
- Cost advantages compared to alternative approval methods,
- Wide availability over a widespread network independent of time and location,
- Ease of auditing and management,
- Integration with options such as the internet of things, smart sensors, and applications for ensuring the execution and monitoring of the contract in the real world,
- Low error tolerance because rules and parameters are initially defined and automatically executed.

The disadvantages are:

- The creation, design, and digitization of contract rules require a comprehensive process analysis and an intensive workforce.
- Changes to contracts that are already in effect cannot be made without reviewing all the rules and conditions that the contract is bound to.
- Transactions in open and large blockchain networks can be slow.
- If the scenario that forms the contract process is not examined adequately, the contract may not be executed, and it may take time to detect the cause of unexpectedly arising conditions.

Institutions that have established contract management processes and are managing their contracts through an application, even if not on blockchain technology, can still manage their contracts with smart contract designs on blockchain technology faster and more comprehensively than institutions that track all contract processes physically. When departments take ownership of the applications they use while performing their primary duties, they can develop them much faster over time, whereas it takes much longer for applications with interdepartmental structures like contract management to be accepted quickly by all departments. Recently, many institutions have started to describe contract management as one of the critical infrastructures of the institution and have created departments that only deal with contract management processes.

From a management perspective, designing structures on the blockchain infrastructure that can autonomously perform contract management activities that many departments spend time on for preparation, audit, and management will bring time, labor, and financial advantages (Raskin, 2017). Even considering the negative impact of initial investment costs and the labor and time lost during the design and analysis phase, designs that are successfully analyzed and applied will bring more benefits to the institution than costs. In addition, minimizing the contribution of human factors will result in processes being free of human errors and operating much more efficiently.

References

Anderson, L., Holz, R., Ponomarev, A., Rimba, P., Weber, I. et al. (2016). New kids on the block: an analysis of modern blockchains. CoRR abs/1606.06530.

Bitcoin contract. https://en.bitcoin.it/wiki/Contract. Accessed 10 Jan 2023.

Chu, Y., Ream, J. and Schatsky, D. (2022). Getting smart about smart contracts. https://www2.deloitte.com/content/dam/Deloitte/tr/Documents/finance/cfo-insights-getting-smart-contracts.pdf, 10.12.2022.

Clack, C. D., Bakshi, V. A. and Braine, L. (2016). Smart contract templates: foundations, design landscape and research directions. CoRR abs/1608.00771.

Delmolino, K., Arnett, M., Kosba, A., Miller, A., Shi, E. et al. (2016). Step by step towards creating a safe smart contract: lessons and insights from a cryptocurrency lab. pp. 79–94. *In*: Clark, J., Meiklejohn, S., Ryan, P. Y. A., Wallach, D., Brenner, M., Rohloff, K. et al. (eds.). FC 2016. LNCS, vol. 9604. Springer, Heidelberg. https:// doi.org/10.1007/978-3-662-53357-46.

Donercark, M. and Selimoglu, D. (2022). Contract Management. https://microdestek.com.tr/sozlesme-yonetimi-sistemi.html, 23.12.2022.

IBM Blockchain - Enterprise Blockchain Solutions & Services IBM. (2023 March 13). Retrieved from https://www.ibm.com/blockchain.

Lin, I. C. and Liao, T. C. (2017). A survey of blockchain security issues and challenges. IJ Network Security 19(5): 653–659.

Nair, G. R. and Sebastian, S. (2017). Blockchain technology centralised ledger to distributes ledger. International Research Journal of Engineering and Technology (IRJET) 4(3): 2823–2827.

O'Connor, R. (2017). Simplicity: A new language for blockchains. Proceedings of the Workshop on Programming Languages and Analysis for Security Pages 107–120, https://doi.org/10.1145/3139337.3139340.

Raskin, M. (2017) The law and legality of smart contracts. 1 Georgetown Law Technology Review 304. http://dx.doi.org/10.2139/ssrn.2842258.

Ünal, G. and Uluyol, Ç. (2020). Blok Zinciri Teknolojisi. Bilişim Teknolojileri Dergisi 13(2): 167–175. DOI: 10.17671/gazibtd.516990.

Chapter 9
Blockchain Applications in Marketing

Merve Coskun Ekinci

9.1 Introduction

Due to the rapid advancement of information and communication technologies, organizations need to stay informed about the evolving dynamics of the business environment (Darley et al., 2010). Businesses are creating numerous technologies across various social media platforms and marketing efforts to brand and market their products, services, and ideas. Businesses can employ social networking platforms that are always growing for modern, creative, efficient, and effective customer engagement with the help of digital marketing (Idrees and Nowostawski, 2022; McAllister and Turow, 2002).

While technological advancements provide businesses with a number of advantages, they also leave them in a challenging competitive environment where they must adapt quickly to the changing desires and needs of their customers (Martinez-Ruiz and Moser 2019). The emergence of the internet, information technologies and social media networks has significantly altered how marketers communicate with customers and run their marketing campaigns in the digital age (Antoniadis et al., 2019; Belch and Belch, 2014; Aspasia and Ourania, 2014). While marketing campaigns in the digital environment evolve, digital data management becomes more crucial for businesses. The digital world is filled with enormous volumes of data on clicks, customer ratings, customer reviews, blogs, likes, comments, shares, retweets, and other consumer behaviors that are related

Assistant Professor, University of Bakırcay, Turkey.
Email: merve.coskun@bakircay.edu.tr

to the company and its competitors. This data serves as the main sources for companies to establish their marketing mix elements. Marketing in a data-driven digital world has brought on some challenges regarding the Big Data and how it is used to create marketing campaigns with data analytics (Shah and Murthi, 2021). Modern technologies have heightened the importance of security, transparency, trust, and privacy issues in this data-driven world of marketing. Companies are required to implement a solid technology foundation that fixes current security problems and fosters consumer trust in the marketing environment (Cvitanović, 2018). Technologies have been crucial in offering new products, services, quality, and data protection while facilitating a more flexible and economical production process in order to gain a competitive advantage. New technologies can therefore fundamentally alter the marketing landscape (Stallone et al., 2021). Developing technologies like Blockchain have had a significant transformative impact on the conventional marketing mix such as branding, loyalty and digital assets, and product and branding strategies. They have also affected, digital payments, pricing strategies, e-commerce approaches, place strategies, and digital advertising and social media applications, thus shaping the way businesses promote their products and engage with their customers.

Besides marketing mix, consumer trust, transparency and privacy issues are the main challenges that companies may handle by the Blockchain applications. As a result of blockchain technology, numerous sectors are changing quickly. Although the word "Blockchain" is usually used in connection with the financial industries, it has broader applications (Rabby et al., 2022). Numerous industries, including retail, insurance, communications, entertainment, transportation, healthcare, real estate, pharmaceuticals, education, public procurement and distribution services, energy, and marketing have shown interest in blockchain applications (Madhani, 2022a).

Blockchain technology has a significant impact on digital marketing (Rabby et al., 2022). The implementation of blockchain has the potential to fundamentally alter how marketers interact with consumers, manage elements of the marketing mix, and execute marketing campaigns. Blockchain technology promotes disintermediation, raises transparency and trust, prevents ad fraud, and lowers overall marketing costs. Despite the significance and promise of this novel technology for marketing, research on this topic is limited and there are few comprehensive study papers on Blockchain technology as a tool for marketing support (Antoniadis et al., 2019; Casino et al., 2019; Li et al., 2018; Madhani, 2022b). The structure of this chapter is as follows: first it provides the basic characteristics and various types of blockchain technology that can be used in the marketing field, then, by using actual company examples, discusses the various marketing applications of blockchain technology and finally its specific benefits are discussed to understand how companies use blockchain to conduct their marketing mix strategies by giving details for each marketing mix element (product, price, place and promotion).

9.2 Blockchain Technology in Marketing: Basic Characteristics and Various Types

The implementation of blockchain technology by businesses may alter how they connect with stakeholders, changing communication plans and other marketing strategies to create value for consumers (Lemos et al., 2022). Blockchain as a massive decentralized digital database (called ledger) keeps transaction records (Pilkington, 2016) and these transactions are recorded and stored in chronological order to produce permanent and immutable records (Treiblmaier, 2018). Blockchain is made up of an expanding collection of records and data frameworks known as "blocks" that are connected and protected by cryptography (Maslova, 2018; Madhani, 2022a). A blockchain is used to securely record transactions involving money, property (digital or non-digital), any information, and authorization by eliminating third-party middlemen such as banks or governments (Peres et al., 2022; Zheng et al., 2018). A block in the blockchain contains transaction data that has been coded. The data within the block may also contain any kind of picture, text, sound, or other pertinent information in addition to the date, time, place, money exchanged and identities of the buyer and seller (Peres et al., 2022).

Businesses that wish to succeed in the fiercely competitive environment of business-to-consumer (B2C) industry, must adopt a customer-centered strategy (Rabby et al., 2022; Sheth, 2002). Customers can engage and communicate with businesses directly by reacting to their marketing initiatives with genuine and verifiable product or service evaluations (Deighton and Kornfeld, 2008). The implementation of blockchain technology has the potential to fundamentally alter how marketers interact with their consumers, suppliers, and all stakeholders, manage elements of their marketing mix, and execute their marketing campaigns (Madhani, 2022a). With the help of different features, blockchain technology can have a significant impact on a company's branding and marketing efforts since it encourages disintermediation between peers, helps prevent click fraud and strengthens trust and transparency in digital marketing platforms. In addition, it provides improved privacy protection and facilitates security while benefiting Big Data and supports innovative loyalty programs (Madhani, 2022b; Sprinklr, 2019).

Blockchain as a technology that prioritizes security and facilitates secure exchanges has some basic features with such advantages to marketing as disintermediation (cost reduction), immutability of data (enhanced security), decentralization of records (transparency), distributed ledger (single source of truth), consensus algorithms (fraud prevention), tokenization (transactional convenience), smart contracts (faster settlements), real-time updates (effective collaboration), provenance (traceability) and security (data confidentiality) (Madhani, 2022b).

There are various blockchain types, such as private, public, and consortium (hybrid), that can be used for marketing activities in terms of the ability to access blockchains, add transactions to them, and take part in the consensus mechanism. It is important to consider the needs of various marketing applications when selecting the right blockchain type (Madhani, 2022a). Blockchains offer promising marketing benefits, but this is dependent on marketers' choice to use public blockchain, private blockchain or hybrid blockchain models (Al-Ahwal et al., 2022). Anyone with Internet connectivity can access a public (or permissionless) blockchain and share it publicly. In publicly open blockchains, users can maintain their anonymity, yet every transaction is visible to everyone. Brands that want to leverage transparency to offer consumers value may find public blockchains particularly helpful. Marketers can design product packaging with blockchain-based information transparency using public blockchains (Madhani, 2022a).

In a constrained setting, private (or permissioned) blockchain technology protects customer privacy and complies with regulatory requirements. A private blockchain is only accessible to a select group of users as joining requires an invitation or approval from other participants (Hyperledger Fabric). The goals of private blockchains are to increase privacy, handle massive volumes of data, and improve current and future recordkeeping. A combination of both public and private blockchains is called hybrid-consortium blockchain. It enables businesses to decide which data will be made publicly available and who has access to particular data stored on the blockchain (e.g., XinFin). The ideal blockchains for multidisciplinary applications in industries like media are consortium blockchains since they restrict access and consensus to certain people while enabling businesses to benefit from a distributed network (Madhani, 2022a).

9.3 Blockchain Benefits to the Marketing

Blockchain implementation has an impact on marketing since it creates a distinctive ecosystem through which numerous advantages can be gained. The fundamental characteristics of blockchain technology are transparency, privacy, immutability, and security, which make it a trustworthy system based on its distributed and decentralized data storage. In every market industry, these characteristics are essential for information protection (Grover et al., 2019; Lemos et al., 2022; Yanik and

Kilic, 2018). Among its numerous benefits, this technology can increase profit margins in the distribution chain management while decreasing operational and financial costs. Additionally, it improves brand reputation and consumer confidence by reducing fraud (Ertemel, 2018). Blockchain's unique characteristics, technological advancements, and elimination of intermediaries have shown that it is possible to safeguard consumer privacy and also boost marketing security (Boukis, 2020).

Previous research has emphasized different marketing applications that benefit from blockchains (Antoniadis et al., 2019; Lemos et al., 2022; Rejeb et al., 2020). This research has identified blockchain technology benefits to marketing in terms of changing market structures, better data quality and improved customer relationships from the consumer-centric perspective. Peer-to-peer communication as the foundation of blockchain technology, changes market structures by promoting the elimination of middlemen that interfere with data sources and add cost. Blockchain technology can also aid in enhancing data quality and easing data access by producing immutable and distributed data records. By enhancing data transparency, privacy, and security, blockchain technology has the potential to profoundly redefine consumer relationships. Additionally, it enables businesses to provide value through creative approaches to consumer loyalty programs (Rejeb et al., 2020). Companies and marketers may be able prevent ad fraud and save money with the help of blockchain's advantages like decentralization, transparency, and permanence. They may also be able to create long-term strategies based on a closer connection with their customers by winning back their confidence (Al-Ahwal et al., 2022). Table 9.1 shows the important blockchain technology characteristics, how they work and their advantages to the marketing field with specific benefits to the companies and consumers.

9.3.1 *Promoting Disintermediation*

Disintermediation refers to the removal of numerous "middlemen" (intermediaries) and the creation of a better distribution network where customers engage directly with service providers (Al-Ahwal et al., 2022; Jallat and Capek, 2001). Technological advances and the emergence of the Internet allowed disintermediation and fundamentally altered how businesses disseminate their goods and services (Buhalis and Licata, 2002; Rejeb et al., 2020). New technologies have replaced traditional intermediaries and formulated different types of online intermediaries that provide a new range of products and services as re-intermediation in digital environments such as Google, Facebook, Amazon, Alibaba, Airbnb, Uber, Twitter, Youtube (McCole, 2004; Rejeb et al., 2020; Rosenbloom, 2007). With the help of these online intermediaries, interaction and communication between buyers and sellers are now simpler, quicker

Table 9.1. Blockchain characteristics and key advantages to the marketing field (Source: "Prepared by Author").

Blockchain Characteristic	How It Works	Marketing Advantages
Distributed Ledger	- A digital database (or ledger) that keeps transaction records is made up of a growing collection of data structures called "blocks" that are connected and safeguarded by cryptography.	- Single source of truth and trust between actors in the network - All network users have access to and can see transactions.
Decentralization	- With a blockchain, the record is saved as copies distributed across a network of computers rather than being kept in a single master location as the central server or under the control of a single person.	- Transparency and trust between all parties - Decreases the risks of malicious attacks in the network
Immutability	- Data integrity for old and new transactions prevents data manipulation since information cannot be altered or manipulated. Smart contracts should be embedded for immutability.	- Enhanced security between buyer and seller - Trustworthy promotion with less fraudulent actions
Smart Contracts	- A digitalized collection of agreements between parties- as digital contracts that do not require intermediaries for validation or verification.	- Targeting users' actions depending on their habits- viewer trends, online/ website engagement without disruptive ads—there is no need for an intermediary such as Google - Dynamic pricing plans for sales promotions based on real-time demand from customers. - Assist in tracking retailers and suppliers in a robust way, eliminating fraud and other problems that harm a company's reputation.
Disintermediation	- Creating a decentralized environment since no single organization is in charge of the entire system, which provides transactions with credibility.	- Cost reduction within the supply chain—in turn reduces the prices for consumers - High transparency across the value chain members

Table 9.1 contd. ...

...Table 9.1 contd.

Blockchain Characteristic	How It Works	Marketing Advantages
Tokenization	- Token is a digital asset kept on a blockchain. - For the purposes of transactions and records, the non-digitized product can be virtualized (transformed into virtual tokens).	- Convenience in transactions in terms of digital payments - Tokens would result in a more comprehensive loyalty program that would transparently and easily track every customer interaction with the company (Word-of mouth, customer review data) without any third parties.
Consensus Mechanisms	- Participants can independently track and confirm transactions thanks to the peer-to-peer structure and distributed ledger network.	- Fraud prevention in terms of personal identifiable information disclosure, advertising management and also review and credential management - Increased authenticity and verification of data (proof-of-identity, proof-of-work and more)
Security	- Encrypting all transactions with mathematical codes will help to prevent hacker fraud - Data integrity is improved via hash algorithms and cryptographic digital signatures, which also prevent block modification	- Data confidentiality - Real-time updates about data to all network members are always available
Provenance	- Transactions are timestamped to make tracking and auditing possible at any time in the future	- Product traceability—easier verification of data about the product's journey through the entire supply chain - Full transparency for ethical consumption - Ensuring consumers that a product's legitimacy can be verified

and even more engaging than ever but with more cost to the brands and customers (Al-Ahwal et al., 2022). Furthermore, the popularity of social media platforms has highlighted how important it is for companies to connect with their target audiences on sites like Facebook, Instagram, Twitter, and YouTube. These online platforms rely on revenue from data and targeted advertisements rather than receiving money from users who pay for content and services (Rejeb et al., 2020). They make money off personal user data, purchasing patterns, and history of interactions, but they also get a share of the transaction value.

Customers can object to these online intermediaries monetizing their data. Consumers are frequently prevented from enjoying the advantages of connecting directly with companies, such as collaboration, better customer-driven assistance, and broader and dynamic customization (Rejeb et al., 2020). Blockchain can promote true disintermediation due to its decentralized structure and allows content creators to completely take advantage of their effort that online intermediaries have impeded (Al-Ahwal et al., 2022). As marketers are required to pay transaction fees to online payment operators and credit card firms, the cost of sales rises, leading to higher pricing, decreased revenues, and a loss of customers (Madhani, 2022b). Disintermediation leads to lower prices for both consumers and marketers by eliminating a portion of the total cost that intermediaries or third parties add on. Brands can reduce or eliminate costs and get rid of non-value-adding operations at the intermediation layer with the use of blockchain technology. For instance, ride-sharing service company Uber, takes 25 percent from each trip and the drivers—the ones who deliver the services—lose a significant portion of the value. Since a third party is used as an intermediary in the car booking process, transparency is not offered. The ride-sharing systems La'Zooz and Arcade City already operate autonomously of any central organization by leveraging blockchain to manage interactions and transactions between drivers and customers (De Filippi, 2017; L'Hermitte and Nair, 2021). Blockchain technology has made significant strides in the ride-sharing industry, enabling direct communication between drivers and consumers without intermediaries. This technology allows drivers to share rides and earn profits by exchanging tokens, which serve as digitalized financial assets (Al-Ahwal et al., 2022). Additionally, consumers can access ride offers through public transactions and make bookings using their own tokens (Shaikh and Mohammad, 2020).

9.3.2 Preventing Click Fraud

In addition to its disintermediation benefits, blockchain technology has the potential to enhance monitoring of marketing and advertising activities, providing more accurate performance measurement (Antoniadis et al., 2019). Brands may now advertise their goods and services on online platforms and also build and sustain relationships with their customers thanks to the Internet's growth as a marketing and advertising channel (Geiger and Martin, 1999; Rejeb et al., 2020). Using the Internet, businesses can keep their customers updated about their most recent offerings via digital advertisements. By 2027, the size of the worldwide digital advertising and marketing industry is expected to increase by more than twofold from where it was in 2020, reaching 946.9 USD billion (Report Linker, 2022). However, difficulties and inefficiencies have increased along with the industry's growth. For instance, there is a significant problem with advertising fraud, which costs the industry billions of dollars each year. The value of having an online presence cannot be overstated, the advertising and marketing sector's reputation has been damaged by ad frauds as deceptive tactics (Hongwei and Peiji, 2011; Rejeb et al., 2020). Advertising fraud and paying for fake clicks are the major problems for marketers and advertisers today. It was discovered that one out of every five pay-per-click campaigns in January 2017 alone were fake and 36 percent of clicks on display ads were inaccurate or invalid in 2021 (Kuno Creative, 2018; Lunio, 2021).

Ad fraud or click fraud can be considered as a malicious act in which an organic person or institution attempts to make unauthorized gains by using computer programs, bots or natural people that produce fictitious traffic and deplete a specific advertiser's or a competitor's advertising budget (Al-Ahwal et al., 2022; Hongwei and Peiji, 2011; Rejeb et al., 2020). Fraudulent clicks on Pay-Per-Click commercials have renewed debate over the efficacy of online advertising because they can be produced by partners in search engine networks, rivals, and frustrated staff members (Al-Ahwal et al., 2022; Kshetri, 2010).

Click fraud is thought to be reduced by blockchain technology due to its immutability, transparency, and decentralization (Al-Ahwal et al., 2022). By using blockchain technology, it is feasible to guarantee transparency and trust for activities connected to online advertising, such as click-authentication (Madhani, 2022b). By verifying the sources of information blockchain can aid in online advertising to ensure that the recipients of promotional messages are the actual target audience (Peres et al., 2022; Rejeb et al., 2020). Blockchain technology might make it possible for marketers to check their ads to determine if their intended audience has been reached or even whether the ads have been displayed at all (Brauer and Linnala Eriksson, 2020; Kshetri and Voas, 2019). Due to the nature of the technology, advertisers will also be able to monitor who opens their ads, get more precise conversion rates, and find out where potential customers might be (Brauer and Linnala Eriksson, 2020; Kshetri and Voas, 2019).

Blockchain enables marketers to pay consumers in Basic Attention Tokens (BATs) for their attention, ensuring that the advertising budget is effectively spent by proving that adverts are seen by the target market. Marketers would thus be able to manage the delivery of their advertising by keeping track of the exact locations where they are being displayed, reducing ad fraud from spambots by making sure that actual customers are interacting with their ads. A browser like Brave, which affects how people engage with online advertising, provides their users with the options to choose to see ads and receive Basic Attention Tokens (BATs) in exchange for it rather than seeing ads every time they scroll down a page or being bombarded with them (Rabby et al., 2022).

Blockchain technology provides advertisers transparent and auditable transactions. For instance, complete transparency may be guaranteed for actions connected to internet advertising, including the verification of clicks. Campaign audits and nearly real-time impression tracking are made possible for ad space users thanks to the "adChain" platform (Goldin et al., 2017; Rejeb et al., 2020). In addition to preventing fraud and lowering costs, using blockchain to track ad clicks also gives advertisers a greater understanding of consumer behavior, enabling them to create more precise targeted campaigns, maximize effective spending, and develop long-term plans (Al-Ahwal et al., 2022; Antoniadis et al., 2019). For instance, in a pilot project with the blockchain-based business Lucidity, the automaker Toyota and the international advertising agency Saatchi & Saatchi have teamed up (Alexandre, 2018; Al-Ahwal et al., 2022). The project's goal was to optimize Toyota's advertising campaigns with a 21-percentage boost by using the blockchain to verify the integrity of ad clicks, stop overpaying, and eradicate fraud (Al-Ahwal et al., 2022; Lucidity, 2018).

9.3.3 Increasing Transparency and Trust

Trust is the biggest obstacle in the modern, sophisticated marketing world, especially in online settings (Lee and Turban, 2001; Rabby et al., 2022). The success of a brand depends on consumers' trust because their purchasing decisions are mostly influenced by what brands promise (Al-Ahwal et al., 2022; Kim et al., 2008). The Internet today makes it possible to conduct transactions without meeting in face to face. Previous studies claim that an essential condition for trusting a brand is the degree of transparency for openness, communication, and accountability (Kang and Hustvedt, 2014). Transparency implies being open and honest to all partners and consumers about the distribution chain, labor practices, product authenticity, and other issues (Kang and Hustvedt, 2014; Madhani, 2022b).

Blockchain reduces the possibility of supply chain disruptions while facilitating data storage, retrieving, tracking, and auditing across the value chain (Madhani, 2022b). Companies can leverage the capabilities of blockchain to verify specific details such as the exact location of product manufacturing or cultivation, the materials utilized, and the wages paid to employees involved in the process (Newman, 2019). Product legitimacy can be checked using blockchain technology (Al-Ahwal et al., 2022). Blockchain technology can aid in the prevention of fraudulent marketing of counterfeit goods that violates the original manufacturer's intellectual property (IP) rights and copyright laws. This is due to the technology's capacity to provide complete product traceability (Galvez et al., 2018; Rejeb et al., 2020). Through its transparency of transactions and the ability to enable end-to-end surveillance of products blockchain technology has the potential to reduce the prevalence of counterfeiting in various industries such as automotive, pharmaceuticals, and food supply chains (Madhani, 2022b). Blockchain's transparency features enable authentication and verification of brand claims related to production processes, product features like organic or halal certifications, and company practices such as fair trade or sustainability (Rejeb et al., 2020; Treiblmaier, 2019). For instance, IBM has introduced a blockchain technology that retail giants like Walmart use to trace the route of food products from producers to the final selling point (Antoniadis et al., 2019).

Due to the sale of counterfeit goods on their platforms, large online retailers like Alibaba face significant difficulties and complaints. Too many global firms, whose products are offered on Alibaba, the largest e-commerce site in the world, have continuously urged the company take preventive action against fake products from damaging their brands' sales and reputation (Schuman, 2015; Al-Ahwal et al., 2022). The United States Trade Representative listed the giant e-retailer in a blacklist for counterfeiting due to the volume of fake items sold on Alibaba's Taobao (Reuters, 2018). Alibaba, like many other businesses, began to use blockchain as a way to deal with this mounting pressure. In order to track and verify the authenticity of two food products from Australia and New Zealand, the business is now operating a blockchain pilot powered by IoT to give customers a chance to scan the product's tag with their smartphones to learn where it came from. This framework, based on its success, might serve as the foundation for a global supply chain model that is used throughout the whole e-commerce market of Alibaba Group (Al-Ahwal et al., 2022; Millward, 2018). Starbucks is also trying to provide their customers with additional details about its coffee products by implementing a blockchain system that would trace beans from farmers to the final cup (Palmer, 2021). For this project, Starbucks is working with Microsoft Azure Blockchain Service to bring real-time traceability to their supply chains. With the help of Microsoft's blockchain solution, all partners will have a clear view of the supply chain because all changes made to the coffee's journey will be tracked on a shared ledger. Starbucks will add a new feature to its mobile app that will notify customers about the origin and roasting locations of their coffee as well as the flavor notes. In keeping with its dedication to ethical sourcing, Starbucks also hopes that the blockchain technology would help farmers see where their beans end up in consumers' cups (Palmer, 2021).

9.3.4 Improving Privacy Protection

Although internet technology has revolutionized communication, information sourcing, shopping and trading, it has also led to concerns about privacy invasion and excessive exposure of personal data (Al-Ahwal et al., 2022; Ravasan et al., 2014). The complex issue of privacy poses concerns for individuals when using online technology services, particularly regarding the anonymity and security of their transactions (Ratnasingham, 1998; Rejeb et al., 2020). The proliferation of e-commerce and social media platforms has led to significant personal data flows, giving rise to apprehensions about potential abuse and misuse.

A common business practice for many firms is the trading of personal and behavioral consumer data. Brands can more easily recognize, track, gather, and analyze customer data thanks to significant advancements in data gathering technologies and new data mining methods (Antoniadis et al., 2019; McParland and Connolly, 2007; Rejeb et al., 2020). Data is gathered by the so-called data brokers around the world, who then sell it to advertising companies that bombard customers with ads. Around 500 million individuals' personal information and purchasing preferences are gathered from search engines or social media networks such as Google and Facebook, and sold through brokers (like Acxiom) to the highest bidder (Al-Ahwal et al., 2022; Singer, 2012). Consumers exhibit a great desire to have control over their own private data in response to this privacy intrusiveness and sometimes provide fake information on a website in an effort to disable cookies or block online advertising practices (Rejeb et al., 2020). This fake information makes some companies' advertising campaigns a massive waste of money (Geyser, 2022).

Blockchain technology holds promise in addressing privacy concerns as it operates in a decentralized manner, thereby reducing the risk of data breaches and unauthorized access to personal information (Madhani, 2022b). Blockchain technology embraces a privacy-by-design framework by leveraging its pseudonymization function as highlighted by Antoniadis et al., 2019. The pseudonymity feature allows people to exercise greater control over their data, enabling them to store it securely in a cryptographic wallet or on their mobile devices (Ertemel, 2018). Information can be made accessible only to people with the proper authorization by using pseudonymity, encryptions, and smart contracts. This means that even if all information is kept in the ledger, the person who owns it has control regarding who will be able to see it. This is preferred in many privacy-sensitive marketing scenarios, especially regarding the handling of customer data in situations where fraud is a big issue (Marthews and Tucker, 2022; Peres et al., 2022).

At the protocol level, the use of proof-of-identity mechanisms allows individuals to verify their identity while retaining the option to remain anonymous to third parties. While individual transactions are kept private, they are also verified by a majority of network users ensuring the security and integrity of the blockchain. Users can trust blockchain platforms with their personally identifiable information because blockchain transactions are not directly linked to real individuals. This provides a layer of privacy and security (Ertemel, 2018; Kosba et al., 2016; Rejeb et al., 2020). With blockchain technology, consumers have the opportunity without revealing personal information to external parties. The use of cryptocurrencies like Basic Attention Token (BAT) allows users to earn rewards in the form of tokens when sharing data with businesses. By leveraging the transactional history stored on the blockchain, customers can benefit from more accurate forecasts and in-depth analytics on their expectations, preferences, and brand opinions. This enhances customer trust and enables businesses to better understand their target audience (Rejeb et al., 2020; Braurer and Linnala Eriksson, 2020).

With the help of this ecosystem of blockchain, it will be a win-win situation for both customers and companies that are transacting on the blockchain. Customers would be more likely to interact with companies and supply precise data for better analytics, enabling marketers to create campaigns that are both efficient and cost-effective. As only interested consumers see brand advertisements, it results in cost savings for businesses. Moreover, blockchain technology fosters a sense of engagement and commitment among leading them to provide accurate information, actively interact with advertisements, and ultimately generate more revenue (Al-Ahwal et al., 2022).

Several blockchain startups have worked to present solutions that protect privacy. For instance, Wibson created a blockchain-based marketplace in 2017 that uses smart contracts to enable the transfer of personal data between sellers and buyers (like advertising agencies), using Wibson Tokens (WIB) as the method of payment (Al-Ahwal et al., 2022; Futoransky et al., 2020). Blockstack is another cutting-edge innovation that uses blockchain to defend the digital rights of users and build new kinds of networks for decentralized applications. When using some applications in the past, users would typically supply their data, which would then remain on the application's server and be completely out of their control. However, with Blockstack, the data immediately returns to the user when it is used by applications (apps) (Newman, 2019).

9.3.5 Strengthening Digital Marketing Security

Data security and cybercrimes are major issues on a global scale (Al-Ahwal et al., 2022). One of the most important success factors for brand trust in the digital age is the delivery of goods and services with clear security protocols (Rejeb et al., 2020). Information security issues have been demonstrated to be a substantial obstacle to internet marketing in previous studies (Rejeb et al., 2020; Udo, 2001). Numerous studies indicate that consumers' trust has been eroded by online cybercrimes, such as the theft of their personal data, bank accounts and credit cards which has hampered their online presence (Chehrehpak et al., 2014; Rejeb et al., 2020; Smith, 2017; Yousafzai et al., 2003). Almost every industry, including e-commerce, is affected by cybercrimes because they are so pervasive (Huntsman, 2019). This is due to the fact that e-commerce and online buying rely on user credentials and sensitive data, such as credit card numbers and home addresses (collectively PII), which many customers are very hesitant to provide.

Marketing and IT professionals suggest that the long-standing issue of data security could be resolved by using blockchain in marketing (Al-Ahwal et al., 2022; Antoniadis et al., 2019; Ertemel, 2018). The Information Security Triad (IST) concept of Confidentiality, Integrity, and Availability (CIA) is enforced by blockchain technology (Du Toit, 2018; Madhani, 2022a). Based on its distributed and decentralized data storage, blockchain technology has strong security capabilities (Rejeb et al., 2020; Yanik and Kilic, 2018). Confidentiality refers to limiting access to the data to those who are permitted to see it. Additionally, integrity refers to the guarantee that the data reflects the truth and that no modifications intended or unintended to its content have taken place. Data integrity is ensured by the strict consensus process and immutability of the blockchain. Particularly on public blockchains, it is extremely difficult to modify user data or steal their login information. Finally, data availability refers to making data available to authorized users in a timely manner (Al-Ahwal et al., 2022; Madhani, 2022a).

Blockchain technology's ability to make information widely accessible and available boosts transparency and offers more precise tracking and evaluation in the event of mistakes and abuse (Omran et al., 2017). This indicates that, even in the worst-case scenarios, technology can offer customers and companies some remedies and alternatives. For instance, Keybase.io as a blockchain platform that promotes marketing efficiency and trustworthy models of advertisements while also identifying fraudulent rollbacks in social media users' signature chains (Keybase.io, 2019; Rejeb et al., 2020).

9.3.6 Encouraging Creative Loyalty Programs

Brands work to maintain consumer loyalty to their goods and services in an environment of market competition that is becoming more intense (Tahal, 2014). A brand promises to reward its customers for their purchases through a loyalty program and customers seek loyalty programs to pick one brand over another that provides identical product quality and customer experience (Kuno Creative, 2018). Brands have been deliberately gathering and keeping their customer data such as buying habits, previous transactions and preferences mainly through loyalty programs, to increase consumer retention (Cvitanović, 2018). These methods help companies broaden their customer base, enhance brand loyalty, lower price sensitivity, and promote word-of-mouth referrals (Rejeb et al., 2020; Uncles et al., 2003). Points, immediate discounts, and refunds are just a few ways of rewarding customers through loyalty programs (Tahal, 2014). A strong loyalty program encourages ongoing repurchases from the satisfied consumers, but if customers are dissatisfied with the loyalty programs, they can leave the brand and switch to another brand (Al-Ahwal et al., 2022; Goodman and Newman, 2003).

Customers who express dissatisfaction with loyalty programs frequently claim that the businesses do not fulfill their commitments. The promised rewards are worthless, and the provided level of privacy is low (Al-Ahwal et al., 2022; Stauss et al., 2005). The companies that establish successful and attractive loyalty programs are constantly trying to figure out the best methods to engage with their customers efficiently. The development of efficient and personalized loyalty programs has been made easier by technological advancements such as database management software in the acquisition of consumer data including buying habits, transactional records and personal preferences (Buss, 2002; Rejeb et al., 2020). Even though these technological advancements have increased consumers' interest and access to data about loyalty rewards, some businesses experience difficulty in managing their loyalty programs. One of the biggest issues with loyalty programs occurs when customers try to redeem their loyalty points (Madhani, 2022b). It was previously reported that more than 25 percent of the consumers in loyalty programs never use their loyalty points due to the strict, deadline-based procedures for redeeming rewards (Bond Brand Loyalty, 2016; Rejeb et al., 2020) that may cause significant dissatisfaction among devoted consumers (Colman, 2015; Rejeb et al., 2020).

The use of blockchain in marketing transforms how consumer loyalty programs are created, regulated, and shared (Madhani, 2022b). Customers can use their reward points regardless of their location since these points are deposited in real-time. With the use of blockchain technology and smartphone apps, loyalty programs can also be transformed. Marketers will be able to create more enticing, worthwhile, and personalized loyalty programs by having real-time access to the blockchain platform enabling them to view member profiles, points, purchase habits, payment histories, and campaign reactions.

Tokenization will be advantageous in consolidating all customer loyalty programs such as gift cards into a single system that can incorporate not merely purchases but also a consumer's wholehearted connection with the company or retailer to integrate online marketing and social media platforms (Antoniadis et al., 2019; Campbell et al., 2018; Mire, 2018). Pei and REM Loyalty are two blockchain start-ups that provide loyalty program platforms that are believed to enhance loyalty programs to new heights (Mire, 2019). Pei has teamed up with well-known companies such as Starbucks, Taco Bell, Target and H&M in an attempt to provide consumers with a novel loyalty program that is quick, simple, and gives immediate rewards for each purchase in the form of bitcoin or US dollars. Through the REM Loyalty platform, consumers have a single access point to loyalty programs from each airline and hotel company operating globally. This blockchain platform formed a collaboration with numerous well-known companies, including Apple, Amazon, Uber, Virgin Atlantic, Hyatt, and Tesco. The rewards take the form of everlasting REM tokens that can be used anytime or traded (Al-Ahwal et al., 2022). Shake Shack, a well-known burger company, has introduced a new rewards program based on Bitcoin to bring in younger and more tech-savvy consumers (Wright, 2022). Additionally, in 2021, Burger King established a cryptocurrency-based loyalty program with investment app Robinhood, rewarding users with a deposit of cryptocurrency into their Robinhood wallets for every purchase above 5 USD. Burger King's application downloads increased by 30 percent because of the Burger King-Robinhood promotional collaboration (Blacker, 2021). Likewise, in 2021, Starbucks introduced a program in collaboration with the digital wallet service Bakkt that allowed users to convert Bitcoin to dollars. Then it allowed them to load the money onto their Starbucks cards, which could be accessed through their Starbucks application (app) (Wright, 2022).

Based on the above-mentioned concerns and application areas of blockchain in marketing, Figure 9.1 summarizes the benefits of blockchain deployment to marketing given by consumer and company perspectives.

9.4 Blockchain Applications for Marketing Mix Strategies

The blockchain technology can increase the efficiency of each marketing mix element (4Ps—product, place, price, and promotion) (Madhani, 2022b; Peres et al., 2022).

9.4.1 Product

Blockchain technology benefits product strategies in terms of product verification, product design and branding (Peres et al., 2022). Consumers don't need to rely solely on brand claims when they have access to such information. Because of the transparency that blockchain technology offers, businesses can stop the sale of counterfeit items. Customers can use blockchain to track components, products, and raw materials back to their

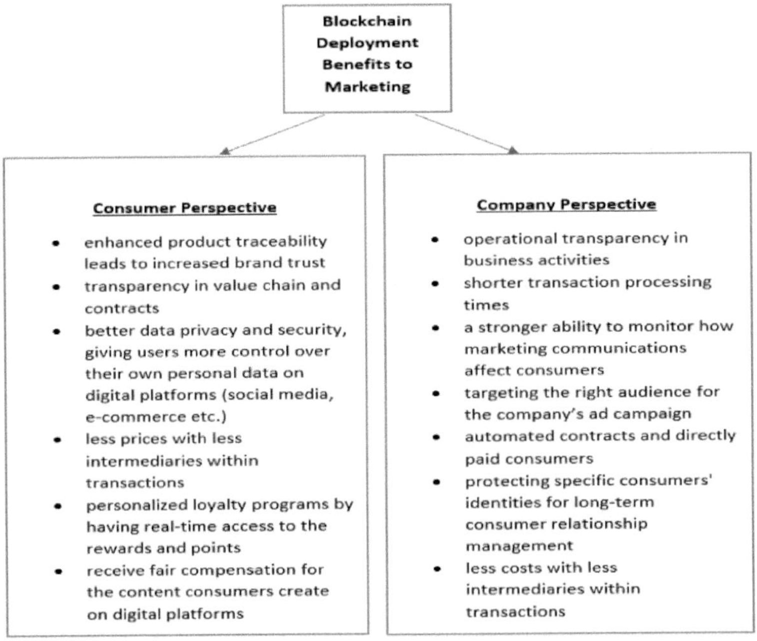

Figure 9.1. Blockchain deployment benefits to marketing with consumer and company perspectives (Source: "Prepared by Author").

source to validate marketing claims. The use of blockchain in marketing increases buying process transparency by allowing customers to validate products. Customers may confirm product information such as country of origin, whether an item is organic or not and sustainability alternatives, thanks to the decentralized nature of blockchain technology.

In terms of product design, with the help of blockchain technology, it is possible for many parties to collaborate productively on the design of a product, with each participant contributing a portion of the final product and receiving compensation in line with their contribution (Bayus, 2013). A blockchain-based platform, for example, can enhance the monitoring of the design procedure by assessing the connectivity of efforts and identifying if design stakeholders build upon each other's ideas or focus on creating their own set of attributes. It can also determine which features are prioritized (Bayus, 2013; Peres et al., 2022).

Almost all non-digital goods can be virtualized (using tokenization) by marketers in order to create non-fungible tokens (NFT) for sale (Madhani, 2022b). Some research discussed the potential benefits of blockchain to businesses for their product and branding strategies (Peres et al., 2022; Colicev, 2022). Blockchain enables the conversion of physical assets and intangibles into digital tokens or equivalents for transactions (Madhani,

2022b). A token is a type of digital good kept on a blockchain. Any digital object can serve as a token including a digital coin, picture, vote, or a song license. The currently existing cryptocurrencies are the most widely used tokens (e.g., Bitcoin, Ethereum) (Peres et al., 2022). There are two types of tokens: fungible and non-fungible. Cryptocurrencies considered to be fungible, can be exchanged, and utilized as a medium for business transactions. Non-fungible tokens (NFT) on a blockchain are cryptographic commodities that are unique and cannot be bought or exchanged for equivalent value that can be distinguished from one another by their distinctive identifying codes (Colicev, 2022). In terms of branding, NFTs can be viewed as representations of brand elements like design of the product, brand logo, or any image in a virtual environment. A ticket to a concert, a digital representation of a brand's logo in visual form, or a digital twin of a physical object are a few examples of branded NFTs (AdAge, 2022; Colicev, 2022). The NFTs can also influence customers to purchase the brand's physical goods, providing cross-selling potential. When a branded NFT is introduced, it can increase brand recognition and draw in previously untapped markets like Gen-Z (Colicev, 2022).

Online fashion companies like Adidas and Nike, which have released numerous pairs of physical shoes as NFTs can increase customer loyalty by strengthening the perception that they own particular brand components like the logo or design (McKinsey, 2022). Incorporating blockchain technology, Nike has introduced. SWOOSH, a new online community for the brand. At welcome.swoosh.nike, Nike members can access the domain and start collecting virtual items, such as digital sneakers or jerseys (Meara, 2022). Brands can choose to build a single NFT-based product line, a bundle that includes both the physical product and a NFT, or just a NFT replica of the physical product also known as a digital twin. Recently, Dolce & Gabbana offered NFT-based digital couture valued at millions of dollars which featured both new products and electronic copies (FashionUnited, 2021). A bundle of NFT and tangible goods can likewise be sold by brands to customers with a variety of distinctive symbolic and practical advantages. By developing distinctive features for each NFT and merging them with the tangible product, brands may provide symbolic value. As an illustration, the Gucci Garden on Roblox has specialized areas that promote Gucci advertising campaigns and let users browse, try on, and purchase Gucci items for their avatars (Colicev, 2022; Webster, 2021).

9.4.2 Price

In a competitive market, supply and demand will eventually determine the price of any asset (Zhang, 2022). Marketing can reduce transactional costs with blockchain technology's disintermediation and decentralization features, and thus decrease product prices (Madhani, 2022b). With the application of blockchain technology and the creation of smart contracts, the key aspects of decentralization and disintermediation emerge, accelerating the process toward pervasive trade (Lemos et al., 2022). Additionally, the removal of intermediaries will save operating and finance expenses, boosting profitability for each transaction (Antoniadis et al., 2019; Gupta, 2017).

Blockchain technology is the foundation of the digital payment system utilized by cryptocurrencies and smart contracts. These agreements guarantee the speed and security of transactions while lowering the cost of transactions between parties. A smart contract between parties is a piece of software that contains the rules and guidelines for agreeing on conditions and taking actions. It carries out the transactions and automatically checks to see if the terms of the contract have been met (Rijanto, 2021). With the use of smart contracts, cryptocurrency can be used for business-to-business (B2B) and business-to-consumer (B2C) transactions, facilitating the building of trust between the parties involved and ensuring speedy transactions and security (Antoniadis et al., 2019; Pilkington, 2016). These contracts boost brand image, secure data, and safeguard suppliers and customers from fraud. Smart contracts within blockchain technology, assist lower transaction costs while increasing trust in the whole system and its results. Blockchain enables marketers to disseminate digital customer coupons with expiration dates that can be tracked, shared, and distributed without manipulation with the help of smart contracts, building long-term trust and customer relationships (Madhani, 2022b).

Retailers typically pay intermediaries such as credit card firms approximately three percent for payment processing costs, with other services imposing listing fees or marketing expenses. These types of payment charges can be avoided with the aid of smart contracts, and transaction costs can be decreased, which in turn decreases the prices of goods and services offered to consumers (Oymak and Kazançoğlu, 2021). Blockchain technology also enables newer and smaller businesses to avoid third-party platforms like Google and Facebook and save on their transaction fees which they can pass on to customers in the form of lower prices (Madhani, 2022b). Regardless of the currency value, retailers and digital services have been urged to accept digital payments (Hawlitschek et al., 2018; Rosario and Raimundo, 2021). The adoption of cryptocurrencies as a means of payment by more than 36 percent of supply chain members in the US, includes well-known companies like Expedia, Subway, Shopify, and Microsoft (Li et al., 2021). Microsoft, for instance, has embraced blockchain technology to accept payments for several services, such as Xbox Live and Skype (Walsh, 2021).

Online shopping is becoming a significant part of daily individual activities because of the rapid advancement of Internet technology. The fact that consumers find it challenging to confirm the validity of an agent's price information when purchasing online is a significant issue. Many buyers are enticed by deceptive discounts only to discover that the regular retail price might be lower than the marked-down price they paid. Consumers lose faith in online buying because of price competition amongst agents, thus online sales fall (Wang et al., 2022). Blockchain technology can be utilized to create a trustworthy cooperation mechanism that fosters strong customer and agent trust, solving the issue of price information disparity on online marketplaces (Sikorski et al., 2017; Wang et al., 2022).

9.4.3 Place

Supply chain management and logistics have dominated discussions of blockchain application in the context of retailing (Caro et al., 2018; Peres et al., 2022). Building effective relationships between suppliers and customers benefits businesses that can manage the distribution chain effectively, giving them a competitive advantage. Retail businesses may use blockchain to increase supply chain transparency, prevent fraud, strengthen loyalty programs, and boost overall operational effectiveness (Makarov, 2022). Retailers can provide end-to-end tracking, verification, and timely recording of items as they transit through the whole value chain since blockchain technologies provide transparency, traceability, and authenticity (Lemos et al., 2022; Peres et al., 2020; Rosario and Raimundo, 2021).

Due to its capacity to foster greater trust and transparency among retailers, customers and other partners in the supply chain, blockchain technology in retail industry has tremendous potential. Without giving authority to any single party, blockchain enables all retail network users to monitor system activity in closeness to real-time. A trustworthy mechanism for tracing a product's provenance does not exist in a traditional supply chain. Contrarily, decentralized blockchain-based systems for product traceability enable businesses to securely track and verify a product (Makarov, 2022). Smart tags, which can track a product's location in almost real-time, are an essential component of a successful blockchain-based tracking system. Smart tags can be used in the form of Quick response (QR) codes that can be read by any smart phone today, Radio frequency identification (RFID) tags and Near-field communication (NFC) chips. All products can be given smart tags, thereby tokenizing them. To sign transactions involving a particular token, each blockchain participant also has a special identity in the form of special signatures allowing them to track the product's history (Makarov, 2022). As an example, retailer Carrefour utilized blockchain technology to control the entire production process and manage its distribution network (Lemos et al., 2022; Wilson and Auchard, 2018). Carrefour, Europe's largest retailer, has implemented blockchain ledger technology developed by IBM Food Trust to trace its food items such as chicken, eggs, and tomatoes as they move from the fields to retail stores (Wilson and Auchard, 2018). Also, Project Provenance as a blockchain-based company assists brands with product origin verification and product journey reports for consumers (Mire, 2018).

The elimination of fraud and fake goods is another advantage of blockchain in retail. Counterfeiting has a particularly detrimental effect on the retail industry. This results in product recalls, harm to a brand's reputation, a decline in customer trust, and eventually, large financial losses. By accurately identifying the proof-of-origin of a product, blockchain in retail can aid businesses in taking preventive measures against counterfeiting. RFID technology as smart tags can be a solution to this counterfeiting problem in the retail industry. It is simple to identify fake goods since tags carry immutable data regarding the final destination of a product's journey (Anwar, 2020).

According to recent studies, blockchain will also significantly affect e-commerce described as the practice of purchasing, selling, transferring, or exchanging goods, services, and/or information using computer networks, such as the Internet (Liu and Li, 2020; Subramanian, 2018; Treiblmaier and Sillaber, 2021). Blockchain is a set of technologies that has an impact on e-commerce in terms of technical, legal and consumer problems. Data management (accessibility and traceability of data), security and privacy concerns of consumers are the major difficulties for e-commerce companies. Blockchain technology is an opportunity to enable real peer-to-peer sales, with a lesser need for intermediaries within platforms like Amazon.com or AliExpress, in addition to the enhanced reliability and security in tracking transactions (Ertemel, 2018). In this type of system, tokenizing user reviews and using designated currencies for speedy transactions and reducing processing costs are also possible (Ertemel, 2018; Peres et al., 2022). Using blockchain technology, marketplaces like Open Bazar enable sellers to sell their goods directly to buyers without having to pay the platform fees to a third party. Additionally, it contains a built-in Bitcoin wallet that makes it easier to earn and purchase with cryptocurrencies (Kuno Creative, 2018).

There is a lot of data in the online shopping environment of today, including information on customer reviews, ratings, likes, shares, retweets, and other behaviors (Dinh et al., 2018). The perception of many forum sites as being unreliable creates another challenge to e-commerce businesses. With the use of Blockchain, it is possible to apply initiatives like a worldwide credibility score that can communicate with different parties involved in the same transaction system. It is possible that the counterparty's reported identity is fraudulent, and this is known as counterparty risk. Blockchain technology allows the tracking and verification of the real identity of the content provider. By incorporating proof of identity at the protocol level, blockchain pseudonymity reduces the threat in marketing contexts and improves trust between businesses and customers (Brauer and Linnala Eriksson, 2020; Ertemel, 2018).

9.4.4 Promotion

The development of technology throughout the years has prompted promotion strategies in all aspects of businesses. With only one click, customers may access the entire world thanks to the shift of advertising from a traditional to the digital environment (Chaudhary and Sharma, 2018; Kumar and Brar, 2018). Despite its many advantages, consumers' trust in the transparency and privacy of the digital advertising sector has been questioned. The biggest challenges for the advertising industry continue to be reducing click fraud and making sure that advertising funds are directed to the right people. Hence, blockchain technology is perceived as a significant solution to these problems (Antoniadis et al., 2019).

Due to the disintermediation aspect of blockchain technology, marketers may display ads and buy advertising space simply from the platform, eliminating third parties and buying networks. Due to the immutability of blockchain technology, marketers may eliminate fraudulent likes and followers from their promotion mechanism. Additionally, it would permit marketers ensure that their advertising budget is used successfully to target the right market. With the adoption of blockchain, consumers are more likely to believe in marketing promotion techniques and statements that they can verify independently. Platforms where users are paid for viewing advertisements could be developed by using tokenized advertising reach data (Ghose, 2018). By utilizing the properties of the blockchain to build a decentralized search engine, BitClave enables advertisers to access the right target audience. People, based on their own interest, watch the advertisements accessed from BitClave, and then are compensated in the form of CAT tokens for providing their personal data to the advertisers (Kuno Creative, 2018). As a result, more accurate determination of the target audience and tracking its reactions to advertisements is possible, which will likely improve behavioral targeting strategies (Peres et al., 2022; Rejeb et al., 2020).

Digital marketing is a dynamic, technologically empowered process in which businesses work with partners and customers to develop, communicate and maintain a competitive edge over competitors (Zheng et al., 2018). The term "digital marketing" refers to a broad range of subjects, including social media marketing, internet marketing, customer data mining, e-commerce and digital advertising. The focus of modern businesses is on digital marketing for digital, Internet-based search, influencer, user generated content, mobile, and email marketing (Brauer and Linnala Eriksson, 2020; Kumar and Brar, 2018).

Adledger (https://adledger.org), created by IBM and Salon, and blockchain-enabled markets for advertising and media planning, like the NYIAX (New York Interactive Advertising Exchange), which was introduced by NASDAQ, are examples of new blockchain platforms being developed that will benefit advertisement management (Antoniadis et al., 2019). Blockchain technology will enable more effective online marketing strategies and thorough assessment of digital advertising and promotional initiatives. Decentralization and smart contracts will ensure that businesses can manage their email, influencer, and digital marketing campaigns, and monitoring will assist the sector prevent fraud and save money (Anthes, 2018; Antoniadis et al., 2019).

Compared to conventional marketing channels, social media platforms tend to have a stronger influence on word-of-mouth referrals. Social media marketing is used by companies to boost customer involvement, raise brand awareness, and enhance brand image. Companies can execute social media marketing strategies by creating, developing, or promoting content on social media network sites (Felix et al., 2017; Kumar and Brar, 2018; Kuno Creative, 2018; Rabby et al., 2022). Blockchain-enabled social media networking can compensate users that create any content. Users can receive payment in the form of tokens in exchange for their contributions. Incentives are offered for creating trustworthy user content, particularly for social media influencers. Blockchain identity applications can help to verify reviews and enhance their legitimacy for both customers and businesses (Antoniadis et al., 2019; Berkowitz, 2017). Users of blockchain-based social media networks like Steem and Peepeth can maintain control over their data and receive monetary rewards for their contributions (Peres et al., 2022). Also, like YouTube, DTube5 is a video sharing website where users may watch and publish videos as well as interact with other users' content (comments and likes on their videos), and finally allows them to earn rewards for their content contributions (Kollmann et al., 2020; Stallone et al., 2021).

Influencer marketing as one of the many applications of social networking has an authenticity issue (Sprinklr Team, 2019). With the use of blockchain technology, marketers can validate the legitimacy of influencers and measure the reaction they receive to their campaigns. This technology is already being developed by a firm called Patron, which wants to assist companies in determining the worth of influencers by tracking and storing their social media data via blockchain. Also, the platform SocialMedia.Market, a decentralized marketplace for influencer marketing, helps users earn money for their influence by using tokens with the help of smart contracts. Such platforms are assisting marketers to confirm the influencers' followers and authenticating their identities as well (Antoniadis et al., 2019; Kuno Creative, 2018).

Emails continue to play a crucial role in maintaining contact besides other new communication channels and it is inevitable that a huge volume is lost in the weeds within spam boxes. This occurs due to the enormous volume of digital communications on a daily basis. Blockchain technology provides better metrics to see how effective or ineffective email marketing is, as long as email campaigns continue to play a significant role in the advertising environment. The blockchain framework has the capacity to gather engagement data and track metadata. This would provide marketers with more knowledge to adjust campaigns for maximum interactions with the target market (Mire, 2018; Pareek, 2019).

9.5 Conclusion

Blockchain technology has the potential to fundamentally alter the global corporate landscape and bring about a paradigm shift in how the business world operates in terms of finance, supply chain management, operations management, and marketing. The use of blockchain technology in business has several advantages. In addition to eliminating middlemen and lowering costs, a well-designed Blockchain network increases speed and reach to better serve as a decentralized, immutable database. The enhancement of transparency and provenance through various operational processes is an added benefit. This chapter explains the fundamental features and various types of blockchain technology that can be used in the marketing field. It addresses the basic concerns of marketers and consumers in today's digital competitive environment in the context of higher prices, data breaches, fraudulent activities, and data privacy. It also discusses how blockchain technology can aid marketers and consumers handle these concerns by identifying various benefits for companies and consumers. Both companies and consumers may have an interest in blockchain technology and its benefit. First the customers who want to protect their privacy while still having quality interactions with businesses, then the businesses who want to successfully use their budgets and gain more control and knowledge over their customer base, and finally the publishers who want to protect their reputation from ad frauds and retain their share of the advertising budgets are the parties most interested in finding solutions to these problems with the help of blockchain (Bezovski et al., 2021).

Also, this chapter discusses how marketers can set their marketing mix strategies and create value by deploying blockchain technology. Blockchain technology will increase operational effectiveness and aid in reducing operating expenses for companies by providing secure platforms that enable product authentication and transmission verification without the use of intermediaries. When incorporating blockchain into a marketing strategy, companies may focus on three different areas: collaborating with decentralized ad exchanges for digital advertising, integrating current touchpoint credentials with decentralized authentication systems, and concentrating on creating distinctive non-fungible token collections for digital branding (Tan and Saraninemi, 2022).

Although blockchain has tremendous potential, it also faces a lot of difficulties and challenges (Brauer and Linnala Eriksson, 2020). The main obstacles for deploying blockchain technology in marketing are seen to be corporate capability and difficulty in implementation (e.g., an absence of digital solutions, infrastructure, adaptability, experience, and high expenses). Marketers must be aware of the regulations and policies that will govern blockchain technology in the event of a failure, particularly when companies conduct business internationally in various countries. In the blockchain, data and transaction storage are currently difficult and expensive. Although so many big companies like Walmart or Starbucks implemented this new technology to their marketing activities, the difficulties in implementing blockchain in industries with complicated supply chain operations, such as those for drugs, food, apparel, and luxury goods, need to be investigated and analyzed, especially for small and medium sized companies in future research. There are currently insufficient empirical studies on the use of blockchain in many business sectors, such as marketing. Future studies should focus on evaluating the overall advantages as well as analyzing the implementation difficulties faced by marketers who pursue blockchain technology with empirical findings (Madhani, 2022a).

References

AdAge. (2022). How brands are using nfts-a continually updated list. Available at: https://adage.com/live-blog/how-brands-marketers-use-nfts-updated-list Accessed on 15.02.2023.

Al-Ahwal, T. M., Mladenović, D. and ZareRavasan, A. (2022). Blockchain implications for marketing; a review and an empirical analysis. Journal of Information Technology Management 14(Special Issue: The Business Value of Blockchain, Challenges, And Perspectives): 83–106.

Alexandre, A. (2018). Toyota uses blockchain tech to reduce fraud in digital advertising campaigns. Available at: https://cointelegraph.com/news/toyota-uses-blockchain-tech-to-reduce-fraud-in-digital-advertising-campaigns. Accessed on 21.02.2023.

Antoniadis, I., Kontsas, S. and Spinthiropoulos, K. (2019). Blockchain applications in marketing. The Proceedings of 7th ICCMI.

Anthes, M. (2018). Three ways blockchain will disrupt traditional business and ımpact marketing ın 2018. Available at: https://www.forbes.com/sites/forbesagencycouncil/2018/01/29/three-ways-blockchain-will-disrupt-traditional-business-and-impact-marketing-in-2018. Accessed on 19.02.2023.

Anwar, H. (2020). Blockchain in retail: use cases and potential applications Available at: https://101blockchains.com/blockchain-in-retail/ Accessed on 19.02.2023.

Aspasia, V. and Ourania, N. (2014). Social media adoption and managers' perceptions. International Journal on Strategic Innovative Marketing 1(2): 61–63.

Bayus, B. L. (2013). Crowdsourcing new product ideas over time: An analysis of the Dell IdeaStorm community. Management Science 59(1): 226–244.

Belch, G. and Belch, M. (2014). The role of new and traditional media in the rapidly changing marketing communications environment. International Journal of Strategic Innovative Marketing 1(3): 130–136.

Berkowitz, D. (2017). Twenty seven ways marketers can use blockchain. Available at: https://adage.com/article/digitalnext/twenty-ways-marketers-blockchain/311105. Accessed on 21.02.2023.

Bezovski, Z., Jovanov, T. and Temjanovski, R. (2021). The impact and the potential disruption of the blockchain technology on marketing. Journal of Economics 6(1): 13–23.

Blacker, A. (2021). Burger King's cryptocurrency play pays off Available at: https://www.qsrmagazine.com/outside-insights/burger-kings-cryptocurrency-play-pays. Accessed on 13.02.2023.

Bond Brand Loyalty. (2016). The 2016 Bond Loyalty Report. Available at: https://cdn2.hubspot.net/hubfs/352767/Resources/2016_Bond_Loyalty_ Report_Executive_Summary_CAN_Launch_Edition.pdf Accessed on 19.02.2023.

Boukis, A. (2020). Exploring the implications of blockchain technology for brand–consumer relationships: a future research agenda. Journal of Product & Brand Management 29(3): 307–320.

Brauer, J. and Linnala Eriksson, B. (2020). Blockchain's Influence on Digital Marketing: An Exploratory Study Examining Blockchain in Relation to Big Data and Digital Marketing. Ms Thesis, Umea School of Business, Umea University, Sweden.

Buhalis, D. and Licata, M. C. (2002). The future eTourism intermediaries. Tourism Management 23(3): 207–220.

Buss, D. (2002). As loyalty programs expand, customer fatigue forces creativity and caution. Resource Center Article, MCI. COM.

Campbell, R. H., Moorman, C. and Toledo, M. (2018). How blockchain can help marketers build better relationships with their customers. Available at: https://hbr.org/2018/10/how-blockchain-can-help-marketers-build-betterrelationships-with-their-customers Accessed 22.02.2023.

Caro, M. P., Ali, M. S., Vecchio, M. and Giaffreda, R. (2018). Blockchain-based traceability in Agri-Food supply chain management: A practical implementation. pp. 1–4. In 2018 IoT Vertical and Topical Summit on Agriculture-Tuscany (IOT Tuscany). IEEE.

Casino, F. (2019). Thomas k. Dasaklis, and Constantinos Patsakis. A systematic literature review of blockchain-based applications: Current status, classification, and open issues. Telematics and Informatics 36: 55–81.

Chaudhary, S. and Sharma, R. (2018). Digital marketing revolutionising fashion industry: the synthesis of the theory and practice. Pramana Research Journal 8(4): 259–266.

Chehrehpak, M., Afsharian, S. P. and Roshandel, J. (2014). Effects of implementing information security management systems on the performance of marketing and sales departments. International Journal of Business Information Systems 15(3): 291–306.

Colicev, A. (2022). How can non-fungible tokens bring value to brands. International Journal of Research in Marketing. (In-press).

Colman, A. M. (2015). A Dictionary of Psychology. Oxford Quick Reference. Oxford University Press, NY.

Cvitanović, P. L. (2018). New technologies in marketing as competitive advantage. ENTRENOVA-ENTerprise REsearch InNOVAtion 4(1): 266–274.

Darley, W. K., Blankson, C. and Luethge, D. J. (2010). Toward an integrated framework for online consumer behavior and decision making process: A review. Psychology & Marketing 27(2): 94–116.

De Filippi, P. (2017). What blockchain means for the sharing economy. Harvard Business Review 15(03).

Deighton, J. and Kornfeld, L. (2008). Digital Interactivity: Unanticipated Consequences for Markets, Marketing, and Consumers. Boston: Harvard Business School.

Dinh, T. T. A., Liu, R., Zhang, M., Chen, G., Ooi, B. C. et al. (2018). Untangling blockchain: A data processing view of blockchain systems. IEEE Transactions on Knowledge and Data Engineering 30(7): 1366–1385.

Du Toit, A. (2018). Confidentiality, Integrity and Availability (CIA) of Data Cyberdirective. Available at: https://cyberdirective.com/confidentiality-integrity-and-availability-ciaof-data Accessed on 18.02.2023.

Ertemel, A. V. (2018). Implications of blockchain technology on marketing. Journal of International Trade, Logistics and Law 4(2): 35–44.

FashionUnited. (2021). Dolce & Gabbana sells 6 million dollar fashion NFT. Available at: https://fashionunited.uk/news/business/dolce-gabbana-sells-6-million-dollar-fashion-nft/2021100858280 million-dollar-fashion-nft/2021100858280 Accessed 16.02.2023.

Felix, R., Rauschnabel, P. A. and Hinsch, C. (2017). Elements of strategic social media marketing: A holistic framework. Journal of Business Research 70: 118–126.

Futoransky, A., Sarraute, C., Fernandez, D., Travizano, M., Waissbein, A. et al. (2020). Fair and decentralized exchange of digital goods. arXiv preprint arXiv:2002.09689.

Galvez, J. F., Mejuto, J. C. and Simal-Gandara, J. (2018). Future challenges on the use of blockchain for food traceability analysis. TrAC Trends in Analytical Chemistry 107: 222–232.

Geiger, S. and Martin, S. G. (1999). The internet as a relationship marketing tool-some evidence from Irish companies. Irish Marketing Review 12(2).

Geyser, W. (2022) Everything You Need to Know About Blockchain Marketing. Available at: https://influencermarketinghub.com/blockchain-marketing/ Accessed on 20.02.2023.

Ghose, A. (2018). What blockchain could mean for marketing. Harvard Business Review 5: 2–5. Available at: https://hbr.org/2018/05/what-blockchain-could-mean-for-marketing Accessed on 17.02. 2023.

Goldin, M., Soleimani, A. and Young, J. (2017). The Adchain Registry. Whitepaper. Available online at: https://blockchain-x.eu/wp-content/uploads/2018/02/The_adChain_Registry_ENG.pdf Accessed on 22.02. 2023.

Goodman, J. and Newman, S. (2003). Understand customer behavior and complaints. Quality Progress 36(1): 51–55.

Grover, P., Kar, A. K., Janssen, M. and Ilavarasan, P. V. (2019). Perceived usefulness, ease of use and user acceptance of blockchain technology for digital transactions–insights from user-generated content on Twitter. Enterprise Information Systems 13(6): 771–800.

Gupta, V. (2017). The Promise of Blockchain is a World Without Middlemen. Available at: https://hbr.org/2017/03/the-promise-of-blockchain-is-a-world-without-middlemen Accessed on 19.02.2023.

Hawlitschek, F., Notheisen, B. and Teubner, T. (2018). The limits of trust-free systems: A literature review on blockchain technology and trust in the sharing economy. Electronic Commerce Research and Applications 29: 50–63.

Hongwei, L. I. N. and Peiji, S. H. A. O. (2011). The study on supervision model for online advertising click fraud. Management Science and Engineering 5(3): 111–119.

Huntsman. (2019). Cyber crime affects every sector. Available at: https://www.huntsmansecurity.com/blog/cyber-criminals-target-all-sectors/ Accessed on 21.02.2023.

Idrees, S. and Nowostawski, M. (2022). Transformations through Blockchain Technology. Springer: Berlin/Heidelberg, Germany.

Jallat, F. and Capek, M. J. (2001). Disintermediation in question: new economy, new networks, new middlemen. Business Horizons 44(2): 55–55.

Kang, J. and Hustvedt, G. (2014). Building trust between consumers and corporations: The role of consumer perceptions of transparency and social responsibility. Journal of Business Ethics 125: 253–265.

Keybase.io. (2019). Keybase. Availble at: https://keybase.io/docs/server_security. Accessed on 21.02.2023.

Kim, D. J., Ferrin, D. L. and Rao, H. R. (2008). A trust-based consumer decision-making model in electronic commerce: The role of trust, perceived risk, and their antecedents. Decision Support Systems 44(2): 544–564.

Kollmann, T., Hensellek, S., de Cruppe, K. and Sirges, A. (2020). Toward a renaissance of cooperatives fostered by Blockchain on electronic marketplaces: a theory-driven case study approach. Electronic Markets 30: 273–284.

Kosba, A., Miller, A., Shi, E., Wen, Z., Papamanthou, C. et al. (2016). Hawk: The blockchain model of cryptography and privacy-preserving smart contracts. pp. 839–858. In 2016 IEEE Symposium on Security and Privacy (SP). IEEE.

Kshetri, N. (2010). The economics of click fraud. IEEE Security & Privacy 8(3): 45–53.

Kshetri, N. and Voas, J. (2019). Online advertising fraud. Computer 52(1): 58–61.

Kumar, A. and Brar, V. (2018). Digital marketing and role of blockchain in digital marketing industry. International Journal of All Research Education and Scientific Methods 6(12): 23–26.

Kuno Creative. (2018). 6 Ways to Benefit from Blockchain Marketing Technology. Available at: https://www.kunocreative.com/blog/blockchain-marketing. Accessed on 09.02.2023.

L'Hermitte, C. and Nair, N. K. C. (2021). A blockchain-enabled framework for sharing logistics resources during emergency operations. Disasters 45(3): 527–554.

Lee, M. K. and Turban, E. (2001). A trust model for consumer internet shopping. International Journal of Electronic Commerce 6(1): 75–91.

Lemos, C., Ramos, R. F., Moro, S. and Oliveira, P. M. (2022). Stick or Twist—the rise of blockchain applications in marketing management. Sustainability 14(7): 4172.

Li, Y., Marier-Bienvenue, T., Perron-Brault, A., Wang, X., Paré, G. et al. (2018). Blockchain technology in business organizations: A scoping review. Proceedings of the 51st Hawaii International Conference on System Sciences, Hawaii.

Li, Y., Jiang, S., Shi, J. and Wei, Y. (2021). Pricing strategies for blockchain payment service under customer heterogeneity. International Journal of Production Economics 242: 108282.

Liu, Z. and Li, Z. (2020). A blockchain-based framework of cross-border e-commerce supply chain. International Journal of Information Management 52: 102059.

Lucidity. (2018). Lucidity's Blockchain Pilot with Toyota Results in 21% Lift in Campaign Performance. Available at: https://www.prnewswire.com/news-releases/luciditys-blockchain-pilotwith-toyota-results-in-21-lift-incampaign-performance-300731983.html. Accessed on 25.01.2023.

Lunio. (2021). Available at: https://lunio.ai/statistics/ad-fraud-statistics/ Accessed on 08.02.2023.

Madhani, P. M. (2022a). Effective marketing strategy with blockchain implementation: enhancing customer value propositions. IUP Journal of Business Strategy 19(1): 7–35.

Madhani, P. M. (2022b). Blockchain implementation in marketing: enhancing effectiveness of marketing mix strategy. Marketing Mastermind 19(2): 29–40.

Makarov, A. (2022). Blockchain in Retail: 4 Use Cases and 6 Real-Life Examples. Available at: https://www.itransition.com/blockchain/retail. Accessed on 14.02.2023.

Marthews, A. and Tucker, C. (2022). What blockchain can and can't do: Applications to marketing and privacy. International Journal of Research in Marketing (In-Press).

Martinez-Ruiz, M. P. and Moser, K. S. (2019). Studying consumer behavior in an online context: The impact of the evolution of the world wide web for new avenues in research. Frontiers in Psychology 10: 2731.

Maslova, N. CMA and CTP, P. (2018). Blockchain: Disruption and opportunity. Strategic Finance 100(1): 24–29.

McAllister, M. P. and Turow, J. (2002). New media and the commercial sphere: Two intersecting trends, five categories of concern. Journal of Broadcasting & Electronic Media 46(4): 505–514.

McCole, P. (2004). Marketing is not dead: a response to Elegy on the death of marketing. European Journal of Marketing 38(11/12): 1349–1354.

McKinsey. (2022). Value creation in the metaverse Report. Available at: https://www.mckinsey.com/capabilities/growth-marketing-and-sales/our-insights/value-creation-in-the-metaverse. Accessed on 14.02.2023.

McParland, C. and Connolly, R. (2007). Online privacy concerns: threat or opportunity. In Proceedings of 2007 Mediterranean and Middle Eastern Conference on Information Systems. EMCIS2007. Citeseer.

Meara, K. (2022). Nike Enters the Blockchain with New Digital Community. Available at: https://dealerscope.com/2022/11/nike-enters-the-blockchain-with-new-digital-community/ Accessed on 15.02.2023.

Millward, S. (2018). Alibaba rolls out blockchain pilot to tackle fake food products. Available at https://www.techinasia.com/alibaba-fake-food-blockchain-pilot. Accessed on 21.02.2023.

Mire, S. (2018), Blockchain in marketing: 7 possible use cases. Available at: https://www.disruptordaily.com/blockchainuse- cases-marketing/, Accessed on 21.02.2023.

Mire, S. (2019). Blockchain in marketing: 23 startups to watch in 2019. https://www.disruptordaily.com/blockchain-startups-marketing/ Accessed on 20.02.2023,

Newman, D. (2019). How Blockchain is changing digital marketing. Available at: https://www.forbes.com/sites/danielnewman/2019/09/18/how-blockchain-is-changing-digital-marketing/?sh=249438c716eb Accessed on 19.02.2023.

Omran, Y., Henke, M., Heines, R. and Hofmann, E. (2017). Blockchain-driven supply chain finance: Towards a conceptual framework from a buyer perspective. Working Paper https://www.alexandria.unisg.ch/251095/1/WP29-Blockchain-driven%20supply%20chain%20finance%20Towards%20a%20conceptual%20framework%20from%20a%20buyer%20perspective.pdf.

Oymak, B. B. and Kazançoğlu, İ. (2021). The use of blockchain technology in marketing: advantages and barriers. Ardahan Üniversitesi İktisadi ve İdari Bilimler Fakültesi Dergisi 3(2): 164–174.

Palmer, D. (2021). Starbucks to track coffee using Microsoft's blockchain service. Available at: https://www.coindesk.com/markets/2019/05/07/starbucks-to-track-coffee-using-microsofts-blockchain-service/ Accessed on 19.02.2023.

Pareek, A. (2019). How blockchain is having an ımpact on digital marketing? Available at: https://customerthink.com/how-blockchain-is-having-an-impact-on-digital-marketing/ Accessed on 22.02.2023.

Peres, R., Schreier, M., Schweidel, D. A. and Sorescu, A. (2022). Blockchain meets marketing: Opportunities, threats, and avenues for future research. International Journal of Research in Marketing (In-Press).

Pilkington, M. (2016). Blockchain technology: principles and applications. pp. 225–253. In Research Handbook on Digital Transformations. Edward Elgar Publishing.

Rabby, F., Chimhundu, R. and Hassan, R. (2022). Blockchain technology transforms digital marketing by growing consumer trust. Transformations Through Blockchain Technology: The New Digital Revolution 265–289.

Ratnasingham, P. (1998). Trust in Web-based electronic commerce security. Information Management & Computer Security 6(4): 162–166.

Ravasan, A. Z., Rouhani, S. and Asgary, S. (2014). A review for the online social networks literature (2005–2011). European Journal of Business and Management 6(4): 22–37.

Rejeb, A., Keogh, J. G. and Treiblmaier, H. (2020). How blockchain technology can benefit marketing: Six pending research areas. Frontiers in Blockchain 3.

Report Linker. (2022). Global Digital Advertising and Marketing Industry Available at: https://www.reportlinker.com/p03646022/Global-Digital-Advertising-and-Marketing-Industry.html?utm_source=GNW. Accessed on 19.02.2023.

Reuters. (2018). U.S. puts Alibaba's taobao on blacklist for counterfeit. Available at: https://www.reuters.com/article/us-alibaba-ustr-idUSKBN1F12DE. Accessed on 18.02.2023.

Rijanto, A. (2021). Blockchain technology adoption in supply chain finance. Journal of Theoretical and Applied Electronic Commerce Research 16(7): 3078–3098.

Rosenbloom, B. (2007). The wholesaler's role in the marketing channel: Disintermediation vs. reintermediation. International Review of Retail, Distribution and Consumer Research 17(4): 327–339.

Rosário, A. and Raimundo, R. (2021). Consumer marketing strategy and E-commerce in the last decade: a literature review. Journal of Theoretical and Applied Electronic Commerce Research 16(7): 3003–3024.

Schuman, M. (2015). Why Alibaba's massive counterfeit problem will never be solved. Forbes. Available at:. https://www.forbes.com/sites/michaelschuman/2015/11/04/alibaba-and-the-40000-thieves/?sh=675661e929dc Accessed on 18.02.2023.

Shah, D. and Murthi, B. P. S. (2021). Marketing in a data-driven digital world: Implications for the role and scope of marketing. Journal of Business Research 125: 772–779.

Shaikh, E. and Mohammad, N. (2020). Applications of Blockchain Technology for Smart Cities. 2020 Fourth International Conference on Inventive Systems and Control (ICISC), Institute of Electrical and Electronics Engineers (IEEE), pp. 186–191.

Sheth, J. N. (2002). The future of relationship marketing. Journal of Services Marketing 16(7): 590–592.

Sikorski, J. J., Haughton, J. and Kraft, M. (2017). Blockchain technology in the chemical industry: Machine-to-machine electricity market. Applied Energy 195: 234–246.

Singer, N. (2012). You for Sale: Mapping, and Sharing, the Consumer Genome. New York Times, 16: 2012.

Smith, T. D. (2017, December). The blockchain litmus test. pp. 2299–2308. In 2017 IEEE International Conference on Big Data (Big Data). IEEE.

Sprinklr. (2019). The future of blockchain in marketing. Available at https:// www.sprinklr.com/blog/blockchain-cryptocurrency-marketing/ Accessed on February 7, 2023.

Stallone, V., Wetzels, M. and Klaas, M. (2021). Applications of Blockchain technology in marketing—A systematic review of marketing technology companies. Blockchain: Research and Applications 2(3): 100023.

Stauss, B., Schmidt, M. and Schoeler, A. (2005). Customer frustration in loyalty programs. International Journal of Service Industry Management 16(3): 229–252.

Subramanian, H. (2018). Decentralized blockchain-based electronic marketplaces. Communications of the ACM 61(1): 78–84.

Tahal, R. (2014). Loyalty programs in e-commerce and their perception by the young adult internet population. Central European Business Review 3(2): 7–13.

Tan, T. M. and Saraniemi, S. (2022). Trust in blockchain-enabled exchanges: Future directions in blockchain marketing. Journal of the Academy of Marketing Science 1–26.

Treiblmaier, H. (2018). The impact of the blockchain on the supply chain: a theory-based research framework and a call for action. Supply Chain Management: an International Journal 23(6): 545–559.

Treiblmaier, H. (2019). Combining blockchain technology and the physical internet to achieve triple bottom line sustainability: a comprehensive research agenda for modern logistics and supply chain management. Logistics 3(1): 10.

Treiblmaier, H. and Sillaber, C. (2021). The impact of blockchain on e-commerce: A framework for salient research topics. Electronic Commerce Research & Applications 48: 101054.

Udo, G. J. (2001). Privacy and security concerns as major barriers for e-commerce: a survey study. Information Management & Computer Security 9(4): 165–174.

Uncles, M. D., Dowling, G. R. and Hammond, K. (2003). Customer loyalty and customer loyalty programs. Journal of Consumer Marketing 20(4): 294–316.

Walsh, D. (2021). Paying with Bitcoin: these are the major companies that accept crypto as payment. Available at: https://www.euronews.com/next/2021/12/04/paying-with-cryptocurrencies-these-are-the-major-companies-that-accept-cryptos-as-payment. Accessed on 18.02.2023.

Wang, L., Xie, G. and Chen, C. (2022). Price competition and blockchain technology adoption strategies of agents on the digital platform. Frontiers in Psychology 13.

Webster, A. (2021). You can now explore a surreal gucci garden inside Roblox. Available at: https://www.theverge.com/2021/5/17/22440134/gucci-garden-roblox-experience-metaverse-date. Accessed on 20.02.2023.

Wilson, T. and Auchard, E. (2018). Chickens and Eggs: retailer Carrefour adopts blockchain to track fresh produce. Available at: https://www.reuters.com/article/us-carrefour-blockchain-ibm-idINKCN1MI162. Accessed on 18.02.2023.

Wright, W. (2022). Shake Shack starts serving Bitcoin to app users. Available at https://www.thedrum.com/news/2022/03/07/shake-shack-starts-serving-bitcoin-app-users#:~:text=Shake%20Shack%20will%20begin%20offering,%2C%20Inc%20(formerly%20Square). Accessed on 19.02.2023.

Yanik, S. and Kilic, A. S. (2018). A framework for the performance evaluation of an energy blockchain. Energy Management—Collective and Computational Intelligence with Theory and Applications 521–543.

Yousafzai, S. Y., Pallister, J. G. and Foxall, G. R. (2003). A proposed model of e-trust for electronic banking. Technovation 23(11): 847–860.

Zhang, Z. J. (2022). Cryptopricing: Whence comes the value for cryptocurrencies and NFTs? International Journal of Research in Marketing (In-Press).

Zheng, Z., Xie, S., Dai, H. N., Chen, X. and Wang, H. (2018). Blockchain challenges and opportunities: A survey. International Journal of Web and Grid Services 14(4): 352–375.

Chapter 10
Blockchain Applications in Banking

Bülent Balkan

10.1 Introduction

Banks are financial intermediation institutions based on trust. Blockchain technology, on the contrary, has a decentralized structure where the need for 'trust' held by a central structure is minimized. For this reason, Blockchain technology creates an opportunity with the efficiency and productivity of technological development in the context of banking, and a threat potential from competition by eliminating the centralized structure and eliminating intermediaries.

This is the age of technology and banks are widely using technology to compete and differentiate themselves. While Blockchain technology poses a threat to banks, it also creates a crucial opportunity for change. Blockchain technology, which is essentially a record-keeping technology, is a new option for keeping financial records in the market. This option uses distributed ledger technology to replace traditional centralized bookkeeping.

Blockchain DLT technology has the potential to be an ideal technology for banking applications with its features such as security, immutability and auditability.

Cryptocurrency is excluded from the scope of this article and instead the impact of block chain application on banking practices is examined.

Atty. PhD, CIP, CCEO.
Email: bulentbalkan@bkare.com.tr

10.2 Purpose

Firstly, we aim to analyze the applications of Blockchain technology in the Banking industry and evaluate their benefits and disadvantages.

This includes examining the potential changes that blockchain technology would bring to these banking applications. An inventory of Blockchain's benefits, drawbacks, and issues will be taken, including a discussion of how Blockchain will give a new direction to banks and the banking sector.

Finally, we will also explore the impact of blockchain applications on the overall banking sector. The effects and the consequences that may arise from these changes will also be evaluated.

10.3 Methodology

In this study, secondary data from books, journals, and websites was used. Multiple databases were utilized. In the study, the benefits and threats of Blockchain applications to banking were analyzed simultaneously.

10.4 Findings

In this section, we will present the relevant findings, analyze and discuss them, and finally share our conclusions.

10.4.1 Blockchain Technology and Characteristics

Although blockchain is not called by this name, it was first described in the article Bitcoin, written under the pseudonym Satoshi Nakamoto. In Nakamoto's system, transactions are recorded and added chronologically so that the records are permanent and tamper-proof (Nakamoto, 2008).

To understand Blockchain and its importance, we need to understand its characteristics. Puthal et al. state that the main characteristics of Blockchain are decentralization, distributed digital ledger, transparency, verifiable time-stamps, secure, irrevocable and auditable, immutable and non-repudiable, consensus based, and reduces dependencies on 3rd parties (Puthal, 2018).

Saberi et al. emphasize the features that distinguish Blockchain from existing systems; security, verifiability, non-localization, and smart execution (Saberi et al., 2018). Blockchain allows the "transaction" to be controlled, materialized and decentralized. The basic concept of the blockchain is to first break down the data into small nodes to encrypt it. This is important for security and to prevent hacking. Each node means a new encryption, a new layer of security. The data is open but encrypted, so it cannot be "cracked" and the information cannot be leaked (Shukla and Balwani, 2022).

Blockchain technology can be defined as a record-keeping technology. While in the traditional method, ledgers are kept centrally, blockchain uses a distributed ledger. In a traditional database, a client performs four functions; "Create, Read, Update, and Delete".[1] Users of Blockchain technology can create and read only. In other words, previous data cannot be changed or deleted and is stored permanently. This is the main safeguard against manipulation and fraud (Mehrotra and Bhatia, 2022)

Kaur et al. state the features of blockchain are; "Distributed database, Peer to peer Transmission, Transparency, and Computational logic" (Kaur et al., 2022). In another approach, according to Pisa and Juden (2017), the main technological features of blockchain include a peer-to-peer network, distributed ledger, consensus mechanism, and cryptography technologies.

When evaluating the features of Blockchain technology in the context of banking, the following features are important and can affect banking applications: Decentralization, Distributed Digital Ledger, Cryptography Technologies, Security, Verifiability, Immutable and Non-Repudiable, Transparency, Time-stamped, Auditable (Figure 10.1).

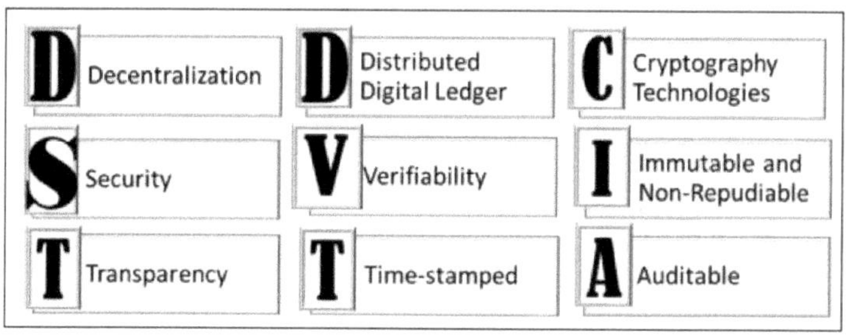

Figure 10.1. Features of Blockchain that are important for Banking. Source: Prepared by author.

10.4.2 Blockchain Technology in Banking

Banking is one of the sectors that has adopted Blockchain technology extensively, driven by the sector's interest in technological advancements and its aspiration to use these as a competitive edge.

Banking has been significantly affected by technological developments throughout the years. In the 1990s, automation through ATMs and computers revolutionized the industry. The 2000s saw the rise of online banking and internet applications, further transforming banking practices. Mobile banking emerged as a game-changer in the 2010s. As we enter the 2020s, technologies like artificial intelligence, cybersecurity, and blockchain are reshaping the sector, presenting both disruptive challenges and promising opportunities.

[1] Acronym for "Create, Read, Update, and Delete" which is known as CRUD commands.

The emergence of blockchain technology is indeed linked to the 2008 financial crisis in which the Lehman Brothers went bankrupt. Following the crisis, which led to liquidity shortages and the struggles of systemically important financial institutions, central banks and governmental authorities intervened to support these institutions using taxpayer funds. Satoshi Nakamoto's paper was published immediately after the bankruptcy of Lehman Brothers as a proposal for an alternative to the centralized system during this period of financial crisis (Seretakis, 2017)

> According to a study conducted by Arman and Kundakçı in 2022 the top three criteria of highest importance for the banking industry's adoption of Blockchain technology are high security, efficiency and a smart system. On the other hand, the criteria of lowest level importance were found to be government support, customer satisfaction and IT readiness (Arman and Kundakcı, 2022).

10.4.3 Blockchain as a Disruptive Technology for Banking

Disruptive technology basically refers to the use of more efficient technology to create a better financial system.

Many authors characterize Blockchain as a disruptive technology in the banking industry. While disruption is inevitable, there is also the potential for banks to transform themselves and adapt to the changes brought by blockchain, rather than being completely displaced. This acceptance and cooperation with disruptive innovation is often referred to as the "grief cycle" of banks (Sironi, 2018).

Khatri and Kaushik also acknowledge blockchain as an influential and disruptive technology. They hihghlight that while blockchain enhances efficiency and speed in banking, it also disrupts the industry, shaping its future (Khatri and Kaushik, 2021).

Gupta and Gupta conclude that Blockchain will transform the Indian Banking sector as a "disruptive force by making banking transactions securer, faster, transparent and cost-effective" (Gupta and Gupta, 2018).

In the blockchain space, numerous startups have begun developing products in the financial sector, while at the same time, major banking groups have initiated blockchain projects by forming strategic partnerships (Sarto and Gai, 2022).

Degener advocates collaboration with Fintech organizations to maximize the benefits of blockchain, rather than its isolated implementation by the banks (Degener, 2018).

10.4.4 Banking Applications and Blockchain

Blockchain technology has the potential to revolutionize and reshape the core services offered by banks, particularly in the realm of payments.

Payments: Blockchain technology offers the potential for significantly lower costs in payment transactions compared to traditional systems. The existing SWIFT protocol used in banking primarily facilitates payment orders rather than actual fund transfers. This leads to additional costs as intermediaries are involved in the subsequent transmission of money. Blockchain can streamline this process and reduce associated expenses (CB Insights, 2022).

Clearing and Settlement Systems: Blockchain technology specifically distributed ledgers, has the potential to reduce the costs of clearing and settlement processes in banking on the one hand and providing real-time transactions on the other.

Loans: This represents a significant area where FinTechs are poised to compete with banks, and the utilization of Blockchain technology can potentially lead to lower interest rates by removing intermediaries in the loan process.

Syndicated lending: Blockchain technology can enhance efficiency in syndicated loans by reducing the need for extensive regulatory meetings, thereby saving time and costs associated with the process (Palihapitiya, 2020).

Crowdfunding: Palihapitiya (2020) suggests that crowdfunding, a method of raising funds through small contributions, is utilized by banks as a financing approach suitable for the implementation of Blockchain technology. This is due to the decentralized and transparent nature of financing facilitated by Blockchain in crowdfunding processes.

10.4.4.1 *Know Your Customer (KYC) Practices in Banking*

Before accepting customers, banks are required to verify customer information and identities as well as conduct necessary checks to prevent money laundering and financing of terrorism. This process, commonly referred to Know Your Customer (KYC), imposes significant costs and consumes a substantial amount of time for banks. Each bank independently carries out this process for every customer, resulting in duplicated efforts and increased time and transaction expenses.

Blockchain technology can decrease the costs associated with Know Your Customer (KYC) processes. By storing customer information on a decentralized Blockchain, and allowing authorized parties to access and utilize that information, the need for individual banks to repeatedly perform KYC procedures for each bank can be eliminated.

KYC verifications encompass several processes such as identity verification, address verification, biometric verification, and document validation which can be time consuming and may take up to 3 months. Disruptions in KYC practices have been found to result in a 12 percent attrition rate, as indicated by a survey conducted by Thomson Reuters. It is important to note that KYC practices not only lead to loss of time and customers but also incur significant costs for banks. According to the same survey, banks spend upto $500 million dollars annually on KYC compliance practices and due diligence efforts for their customers. According to Goldman Sachs, banks can potentially save up to $160 million annually and reduce staffing needs by 10% by leveraging blockchain technology for KYC (CB Insights, 2022).

Marr points to Blockchain's ability to prevent duplication. This is because Blockchain technology allows other banks to access the verification record made by one bank (Marr, 2017).

Walker points out that KYC processes are both expensive and inefficient and can result in banks working with weak customers. By leveraging Blockchain, a single and standardized information source can be established for account opening purposes. This would enable the creation of a single "KYC" file within banks which will strengthen their overall regulatory compliance efforts (Walker, 2018).

Recently, several Blockchain-based credit scoring platforms such as Bloom, Bloom app OnRamp, Quadrata, and Plaid have emerged. These platforms enable customers to create Blockchain-based profiles through mobile applications (apps). Alongside identity verification, these apps can also conduct checks for Politically Exposed Persons (PEP). For example, Quadrata Passport has developed an application that verifies KYC/AML credentials and stores them as non-fungible tokens (NFTs). Similarly, banks are also exploring ways to leverage Blockchain technology for sharing KYC information among themselves. For instance, Deutsche Bank, HSBC Mitsubishi UFJ Financial Group and IBM have collaborated to create a platform where KYC information can be digitized and stored on a unified platform (CB Insights, 2022).

10.4.4.2 Fraud Prevention

Blockchain technology has the potential to significantly enhance fraud prevention in the banking sector. In traditional centralized systems, where all information is stored in a central ledger, the data is more vulnerable to attacks. However, with the implementation of distributed ledger technology, customer information is stored in decentralized blocks, making it more resilient against attacks. Due to this distributed ledger technology, it is very difficult for a hacker to access all customer information simultaneously.

10.4.4.3 The Use of Blockchain in Bank Audits

Auditability is a critical component of good corporate governance (Good Governance), ensuring effective management of banks. Blockchain technology has the potential to offer technical solutions for more efficient and cost effective auditing of banks and banking transactions. This includes internal audits, independent audits, and regulatory authority audits.

Blockchain technology will facilitate the identifaction and prevention of fraud in financial reports (Kılınç, 2020). Additionally, it enables automated monitoring control of a large volume of transactions, such as real-time calculation of stock movements from remote locations and in real-time. By providing a reliabile and transparent audit trail, Blockchain reduces the costs associated with monitoring and control. It ensures the timeliness of the data, thereby enhancing the efficiency of financial reporting and control processes (Cagle, 2020).

Blockchain technology is known for its ability to enhance efficiency and reduce audit costs, primarily due to the real-time audit trail it provides. The real-time audit trail guarantees the accuracy of transactions through timestamping, ensuring that, auditors spend less time verifying the correctness of transactions. Thus, they can allocate more time to audit techniques and other essential steps, enabling them to conduct more effective audits (Gokoglan et al., 2022).

10.4.5 Bancassurance and Blockchain

Blockchain is also being used in bancassurance. The use of blockchain in bancassurance will reduce human error as well as fraud, speed up transactions and reduce costs. Bancassurance has become a very popular product, especially in Asia, with banks offering various products such as life insurance and housing insurance to their customers, for example, China construction bank has created a bancassurance model built with Blockchain (Verma and Kansra, 2022).

10.4.6 Smart Contracts

The main feature of smart contracts is that they are secure and costless contracts that are self-executing under certain conditions. They can be used in banking applications, especially in areas such as loan transactions and KYC compliance transactions. For example, when the collateral of a loan falls below a certain rate according to the contract, a smart contract sends a notice to customers to fulfill their collateral.

Because smart contracts are computer-coded, they are paperless, unlike traditional contracts, stored on a blockchain, smart contracts automatically go into effect when specified conditions are met. The most important feature of smart contracts for banking is their ability to automate business processes. In particular, smart contracts can be used in banking to assess loan eligibility, claims processing and KYC compliance. Smart contracts are self-executing, independent contracts with no intervention from any party. They are free contracts that are executed transparently. All information can be tracked on the Blockchain platform. These tamper-proof contracts are secure applications that allow the contract to be self-authenticated. These contracts are accepted by signing with a cryptographic digital signature (Khan et al., 2021).

Smart contracts create and algorithmically enforce the terms of the agreement without the need for any legal documents. This is completely unlike traditional contracting practices and allows transactions to be carried out without the need for a lawyer or notary public. Many platforms have been created to store smart contracts (Makridakis and Christodoulou, 2019).

10.4.7 *Electronic Check Applications*

Blockchain technology offers suitability for the issuance of electronic cheques. The use of timestamps in each transaction ensures that the date and information associated with the electronic cheque cannot be altered. Furthermore, if the device used for issuing the elrctronic cheque has a GPS feature, it becomes possible to clearly identify the place where the electronic cheque was issued. In addition, the electronic check can be delivered immediately to the parties, especially to those located in different countries or continents. Thus, the electronic issuance or check transfer can be realized within seconds. Smart contracts can also be used in the electronic check application. In the presence of the conditions predetermined by the parties, a smart contract can be created that autonomously sends the check to the beneficiary and informs the relevant parties (Ber, 2022).

10.5 Advantages and Disadvantages and Opportunities that Blockchain will Bring to Banking and Banks

10.5.1 *Advantages of the Blockchain*

Overall, Blockchain technology improves people's standard of living, reduces costs, increases speed, fosters trust, and improves the economy (Makridakis and Christodoulou, 2019).

Blockchain plays a role in safeguarding intellectual property rights by offering features such as traceability, provability, and transparency in trade (Copigneaux et al., 2020). Blockchain also contributes to social and economic development around the world by increasing accessibility to financial services (Kumar and Kaur, 2022).

Shukla and Balwani state that the cost of bank infrastructure can be reduced by 30% with Blockchain adoption (Shukla and Balwani, 2022) Blockchain in general is a tamper-proof system, able to operate on millions of devices simultaneously. Blockchain is a technology that provides transparency, security, and auditability through its architectural design (Mehrotra and Bhatia, 2022).

After evaluating the literature in general, we can summarize the advantages and disadvantages of Blockchain as follows;

***Advantages of Blockchain*:** Transparency, Trust, Decentralized structure, Traceability, Data integrity, Auditability, Cost reduction, Increased accessibility to financial services, Reduction of fraud, Enhanced speed.

***Disadvantages of Blockchain*:** Scalability, Privacy Issues, Size and Bandwidth, Legal uncertainties, Cost and efficiency, Security and Privacy, Energy and resource consumption, Achieving consensus, Design standardization.

***Transparency*:** As all changes are reflected in the ledger and can be audited by anyone participating in the Blockchain network (Makridakis and Christodoulou, 2019) sharing transactions increases transparency and transparency in turn reduces risks.

***Trust*:** Trust is a fundamental and indispensable characteristic of the banking sector, and banks are defined as institutions of trust (Battal, 2001). In the article "The Trust Machine" published in The Economist, it argued that Blockchain's biggest impacts are on trust (Economist, 2015).

In this context, it is of great importance to prevent fraud and other financial crimes and to establish integrity, reliability, responsibility, and predictability, which are the precursors of trust (Beck, 2018).

Blockchain's ability to enable low-risk transactions and increase the cost of compliance departments are factors that increase trust in banking practices (Marr, 2017).

***Decentralized Structure*:** Transactions are verified by the participants through predefined consensus mechanisms, without being approved and verified by any authority. This reduces both costs and the possibility of information loss (Puthal, 2018). Due to the decentralized structure based on distributed ledger technology, banks will become stronger against attacks and fraud as information is not collected in a single center.

Benefits of Blockchain	Disadvantages of Blockchain
• Transparency	• Scalability
• Trust	• Privacy Issues
• Decentralized Structure	• Size and bandwidth
• Traceability	• Legal uncertainties
• Data integrity	• Cost and efficiency
• Auditability	• Security and Privacy
• Cost Reduction	• Energy and resource consumption
• Increased accessibility to financial services	• Achieving consensus
• Reduction of fraud	• Design standardization
• Enhanced speed	

Figure 10.2. Benefits and disadvantages of Blockchain. Source: Prepared by author.

***Traceability*:** The distributed structure and transparency of the Blockchain increases traceability (Banker, 2019).

***Data integrity*:** Blockchain provides the necessary infrastructure for data integrity due to its high confidentiality and its ability to work together with distributed cloud technologies (Gaetani et al., 2017).

***Auditability*:** Blockchain technology has a significant impact on auditing. It enables documentation services, facilitates auditing of all transactions, allows real-time auditing, reduces transaction risks, and ensures immutability of transactions. These features enable auditors to focus on new audit models and provide more accurate opinions on transactions (Gokoglan et al., 2022). A key feature of blockchain is its ability to verify and audit transactions without the need for a third party. This characteristic instills trust and enhances the effectiveness of the auditing process. Transactions recorded in the blockchain are immediately verifiable and traceable, making it more challenging for financial report fraud to occur and easier to identify the fraudulent activities (Kılınç, 2020). The fact that the data used is reliable and transparent will lead to more widespread use of Blockchain in auditing and will have a reducing effect on the cost of monitoring and control activities (Cagle, 2020). Given its ability to enhance trust and transparency, auditability stands out as one of the most significant contributions of Blockchain technology to corporate governance.

***Cost reduction*:** Ucoglu (2022) and Demarco (2019) state that SWIFT costs in payment systems and KYC processes can be expensive, while blockchain technology can reduce costs by eliminating intermediaries and streamlining account information and verification. According to Accenture consulting (Accenture, 2017), blockchain, along with technologies like DBT and smart contract, can save between 30% and 50% by reducing transaction fees and losses. Chowdhury et al. (2021) suggest that blockchain technology can decrease centralized financial reporting by up to 70%, and cut Business operation and compliance costs by less than half.

Increased accessibility to financial services: Blockchain has enabled many people who could not get bank loans prior to it benefit from financial services (Palihapitiya, 2020). According to a study by the World Bank, 18% of citizens cannot benefit from financial products as they are not entitled to digital identitifications (Üçoğlu, 2022). According to Appaya, Blockchain increases accessibility to financial services and financial inclusion. Hence it can accelerate economic development and growth (Appaya, 2021).

Enhanced speed: Blockchain applications, especially in payments, enable payments to be made to recipients with fewer business processing steps faster.

10.6 Disadvantages of Blockchain

Shukla and Balwani identified 13 barriers to Blockchain in banking by past research and interviews with experts (Shukla and Balwani, 2022). Of these 13 barriers, Scalability, Cost, and Efficiency were evaluated as important factors in terms of banking and were included in the list of disadvantages.

Biella and Zinetti's study (Biella and Zinetti, 2016) highlights throughput and latency, privacy, size and bandwidth, and security as factors limiting the implementation of Blockchain in financial institutions.

Scalability: Scalability is fundamentally an efficiency issue. Due to the limited capacity of the networks, Blockchain cannot process large amounts of transactions in banking in a short period of time and transactions are delayed, reducing efficiency and effectiveness.

Scalability is an imperative factor affecting computing capacity (Garg et al., 2020). In order to reduce the possibility of double spending, a certain number of verifications are required, which can take from a few seconds in credit card payment networks to up to ten minutes (Biella and Zinetti, 2016).

Privacy: In the context of blockchain technology, privacy concerns arise due the nature of storing each transaction in each node for control purposes. These concerns pose problems for banking in two dimensions. Biella and Zinetti (2016) address the regulatory limitations associated with blockchain technology. According to legislation, certain information must be kept confidential. The second issue arises from the strategy that banks seek to maintain competitive advantage by safeguarding customer information from their competitors.

Size and bandwidth: High transaction speeds and the use of smart contracts increase the amount of data which in turn creates a burden on the hardware.

Legal uncertainties: Legal uncertainties arise due the lack of detailed national and international regulations for blockchain. This creates ambiguity, particularly in cases of financial failure like fraud and bankruptcy, where it is unclear which country's law will be apply and how regulations will be followed.

The absence of clear guidance from governments makes blockchain a gray area in terms of legal regulations (Arjun and Suprabha, 2020).

The decentralization of the system poses a significant challenge to regulation. Additionally, regulatory authorities may struggle with over-regulation and inflexibility, making it difficult to effectively regulate the field (Mehrotra and Bhatia, 2022).

Blockchain applications pose significant challenges in terms of legal regulation due to their decentralized structure. The intricate identification of parties involved in blockchain transactions, as well as their establishment creates complexities that hinder regulatory efforts. Consequently, regulators play a crucial role in this context. Their primary responsibilities include ensuring the safety of participants, reducing uncertainties, and safeguarding the decentralized nature of blockchain technology from being compromised.

Cost and efficiency: Cost and efficiency are crucial competitive factors in the banking industry. Banks must carefully consider the relationship between these two elements to ensure optimal performance. Costs encompass various aspects, including transaction costs, initial capital, and infrastructure investments.

The literature has placed particular emphasis on transaction costs, start-up capital, and infrastructure costs (Garg et al., 2020; Reyna et al., 2018). Another major issue in terms of throughput is high energy consumption associated with banking processes (O'Dwyer and Malone, 2014).

Security and Privacy: Security and privacy are critical considerations in the banking industery., and blockchain technology is generaly regarded as highly secure (Kakavand et al., 2017). However, it is important to acknowledge that blockchain is not immune to cyber-attacks. Given the significance of security and privacy in banking, any vulnerability in this area is deemed unacceptable. Numerous authors have addressed the issue of security in the literature (Deshpande et al., 2017).

Energy and resource consumption: Blockchain technology is known for its high energy consumption due to its computational requirements.

While this poses cost considerations for banks, it also raises significant sustainability concerns.

When implementing Blockchain technology, banks need to be aware that it will result in substantial energy consumption and contribute to a significant carbon footprint (Jayasuriya and Sims, 2021; Palihapitiya, 2020; Deshpande et al., 2017).

Achieving consensus: Achieving consensus in blockchain involves obtaining approval from all parties in the network for any protocol changes; otherwise, the changes will be rejected. However, the process of updating records can create a security gap due to its complexity and waste of time (Kumutha and Jayalakshmi, 2021).

Design standardization: Standardization is imperative in banking. In order to adopt blockchain in banking, design standardization must be ensured. Otherwise, it will not be widely accepted and implemented in the sector (Mehrotra and Bhatia, 2022).

10.7 Opportunities of Blockchain for Banks and Banking Industry

Blockchain technology presents a significant opportunity for the banking industry, primariy in terms of enabling new products, and potential sources of income (Brennan and Lunn, 2016). Blockchain will likely revolutionize the way banks conduct business and reshape their existing business models.

Kahyaoğlu argues that Blockchain technology can "reduce cost and risk, create new opportunities for innovation and growth, and ultimately radically improve banking" (Kahyaoglu, 2017).

The immutability feature of blockchain is particularly noteworthy, offering several opportunities for the industry. The inability to alter or delete transactions enhances the reliability of financial analysis, especially in reporting, providing auditors with a more robust foundation. Smart contracts, better improved regulatory compliance practices, increased transparency, and reduced risk of errors and fraud all contribute to significant cost savings and competitive advantages in banking. Opportunities for immutability can also increase customer trust and loyalty and customer engagement.

10.8 Sustainable Banking and Blockchain

Meenakshi et al. emphasizes that the implementation of blockchain technology in the banking sector will not only enhance the financial performance but also improve environmental performance, leading to sustainable banking practices. The authors state that Blockchain technology will create paperless banking by eliminating unnecessary procedures and intermediaries reducing the carbon footprint of the sector. They argue that Blockchain applications will contribute to sustainable banking by shortening transaction times, reducing registration and maintenance costs due to the digitalization of transactions, preventing and quickly detecting fraudulent activities, and reducing the use of natural resources (Meenakshi et al., 2018).

10.9 Blockchain and Corporate Governance

Blockchain technology can also provide a solution to corporate governance problems between shareholders and organizations, both for banks and their customers. The use of Blockchain ensures the integrity of the process as transactions cannot be altered and will be transparent, allowing accurate, consistent and timely information provision. Blockchain supports good governance practices in banking by increasing the efficiency and reliability of banking supervision with the aforementioned features.

10.10 Blockchain's Impact on Banking through FinTech Companies

Part of the impact of Blockchain on Banking endures through technology companies. Competition or cooperation, the disappearance of old business models, or the emergence of new business models are the main factors shaping this relationship.

Technology is not only adopted by Banks; FinTech companies have been using this technology even before Banks. FinTech firms pose the most significant threat to the banking sector, particularly in terms of competition. They can capture market shares from banks and reduce their profit margins. Furthermore, it should be noted that this technology also amplifies cyber risks.

Iskandar points out that blockchain technology will reduce transaction costs and enable cost savings, potentially facilitating the establishment of new banks by FinTech startups. By reducing the costs associated with establishing a bank FinTech organizations are likely to become competitors, thereby and increasing competition in the sector (Iskandar, 2017).

Rega's research indicates that technological innovations through FinTech companies positively affect the profitability of banks (Rega, 2017).

Kocianski (Kocianski, 2018) argues that banks' applications of Blockchain will increase their strength in competition with FinTechs, as the banks will develop new business models with the technology brought by Blockchain. In sum, the use of Blockchain will drive banking forward.

However, instead of identifying FinTech firms as competitors, working in cooperation can provide many advantages to the banking sector. First of all, it allows them to offer less costly services, as they become more flexible and therefore can offer better services. In brief, competition always contributes to doing better.

10.11 Conclusion

Owing to its decentralized structure, blockchain has emerged as a highly significant alternative to banking services, particularly in fundamental areas such as payment systems, swift transactions, cryptocurrencies that can replace credit cards as well as lending and borrowing. This powerful alternative has the potential to bring about transformative changes in the banking industry, impacting banks themselves and the overall structure of the banking sector.

When evaluated extensively, Blockchain technology reduces costs in banking and increases speed and efficiency. Due to the decentralized structure based on distributed ledger technology, banks will become much stronger against attacks and fraud as information is not collected in a single center. Blockchain technology will increase the effectiveness and reliability of auditing in banking with the application of time stamping and strengthen corporate governance.

Blockchain technology will provide major cost reductions by removing intermediaries in payment systems, especially SWIFT. Immense cost savings could be provided by the fact that KYC applications can be carried out from a single center with certain standards thanks to Blockchain technology. Smart contract applications will also provide significant savings by the automation in the banking operations. Additionally, we can mention the reduction in infrastructure costs in the list of benefits.

The most significant Blockchain aspect that needs resolution in the context of Banking are the regulatory uncertainties. Banking is a sector built on rules and regulations, so the regulatory authorities' approach to Blockchain is a matter of prime importance.

The fact that the actors in distributed ledger technology are located in different countries will pose a major problem as to which country's law will be applied. This problem needs to be resolved in order for Blockchain applications to disseminat further in banking.

Blockchain's high energy consumption makes it questionable in terms of sustainability and the environment.

If standardization is not achieved, the probability of implementation in banking, where standards are important, will decrease considerably.

In the near future, applications such as smart contracts, electronic checks and electronic bills of lading will find a greater place in banking.

Blockchain technology creates an opportunity with the efficiency and productivity it will create in terms of technological developments in the banking indusrty by eliminating the centralized structure and excluding intermediaries.

Blockchain technology can be effectively implemented in applications such as Know Your Customer systems, AML (antimoney laundering), personal data protection, identity recognition, smart contracts, electronic cheques, sustainable finance and decentralized finance (DeFi).

The banking sector can perceive Blockchain applications as a threat, or it can overcome its shortcomings by strengthening the above-mentioned products with Blockchain technology.

The key question is whether traditional banking will be able to adopt and implement Blockchain technology, or will Blockchain technology replace traditional banking. Many authors describe Blockchain as a disruptive technology for banking. As a matter of fact, this refers to the destruction of old technology and the activation of a more efficient one to create a better financial system.

There are three possible ways of utilizing of Blockchain in the banking sector. The first option is adopting Blockchain in isolation by banks. The second option is to offer Blockchain services to access external platforms, that is, to integrate the services developed by FinTech organizations with their own systems or to join the Blockchain platforms created by FinTech organizations. The third option is to implement the first two options together, that is, to establish their own isolated Blockchains for some products and services, while integrating the services of FinTech organizations with their own services or joining the platforms created by them. From our point of view, the third option, which can be called the hybrid option, seems to be the most flexible and effective option for banks.

References

Accenture. (2017). Banking on blockchain a value anaysis for investment banks. https://www.accenture.com/_acnmedia/accenture/conversion-assets/dotcom/documents/global/pdf/consulting/accenture-banking-on-blockchain.pdf accessed december 20.2022.

Arman, K. and Kundakcı, N. (2022). Evaluation of critical factors affecting the adoption of blockchain technology in the banking industry with the fuzzy PIPRECIA method. Balıkesir Üniversitesi Sosyal Bilimler Enstitüsü Dergisi 25(47): 79–92. DOI: 10.31795/baunsobed.975891.

Arjun, R. and Suprabha, K. R. (2020). Innovation and challenges of blockchain in banking: a scientometric view. International Journal of Interactive Multimedia and Artificial Intelligence 6(3): 7–14.

Appaya, S. (2021) On fintech and financial inclusion. Accessed December 12 2022 from https://blogs.worldbank.org/psd/fintech-and-financial-inclusion.

Banker, S. (2019). 2019 Is The Year For Blockchain For Traceability, But Will It Have Legs?, Forbes Magazine,. https://www.forbes.com/sites/stevebanker/2019/02/02/2019-is-the-year-for-blockchain-for-traceability-but-will-it-have-legs/?sh=43c73af53dcc. accessed december 2023.

Battal, A. (2001). Legal Liability of Banks in the Light of Trust Institution Qualification. (Güven Kurumu Nitelendirmesi ışığında Bankaların hukuki sorumluluğu) Ankara: Banka ve Ticaret Hukuku Araştırma Enstitüsü.

Beck, R. (2018). Beyond Bitcoin: The Rise of Blockchain World. Computer 51(2): 54–58. https://www.researchgate.net/publication/323371689_Beyond_Bitcoin_The_Rise_of_Blockchain_World. accessed December 18 2022.

Ber, A. S. (2022) Electronic Check within the Scope of Blockchain Technology Journal of Marine and Engineering Technology (JOINMET) 2(1).

Biella, M. and Zinetti, V. (2016). Blockchain Technology and Applications from a Financial Perspective. Unicredit. https://www.the-blockchain.com/docs/UNICREDIT%20-%20Blockchain-Technology-and-Applications-from-a-Financial-Perspective.pdf.

Brennan, C. and Lunn, W. (2016) Blockchain: The Trust Disrupter. London: Credit Suisse. As of 12/15/2022 :https://www.finextra.com/finextra-downloads/newsdocs/document-1063851711.pdf.

Cagle, M. N. (2020). A Mapping analysis of blockchain applications within the field of auditİng. Muhasebe Bilim Dünyası Dergisi 22(4): 695–724.

CB Insights. (2022). How Blockchain Could Disrupt Banking. from https://www.cbinsights.com/: https://www.cbinsights.com/research/blockchain-disrupting-banking/#:~:text=Blockchain%20tech%20removes%20the%20middleman,in%20global%20trade%20processing%20costs. accessed january 10, 2023.

Chowdhury, M. U., Suchana, K., Alam, S. M. E. and Khan, M. M. (2021). Blockchain application in banking system. Journal of Software Engineeringand Applications 14: 298–311. https://doi.org/10.4236/jsea.2021.147018.

Copigneaux, B., Vlasov, N. and Bani, E. (2020). Blockchain for Supply Chains and International Trade. Scientific Foresight Unit of European Parliamentary Research Service. https://www.europarl.europa.eu/RegData/etudes/STUD/2020/641544/EPRS_STU(2020)641544_EN.pdf accessed December 13 2022.

Degener, S. M. (2018). How blockchain affects business models in international banking. 11th IBA Bachelor Thesis Conference. Enschede, The Netherlands.: University of Twente.

Demarco, A. E. (2019). Analysing blockchain/distributed ledger technology in capital markets and know your customer process. Journal of Securities Operations & Custody 12(1): 58–71.

Deshpande, A., Stewart, K., Lepetit, L. and Gunashekar, S. (2017). Distributed LedgerTechnologies/Blockchain: Challenges, opportunities and the prospects for standards. https://www.bsigroup.com/LocalFiles/zh-tw/InfoSec-newsletter/No201706/download/BSI_Blockchain_DLT_Web.pdf accessed December 25 2022.

Economist. (2015). The trust Machine, https://www.economist.com/leaders/2015/10/31/the-trust-machine accessed December 14 2022.

Gaetani, E., Aniello, L., Baldoni, R., Lombardi, F., Margheri, A. et al. (2017). Blockchain-based database to ensure data integrity in cloud computing environments. In Proceedings of the First Italian Conference on Cybersecurity (ITASEC17), Venice, Italy.

Garg, P., Gupta, B., Chauhan, A. K., Sivarajah, U., Gupta, S. et al. (2020). Measuring the perceived benefits of implementing blockchain technology in the banking sector. Technological Forecasting and Social Change 120407.

Gokoglan, K., Cetin, S. and Bilen, A. (2022). Blockchain technology and its impact on audit activities. Journal of Economics, Finance and Accounting (JEFA) 9(2): 72–81.

Gupta, A. and Gupta, S. (2018). Blockchain technology: application in Indian banking sector. Delhi Business Review 19(2): 89–94.

Iskandar, K. (2017). What Will Blockchain Mean for Banks? Available via: https://www.linkedin.com/pulse/what-blockchain-mean-banks-karim-iskandar (accessed 25 december 2022).

Jayasuriya and Sims, A. (2021). Fantastic beasts: blockchain based banking. Journal of Risk and Financial Management 14(4): 170.

Kahyaoglu, S. B. (2017). Possible effects of blockchain technologies on Financial Markets. (Blok zinciri teknolojilerinin Finansal Piyasalara olası etkileri.) Çalıyurt, K. T. and Günay, S. G. (eds.). Prof. Dr. Fehmi Yıldız AnısınaMuhasebe Finans ve Denetimde Güncel Konular (s. 204–228). Edirne: Trakya Üniversitesi.

Kakavand, H., Kost De Sevres, N. and Chilton, B. (2017). The Blockchain Revolution: An Analysis of Regulation and Technology Related to Distributed Ledger Technologies. https://ssrn.com/abstract=2849251 accessed 25 12 2022.

Kaur, S., Jaswal, N. and Singh, H. (2022). Blockchain technology: principles, applications, and advantages of blockchain technology in the digital era. pp. 204–212. *In*: Kukreja, G., Kansra, P., Kukreja, G., Gupta, S., Kansra, P. and Kukreja, G. (eds.). Applications, Challenges, and Opportunities of Blockchain Technology in Banking and Insurance. Hershey USA: IGI Global.

Khan, S. N., Loukil, F., Ghedira-Guegan, C., Benkhelifa, E., Bani-Hani, A. et al. (2021). Blockchain smart contracts: Applications, challenges, and future trends. Peer-to-peer Networking and Applications 14: 2901–2925.

Khatri, A. and Kaushik, A. (2021). Systematic literature review on blockchain adoption in banking. Finance and Accounting (JEFA) 8(3): 126–146.

Kılınç, Y. (2020). Blockchain technology: a review in terms of accounting and auditing profession (Blockchain Teknolojisi; Muhasebe ve Denetim Mesleği Açısından Bir İnceleme). Journal of Accounting and Taxation Studies 989–1011.

Kocianski, S. (2018). The blockchain in banking report: The future of blockchain solutions and technologies. Available via: http://uk.businessinsider.com/blockchain-in-banking-2018-5 [Accessed: 20.12.2022].

Kumar, T. and Kaur, S. (2022). Blockchain technology: present and future perspectives chapter in book. pp. 258–265. Gupta, S. L., Pooja Kansra and Gagan Kukreja (eds.). Applications, Challenges, and Opportunities of Blockchain Technology in Banking and Insurance. Hershey USA: IGI Global.

Kumutha, K. and Jayalakshmi. (2021). Blockchain technology and academic certificate authenticity—a review. Expert Clouds and Applications pp. 321–334.

Makridakis, S. and Christodoulou, K. (2019). Blockchain: Current challenges and future prospects/applications. Future Internet 11(12).

Marr, B. (2017). Practical Examples of How Blockchains are Used in Banking and the Financial Services Sector. Available via: https://www.forbes.com/sites/bernardmarr/2017/08/10/practical-examples-of-how-blockchains-are-used-in-banking-and-the-financial-services-sect#f1b3383831a116. accessed December 12.2022.

Meenakshi, K., George, A. R., Nandini, G. and Thangjam, R. (2018). Green banking through blockchain. International Journal of Research and Analytical Reviews 1(12): 212–220.

Mehrotra, V. and Bhatia, M. (2022). Blockchain and financial market innovation. pp. 128–150. *In*: Gupta, S., Kansra, P. and Kukreja, G. (eds.). Applications, Challenges, and Opportunities of Blockchain Technology in Banking and Insurance. Hershey USA: IGI Global.

Nakamoto, S. (2008). Bitcoin: A Peer-to-Peer Electronic Cash System. Retrieved 12 01, 2022, from https://bitcoin.org/bitcoin.pdf: https://bitcoin.org/bitcoin.pdf.

O'Dwyer, K. J. and Malone, D. (2014). Bitcoin mining and its energy footprint. ISSC 2014/ CIICT 2014, Limerick, June 26–27.

Palihapitiya, T. (2020). Blockchain in Banking Industry October 2020 Conference: Blockchain in Banking Industry At: Colombo, Sri Lanka.

Pisa, M. and Juden, M. (2017). Blockchain and economic development: hype vs. reality. Center For Global Development, Paper No: 107: 5–7.

Puthal, D. N. (2018). The Blockchain as a decentralized security framework. IEEE Consumer Electronics Magazine 7(2): 18–21. doi:10.1109/MCE.2017.2776459.

Rega, F. G. (2017). The bank of the future, the future of banking-An empirical analysis of European banks. Available via: https://papers.ssrn.com/sol3/papers.cfm?abstract_id=3071742.

Reyna, A., Martín, C., Chen, J., Soler, E., Díaz, M. et al. (2018). On blockchain and its integration with IoT. Challenges and opportunities. Future Generation Computer Systems 88: 173–190.

Saberi, S., Kouhizadeh, M., Sarkis, J. and Shen, L. (2018). Blockchain technology and its relationships to sustainable supply chain management. International Journal of Production Research 57(7): 2117–2135. doi:10.1080/00207543.2018.1533261.

Sarto, N. D. and Gai, L. (2022). Blockchain for SMEs: Threats, Opportunities, and Future Research Trajectories. pp. 69–82. *In*: Gupta, S. L., Kansra, P. and Kukreja, G. (eds.). Applications, Challenges, and Opportunities of Blockchain Technology in Banking and Insurance. Hershey USA: IGI Global.

Seretakis, A. (2017). Blockchain, securities markets and central banking. Journal of Financial Economics 1: 425–435.

Shukla, G. P. and Balwani, N. (2022). Analysis of key barriers in blockchain in banking: ISM ranking. pp. 83–89. *In*: Gupta, S. L., Kansra, P. and Kukreja, G. (eds.). Applications, Challenges, and Opportunities of Blockchain Technology in Banking and Insurance. Hershey USA: IGI Global.

Sironi, P. (2018) Disruptive & Sustainable innovation and coopetition Finteech (Findings and Recommendations for Traditional Structures.) This study summary of the first part of the book "FinTech Innovation" by Sironi P. Summarized by Ahmet Usta. (Istanbul: BKM Bankalararası Kart Merkezi.) Available via: https://bkm.com.tr/wp-content/uploads/2017/06/FINTECH-PAOLO-SIRONI-eng3.pdf [Accessed: 20.12.2022].

Üçoğlu, D. (2022). Blockchain technology and future banking: opportunities and challenges chapter in book. pp. 43–68. Gupta, S. L., Pooja Kansra and Gagan Kukreja (eds.). Applications, Challenges, and Opportunities of Blockchain Technology in Banking and Insurance. Hershey USA: IGI Global.

Verma, D. and Kansra, P. (2022). Blockchain technology in digitizing bancassurance: a theoretical perspective of prospects and confronts in India. pp. 193–203. *In*: Gupta, S. L., Kansra, P. and Kukreja, G. (eds.). Applications, Challenges, and Opportunities of Blockchain Technology in Banking and Insurance. Hershey USA: IGI Global.

Walker, G. (2018). Is KYC using blockchain the answer for banks? Available via: https://www.refinitiv.com/perspectives/regulation-risk-compliance/kyc-using-blockchain-answer-banks/. accesed December 12 2022.

Chapter 11
Blockchain Applications in Finance

Osman Tüzün[1,*] and *Ramazan Ekinci*[2]

11.1 Introduction

The adoption of digital technology in social and economic life causes structural changes. Particularly since the beginning of the twenty-first century, there has been an acceptance that this change has started the process of "creative destruction" in all industries. As a result of this process, new technologies such as artificial intelligence, big data, the internet of things (IoT), blockchain, and cloud computing have evolved. These technologies have a substantial impact on an organization's procedures, time management, network connectivity, and performance (Urbach et al., 2017). These new development trends have resulted in structural changes in the financial industry as well as an increase in the influence of technical innovations on economies. The structural transformation of technology improvements in finance, on the other hand, has had a stronger impact on transforming the link between financial interactions and markets. In this process, both internal and foreign technical developments has had a colossal impact on the financial sector following the cost reduction. However, technological advances have had a significant impact on the productivity of capital, resulting in a decline in interest rates, particularly in developed countries. This phenomenon has been seen as a drawback of technological progress, despite its advantages for the financial sector.

[1] University of Usak, Department of Economics.
[2] University of Bakircay, Department of Economics.
Email: ramazan.ekinci@bakircay.edu.tr
* Corresponding author: osman.tuzun@usak.edu.tr

Digital innovation reflects shifts in consumer demand and sets the path for the establishment of a financial infrastructure that will improve both time and cost effectiveness. This situation calls attention to the topic of "Financial Technology (FinTech)," which will drastically alter and even completely revolutionize the financial industry. FinTech, which stands for financial technology, is a technologically effective financial innovation that has the potential to provide new business models, applications, processes, goods, or services for financial markets as well as the delivery of financial services. It refers to digital currencies, robo-consulting, financial applications of blockchain and distributed ledger technology, and online peer-to-peer financing (Schindler, 2017). Blockchain or distributed ledger technology, which permits future development of FinTech technologies, lies at the heart of all of these financial advancements.

Financial technology is a fundamental factor that determines the structure, system, process and institutional structure of the financial sector as a whole. The important feature of this factor is the rate of change that it has revealed along with the speed of development. Depending on the information provided by the history of economics, technological changes are the main variable that initiates cyclical and structural changes in the economy. In this context, with the economic crisis in 2008, the technological developments that started this change began to be discussed. Blockchain technology, initially gained popularity throughout the world in 2008. It has a significant capacity to alter the financial system formed by the interaction of the elements within this structure, and the processes that make up the functioning within it. Blockchain technology is a form of information technology that enables individuals to carry out financial transactions on their own without requiring the consent of a third party with the authority to centrally manage all transactions. This technology-enhanced distributed ledger is a data storage mechanism that maintains data integrity. This system allows for the decentralized storage of information about previous transactions. Blockchain technology has various applications, including facilitating cross-border payments, expanding access to financial resources, enhancing secure asset management, and ensuring compliance with relevant laws and regulations in legal reporting activities (World Economic Forum, 2016). Blockchain technology has brought about trust and transparency in economic relationships, which in turn leads to a reduction in transaction costs. This reduction is expected to drive significant development acceleration, benefiting both external and internal economies in the future. Consequently, advancements in the field of FinTech will serve as the foundation for emerging trends in the upcoming period.

This paper examines the characteristics of Blockchain technology and their implications for the financial industry. Research on blockchain technology in the financial sector has been increasing rapidly in recent years. It is important to explain the reasons for the increasing interest in this situation, which is a new scientific phenomenon. Therefore, these reasons will be revealed in the study. Thus, the purpose is to explore the potential of blockchain technology in the financial sector and offer insights into its main components, key challenges and current research gaps.

11.2 FinTech (Financial Technology)

In the past decade, the global economy has experienced a profound and rapid transformation on a global scale. The concept of Financial Technology refers to the continuous application of technology within this framework, which has begun to change processes with the approaches put forward for business solutions. Financial technologies are financial products used with technologies available in the market or applications that enable the use of financial services with more advanced technologies (Knewtson and Rosenbaum, 2020). The use of the word "FinTech" dates back to the early 1990s (Cai, 2018). In addition to their regulatory effects, the developments in the FinTech field have had a significant impact on the development of the financial services sector, with the new infrastructure enabling transactions to be made regardless of time and place. From this point of view, it can be stated that Fintech covers the digital innovations and technology-intensive advances that the global economy has created in the financial sector (Philippon, 2016). Such advances and business model innovations have led to a significant breakdown in the financial sector, improving the scope of financial services and leading to significant changes in the products and services provided by firms.

According to Zetzsche et al. (2017), the field of FinTech is progressing along two major lines. The first line involves technological advancements such as Big Data, machine learning, and Artificial Intelligence (AI).These technologies are transforming the financial industry by enabling new capabilities and insights. The second line of progress involves the entry of non-financial companies into the financial services sector, bringing new investments and innovations. Fintech has played a crucial role in the development of Industry 4.0, which encompasses the integration and utilization of various technologies such as Fintech, AI, and data science (Dhanabalan and Sathish, 2018). Within the financial sector, Blockchain technology has demonstrated significant progress and development serving as a counterpart to the advancements in Industry 4.0.

11.3 Blockchain

Blockchain technology is one of the key technological trends that have emerged in the last decade. The main innovation that started this trend is the new blockchain-enabled financial relationship network launched by Nakamoto in 2008. This financial relationship network has become important with the prevalence of a unit of value used in exchange between people as money in practice, which is defined as Bitcoin. Basically, the infrastructure of this financial relationship network Blockchain and the opportunities it has created have been internalized in relation to the finance sector and started the new trend.

Nakamoto defined blockchain as a decentralized and trustless payment system mechanism in his article titled "Bitcoin in 2008: A Peer-to-Peer Electronic Cash System" published in 2008. Nakamoto (2008) invented a ledger and termed it the "blockchain," which eventually became known as Blockchain (The Economist, 2015). Blockchain refers to a distributed ledger technology where every transaction and related information is encrypted by hashing and all network members have access to the same information (Zheng et al., 2018). This ledger technology offers an infrastructure where there is no possibility of outside intervention, thus reducing the possibility of manipulation. Thus, it has become possible for each network member to constantly check the integrity of the data. The mutual relationship between the said infrastructure and the units that use or provide this infrastructure constitutes the Blockchain system. The most important feature of the system is that the user is the basic unit. The growth of this basic unit has the effect of generating economies of scale, but more importantly, increased yields. The rising number of participants in the system's operation, as well as the ongoing replacement of the infrastructure, are the most essential aspects that reveal the increased efficiency. When evaluated from this point of view, technological investments with each participant will reveal a higher income trend than itself. This situation will accelerate a significant profitability rate in the financial sector and at the same time capital accumulation in the coming period. Transferring this accumulation, both as information and as capital, will accelerate the use of Blockchain in economies.

Although blockchain is a technological development, it has turned into an internal and capitalized production factor beyond being an external factor. In this respect, it is necessary to introduce a new understanding that will reveal increased yields due to the fact that the increase in the production factor in question causes a production increase that is greater than itself.

Blockchain, a rapidly developing financial technology, has increased the financial inclusion that has emerged within the framework of people's ability to deal with financial transactions (Antonio and Dinizo, 2018). Thus, the constraints of space, time and communication have accelerated the use of this technology together with internet technology. Blockchain is considered a fundamental technology for bitcoin and other cryptocurrencies (Staples et al., 2017) as it is beginning to be seen as the basis of financial transactions around the world (Nguyen, 2016). Blockchain is a perpetual database of accounts that is complete, distributed, and immutable (Yoo, 2017).

The most important feature of blockchain is that it is a decentralized system with a very long security chain. Another innovation provided by blockchain technology is the distributed trust that the system offers. This system-developed safety net eliminates trusted third parties to facilitate transactions and reduces transaction and time costs (Staples et al., 2017). Another innovation provided by blockchain technology is the distributed trust that the system offers. This system-developed safety net eliminates trusted third parties to facilitate transactions and reduces transaction and time costs (Staples et al., 2017).

11.4 Blockchain in the Financial Industry

Blockchain technology has opened up new opportunities for all sectors. All institutions strive to take advantage of these opportunities. Financial markets are at the top of the areas that are thought to benefit the most from the expected benefits of blockchain technology. Blockchain technology derives all its functionality mainly from the "Distributed Ledger" approach. Thanks to distributed ledgers, transactional data is distributed between peers (P2P) without any intervention (Cosares et al., 2021). However, while Blockchain technology offers opportunities, there are some threats within the system. Both in financial system and at the monetary policy level, risk management strategies need to be reconsidered to include blockchain technology.

The economic contraction and increasing regulations brought about by the 2008 financial crisis made it necessary for financial service providers to take new measures. As a result, the financial sector is increasingly using advanced technologies that will increase transparency and security, thereby resulting in cost savings and increased productivity (Schneider et al., 2017). Blockchain has gained significant attention in the financial sector recently because of its ability to improve process automation and streamlining, remove manual office procedures, cut down on time, and boost transparency and security (Walker et al., 2016). In the banking and finance sector, blockchain frequently serves as the foundation of innovative business models. The system already has an impact on payments, interbank operations, and several financial services (Cucari et al., 2021; Holotiuk et al., 2019; Yu et al., 2018).

One of the innovations at the center of current Fintech trends is blockchain technology, which serves as the foundation for cryptocurrencies (Bozkus Kahyaoglu, 2019). The procedures of different financial services firms have been significantly impacted by the developing financial technology element known as blockchain (Tapscott and Tapscott, 2016). Blockchain's innovations in data transmission and storage have the potential to have a big influence on how the financial sector operates (Mu, 2016). Blockchain-based distributed ledger technology's advancements and innovations can be applied to a number of financial services provided by businesses, including financial solutions, investment product design, paying and clearing securities, payments between geographical regions, financial participation, and more (Chang et al., 2020). Cocco et al. (2017) claim that blockchain has the ability to strengthen global financial infrastructure or shift assets more efficiently from the current financial system. Research on the effects of blockchain on the financial sector has revealed that it can save costs and create big improvements in finance in the long term (Nguyen, 2016). According to Schuetz and Venkatesh (2020), organizations must place greater emphasis on Blockchain technology in order to enhance their market share and compete on a global scale.

With the increasing use of blockchain in finance, commercial banks are increasingly using this technology to improve their existing central banking system (Kahyaoglu, 2021). By using the security, immutability and transparency of Blockchain, financial institutions have begun to use fewer intermediaries in their financial transactions (Underwood, 2016). Hassani et al. (2018), on the other hand, states that Blockchain has both advantages and drawbacks over the financial system. The main activities of banks are to fulfill their intermediary duties. Although this mediation task is an effect that reduces moral risk factors such as asymmetric information and adverse selection, it will be easier with the reduction and effective control of these effects with Blockchain. However, since Blockchain technology has eliminated the intermediary function in financial transactions and reduced the central role of financial institutions, the attitudes of banks towards Blockchain are primarily negative, but with the increase in its use in the sector, it has turned into an advantage. Blockchain technology is expected to bring significant benefits to consumers, existing banking systems and society in general. In addition to the security and transparency it provides between the parties, it is expected to have a decisive effect on pricing and cost analysis in the market (Glaser et al., 2014). It has even led to some services being provided free of charge. At the same time, Blockchain provides the opportunity to reduce the risk of fraud by protecting the secure payment histories of customers with transactions in different regions and different banks (Zohar, 2015; Lindman et al., 2017). Other benefits of the technology include greater transaction speed, improved traceability, and transparency. It is necessary to thoroughly research and practically examine each of its advantages for a variety of use cases and applications. The advantages of blockchain technology and its effects across the board on the financial sector are extremely difficult to measure. As a result, it is necessary to create theoretically valid and practically usable blockchain technology impact indicators to assess how these technologies are evolving across many areas.

The main effects that lead to the increasing use of blockchain technology by financial institutions can be listed as follows: First, it can reduce costs. Due to high terminal maintenance and acquisition costs, banks often must spend much on a central database. Too many bookkeeping and accounting transactions, on the other hand, raise labor expenses and operational risk. Thanks to the decentralized ledger system of blockchain technology, a low-cost and transparent model can be created and these costs can be reduced (Nguyen, 2016). Second, it can more effectively manage risks. Banks give importance to the monitoring and follow-up of loans. However, non-performing loans are one of the most important risk items for banks. Banks can benefit from Blockchain technology in reducing non-performing loans. Thus, banks have the opportunity to monitor risk assessment in the use of resources and to use early warning systems effectively. The polycentric structure of blockchain connects each user as a type of node around the blockchain, allowing for direct transactions between borrowers and lenders. Thus, credit risk can be greatly decreased, and fund management effectiveness can be improved (Nguyen, 2016).

Finally, it can develop mechanisms to increase the level of profitability. The financial sector is a market structure in which monopolistic or oligopolistic competition is intense, since entrances and exits are prohibited by law. In this market, innovations such as Blockchain technology come to the fore as tools that provide a significant advantage, since there is more product differentiation and a quality-oriented competitive structure. Using the advantage of the said technology in terms of increasing the diversity of financial products, accelerating the access to financial products on a global scale, and turning it into a service will increase the competition in the sector and accelerate the use of this technology. For the competitive analysis of the use of these models in terms of economics, it should be examined with tools for game theory and analysis of market structure. Within the scope of this study, the usage of Blockchain in the banking and financial industry, as well as its benefits and drawbacks, will be explained. In the next part of the study, explanations for this are made.

11.5 Applications of Blockchain Technology on the Financial Sector

Blockchain technology has opened up new opportunities for all sectors. All institutions strive to take advantage of these opportunities. Financial markets are at the top of the areas that are thought to benefit the most from the expected benefits of blockchain technology. The increasing use of blockchain technology in financial operations such as money transfers, international payments, identity verifications, trade financing, insurance, smart contracts, auctions, and trading currencies has resulted in a fast expansion of financial applications. Blockchain technology derives all its functionality mainly from the "Distributed Ledger" approach. Thanks to distributed ledgers, transactional data is distributed between peers (P2P) without any intervention (Cosares et al., 2021). However, while Blockchain technology offers opportunities, there are some threats within the system. Both in the financial system and at the monetary policy level, risk management strategies need to be reconsidered to include blockchain technology.

Blockchain technology is considered as the "creative destruction" process brought by Financial Technology (FinTech) (Gomber et al., 2018). The creative destruction that comes with blockchain technology is a candidate to cause various changes in financial markets. These changes can be listed as follows; reducing transaction costs, ensuring continuous transparency, making fund transfers instantly without time limits, and making contracts securely without any need for intermediaries (Chen and Bellavitis, 2020; Tapscott and Tapscott, 2017). Blockchain technology makes the changes with specific applications for financial markets. Figure 11.1 shows applications that are increasingly used in financial markets.

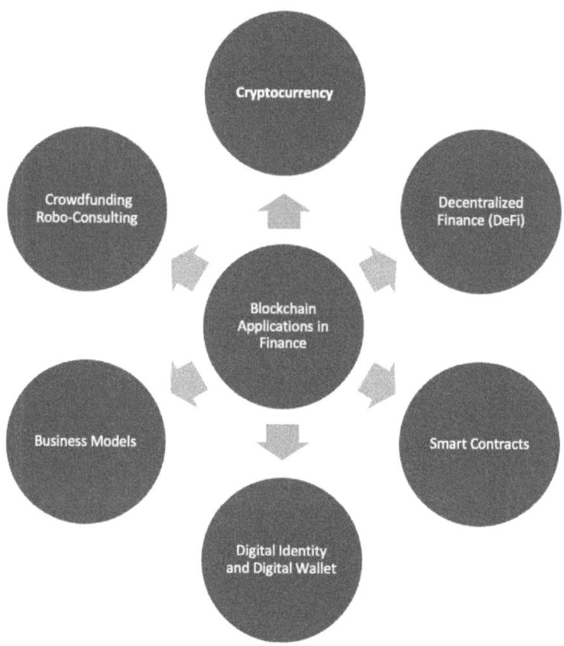

Figure 11.1. Blockchain applications in finance. Source: The authors' assessments.

11.5.1 Cryptocurrency

The common name used in the financial industry to describe all digital assets is digital currency. The functionality of digital currencies is similar to physical currency. However, digital currencies instead of physical money have some advantages. One of these advantages is the simultaneous ability of cross-border money transfers and transactions with lower cost and time. It is used in various forms, including digital currencies, virtual currencies also known as cryptocurrencies and central bank digital currency. Bitcoin was the first cryptocurrency to appear in 2008. It is not an entity that is tied to a particular central bank or intervened by the monetary authority. The most important feature of Bitcoin and other cryptocurrencies is that they have the ability to send money end-to-end without the need for intermediaries. Thanks to this feature, the time and cost of any payment transaction can be significantly reduced. Also, bitcoin has the basic functions of money as a medium of exchange, being a unit of value. However, it has a certain value when interest rates are negative at the international and global level. It will be discussed as an alternative financial instrument if interest rates increase in international markets and provide a positive real return. We can say that the monetary policies to be implemented by the central banks towards inflation in the coming years may have an effect in this direction.

The spread of financial instruments, which are defined as crypto money and based on blockchain technology can be expressed as a structural change in money and financial markets. However, these tools, which are defined as crypto money, are defined depending on the fact that money is a "store of value" tool. According to this definition; cryptocurrencies represent an asset in terms of its holder. This asset is also a financial instrument since its price is determined depending on the value created by the payment commitment given by the counterparty when it is sold (Bozkus Kahyaoglu and Ekinci, 2021).

In addition to the benefits it provides, a cryptocurrency can also cause risks within the financial system. In particular, its unpredictability due to its volatility harms investors and firms' balance sheets. Although the developments at the time of writing of this study provided information about the fluctuation that may occur in the value of this currency, especially against the increase in interest rates, the accumulation of data for the analysis of mapping was necessary. In this respect, this issue will be discussed empirically in the coming periods.

In general, the demand for these products tends to increase due to the increasing financial risks all over the world. However, the fact that these products do not have any basis and the market structure based on the principle of mutual consent has started to be discussed as a new source of financial risk in the world (Castren, 2022). In particular, the use of blockchain by central banks for digital money and its applications causes a significant fluctuation in the digital currency markets. On the other hand, cryptocurrencies are constantly on the agenda due to the frauds and scandals that have emerged recently. However, within the framework of the developments in the financial system, the need for cryptocurrencies is accepted and offers experience in the creation of new financial products. Especially in financial markets, the integration of algorithm-based financial transactions with the Blockchain has led to an increase in the liquidity and transaction volume of the markets (Rose, 2015). This increase can be expressed as an advantage as well as a source of new risks.

The fact that central banks began to enter the financial markets, but before that, the change in interest rate policies, especially the tendency of the FED and the ECB to abandon their purchases of financial assets, led to the volatile risk in cryptocurrencies. Central banks have started to use stablecoins as a new currency and exchange tool for cryptocurrencies, which have started to have an important function in the financial system.

Stablecoins have started to gain importance as a tool that enables transactions based on the credibility of central banks in financial markets. The main reason for central banks to issue this tool is to limit the influence of other digital currencies in financial markets globally. Thus, central banks aimed to reduce the negative effects of digital currencies on the seigniorage incomes of countries. The fact that the institutions that support stablecoins are central banks makes them resistant to price movements. For this reason, the value of such cryptocurrencies can be indexed to different currencies, usually under the assurance of central banks. Most stablecoins are indexed in the US dollar. Stablecoins have started to be used not only by the private sector but also by the central banks in different countries. Depending on the development at the global level, the business models of financial institutions in the financial system and the innovations in the processes of these business models have not started to differentiate.

11.5.2 Decentralized Finance (DeFi)

In Centralized finance (CeFi), there are institutions that mediate a transaction between the parties. However, Decentralized finance (DeFi) uses blockchain technology (BT) to make financial services decentralized, open, and borderless. In Decentralized Finance (DeFi), financial transactions are not carried out by centralized financial institutions, but by decentralized peers. Decentralized distributed networks in blockchain technology facilitate peer-to-peer transactions. On the other hand, BT promises to strengthen access, to reduce transaction costs, to expand financial inclusion, and to encourage unauthorized innovation. Increasing prevalence of DeFi processes leads to start a discussion about regulation of BT in financial markets (Chen and Bellavitis, 2019:2–5).

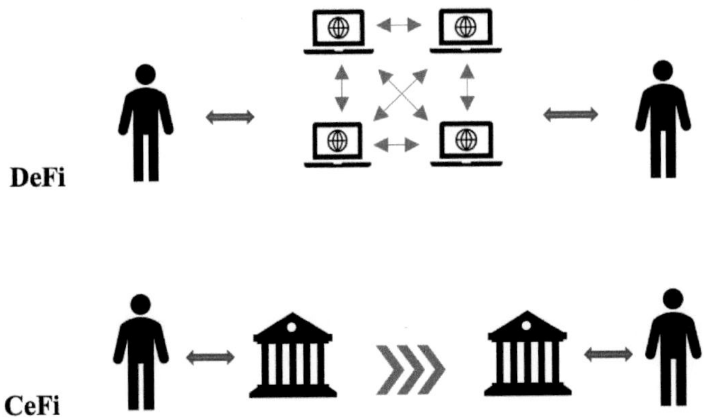

Figure 11.2. Operation process in Defi and Cefi. Source: Adopted from Qin et al. (2021).

As seen in Figure 11.2, contrary to CeFi, in DeFi, the parties carry out their transactions from peer to peer without any intermediary institution by smart contacts. This structure also demonstrates how the credit-debt relationship of the decision units will be made. In addition, although crypto currency exchanges are generally centralized, decentralized exchanges and decentralized funds are also emerging (Sanlisoy ve Ciloglu, 2019:70–71).

The global financial system serves billions of people every day while managing trillions of moneys. The existence of such a large market brings with it some difficulties. The term "Blockchain in finance" refers to the use of blockchain technology in the banking industry. The use of blockchain technology in the financial industry has led to the development of DeFi. DeFi is a financial transaction that uses blockchain technology and smart contracts to eliminate the need for intermediaries in the provision of financial services (Akash, 2022).

DeFi refers to financial applications known as "smart contracts" that are processed by computer code on blockchains with little or no intervention from centralized intermediaries. DeFi's primary features include automated and decentralized record keeping, risk taking, and decision making in the crypto ecosystem. Changes to collateral requirements or practices such as dividends are usually made by voting users who accompany the use of the platform. Furthermore, DeFi provides broad access to users of all sizes and does not require storage services. This has the potential to improve efficiency and financial inclusion. Three major technological advances have considerably facilitated in the broad adoption of DeFi. First, the use of blockchain technology has created a digital infrastructure that records data through a publicly distributed system, where transaction records of crypto assets are confirmed without the requirement for a single trusted entity. This has provided a digital infrastructure that records data through a publicly distributed system, where transaction records of crypto assets are verified without the need for a single trusted entity. Second, thanks to its smart contract implementation, blockchain technology has revolutionized the way financial intermediary transactions are conducted. A smart contract is computer code that permits transactions to be completed when certain predetermined requirements are satisfied. DeFi is the use of smart contracts for financial intermediation such as deposit taking, lending, derivatives, and the exchange of crypto assets. Third, under DeFi, stablecoins may be used as a unit of account, medium of trade, and store of value. The introduction of stablecoins took place with the development of DeFi.

11.5.3 Smart Contracts

Smart contracts are contracts that allow the transfer of the parties' contracts and the obligations arising from this contract to the distributed ledgers. This system is a continuously digitized contract system that is stored across all peers. Thus, smart contracts provide assurance to contracting parties. The reason for smart contracts to be stored on the blockchain, is to ensure that users cannot alter the contract after it is distributed to peers (Khacef and Pujolle, 2019). According to the ESMA (2017) the distributed storage of smart contracts also reduces the possibility of errors. However, the regulation and supervision of the system remains important to the efficient functioning of the system.

Leading cryptocurrencies such as Ethereum have also led to the spread of smart contracts. Afterwards, many cryptocurrencies have entered the market over time and transaction volumes have increased substantially. Futures and options contracts, real estate sales, financial derivatives, insurance premiums, and crowdfunding contracts are examples of the usage of smart contracts in the finance industry.

According to the BIS (2017), smart contacts provide some advantages, such as;

- Time and cost advantages; no need for intermediary institution
- Reliability: avoiding mistakes and abuses
- Reduced risks of manipulation and external attacks

Additionally, there are also some risks and areas for improvement of smart contacts, such as;

- Limited competent human resources
- Software errors
- Impacts of irreversible transactions on Financial Legos.

11.5.4 Digital Identity and Digital Wallet

A digital identity diagnoses of an owner stores identity information by using codes in the blockchain. In particular, digital identities and instant verification of these identities are prominent for peers transacting in financial markets. Besides, in order to fulfill digital financial services in the financial markets, digital identity applications need to be widespread (Wolfond, 2017:36).

A digital wallet is another fintech application. Digital coins and assets are stored in this wallet. Thanks to the digital wallet, the payment process is carried out quickly without any intermediaries. Digital wallets use the blockchain network for a transaction and they run with encrypted codes within this network. However, digital wallets are not considered as traditional deposit wallets. Being regulated like traditional ones will increase the reliability of the system.

11.5.5 Business Models

Blockchain will cause a structural change in the alignment and transformation of the banking and financial sector's working and innovation processes. Features such as decentralized structure, inter-institutional trust through distributed ledger technology, and less information asymmetry have resulted in the inclusion of blockchain technology in finance business models and processes more intensively. A blockchain-based financing system could improve information asymmetry and transaction cost issues and lead to a more decentralized and efficient entrepreneurial financing process (Ahluwalia et al., 2020). Blockchain technology, which is also used in the derivatives market space, can increase investor control and expand the distribution of systematic risk. In addition, it will enable more effective risk management by ensuring the diversification of new financial derivative instruments. Increasing the relationship of these derivative markets with digital currency markets will also be an effective tool against the volatility risk that may arise in the currencies' market such as bitcoin. In addition, it will be possible to provide liquidity in derivative markets and increase the depth with new participants (Avgouleas and Kiayias, 2019).

On the other hand, blockchain-based credit analysis can be used to ensure the effective functioning of the credit distribution mechanism. Thanks to this system, financial institutions can collect information about customers, analyze customers' eligibility, calculate customers' credit scores, and thus conduct a more efficient and transparent loan allocation process (Chakraborty et al., 2019). One of the most important effects of blockchain is that it will create a more efficient means of allocating credit for converting savings into investments in the economy. Thus, a structural change will occur in the functioning of the monetary transmission mechanism and the credit channel with Blockchain. It is clear that business models and processes in the financial sector will also change. This is an effect that will lead to the differentiation of the relationship between money market and financial markets within the economy as a whole. In this context, the business models of the financial sector and the monetary policy instruments of central banks will also differ. In particular, instantaneous withdrawal and evaluation of data from the system will enable risk management and assessment to be carried out instantly. At this point, the high size and frequency of the information coming from the financial markets requires this information to be processed quickly. This requires business models to be algorithm-based and at the same time very fast. The necessity of speed is an important effect that will lead to high frequency of process innovations.

11.5.6 Crowdfunding and Robo-Consulting

Crowdfunding can be defined as the accumulation of investable liquidity obtained through contributions from numerous investors who provide the financial resources required by entrepreneurs. Blockchain-based crowdfunding can be carried out through many networks for the purpose of financing start-ups, by bringing together new generation business ideas and funds (Hartmann et al., 2019).

In Figure 11.3 an illustration of crowdfunding is demonstrated. Project developers look for investors to finance their business ideas. According to the blockchain-based crowdfunding model Hassija et al. (2020) proposed, projects have a deadline and possibility of not reaching adequate funding. If so, the project cannot be funded. If the project reaches the goal a smart contract is generated and blockchain-based crowdfunding is realized.

Robo-consulting or Robo-Advisor is essentially the digital form of investment consultancy or portfolio management. In Robot-Consulting, Robo-consultants collect data such as investors' risk appetite, financial position, and the return they expect from the investment and determine a

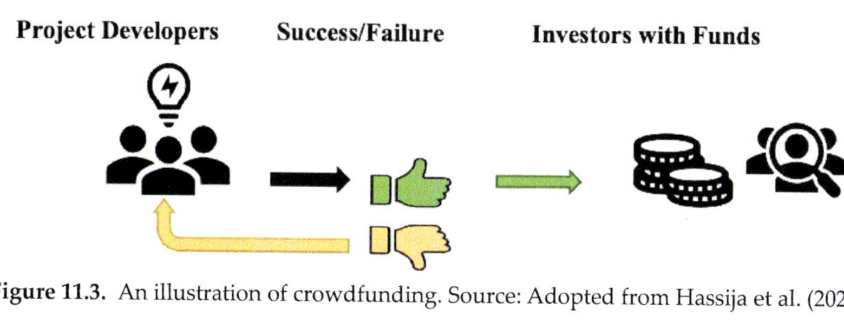

Figure 11.3. An illustration of crowdfunding. Source: Adopted from Hassija et al. (2020).

path through algorithms. Algorithms monitor all financial data instantly and move the investments to the right options.

Robo-consulting is poised to outshine traditional financial advisory services thanks to its user-friendly and automated processes, low-cost portfolio management and efficient performance. In this regard, it is also another creative destruction FinTech approach. Robo-consulting algorithms run depending on artificial intelligence. Thus, it has the potential for continuous improvement.

11.6 Benefits and Risks of Blockchain in Financial Services

In particular, in the post-COVID-19 era, physical contact between vendors and customers is increasingly being replaced by digital engagement. As a result, financial service providers' demand for digital innovations has increased. For example, the pandemic has accelerated the transition to digital payments (Auer et al., 2020a). It also intensified e-commerce, which could benefit large tech firms and their operations in finance (BIS, 2019). Following the outbreak, countries that have implemented stricter Covid-19 measures and have lower financial participation rates have begun to put more emphasis on digital financial applications (Didier et al., 2021). As a result, the interest of central banks in digital currencies began to increase and the work on central bank digital currencies (CBDC) accelerated (Auer et al., 2020b). Based on these and similar developments, we will mention some benefits, risks and compliance issues of blockchain in finance.

11.6.1 Benefits

Blockchain addresses difficulties in the financing sector by providing a single platform on which all participants can benefit from a competitive advantage. The main advantage of technology is that it is built on distributed trust, which eliminates the need for a third party to supervise payments. This reduces transaction costs and saves time (Li et al., 2020). While the application of technology in a wide area provides an advantage as an economy of space, it provides an increase in efficiency and productivity with the scale effect that allows the costs to decrease rapidly with scale growth. Also, all transactions on the blockchain are visible and irreversible. Its immutability feature facilitates in improving traceability, tracking every financial transaction, and streamlining the compliance procedure for financial institutions. Transactions may be carried out without the involvement of a trusted third party due to distributed open-source protocols' integrity (Hilary and Liu, 2021). The following is a summary of other advantages that might result from the adoption of blockchain technology:

Competition: The digital transformation emerging in financial markets not only makes the market more diverse, competitive, efficient and inclusive, but also increases concentration. Digital innovation has led to increased competition and financial inclusion, particularly in emerging markets (Pazarbasioglu et al., 2020; Frost et al., 2021). Studies show that Fintech is effective in achieving the expected result, especially in markets where the financial system is less developed (FSB, 2020; Didier et al., 2021). However, the new brokerage economy brought about by blockchain technology causes concentration among both traditional and new financial service providers with the effect of economies of scale and space.

Settlement time: Settlement time can be greatly reduced by quickly recording notifications and confirming them on a blockchain. This action can promote greater liquidity in certain types of trades that face long settlement cycles and will encourage better capital utilization.

Faster payments: Global payment systems require multiple regulatory control and clearing cycles. The foreign exchange market is one of the markets that carries out the most brokerage transactions in the world through clearing banks and commercial banks. A DLT technology with digital identities will shorten settlement times for tradable parties.

11.6.2 *Risks and Compliance Issues*

Although blockchain is an innovation that transforms existing FinTech applications to gain competitive advantage, there are still vulnerabilities, disadvantages and some problems to be solved on the system. For example, as the number of shareholders grows, so does the complexity of using blockchain in the financial industry. Complexities vary in terms of method, knowledge, experience, regulatory compliance, and cybersecurity. The following are some examples of risk and compliance challenges experienced in practice.

Regulatory and governance: There is a problem with the acceptance of sanctions and transactions due to the lack of a basic legal infrastructure in the blockchain. For example, the responsible regulatory bodies providing resolution in disputes and their coordination are not clear. In addition, aspects such as the legal status of documents on the blockchain, liability ownership, and regulatory reporting are key regulatory elements that financial intermediaries need to disclose.

There is a lack of a common and transparent governance structure for blockchain. Decision making mechanisms are often left to market dynamics. This, in turn, has emerged as a source that could cause wider financial instability by creating risks of network and infrastructure failure. On the other hand, there are issues as to who will control the distributed ledger system and who will be responsible for it. Also, smart contracts can have multiple parties and governance issues can arise when contracting parties do not comply with the contract or there are coding errors in the contract. It is also discussed that the changes that should be made in the chain as a result of the arrangements to be made can cause problems.

Privacy and security: The most important feature of distributed ledger technology is that all network participants can access the recorded information. However, in the unauthorized ledger, counterparties can access transaction history, including transactions of which they are not a part. Transaction chains are publicly visible and publicly traceable. There was also the risk that smart contracts accessing transaction data might disclose information about what was being handled. On the other hand, trading terms stored in smart contracts are subject to privacy breaches. Blockchain transactions are prone to fraud in terms of security. While it is possible to identify the owner of an address used for money laundering, such transactions cannot be prevented in advance.

Behavioral and transition risk: Most financial institutions have diverging and conflicting interests. These conflicts lead to risks of lack of cooperation among stakeholders such as regulators, exchanges, clearing services, trading firms and banks. In addition, there is a risk that private distributed ledgers can lead to collusion and cartelization, and that algorithms are set up to produce anti-competitive results. Competition risk may arise if a private blockchain becomes a monopoly of a few large firms. Additionally, if there are significant entry barriers into a private blockchain, smaller service providers could be at a disadvantage. Also, it might be quite difficult operationally to migrate the new blockchain-based market structure. Integration with already operating non-blockchain systems can be quite difficult. Financial firms are hesitant to replacing or transforming old systems, such as record-keeping, CRM, business intelligence, risk, and compliance systems.

Systemic risk: Smart contracts can pose systemic risks both because of the digital environment and because this environment is connected to a network. For example, systemic risks arise when multiple obligations and rights are tied into smart contracts over complex proposals. A sudden loss of confidence and the effects that will cause panic in the market in question have revealed the necessity of monitoring the said technology as a source of systemic risk. Also, ledgers based on distributed ledger technology are immutable and cannot be changed or revoked. This creates difficulties in the rapid reversibility of errors. This will lead to an insufficient capacity problem in the digital environment, based on the necessity of storing and preserving transactions in the digital environment.

***Settlement risk*:** Settlement finality is the fulfillment of an obligation through the transfer of funds and securities. Certainty of payment is a legal requirement in post-trade settlement. However, due to its systemic nature, public blockchains cannot guarantee payment certainty. As a result, assigning legal responsibility in blockchain technology is difficult due to the nature of the system. This may adversely affect the balance sheets, creditors and customer rights of the participants. In the absence of guaranteed payment certainty, the participant risks going bankrupt, which creates liquidity and credit problems for other participants.

11.7 Conclusion

Technological developments appear primarily in financial markets among all sectors of an economy. Blockchain technology has executed a revolutionary development in the field of finance and has revealed some innovations for the financial industry, such as cryptocurrencies, decentralized finance, smart contracts, crowdfunding and robo-consulting. Blockchain technology makes financial transactions easier and more efficient with its secure, transparent and accountable structure.

Blockchain technology became popular thanks to cryptocurrencies. However, developments in decentralized finance cause the existing business models and systems to change and new financial, economic and social connections to emerge. Decentralized finance provides secure transactions and cost advantages for parties by eliminating complex bureaucratic processes and central authorities by using distributed ledgers.

Another application of blockchain technology in the financial sector is smart contracts. Smart contracts allow developers to create a variety of decentralized applications. It is applicable on any kind of financial instrument and stored on the blockchain. The distributed structure in the blockchain constantly verifies the contract and ensures that it is stored by each peer. The fact that they are irrevocable and unchangeable with exceptions makes smart contracts secure and transparent. Smart contracts also allow financial investments to be managed. Start-ups and new projects can find financing through crowdfunding. Besides, areas such as portfolio management and investment consultancy become automated with blockchain-based robo-consulting, another financial application of blockchain.

Considering all the developments created by blockchain technology in the financial markets, it is understood that many companies of various scales operating in this field should keep up with this technology. Even some macroeconomic decisions seem inevitable. For instance, monetary authorities must reconsider payment systems. Central banks need to include blockchain-based payment systems and cryptocurrencies in their toolkit. While doing this, all risk factors should be taken into account. As a matter of fact, central banks have started to give some messages regarding their preparation on managing risks. Additionally Blockchain-based transformation should be initiated in areas such as healthcare, insurance, law enforcement and notarizing.

References

Ahluwalia, S., Mahto, R. V. and Guerrero, M. (2020). Blockchain technology and startup financing: a transaction cost economics perspective. Technological Forecasting and Social Change 151. Article 119854.

Akash, T. (2022). How Can Blockchain Revolutionize The Finance Sector? Retrieved from https://www.leewayhertz.com/10-use-cases-of-blockchain-in-finance/ Accessed on February 2, 2023.

Antonio, M. and DiNizo, Jr. (2018). From alice to bob: the patent eligibility of blockchain in a Post-CLS Bank World. Journal of Law, Technology & the Internet, Vol. 9.

Auer, R., Cornelli, G. and Frost, J. (2020a). Covid-19, cash, and the future of payments. BIS Bulletin, no 3, April.

Auer, R., Frost, J., Lammer, T., Rice, T. and Wadsworth, A. (2020b). Inclusive payments for the post-pandemic world. SUERF Policy Note, no. 193, September.

Avgouleas, E. and Kiayias, A. (2019). The promise of blockchain technology for global securities and derivatives markets: the new financial ecosystem and the "holy grail" of systemic risk containment. European Business Organization Law Review 20: 81–110.

[BIS] Bank for International Settlements. (2017). Distributed ledger technology in payment, clearing and settlement an analytical framework. Committee on Payments and Market Infrastructures.

[BIS] Bank for International Settlements. (2019). Big Tech in Finance: Opportunities and Risks. BIS Annual Economic Report, June.

Bozkus Kahyaoglu, S. (2019). An Analysis on the Implementation of New Approaches and Techniques in the Auditing of Business Processes Based on Blockchain Technologies. Cryptocurrencies in all Aspects. Edited By Fatih Ayhan and Burak Darici. Peterlang Publishing. ISBN:978-3-631-78387-0.

Bozkus Kahyaoglu, S. and Ekinci, R. (2021). İnterdisipliner Çalıştay: Anayasa Tartışmaları Gündemine Hukuki, Ekonomik ve Siyasi Bakış Açısıyla Bütünleşik Yaklaşım, Nobel Tıp Kitabevleri, İstanbul.

Cai, C. W. (2018). Disruption of financial intermediation by FinTech: a review on crowdfunding and blockchain. Accounting and Finance 58(4): 965–992.

Castren, O., Kavonius, I. K. and Rancan, M. (2022). Digital currencies in financial networks. Journal of Financial Stability 60(1).

Chakraborty, S., Aich, S., Seong, S. J. and Kim, H. C. (2019). A blockchain based credit analysis framework for efficient financial systems. pp. 56–60. *In*: 2019 21st International Conference on Advanced Communication Technology.

Chang, V., Baudier, P., Zhang, H., Xu, Q., Zhang, J. et al. (2020). How blockchain can impact financial services—the overview, challenges and recommendations from expert interviewees. Technological Forecasting and Social Change 158: 120166.

Chen, Y. and Bellavitis, C. (2019). Decentralized finance: Blockchain technology and the quest for an open financial system. Stevens Institute of Technology School of Business Research Paper.

Chen, Y. and Bellavitis, C. (2020). Blockchain disruption and decentralized finance: The rise of decentralized business models. Journal of Business Venturing Insights 13: 1–8.

Cocco, L., Pinna, A. and Marchesi, M. (2017). Banking on Blockchain: Costs savings thanks to the blockchain technology. Future Internet 9(25): 5, 1–20.

Cosares, S., Kalish, K. and Maciura, T. (2021). Blockchain applications in finance. pp. 275–291. Baker, H. K., Nikbakht, E. and Smith, S. S. (eds.). The Emerald Handbook of Blockchain for Business. Emerald Publishing Limited.

Cucari, N., Lagasio, V., Lia, G. and Torriero, C. (2021). The impact of blockchain in banking processes: the Interbank Spunta case study. Technology Analysis & Strategic Management 34(2): 138–150.

Dhanabalan, T. and Sathish, A. (2018). Transforming Indian industries through artificial intelligence and robotics in industry 4.0. Int. J. Mech. Eng. Technology 9(10): 835–845.

Didier, T., Feyen, E., Llovet Montanes, R. and Ardic Alper, O. P. (2021). Global Patterns of Fintech Activity and Enabling Factors. World Bank Group Fintech and the Future of Finance Report.

[ESMA]. European Securities and Markets Authority. (2017). The Distributed Ledger Technology Applied to Securities Markets. Paris, France.

[FSB]. Financial Stability Board. (2020). BigTech Firms in Finance in Emerging Market and Developing Economies: Market developments and potential financial stability implications. October. https://www. fsb. org/wp-content/uploads/P121020-1. pdf. Accessed on March 5, 2023.

Frost, J., Gambacorta, L. and Shin, H. S. (2021). From Financial Innovation to Inclusion. IMF Finance & Development, Spring/March.

Glaser, F., Zimmerman, K., Haferkorn, M., Weber, M., Siering, M. et al. (2014). Bitcoin – Asset or currency? Revealing users' hidden intentions. The Twenty Second European Conference on Information Systems 2014: 1–14.

Gomber, P., Kauffman, R. J., Parker, C. and Weber, B. W. (2018). On the Fintech revolution: Interpreting the forces of innovation, disruption, and transformation in financial services. Journal of Management Information Systems 35(1): 220–265.

Hartmann, F., Grottolo, G., Wang, X. and Lunesu, M. I. (2019). Alternative fundraising: success factors for blockchain-based vs. conventional crowdfunding. pp. 38–43. In 2019 IEEE International Workshop on Blockchain Oriented Software Engineering (IWBOSE). Hangzhou, China.

Hassani, H., Huang, X. and Silva, E. (2018). Banking with blockchained big data. Journal of Management Analytics 5(4): 256–275.

Hassija, V., Chamola, V. and Zeadally, S. (2020). BitFund: A blockchain-based crowd funding platform for future smart and connected nation. Sustainable Cities and Society 60: 102145.

Hilary, G. and Liu, L. X. (2021). Blockchain and other distributed ledger technologies in finance. *In*: Rau, R., Wardrop, R. and Zingales, L. (eds.). The Palgrave Handbook of Technological Finance. Palgrave Macmillan, Cham.

Holotiuk, F., Pisani, F. and Moormann, J. (2019). Radicalness of blockchain: an assessment based on its impact on the payments industry. Technology Analysis & Strategic Management 31(8): 915–928.

Kahyaoglu, H. (2021). The impact of artificial intelligence on central banking and monetary policies. pp. 83–98. *In*: Bozkus Kahyaoglu (ed.). The Impact of Artificial Intelligence on Governance, Economics and Finance (vol. I). Springer Nature Singapore.

Khacef, K. and Pujolle, G. (2019). Secure peer-to-peer communication based on blockchain. pp. 662–672. In Workshops of the International Conference on Advanced Information Networking and Applications. Cham: Springer.

Knewtson, H. S. and Rosenbaum, Z. A. (2020). Toward understanding FinTech and its industry. Managerial Finance 46(8).

Li, J., Zhu, S., Zhang, W. and Yu, L. (2020). Blockchain-driven supply chain finance solution for small and medium enterprises. Front. Eng. Manag. 7: 500–511.

Lindman, J., Rossi, M. and Tuunainen, V. K. (2017). Opportunities and risks of blockchain technologies in payments: A research agenda. The 50th Hawaii International Conference on System Sciences 1533–1542.

Mu, Q. (2016). Report on Survey of Blockchain Technology: Potential to Disrupt All Industries. [Online] Available: https://www.chainnode.com/doc/415 (Accessed: October 23rd, 2022).

Nakamoto, S. (2008). Bitcoin: A peer-to-peer electronic cash system. Available online: https://ssrn.com/abstract=3440802 (accessed on 25 August 2023).

Nguyen, Q. K. (2016). Blockchain—A financial technology for future sustainable development. pp. 51–54. *In*: Proceedings of the 3rd International Conference on Green Technology and Sustainable Development (GTSD). Kaohsiung, Taiwan. IEEE.

Pazarbasioglu, C., Garcia Mora, A., Uttamchandani, M., Natarajan, H., Feyen, E. et al. (2020). Digital Financial Services. World Bank, p. 54. Available online: http://pubdocs.worldbank.org/en (accessed on 25 December 2022).

Philippon, T. (2016). The fintech opportunity (no. w22476). National Bureau of Economic Research.

Qin, K., Zhou, L., Afonin, Y., Lazzaretti, L., Gervais, A. et al. (2021). CeFi vs. DeFi—Comparing Centralized to Decentralized Finance. arXiv preprint arXiv:2106.08157.

Rose, C. (2015). The evolution of digital currencies: bitcoin, a cryptocurrency causing a monetary revolution. International Business & Economics Research Journal (IBER) 14(4): 617–622.

Sanlisoy, S. and Ciloglu, T. (2019). An investigation on the crypto currencies and its future. International Journal of eBusiness and eGovernment Studies 11(1): 69–88.

Schindler, J. W. (2017). FinTech and Financial Innovation: Drivers and Depth, Finance and Economics Discussion Series 2017–081. Washington, DC: Board of Governors of the Federal Reserve System.

Schneider, j., Blostein, A., Lee, B., Kent, S., Groer, I. et al. (2017). Profiles in Innovation – Blockchain – Putting Theory into Practice. Report, Goldman Sachs. Available at: https://www.gspublishing.com/content/research/en/reports/2019/09/04/916e112c-3150-40df-85df-9630090048de.pdf (Accessed on January 10, 2023).

Schuetz, S. and Venkatesh, V. (2020). Blockchain, adoption, and financial inclusion in India: research opportunities. International Journal of Information Management 52: 101936.

Staples, M., Chen, S., Falamaki, S., Ponomarev, A., Rimba, P. et al. (2017). Risks and Opportunities for Systems using Blockchain and Smart Contracts. Data61 (CSIRO), Sydney.

Tapscott, A. and Tapscott, D. (2017). How blockchain is changing finance. Harvard Business Review 1(9): 2–5.

Tapscott, D. and Tapscott, A. (2016). The impact of the blockchain goes beyond financial services. Harvard Business Review 10(7).

The Economist, The Promise of the Blockchain: the Trust Machine. (2015). Available at: https://www.economist.com/leaders/2015/10/31/the-trust-machine (Accessed on January 12, 2023).

Underwood, S. (2016). Blockchain beyond bitcoin. Commun. ACM 59(1): 15–17. https:// doi.org/10.1145/2994581. (Accessed on January 10, 2023).

Urbach, N., Drews, P. and Ross, J. (2017). Digital business transformation and the changing role of the IT function. MIS Q. Exec. 16(2): 1–4.

Walker, M. J., Burton, B. and Cantara, M. (2016). Hype Cycle for Emerging Technologies Identifies Three Key Trends That Organizations Must Track to Gain Competitive Advantage. Gartner. Available at: https://www.gartner.com/en/newsroom/press-releases/2016-08-16-gartners-2016-hype-cycle-for-emerging-technologies-identifies-three-key-trends-that-organizations-must-track-to-gain-competitive-advantage (Accessed on January 25, 2023).

Wolfond, G. (2017). A blockchain ecosystem for digital identity: improving service delivery in Canada's public and private sectors. Technology Innovation Management Review 7(10).

World Economic Forum. (2016). Blockchain: what it is, how it really can change the world. Retrieved February 2, 2023 from https://www.weforum.org/agenda/2016/06/the-blockchain/.

Yoo, S. (2017). Blockchain based financial case analysis and its implications. Asia Pac. J. Innov. Entrepreneurship 11(3): 312–321.

Yu, T., Lin, Z. W. and Tang, Q. L. (2018). Blockchain: The introduction and its application in financial accounting. Journal of Corporate Accounting and Finance 29: 37–47.

Zetzsche, D. A., Buckley, R. P., Arner, D. W. and Barberis, J. N. (2017). From FinTech to TechFin: the regulatory challenges of data-driven finance. SSRN Electron. J. (6): 1–36.

Zheng, Z., Xie, S., Dai, H. N., Chen, X., Wang, H. et al. (2018). Blockchain challenges and opportunities: a survey. International Journal of Web and Grid Services 14(4): 352–375.

Zohar, A. (2015). Bitcoin: Under the hood. Communications of the ACM 58(9): 104–113.

Chapter 12
Blockchain Applications in Health Services

*Zehra Ozge Candereli** and *Levent B. Kidak*

12.1 Introduction

The healthcare systems are significant to society as they contribute to improvements in people's quality of life and personal satisfaction (Kumar and Tripathi, 2021; Saeed et al., 2022). Recent phenomena such as the emerging COVID-19 pandemic and digital technologies have resulted in both new challenges and opportunities in the global healthcare industry as well as other industries having an influence on society (Hiwale et al., 2021; Levy, 2022; Ng et al., 2021). For example, the COVID-19 pandemic has accelerated the development and adoption of digital health applications while putting a strain on healthcare systems' resources (Hiwale et al., 2021; Jillian Oderkirk and Slawomirski, 2020; Ng et al., 2021). Furthermore, advancements in information and communication technology, such as big data, the Internet of things, machine learning, and cloud computing, are inducing fundamental shifts in established business structures. Along with the aforementioned challenges and motivations, this transformation process has been altering the fundamental tenets of current systems and governance models, thereby questioning the conventional role of centralised institutions (Dwivedi et al., 2019; Kara and Kurutkan, 2021). This transformation is reflected in the healthcare sector through the adoption of prominent approaches based on decentralised structures, such as patient-centred and value-based healthcare (Haleem

Department of Health Management, Izmir Katip Celebi University, Izmir, Turkey.
Email: leventkidak@gmail.com
* Corresponding author: ozgehuccet@gmail.com

et al., 2021; Zhang et al., 2019). The most promising and important example of this decentralised structure from a technological perspective is "blockchain", which is immutable and peer-to-peer distributed ledger technology. It possesses unique features such as transparency, anonymity, tamper-proofing, traceability, and cryptography (Abu-elezz et al., 2020; Arbabi et al., 2022; Hasselgren et al., 2020; Kara and Kurutkan, 2021). Blockchain maintains an immutable historical record of all transactions (blocks), which are distributed across all participating nodes without the need for a central authority or reliable third parties (Namasudra and Deka, 2021). Moreover, a digital ecosystem's technology layer, blockchain, includes related technologies such as consensus algorithms, smart contracts, cryptocurrencies, and distributed ledger technologies as well as platforms such as Hyperledger and Ethereum (Conway et al., 2022; Sharma et al., 2022). With the popularization of Bitcoin considered as an outstanding application example of blockchain (Nakamoto, 2008), the technology has supported the emergence of new organisational structures, work processes, and business models. In addition, it has a great potential to facilitate suitable and reliable direct value transfers between participants (Subic et al., 2018).

The ever-evolving blockchain technology has been described in relation to a variety of current and potential activities. Initially, Blockchain 1.0 was associated with Bitcoin and focused on decentralizing money and payments. Blockchain 2.0, represented by smart contracts, expanded the decentralization concept to markets and the transfer of assets other than currency, such as stocks and smart properties. Blockchain 3.0 refers to the use of Decentralized applications (Dapps) and extends its reach beyond money to encompass markets, finance, government, science, health, education, and culture (Swan, 2015). The third generation of blockchain protocols placed an emphasis on factors including speed, security, scalability, interoperability, and environmental friendliness. Nowadays, Blockchain 4.0 represents a promising new development in the evolution of blockchain with a focus on Web 3.0 and the metaverse. In Blockchain 4.0, the main areas of interest will be speed, user experience, and adoption by a larger and more widespread audience (Banafa, 2022). As a result, the adoption of blockchain applications, which began in the financial sector, has expanded to encompass every industry that relies on human effort today, including healthcare, supply chains, agriculture, and manufacturing (Subic et al., 2018). With Blockchain 3.0, researchers and scholars have commenced applying blockchain technologies to the healthcare field (Farahat et al., 2022). It is also noteworthy as a complementary technology which can be integrated with various technologies (Kara and Kurutkan, 2021). Therefore, it has several application areas and functions in the healthcare industry (Haleem et al., 2021).

The literature on blockchain applications in healthcare has witnessed a significant increase in recent years due to the growing number of studies conducted in this area. However, there are few bibliometric studies that focus on the intersection of blockchain technology and healthcare. Given the considerable attention from scholars and practitioners, it will be important to exhibit a dynamic outline of the area of study and its potential. The purpose of this study is to determine in which areas of healthcare blockchain applications are used. The goal is to achieve this by conducting a bibliometric analysis to unveil the intellectual knowledge structure, development trends, and research focuses within the field.

- In this context the following objectives are sought to be achieved: To identify the blockchain applications that are currently being used in healthcare and their frequency of use for each of these applications.
- To explore the evolving direction of blockchain applications in healthcare.
- To identify the emerging and motor concepts of blockchain applications in healthcare.
- To identify countries conducting studies on blockchain applications in healthcare.
- To identify research areas focused on studying blockchain applications in healthcare.
- To identify scholars conducting effective research on blockchain applications in healthcare.

This study is expected to make several contributions to the research field in various aspects. Firstly, it aims to provide scholars with a comprehensive overview of the current state of research and advancements in blockchain applications within the healthcare industry. Secondly, it can assist researchers in identifying study areas that have significant research hotspots and areas for further exploration. Thirdly, it may aid academics and researchers in identifying the most influential authors, organizations, and countries in terms of developing and disseminating blockchain applications in healthcare. Fourthly, it can guide academics and students in identifying top international journals that focus on the intersection of blockchain technology and healthcare. Furthermore, this research can help inform decisions regarding funding allocation for scientific and technological operations by governments, businesses, and policymakers, by identifying the R & D organizations that are leading in this field.

The research is structured as follows:

1. *Introduction*: Provides an overview of the research topic and its significance.
2. *Background*: Explores the background and context of the research field.
3. *Methodology*: Describes the research including the analyses used, database selection, search criteria, search query, and data collection preparation for analysis.
4. *Findings*: Presents the research findings based on the research questions addressed.
5. *Conclusion*: Offers conclusions drawn from the findings and provides recommendations for future research endeavors.

12.2 Convergence of Blockchain Technology and Healthcare

Data, actors, and technology are the diversified and complex components that built modern healthcare ecosystems. The number of components and their interactions increase day by day. In this context, a wide variety of digital data types have emerged, including personal data, medical records, sensor data, financial and transaction records, consent forms, and clinical trial records. These data have been generated, exchanged, and stored by multiple parties and technologies involved in the healthcare ecosystem. Blockchain has the potential to offer a holistic perspective and awareness of the whole lifecycle of healthcare components due to its unique features (Kassab et al., 2021; Wright, 2019).

Furthermore, in the data-intensive healthcare system, a centralized structure predominates, making it crucial to effectively manage large amounts of siloed data, particularly sensitive patient data. These data are generated, stored, shared, and accessed by various authentic parties. However, this process has also given rise to security, privacy, and access control concerns. Thus, blockchain has significant potential in healthcare, particularly in healthcare information management, which includes electronic health records, personal health records, and electronic medical records (Kassab et al., 2021; Saeed et al., 2022).

Many stakeholders are actively investigating blockchain to reduce costs, raise compliance, enhance patient outcomes, and empower improved use of healthcare-related data (Mackey et al., 2019). According to the Stanford Graduate School of Business Report (2018), health-related blockchain projects began later than those in other industries, but they significantly increased in 2016 and 2017. More blockchain attempts have been drawn to the health sector than any other. In the report, it was stated that the health sector accounted for nearly twice as many blockchain projects (25%) compared to the next most popular industry, which was the financial sector (13%), were devoted to health (Galen et al., 2018).

Blockchain enables secure and efficient access to medical data while simultaneously preserving patient privacy for patients, healthcare practitioners, and third parties (Guo et al., 2021). It also helps with the healthcare information exchange process in terms of preventing time-consuming and repetitive processes (Haleem et al., 2021). Its traceability, immutability, and transparency features make it well-suited for managing the supply chain, including medical supplies, counterfeit drugs and pharmaceuticals, as well as clinical trials and health insurance claim processing (Agbo and Mahmoud, 2020; Zhuang et al., 2022). In particular, it has been effective in combating COVID-19 with supply chain management for medical supplies, vaccines, and identity management (Jillian Oderkirk and Slawomirski, 2020; Razzaq et al., 2022).

The Industry 4.0 revolution, including the internet of things, artificial intelligence, and 5G, has launched technologies with great potential, and this has increased the use of technologies such as smart wearable devices, sensors, and mobile health, providing advanced real-time monitoring of patients. At the same time, advancements in these technologies and processes have presented new challenges in terms of security, privacy, information collection, processing, and transfer speed. These challenges can be addressed by integrating blockchain with these cutting-edge technologies, as blockchain enables autonomous communication among individuals, organisations, and machines (Dwivedi et al., 2019; Guo et al., 2021; Kumar and Tripathi, 2021).

Therefore, blockchain offers a cutting-edge solution for storing healthcare data, conducting healthcare transactions, and establishing trust for healthcare data integration and exchange in a distributed healthcare network setting (Zhang et al., 2021). As a result, blockchain technologies can be applied at various levels of the healthcare sector, encompassing the development and tracing of pharmaceutical and medical products, diagnostic procedures such as medical imaging, e-prescription processes, remote patient monitoring, and health insurance reimbursement procedures. Most importantly, it can be used for better management and protection of health records (Dwivedi et al., 2019; Guo et al., 2021; Hölbl et al., 2018; Kara and Kurutkan, 2021; Saeed et al., 2022).

12.3 Methodology and Data

12.3.1 Bibliometric Analysis

In this study, a bibliometric analysis was conducted. Bibliometrics serves as a crucial tool for evaluating and analysing academic research published in journals, universities, countries, research centres, and research groups

(Martínez et al., 2015). Bibliometric mapping is employed to create a graphical representation of the relationships between disciplines, fields, documents, and authors (Small, 1999). The purpose of scientific mapping is to display the dynamic and structural elements of the scientific field (Martínez et al., 2015). In these studies, data such as topics, keywords, authors, publication dates, and countries of publication are analysed. This approach allows for tracking the conceptual structure and evolution of the field (Cobo et al., 2011). Currently, due to the numerous benefits it offers, bibliometrics provides an opportunity to make predictions for the future and develop policies based on scientific literature. As a result, it is being utilized in various fields, ranging from engineering to social sciences (Kumar and Tripathi, 2021; Kuzior and Sira, 2022; Martínez et al., 2015). In this study, science bibliometrics was applied to thoroughly examine blockchain applications in healthcare.

The data collected from bibliographic sources typically can contain errors, so first a pre-processing process needs to be used. One of the most crucial steps to successful science mapping analysis is pre-processing. The raw data can go through a variety of pre-processing steps, including network reduction, time slicing, data reduction, and the detection of duplicate and misspelled entries (Cobo et al., 2012).

Scientific mapping is performed in different units of analysis depending on the purpose of analysis. One of these is "co-word" analysis, which uses the most important or keywords of scientific publications to reveal the conceptual structure of a field. The analysis is based on visualizing the relationships between keywords in a network by weighting the co-occurrence of keywords from scientific publications. In this way, conceptual closeness and relation clusters are formed. This ensures that the main topics and sub-topics explored within the field of study are revealed (Börner et al., 2003; Martínez et al., 2015). Similarly, "Co-author" analysis study the social networks that scientists build when they work together to publish scientific article. When two writers co-publish an article, a relationship is created between them. Therefore, the social network of actors in a field defines the interaction between two or more people, organizations, or nations in terms of partnerships (Börner et al., 2003; Song et al., 2019). In this study, co-word and co-author analyses were used.

12.3.2 Data Extraction Process

To thoroughly explore international research on blockchain applications in healthcare, the Scopus database was selected. Web of Science (WoS) and PubMed databases are also there in the literature. However, each database has strengths, weaknesses, and some biases depending on the purpose of the study due to the fact that they have different coverage, focuses, and tools. While Scopus and WoS are multidisciplinary, PubMed primarily focuses on life sciences and biomedical disciplines (AlRyalat et al., 2019; Mongeon and Paul-Hus, 2016). The use of bibliographic tags in PubMed data is limited. In studies comparing the other databases, it was found that Scopus containing the majority of the journals indexed in the WoS, covered a much larger number of journals, and had more exclusive journals than the WoS (Mongeon and Paul-Hus, 2016; Visser et al., 2021). However, it was indicated that WoS was the most selective (Singh et al., 2021). Therefore, the authors emphasized that the evaluation of differences between databases should, be based on the purpose of using the data sources. Preliminary analysis was performed with the same query terms in Scopus and WoS databases. 2999 publications were found in WoS, while 5259 publications were found in Scopus. Thus, the Scopus database was selected as the search engine.

In the data extraction phase, firstly, no timeframe was set to find the relationship between blockchain technology and healthcare literature using the Scopus database. The lexical search query was decided based on previous literature and experts' opinions. Initially, in order to address the intersection of healthcare and blockchain more inclusively, the query was expanded with terms such as "emergency service*", "ambulance service*", "primary healthcare*", "general practice", "chronic illness*", "non-communicable disease*", "doctor*" and "physician*" as well as "health", "healthcare", "hospital*" and "medical". However, the search in Table 12.1 was chosen after a preliminary review. Accordingly, in December 2022, the boolean expression (TITLE-ABS-KEY ("blockchain" OR "distributed ledger" OR "cryptocurrenc*") AND TITLE-ABS-KEY ("health" OR "healthcare" OR "hospital*" OR "medical")) was used. The search was conducted using the TITLE-ABS-KEY query field because it allows searching for topic terms in the Article Title, Abstract, Author Keyword and Indexed Keyword fields within a record. This query resulted in 5259 publications for the 2016–2022 time period, as shown in Table 12.1.

Table 12.1. Research strategy in Scopus.

Step	Keyword Search	Publications
1	(TITLE-ABS-KEY ("blockchain" OR "distributed ledger" OR "cryptocurrenc*") AND TITLE-ABS-KEY ("health" OR "healthcare" OR "hospital*" OR "medical"))	5259
2	(TITLE-ABS-KEY ("blockchain" OR "distributed ledger" OR "cryptocurrenc*") AND TITLE-ABS-KEY ("health" OR "healthcare" OR "hospital*" OR "medical")) AND (LIMIT-TO (DOCTYPE, "ar"))	1944
3	After initial analysis of 1944 articles, it was excluded irrelevant articles by examining abstracts	1742

Secondly, when the search was refined by including only articles, 1944 publications remained in the query. By examining the abstracts, articles not related to the subject were removed, and 1742 articles were finally included. Thirdly, these articles were downloaded as Comma-Separated Values (CSV) files with BibTeX format for data processing and data visualization.

Following the data collection phase, a data pre-processing phase was carried out to perform co-occurrence analysis using words and authors as units of analysis. For some articles, it was observed that different keywords in the dataset's keywords reflected words with the same meaning twice or more. In order to avoid inconsistency, separate articles' use of the terms blockchain, blockchains, and block-chain as keywords were merged into a single term "blockchain". The merging process was similarly applied to terms such as "healthcare and health care", "internet of things, iot and internet of things (IoT)".

There are numerous free and commercial software programs that can be used to perform scientific mapping. For the data analysis and visualization, the Bibliometrix package in R (Aria and Cuccurullo, 2017) and VOSviewer version 1.6.18 (van Eck and Waltman, 2010) were used in this study. Biblioshiny is an open-source program written in the R environment that performs a thorough study of the scientific literature in terms of scientific mapping (Aria and Cuccurullo, 2017) and an open-source Java program called VOSviewer is used to examine and display the citation networks of scientific literature (van Eck and Waltman, 2010).

12.4 Analysis and Findings

The findings of the bibliometric analysis were provided based on the research questions they answer, respectively. In this context, the prominent topics, prominent themes, development of the field, motor and emerging themes, and other findings related to the research questions are presented below.

It was found that 1742 articles, and the oldest article about blockchain applications in healthcare were dated back to 2016. Figure 12.1 shows the year-based distribution of publications during the 2016 to 2022 research period. Despite being created in 2008, blockchain did not gain popularity until the recent growth of bitcoin in 2016. After 2017, blockchain has been recognized as one of the secure data protection technologies. As a result, its use in various applications like finance, manufacturing, logistics and energy that prioritise data security increased (Kuzior and Sira, 2022). A similar trend has been observed in the field of healthcare. This situation is demonstrated by the abrupt growth as in Figure 12.1 in 2018 and beyond.

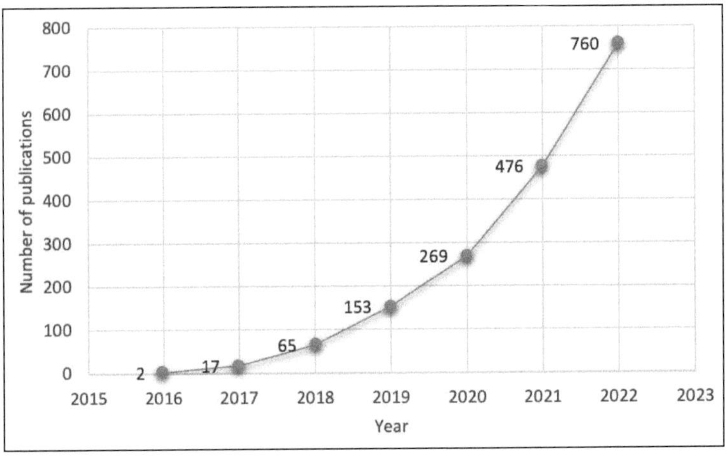

Figure 12.1. Number of articles by year.

After all, the number of publications reached 760 in 2022, up 63% from the previous year.

When the general information regarding bibliometric data was analysed, 1742 articles were produced on 612 different sources by 5222 different authors. The field showed an annual growth rate of 169.13%. The number of author's keywords was 3472.

Prominent Topics

According to Kuhn (2012), a scientific field gradually develops with time, giving rise to new sets of theoretical, conceptual, and methodological foundations. The terminology used by academia to describe a novel phenomenon changes along with the emergence of a new paradigm. Thus, lexical changes play a crucial role in the scientific revolution that ushers in a new era of conventional study. It can forecast the association between keywords and research foci of a particular knowledge domain over time by analysing the frequency of keywords in the intersection between blockchain and healthcare literature (Kuhn, 2012).

The easiest technique to locate and analyse a key term utilizing search engines is to use keywords because they make the research more visible. Author's keywords as units of analysis were used in this study. The term "author's keywords" (DE) refers to a certain list of keywords that the authors of a paper have catalogued to highlight the main points of their research (Tripathi et al., 2018). The study examined the 25 most popular search terms related to blockchain technology in healthcare. According to the examination, blockchain was the most prominent term used (1237 times), as can be seen in Table 12.2. The other keywords with high occurrences include internet of things (258), security (199), healthcare

Table 12.2. Top 25 most used keywords.

Rank	Keywords	Occurrences
1	Blockchain	1237
2	internet of things	258
3	Security	199
4	Healthcare	197
5	smart contract	180
6	Covid-19	157
7	electronic health records	153
8	Privacy	145
9	internet of medical things	80
10	distributed ledger	75
11	artificial intelligence	71
12	Ethereum	68
13	privacy preservation	64
14	electronic medical records	60
15	access control	57
16	e-health	53
17	supply chain	53
18	cloud computing	49
19	data sharing	49
20	machine learning	49
21	hyperledger fabric	45
22	federated learning	43
23	interplanetary file system	42
24	deep learning	40
25	Authentication	38

(197), smart contract (180) and Covid-19 with 157 occurrences. All of these keywords reflect the scope of articles included in the dataset. In this context, it has been revealed that blockchain applications in healthcare are linked with fields like the internet of things, security, smart contract, Covid-19, electronic health records, and privacy. In addition to these keywords, new keywords that are not included in the table but considered important were smart healthcare with 36 occurrences, big data (35), edge computing (35), fog computing (31) and smart city (24).

However, high-frequency keywords alone cannot identify research hotspots in a field and thus co-word analysis should be utilized to further identify the connections between high-frequency keywords (Fang et al., 2021).

Prominent Themes

The frequency of a keyword occurring alongside other keywords is known as a co-occurrence. A network diagram representing a co-occurrence network of keywords can show specific links between keywords (Tripathi et al., 2018). The word's frequency in the article and its association with other keywords are displayed on the keyword co-occurrence map. In this study, the knowledge map of the co-occurrence network of keywords in blockchain applications in healthcare was created using Vosviewer software. A circle is used to symbolise each phrase in the network, and the size of the circle reflects how many publications contain that term. Each colour represents a collection of terms grouped into clusters. The relationships between various topics are depicted by the clusters. The thickness of curved lines indicates the strength of pairs of keywords, while the length of curved lines indicates the approximate connection of the repetition of the keyword. Thus, the co-word analysis revealed study subjects that can be divided into broadly developed issues and specialised peripheral issues (van Eck and Waltman, 2010). Figure 12.2 shows that the researchers associate blockchain with multiple fields of research, and thus seven different clusters were formed.

Cluster 1, represented by red colour, consisted of 20 keywords and the largest and central node in this cluster was Blockchain, highlighting its importance in the topic being studied. It was connected with internet of things (IoT), Covid-19, internet of medical things (IoMT), artificial intelligence, machine learning, federated learning, deep learning, edge computing, big data and fog computing, as can be seen in Table 12.3. Recently, technology has been ever-evolving, and blockchain development has demonstrated a remarkable capacity for adaptation (Rejeb et al., 2021). This cluster was mainly focused on state-of-the-art technologies such as IoT, IoMT, machine learning, federated learning, and big data, as well as new algorithms like edge computing and fog computing. Furthermore, the focus of this cluster on cutting-edge technologies makes blockchain a suitable solution to address current challenges, such as the Covid-19 pandemic, by utilizing the capabilities of IoT and machine learning to analyze data and aid public health decision-making (Bazel et al., 2021).

The rapid growth of remote medical devices such as the internet of medical things, wearable devices, and sensors in healthcare has created challenges related to computing power, data storage, privacy, and security. To tackle these challenges, edge computing, fog computing, and

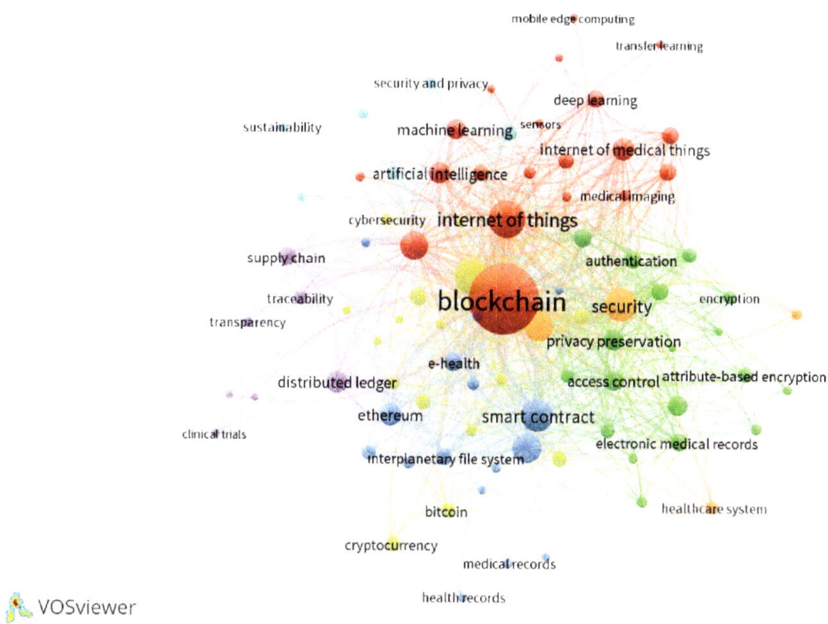

Figure 12.2. Co-occurrence network of keywords.

federated learning, in conjunction with blockchain, have come to the fore (Ahmad et al., 2023; Yang et al., 2022). Healthcare 4.0, taken from Industry 4.0 as a root concept, covers the internet of things, big data, blockchain, 5G, fog computing and more (Koştı et al., 2021; Mahajan, 2022). Therefore, it can be said that these technologies have a high degree of interactivity with blockchain in the healthcare sector.

Cluster 2, labelled in green, was primarily concerned with Privacy Preservation which connected 18 keywords. This cluster emphasized the importance of features such as data sharing, access control, authentication and authorization in sharing electronic medical records and medical data based on privacy preservation. To achieve this, blockchain specifications such as cryptography, attribute-based encryption, encryption, proxy re-encryption, searchable encryption, and consortium blockchain were mainly focused on. Electronic medical records (EMRs), typically viewed as a system used internally by organizations, are a vital component of medical services and provide a foundation for resolving medical disputes as well as providing medical data for diagnosis and scientific study. The most authentic patient records in medical care are now kept in EMRs. Sharing medical data is therefore, of utmost importance for the advancement of human health. Blockchain technology can help EMRs in maintaining control over information access thanks to its decentralized

Table 12.3. Map of co-occurrence keyword clusters.

Clusters	Co-keywords
Cluster 1 (red) (20 items) Blockchain	Blockchain, Internet of things, Covid-19, Internet of medical things, Artificial intelligence, Machine learning, Federated learning, Deep learning, Edge computing, Big data, Fog computing, Hyperledger, Medical imaging, Technology, Healthcare 4.0, 5g, Sensors, Mobile edge computing, Transfer learning, Unmanned aerial vehicles
Cluster 2 (green) (18 items) Privacy Preservation	Privacy preservation, Access control, Data sharing, Cloud computing, Electronic medical records, Authentication, Data privacy, Medical services, Cryptography, Attribute-based encryption, Data security, Encryption, Proxy re-encryption, Searchable encryption, Consortium blockchain, Medical data sharing, Authorization, Data integrity
Cluster 3 (blue) (16 items) Smart Contract	Smart contract, Electronic health records, Ethereum, E-health, Interplanetary file system, Personal health record, Mobile health, Digital health, Telemedicine, Contact tracing, Medical records, Health information exchange, Health records, Hospitals, Merkle tree, Health information management
Cluster 4 (yellow) (16 items) Healthcare	Healthcare, Hyperledger fabric, Medical data, Decentralization, Cryptocurrency, Interoperability, Bitcoin, Scalability, Consensus, Cybersecurity, Decentralized, Integrity, Network security, Permissioned blockchain, Wearable devices, Zero-knowledge proof
Cluster 5 (purple) (7 items) Distributed Ledger	Distributed ledger, Supply chain, Traceability, Transparency, Clinical trials, Distributed systems, Health informatics
Cluster 6 (light blue) (6 items) Smart Health	Smart health, Smart city, Security and privacy, Industry 4.0, Sustainability, Information security
Cluster 7 (orange) (4 items) Security	Security, Privacy, Healthcare system, Homomorphic encryption

nature and various encryption and cryptographic features. It can also maintain a balance between data accessibility and privacy (De Oliveira et al., 2019; Mhamdi et al., 2022; Zou et al., 2021).

Cluster 3, represented by blue colour, consisted of 16 keywords and was labelled Smart Contract. It was connected with electronic health records (EHR), ethereum, e-health, interplanetary file systems (IPFS), personal health record (PHR), and more, as can be seen in Table 12.3. A smart contract is a type of digital transaction that runs, carries out, and logs dynamic operations on a ledger automatically (Sharma et al., 2022). Smart contracts, the second revolution in blockchain technology, are widely used with different platforms like Fabric and Ethereum in healthcare (Prasad and Ramachandram, 2022; Sharma et al., 2022). It is evident that this term has a significant impact on blockchain technology and the healthcare sector. It can be said that smart contracts are commonly used with Merkle trees and IPFS, especially in digital health, such as electronic health records, personal health records, telemedicine, and mobile health. Telemedicine and digital health services can be automated in a reliable and effective manner using blockchain technology and smart contracts, which can replace intermediaries in the current healthcare system and automate business procedures. To build trust, the predefined regulations among the involved organizations can be converted into smart contract functionalities. In addition, blockchain technology paired with smart contracts has expanded the use of decentralized storage systems, such as the Interplanetary File System (IPFS), to store and manage large-size digital assets, like images and audio and video recordings of telemedicine services. Thus, preserving data provenance, enabling data exchange, and producing accurate warnings and notifications can be provided (Hasan et al., 2021; Jain and Tripathi, 2022).

Cluster 4, labelled in yellow, was linked to 16 keywords with Healthcare at its hub. This cluster focused on various fundamental features of blockchain such as decentralization, bitcoin, cryptocurrency, interoperability, consensus, scalability, as well as platforms like Hyperledger Fabric as a permissioned blockchain. Although each topic had a distinct emphasis, the contents were interconnected. It can be said that the cluster was interested in ensuring the security of medical data by means of cybersecurity, network security, zero-knowledge proof, and permissioned blockchain.

Cluster 5, represented by purple colour, consisted of 7 keywords and the largest node was its Distributed Ledger Technology, which highlighted the importance of blockchain. The cluster was connected with supply chain, traceability, transparency, clinical trials and health informatics, as shown in Table 3. It can be said that blockchain's traceability and transparency features have the potential to support supply chain, clinical trials, and health informatics.

Cluster 6, represented in purple colour, consisted of 6 keywords. Sustainability and industry 4.0, important components of smart cities, were linked with Smart Health. Data is a valuable resource in a connected smart city, and healthcare data can help in remote diagnosis and medical research. Privacy is a crucial factor for both individuals and organizations owing to the potentially sensitive nature of healthcare data (Dai et al., 2022). Therefore, it can be said that this cluster focused on information security and privacy in smart health, using blockchain technologies.

Cluster 7, represented by orange, consisted of 4 keywords and the largest and central node in this cluster was Security. This cluster focused on privacy and security in healthcare systems through homomorphic encryption. Hospitals and research facilities are increasingly coming up with innovative ways to share medical data while protecting privacy, and two of these technological solutions are homomorphic encryption and distributed ledger technology. Using homomorphic encryption, data can be computed without ever decrypting (Scheibner et al., 2022). The primary focus areas of blockchain research are currently finding solutions to privacy and security issues because the technology is still in its infancy. It is suggested that addressing these issues is crucial for achieving widespread acceptance and use of blockchain technology in the healthcare sector (Candereli et al., 2020; Rejeb et al., 2021).

Development of Blockchain Applications Used in Healthcare

The co-occurrence of keywords was analysed in terms of the time dimension, as can be seen in Figure 12.3. Keywords represented by dark blue reflect those that appeared earlier, while keywords represented by yellow reflect those that appeared later, based on the time progress colour bar in the bottom right corner of Figure 12.3. In 2020 and before, most studies focused on concepts such as distributed ledger, consensus, and bitcoin, which represent the main features of blockchain. Additionally, research explored areas such as health information management, e-health, m-health, and clinical trials.

The concepts of health informatics, information security, transparency, big data, supply chain, EHR, EMR, and telemedicine were highlighted in the late 2020s. At the beginning of 2021, the concepts of internet of things, artificial intelligence, privacy preservation, smart contract, as well as fog computing, access control, and security and privacy issues, gained momentum. Over time, while privacy and security remained important, the focus shifted to smart health, machine learning, and edge computing. However, recently, internet of medical things, healthcare 4.0, medical imaging, transfer learning, deep learning, federated learning, and unmanned aerial vehicles have gained importance.

Today's healthcare system, which is built on a patient-centered approach, prioritises prevention and follow-up over treatment by empowering patients. This paradigm shift enhances the usage of novel technologies like wearable medical devices, sensors, and the internet of things for remote patient monitoring. One of these is Internet of Medical Things (IoMT), the integration of IoT in the healthcare sector. More importantly, these innovations have major positive effects on health, including enhancing the quality of care and diminishing healthcare costs (El Rifai et al., 2020; Prasad et al., 2022; Taherdoost, 2023). In order

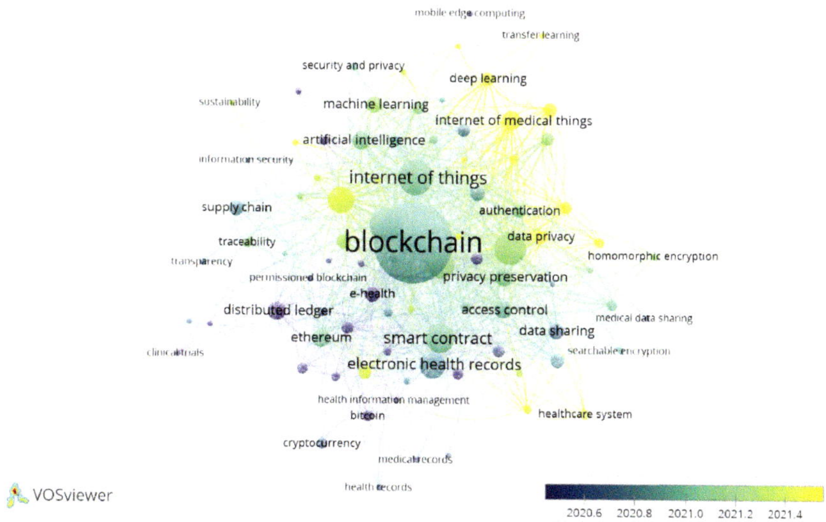

Figure 12.3. Map of co-occurrence of keywords by time dimension.

to exploit the potential of data collected in real-time across different devices and environments and provide meaningful data-driven insights, this data needs to be properly collected, processed, and shared while ensuring privacy and security (Prasad et al., 2022). As a response to these difficulties, new algorithms like federated learning, transfer learning, and deep learning have been tried in healthcare (Farooq et al., 2022; Kumar et al., 2022; ul Haque et al., 2020).

The idea behind federated learning is to lessen the chance of sensitive data being exposed while building machine learning models on distributed devices. Healthcare data is well suited to be processed using the federated learning paradigm due to its private and fragmented structure. Healthcare has begun utilizing federated learning and blockchain to tackle challenges with data privacy and transparency (El Rifai et al., 2020; Liu et al., 2022). It may be claimed that researchers are working to merge the best features of these disruptive technologies with blockchain while also supporting them with new algorithms that can handle data more effectively.

Motor Themes and Emerging Themes

In thematic analysis, each theme identified by this approach is denoted by two parameters: centrality, which indicates the degree of relevance along the horizontal axis, and density, which indicates the level of development along the vertical axis (Cobo et al., 2011). According to the thematic analysis, four clusters emerged, as can be shown in Figure 12.4. Motor themes refer to well-developed and important study fields that have both high centrality

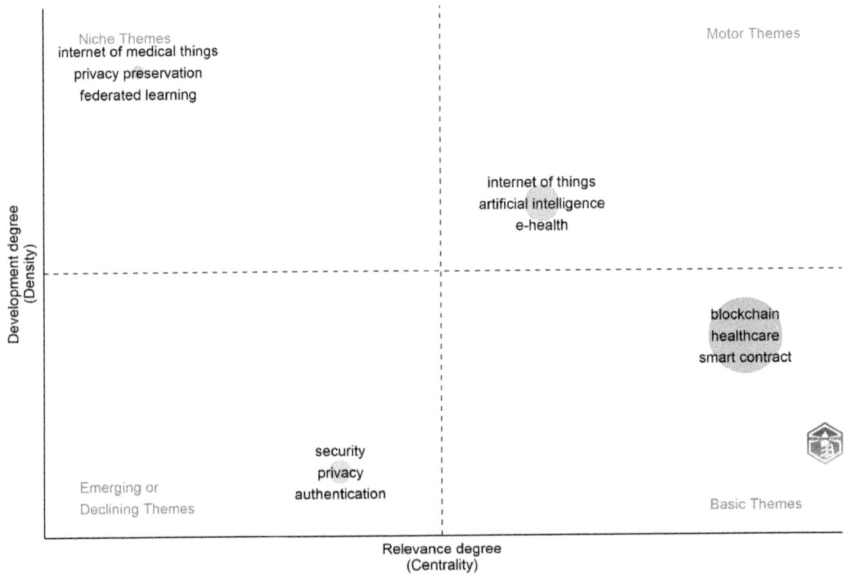

Figure 12.4. Thematic map.

and high density. In this quarter, one cluster emerged, including internet of things (artificial intelligence, machine learning, cloud computing, deep learning, smart healthcare, edge computing, big data, fog computing, and smart city). It can be said that this cluster was related to state-of-the-art technologies along with blockchain in healthcare. Basic themes are key and potentially important for the development of a research area but have not been sufficiently developed internally. The basic theme in this quarter had one cluster: blockchain (healthcare, smart contract, EHRs, Covid-19, distributed ledger, ethereum, EMRs, access control, and e-health). This cluster was related to the core components of blockchain and application areas in healthcare such as EHRs, EMRs, and e-health. Niche themes are highly developed and specialised themes, with groups focused on these issues. Topics such as internet of medical things, privacy preservation, federated learning, data privacy, encryption, medical imaging, internet of healthcare things were in this quadrant. This theme included new algorithms like federated learning, which focus on privacy and new topics like internet of medical things and internet of healthcare things. The fourth quarter has emerging or declining themes. These themes are marginal areas with both weak internal external linkages. The theme was composed of security, privacy, authentication, decentralization, scalability, homomorphic encryption, and consensus. It can be asserted that privacy and security issues were the main challenges of health technologies and blockchain, and therefore, these topics emerged as significant areas of focus.

Research Areas Examining Blockchain Applications in Healthcare

Table 12.4 lists the top 16 journals that published at least 15 articles on the connection between blockchain technology and healthcare. These 16 prominent journals accounted for roughly 30% of the total number of articles analysed. IEEE Access published the most articles, with 145, followed by Sensors and IEEE Internet of Things Journal, with 42 and 40 articles, respectively. When examining the scopes of journals, it was found that journals in the fields of medicine, business, and management were included in the journal list, but those in the fields of computer science and engineering were more prevalent in the analysed research (Goyal et al., 2021; Rejeb et al., 2021). As a result, it was observed that blockchain research covered a multidisciplinary approach.

Table 12.4. Number of publications by source.

Name of Sources	Number of Articles
IEEE Access	145
Sensors	42
IEEE Internet of Things Journal	40
Journal of Medical Internet Research	36
Electronics (Switzerland)	33
Security and Communication Networks	32
Applied Sciences (Switzerland)	30
Computers, Materials and Continua	23
Sensors (Switzerland)	21
Sustainability (Switzerland)	21
Journal of Healthcare Engineering	20
International Journal of Advanced Computer Science and Applications	18
IEEE Journal of Biomedical and Health Informatics	17
IEEE Network	16
Journal of Medical Systems	16
Transactions on Emerging Telecommunications Technologies	15

Countries Studying on Blockchain Applications in Healthcare

In order to reveal their collaborations in blockchain applications in healthcare research, the network maps of countries' and authors' collaborations were created, respectively. According to the co-authorship

Table 12.5. Top 10 countries with the highest number of publications.

Rank	Countries	Clusters-Colours	Articles
1	China	Cluster 1 - Red	410
2	India	Cluster 1 - Red	400
3	USA	Cluster 2- Green	275
4	Saudi Arabia	Cluster 6 – Light Blue	169
5	South Korea	Cluster 7 - Orange	159
6	United Kingdom	Cluster 3 - Blue	129
7	Australia	Cluster 7 - Orange	86
8	Pakistan	Cluster 6 – Light Blue	86
9	Taiwan	Cluster 1 - Red	69
10	United Arab Emirates	Cluster 3 - Blue	69

of the countries' network map, China contributed the most to the field with 410 documents, followed by India (400), the USA (275), Saudi Arabia (169), and South Korea (159), respectively (Table 12.5). China's production was around six times greater than that of the United Arab Emirates, resulting in a relatively large gap between the first and tenth-placed countries in terms of the number of articles published. Additionally, it was observed that countries in Asia had more research on blockchain applications in healthcare.

Seven clusters with different colours were identified by the country collaboration network map in Figure 12.5. In Cluster 1, it was observed that

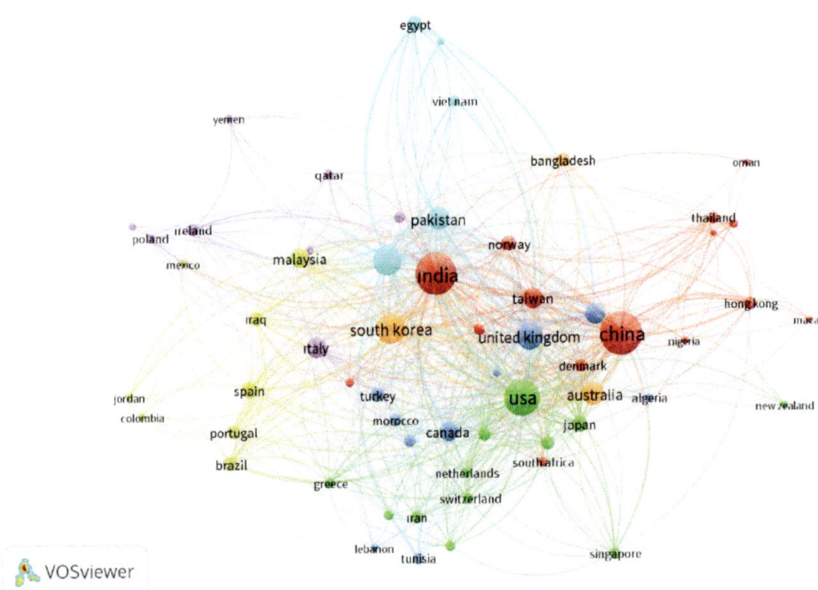

Figure 12.5. Country collaboration network map.

collaborations between Asian countries such as China, India, and Taiwan, and Scandinavian countries such as Norway, Denmark, and Sweden, were more intense. Additionally, collaborations between Asian countries were also more frequent in this cluster. In Cluster 2, it was seen that the USA and countries such as Japan, Germany, and Russia had much more collaboration. There was a collaboration between North Africa, Europe, and Asia in Cluster 3, which has the United Kingdom as its hub.

Most Productive Scientists in Research on Blockchain Applications in Healthcare

The number of articles published by the 10 most productive authors is sorted in descending order, as shown in Table 12.6. Salah, K. was the most productive author with 30 articles, and followed by Jayaraman R. with 28 articles, and Zhang Y. with 25 articles.

The co-author collaboration map is shown in Figure 12.6. It was observed that many authors preferred to collaborate with a small number of people, resulting in six different collaboration clusters that are disconnected from each other. However, Salah K., Jayaraman R., Zhang Y., Kumar N., Liu Y., and Wang W., who are some of the well-known prolific scholars in the field, have a strong collaboration network.

Table 12.6. Top 10 most productive authors.

Rank	Authors	Number of Articles
1	Salah K.	30
2	Jayaraman R.	28
3	Zhang Y.	25
4	Kumar N.	21
5	Liu Y.	20
6	Wang W.	20
7	Tanwar S.	19
8	Wang H.	19
9	Zhang X.	18
10	Yaqoob I.	16

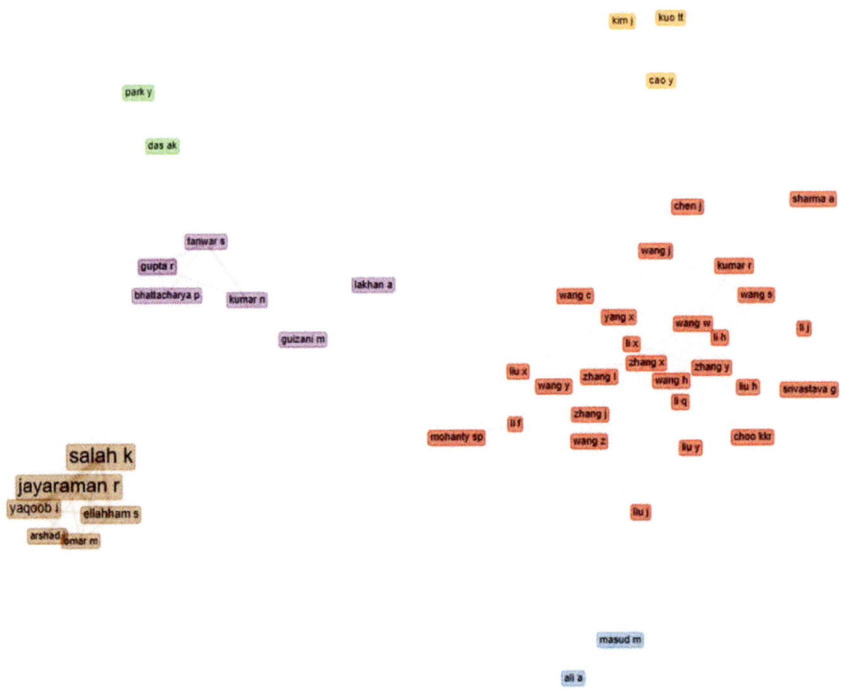

Figure 12.6. Map of author's collaboration network.

12.5 Conclusion

It can be asserted that there are close interactions between blockchain technologies and healthcare technologies such as IoMT, EHR, EMR, e-health, mobile health, telemedicine, and medical imaging, and they are integrated with state-of-the-art technologies. This trend is expected to continue, and the interaction of federated learning focusing on privacy with the Internet of Things will likely grow. However, security and privacy remain important issues in healthcare. This is supported by the fact that there are a variety of security concepts such as privacy preservation, data security, and network security, and technologies that focus on addressing them.

It may be asserted that blockchain applications can help solve security, privacy, interoperability, sharing, and transparency problems in the fields of health information exchange, health information management, and health informatics for the management of sensitive data in the data-intensive healthcare system.

These results indicate that researchers are enthusiastic about using blockchain technology in healthcare to improve security and privacy. Furthermore, the findings suggest that they rely on blockchain technology to secure data from IoMT devices and electronic health records, safeguard individuals' identities and privacy, and guard against data breaches.

In terms of productivity and collaborations, China and India were leaders in this field, but links between researchers were few. In comparison to medicine and social sciences, computer science and engineering were dominant in the field. Therefore, it is thought that it will be important to increase the cooperation between researchers and various disciplines due to the multidisciplinary nature of healthcare.

Limitations

This paper also has some limitations. The data were selected only from the Scopus database and focused solely on scholarly articles. Since the search query was limited, expanding the search criteria could potentially increase the number of studies. For future research, it would be beneficial to expand the data sources to include WoS and PubMed and to utilize more diverse research methods.

References

Abu-elezz, I., Hassan, A., Nazeemudeen, A., Househ, M., Abd-alrazaq, A. et al. (2020). The benefits and threats of blockchain technology in healthcare: A scoping review. International Journal of Medical Informatics 142: 104246. https://doi.org/https://doi.org/10.1016/j.ijmedinf.2020.104246.

Agbo, C. C. and Mahmoud, Q. H. (2020). Blockchain in healthcare. International Journal of Healthcare Information Systems and Informatics 15(3): 82–97. https://doi.org/10.4018/ijhisi.2020070105.

Ahmad, I., Abdullah, S. and Ahmed, A. (2023). IoT-fog-based healthcare 4.0 system using blockchain technology. The Journal of Supercomputing 79(4): 3999–4020. https://doi.org/10.1007/s11227-022-04788-7.

AlRyalat, S. A. S., Malkawi, L. W. and Momani, S. M. (2019). Comparing bibliometric analysis using PubMed, Scopus, and Web of science databases. J. Vis. Exp. (152). https://doi.org/10.3791/58494.

Arbabi, M. S., Lal, C., Veeraragavan, N. R., Marijan, D., Nygård, J. F. et al. (2022). A survey on blockchain for healthcare: challenges, benefits, and future directions. IEEE Communications Surveys & Tutorials 1–1. https://doi.org/10.1109/COMST.2022.3224644.

Aria, M. and Cuccurullo, C. (2017). bibliometrix: An R-tool for comprehensive science mapping analysis. Journal of Informetrics 11(4): 959–975. https://doi.org/https://doi.org/10.1016/j.joi.2017.08.007.

Banafa, A. (2022). Blockchain 4.0. OpenMindBBVA. Retrieved 01.04.2023 from https://www.bbvaopenmind.com/en/technology/digital-world/blockchain-4-0/.

Bazel, M. A., Mohammed, F., Alsabaiy, M. and Abualrejal, H. M. (2021). The role of internet of things, blockchain, artificial intelligence, and big data technologies in healthcare to prevent the spread of the COVID-19. 2021 International Conference on Innovation and Intelligence for Informatics, Computing, and Technologies (3ICT).

Börner, K., Chen, C. and Boyack, K. W. (2003). Visualizing knowledge domains. Annual Review of Information Science and Technology 37(1): 179–255.

Candereli, Z. O., Burmaoglu, S., Kidak, L. B. and Gungor, D. O. (2020). Applying blockchain technologies in healthcare: A scientometric analysis. pp. 69–92. In Multidimensional Perspectives and Global Analysis of Universal Health Coverage. IGI Global.

Cobo, M. J., López-Herrera, A. G., Herrera-Viedma, E. and Herrera, F. (2011). An approach for detecting, quantifying, and visualizing the evolution of a research field: A practical application to the Fuzzy Sets Theory field. Journal of Informetrics 5(1): 146–166. https://doi.org/https://doi.org/10.1016/j.joi.2010.10.002.

Cobo, M. J., López-Herrera, A. G., Herrera-Viedma, E. and Herrera, F. (2012). SciMAT: A new science mapping analysis software tool. Journal of the American Society for Information Science and Technology 63(8): 1609–1630. https://doi.org/10.1002/asi.22688.

Conway, D., Venkataraman, M., Laverick, D., Pelin, G., Hasselgren, A. et al. (2022). Blockchain in Healthcare Today 2022 Predictions. Blockchain in Healthcare Today. https://doi.org/10.30953/bhty.v5.194.

Dai, W., Tuo, S., Yu, L., Choo, K.-K. R., Zou, D. et al. (2022). HAPPS: A hidden attribute and privilege-protection data-sharing scheme with verifiability. IEEE Internet of Things Journal 9(24): 25538–25550. https://doi.org/10.1109/jiot.2022.3197708.

De Oliveira, M. T., Reis, L. H. A., Carrano, R. C., Seixas, F. L., Saade, D. C. M. et al. (2019). Towards a Blockchain-Based Secure Electronic Medical Record for Healthcare Applications. ICC 2019 - 2019 IEEE International Conference on Communications (ICC), China.

Dwivedi, A., Srivastava, G., Dhar, S. and Singh, R. (2019). A decentralized privacy-preserving healthcare blockchain for IoT. Sensors 19(2): 326. https://doi.org/10.3390/s19020326.

El Rifai, O., Biotteau, M., de Boissezon, X., Megdiche, I., Ravat, F. et al. (2020). Blockchain-based federated learning in medicine. Artificial Intelligence in Medicine: 18th International Conference on Artificial Intelligence in Medicine, AIME 2020, Minneapolis, MN, USA, August 25–28, 2020, Proceedings. Springer International Publishing.

Fang, J., Tu, W., Jiao, F. and Ci, Y. (2021). Research Hotspots Mining and Trend Analysis of Blockchain. Journal of Physics: Conference Series.

Farahat, I. S., Aladrousy, W., Elhoseny, M., Elmougy, S., Tolba, A. E. et al. (2022). Improving healthcare applications security using blockchain. Electronics 11(22): 3786. https://doi.org/10.3390/electronics11223786.

Farooq, K., Syed, H. J., Alqahtani, S. O., Nagmeldin, W., Ibrahim, A. O. et al. (2022). Blockchain federated learning for in-home health monitoring. Electronics 12(1): 136.

Galen, D., Brand, N., Boucherle, L., Davis, R., Do, N. et al. (2018). Blockchain for social impact: Moving beyond the hype. Center for Social Innovation, RippleWorks.

Goyal, A., Banerjee, A., Mulik, A., Chhabaria, Y., Tidke Dr, S. K. et al. (2021). Blockchain-based healthcare portal—a bibliometric analysis. Library Philosophy and Practice 1–15.

Guo, Y.-M., Huang, Z.-L., Guo, J., Guo, X.-R., Li, H. et al. (2021). A bibliometric analysis and visualization of blockchain. Future Generation Computer Systems 116: 316–332. https://doi.org/https://doi.org/10.1016/j.future.2020.10.023.

Haleem, A., Javaid, M., Singh, R. P., Suman, R., Rab, S. et al. (2021). Blockchain technology applications in healthcare: An overview. International Journal of Intelligent Networks 2: 130–139. https://doi.org/https://doi.org/10.1016/j.ijin.2021.09.005.

Hasan, H. R., Salah, K., Jayaraman, R., Yaqoob, I., Omar, M. et al. (2021). Blockchain-enabled telehealth services using smart contracts. IEEE Access 9: 151944–151959. https://doi.org/10.1109/access.2021.3126025.

Hasselgren, A., Kralevska, K., Gligoroski, D., Pedersen, S. A., Faxvaag, A. et al. (2020). Blockchain in healthcare and health sciences—A scoping review. International Journal of Medical Informatics 134: 104040. https://doi.org/https://doi.org/10.1016/j.ijmedinf.2019.104040.

Hiwale, M., Phanasalkar, S. and Kotecha, K. (2021). Using blockchain and distributed machine learning to manage decentralized but trustworthy disease data. Science & Technology Libraries 40(2): 190–213. https://doi.org/10.1080/0194262x.2020.1859046.

Hölbl, M., Kompara, M., Kamišalić, A. and Nemec Zlatolas, L. (2018). A systematic review of the use of blockchain in healthcare. Symmetry 10(10): 470. https://doi.org/10.3390/sym10100470.

Jain, A. and Tripathi, A. K. (2022). Blockchain enable smart contract based telehealth and medicines system. pp. 724–739. *In*: International Conference on Emerging Technologies in Computer Engineering: Cognitive Computing and Intelligent IoT. Springer International Publishing. https://doi.org/10.1007/978-3-031-07012-9_60.

Jillian Oderkirk and Slawomirski, L. (2020). Opportunities and challenges of blockchain technologies in health care. *In*: OECD Blockchain Policy Series.

Kara, O. and Kurutkan, M. N. (2021). Applications of blockchain technologies in health services: a general framework for policymakers. pp. 201–232. *In*: The Impact of Artificial Intelligence on Governance, Economics and Finance. Springer Nature Singapore. https://doi.org/10.1007/978-981-33-6811-8_11.

Kassab, M., Defranco, J., Malas, T., Laplante, P., Destefanis, G. et al. (2021). Exploring research in blockchain for healthcare and a roadmap for the future. IEEE Transactions on Emerging Topics in Computing 9(4): 1835–1852. https://doi.org/10.1109/tetc.2019.2936881.

Koştı, G., Burmaoğlu, S. and Kıdak, L. B. (2021). SAĞLIK 4.0: SANAYİDE ÖNGÖRÜLEN GELİŞİMİN SAĞLIK SEKTÖRÜNE YANSIMALARI. Hacettepe Sağlık İdaresi Dergisi 24(3): 483–506.

Kuhn, T. S. (2012). The Structure of Scientific Revolutions. 50th Anniversary. EE. UU.: The University of Chicago.

Kumar, R. and Tripathi, R. (2021). Scalable and secure access control policy for healthcare system using blockchain and enhanced Bell–LaPadula model. Journal of Ambient Intelligence and Humanized Computing 12: 2321–2338.

Kumar, R., Arjunaditya, Singh, D., Srinivasan, K. and Hu, Y.-C. (2022). AI-powered blockchain technology for public health: a contemporary review, open challenges, and future research directions. Healthcare 11(1): 81. https://doi.org/10.3390/healthcare11010081.

Kuzior, A. and Sira, M. (2022). A bibliometric analysis of blockchain technology research using VOSviewer. Sustainability 14(13): 8206. https://doi.org/10.3390/su14138206.

Levy, V. (2022). Global Life Sciences Outlook—Digitalization at Scale: Delivering on the Promise of Science. Deloitte: London, UK.

Liu, Y., Yu, W., Ai, Z., Xu, G., Zhao, L. et al. (2022). A Blockchain-empowered federated learning in healthcare-based cyber physical systems. IEEE Transactions on Network Science and Engineering 1–1. https://doi.org/10.1109/tnse.2022.3168025.

Mackey, T. K., Kuo, T.-T., Gummadi, B., Clauson, K. A., Church, G. et al. (2019). 'Fit-for-purpose?'—challenges and opportunities for applications of blockchain technology in the future of healthcare. BMC Medicine 17(1). https://doi.org/10.1186/s12916-019-1296-7.

Mahajan, H. B. (2022). Emergence of Healthcare 4.0 and Blockchain into secure cloud-based electronic health records systems: solutions, challenges, and future roadmap. Wireless Personal Communications 126(3): 2425–2446. https://doi.org/10.1007/s11277-022-09535-y.

Martínez, M. A., Cobo, M. J., Herrera, M. and Herrera-Viedma, E. (2015). Analyzing the scientific evolution of social work using science mapping. Research on Social Work Practice 25(2): 257–277. https://doi.org/10.1177/1049731514522101.

Mhamdi, H., Ayadi, M., Ksibi, A., Al-Rasheed, A., Soufiene, B. O. et al. (2022). SEMRAchain: A secure electronic medical record based on blockchain technology. Electronics 11(21): 3617.

Mongeon, P. and Paul-Hus, A. (2016). The journal coverage of Web of Science and Scopus: a comparative analysis. Scientometrics 106(1): 213–228. https://doi.org/10.1007/s11192-015-1765-5.

Nakamoto, S. (2008). Bitcoin: A peer-to-peer electronic cash system. Decentralized Business Review 21260.

Namasudra, S. and Deka, G. C. (2021). Applications of Blockchain in Healthcare. Springer.

Ng, W. Y., Tan, T.-E., Movva, P. V. H., Fang, A. H. S., Yeo, K.-K. et al. (2021). Blockchain applications in health care for COVID-19 and beyond: a systematic review. The Lancet Digital Health 3(12): e819–e829. https://doi.org/10.1016/s2589-7500(21)00210-7.

Prasad, B. and Ramachandram, S. (2022). Prevention and detection mechanisms for re-entrancy attack and king of ether throne attack for ethereum smart contracts. Ingénierie des Systèmes d'Information 27(5).

Prasad, V. K., Bhattacharya, P., Maru, D., Tanwar, S., Verma, A. et al. (2022). Federated learning for the internet-of-medical-things: a survey. Mathematics 11(1): 151. https://doi.org/10.3390/math11010151.

Razzaq, A., Mohsan, S. A. H., Ghayyur, S. A. K., Al-Kahtani, N., Alkahtani, H. K. et al. (2022). Blockchain in healthcare: a decentralized platform for digital health passport of COVID-19 based on vaccination and immunity certificates. Healthcare 10(12): 2453. https://doi.org/10.3390/healthcare10122453.

Rejeb, A., Treiblmaier, H., Rejeb, K. and Zailani, S. (2021). Blockchain research in healthcare: a bibliometric review and current research trends. Journal of Data, Information and Management 3(2): 109–124. https://doi.org/10.1007/s42488-021-00046-2.

Saeed, H., Malik, H., Bashir, U., Ahmad, A., Riaz, S. et al. (2022). Blockchain technology in healthcare: A systematic review. PLOS ONE 17(4): e0266462. https://doi.org/10.1371/journal.pone.0266462.

Scheibner, J., Ienca, M. and Vayena, E. (2022). Health data privacy through homomorphic encryption and distributed ledger computing: an ethical-legal qualitative expert assessment study. BMC Medical Ethics 23(1). https://doi.org/10.1186/s12910-022-00852-2.

Sharma, P., Jindal, R. and Borah, M. D. (2022). A review of smart contract-based platforms, applications, and challenges. Cluster Computing. https://doi.org/10.1007/s10586-021-03491-1.

Singh, V. K., Singh, P., Karmakar, M., Leta, J., Mayr, P. et al. (2021). The journal coverage of Web of Science, Scopus and Dimensions: A comparative analysis. Scientometrics 126(6): 5113–5142. https://doi.org/10.1007/s11192-021-03948-5.

Small, H. (1999). Visualizing science by citation mapping. Journal of the American Society for Information Science 50(9): 799–813.

Song, Y., Chen, X., Hao, T., Liu, Z., Lan, Z. et al. (2019). Exploring two decades of research on classroom dialogue by using bibliometric analysis. Computers & Education 137: 12–31. https://doi.org/https://doi.org/10.1016/j.compedu.2019.04.002.

Subic, A., Xiang, Y., Pai, S. and de La Serve, E. (2018). Blockchain and Industry 4.0: Why blockchain is at the heart of the Fourth Industrial Revolution and Digital Economy. Capgemini 2017.

Swan, M. (2015). Blockchain: Blueprint for a New Economy. " O'Reilly Media, Inc."

Taherdoost, H. (2023). Blockchain-based internet of medical things. Applied Sciences 13(3): 1287. https://doi.org/10.3390/app13031287.

Tripathi, M., Kumar, S., Sonker, S. K. and Babbar, P. (2018). Occurrence of author keywords and keywords plus in social sciences and humanities research: A preliminary study. COLLNET Journal of Scientometrics and Information Management 12(2): 215–232. https://doi.org/10.1080/09737766.2018.1436951.

ul Haque, A., Ghani, M. S. and Mahmood, T. (2020). Decentralized transfer learning using blockchain & IPFS for deep learning. 2020 International Conference on Information Networking (ICOIN).

van Eck, N. J. and Waltman, L. (2010). Software survey: VOSviewer, a computer program for bibliometric mapping. Scientometrics 84(2): 523–538. https://doi.org/10.1007/s11192-009-0146-3.

Visser, M., van Eck, N. J. and Waltman, L. (2021). Large-scale comparison of bibliographic data sources: Scopus, Web of Science, Dimensions, Crossref, and Microsoft Academic. Quantitative Science Studies 2(1): 20–41. https://doi.org/10.1162/qss_a_00112.

Wright, S. A. (2019, 4–6 Dec. 2019). Technical and Legal Challenges for Healthcare Blockchains and Smart Contracts. 2019 ITU Kaleidoscope: ICT for Health: Networks, Standards and Innovation (ITU K).

Yang, Y., Shi, R.-h., Li, K., Wu, Z., Wang, S. et al. (2022). Multiple access control scheme for EHRs combining edge computing with smart contracts. Future Generation Computer Systems 129: 453–463. https://doi.org/https://doi.org/10.1016/j.future.2021.11.002.

Zhang, R., George, A., Kim, J., Johnson, V., Ramesh, B. et al. (2019). Benefits of blockchain initiatives for value-based care: proposed framework. Journal of Medical Internet Research 21(9): e13595. https://doi.org/10.2196/13595.

Zhang, R., Xue, R. and Liu, L. (2021). Security and privacy for healthcare blockchains. IEEE Transactions on Services Computing 15(6): 3668–3686.

Zhuang, Y., Zhang, L., Gao, X., Shae, Z.-Y., Tsai, J. J. P. et al. (2022). Re-engineering a clinical trial management system using blockchain technology: system design, development, and case studies. Journal of Medical Internet Research 24(6): e36774. https://doi.org/10.2196/36774.

Zou, R., Lv, X. and Zhao, J. (2021). SPChain: Blockchain-based medical data sharing and privacy-preserving eHealth system. Information Processing & Management 58(4): 102604.

Chapter 13

Good Governance and Ethical Perspective of Block Chain Applications

Lethiwe Nzama[1,*] and *Oznur Tasdoken*[2]

13.1 Introduction

Information technology is a highly complex, rapidly evolving industry; computers have become smaller, faster, and more efficient and can quickly process large quantities of data (Nzama, 2021). Literature also indicates that technology disruptions highly influence the environment of IT consulting firms (Mofokeng et al., 2020). These AI applications resulting in disruptions have opened doors to various risks, in which companies must put measures in place to mitigate these risks (Mofokeng et al., 2020). Blockchain as a digital currency was developed by Satoshi Nakamoto in 2008. Blockchain has very different features from older technology applications, known as a new technology application beyond a digital currency when the ease of use is considered. Therefore, blockchain has increased its use in many areas with key features such as verifiability, transparency, privacy and accountability. As a result of the proliferation and rapid development of blockchain technology, its use has increased in many applications that increase social welfare (Chang et al., 2020; Srivastava et al., 2021; Upadhyay et al., 2021). Blockchain

[1] Department of Commercial Accounting, College of Business and Economics, University of Johannesburg, Johannesburg, South Africa.
[2] Dr. Independent Researcher, Turkey.
* Corresponding author: lethiwen@uj.ac.za

technology is used in the production process of many products (Ronaghi and Mosakhani, 2022), logistics sector (Kim and Laskowski, 2018; Koh et al., 2020), emission systems, increasing economic efficiency (Brynjolfsson et al., 2019), investment decisions (Blohm et al., 2022), the field of marketing (Kumar et al., 2019), the energy sector, and many different sectors.

The increase in social welfare and benefit expectations of individuals are also driving the pace of the development of blockchain technology. Thus, the blockchain shows mutual interaction between the use of technology and the speed of technology development. However, the increasing use of blockchain technology in many different areas, such as organizations, firms, industries, and the economy makes it a situation that must be considered in the risks and problems it creates. In other words, it makes it difficult to follow and determine the appropriate governance method. Therefore, it is necessary to carry out studies on the regulation of governance processes to eliminate these risks and problems.

The remainder of this chapter is organised as follows: Section 2 provides a brief literature review on the good governance and ethical perspective concerning blockchain applications. Section 3 covers the objective and research questions of the study. Section 4 provides brief information about the research process and qualitative method followed in conducting the study. Section 5 is a discussion, and Section 6 provides a conclusion and future research.

13.2 Related Review of Literature

Blockchain technology offers a new alternative to the organisation and storage of information in the system without any institution or organisation. In addition, considering the characteristics of blockchain technology, it is very different from current technological models. In this context, Blockchain technology is decentralized first. In other words, it is a database where transactions or electronic events between all participants in a decentralised system are recorded. Therefore, security problems such as theft or leakage of personal data are eliminated. Secondly, it facilitates the execution of transactions without the need for a third party or intermediary institution. Therefore, it increases the speed of approval of transactions that take place over a long period of time. Transacting institutions and individuals do not have to bear any cost, and the problem of information asymmetry is eliminated. Thirdly, it is a record of all transactions made through the blockchain. Therefore, it provides the opportunity to verify each of the transactions made (Yan et al., 2022). In this context, it eliminates accuracy and reliability problems between individuals or institutions. Fourthly, the use of smart contracts between organizations also facilitates many issues, such as cooperation and information exchange between companies.

The information entered once into the blockchain is recorded simultaneously by each node in the system. Therefore, this information cannot be deleted or changed. In other words, it can be said that all ledgers also protect the recorded information. Therefore, data security, transparency and integrity of all transactions made through the blockchain database are preserved. Therefore, protecting the security and transparency of data in blockchain technology also positively impacts corporate governance (Ronaghi and Mosakhani, 2022).

There are many discussions about the security of blockchain technology. One of these discussions is the 51% attack. In this attack, if a single node controls more than half (51%) of the processing power, the system belongs to a single user and becomes vulnerable. Blockchain is another attack, cyber attack that occurred in 2014, 2016 and 2018 (Zhao et al., 2016:3; Lin and Liao, 2017). Therefore, these attacks on the blockchain indicate that there are security problems in the database (Bassey, 2009; Chang et al., 2020).

System-related malfunctions occur in the blockchain database. These malfunctions are primarily caused by the modification of software to prevent cyber attacks. Secondly, node or network failures occur as a result of a software update. Thirdly, vulnerabilities occur in software due to updating smart contracts. In this context, the existence of these problems in the use of blockchain causes discussions by many users (Sultanik et al., 2022; Yan et al., 2022).

In the blockchain system, terms such as "Permissionless" or "permissioned" are used for users. Permissioned users are allowed to participate in the blockchain by authorized watchdogs rather than anonymous miners. Permissionless users can freely join the blockchain without any conditions. All information on Permissionless users registered on the blockchain is publicly accessible (Helliar et al., 2020; Liu et al., 2022). Therefore, there are differences between users. Therefore, it is held responsible with legal regulations and agreements prepared for immoral and unethical behavior of permissioned users (Hileman and Rauchs, 2017). However, the legal responsibilities do not apply to other blockchain users. This has led to the need for good governance in blockchain to ensure security, and prevent unethical behaviour of users and discrimination between users.

Appropriate governance frameworks need to be established to mitigate the risks that may arise from the use of blockchain. In other words, the blockchain governance process means making ethical responsibilities and legal regulations to solve the problems that may arise due to the software developers responsible for its development and use. Therefore, it is necessary to make arrangements on different issues such as various regulations and guidelines, industry standards, ethical codes, coordination and cooperation procedures among companies for the governance problems that may arise due to the use of blockchain. These regulations reduce the risks that may arise due to the use of blockchain in different areas. The reduction of these risks will also lead to the spread of blockchain applications in the public and private sectors.

Regulations to be made in the blockchain governance process should be created based on moral judgments, considering ethical values. However, it cannot be said that many researchers have reached a consensus on the criteria to be considered in the ethical decision-making process. This is because the ethical decision making process is expressed as individuals using their own moral judgments to decide whether a certain action or event is right or wrong (Lehner et al., 2022). In this context, the existence of different cultural practices in the society in which individuals live or the change in environmental conditions causes moral values and ethical judgments to change (Christopoulos et al., 2016). Therefore, the fact that individuals take into account their own moral judgments in the ethical decision-making process has made it difficult to define a common concept of ethics and moral values in all societies. In other words, it causes different ethical and moral judgments to emerge even in different socio-cultural environments or within the same social structure. This is because the moral preference of the individual in the decision process will be a reflection of his experiences and socio-cultural environment. This situation makes it difficult to evaluate a behavior appropriately by considering ethical judgments (Zollo et al., 2017; McManus, 2018). For this reason, the concept of ethics and moral judgments that will be universally accepted in the blockchain governance process gains importance.

The reliability, verifiability and transparency features of blockchain provide the same conditions to all users. In other words, it gives equal rights to all users. For this reason, the use of blockchain leads to establishing trust in society and reducing prejudice and discrimination. Thus, the key features of blockchain consider the human concerns that are part of society, such as reliability, reputation, and privacy. In this context, it can be said that the applications of blockchain reflect the basic features of ethical principles and moral judgments because blockchain causes institutions or individuals to provide the highest benefit without any conflict of interest. Therefore, the question that needs to be asked is what the ethical judgements and governance method should be in the use of the blockchain system by institutions or individuals. Therefore, it determines how blockchain is used as a reflection of the ethical and moral behavior of institutions and individuals.

Blockchain's decentralization, lack of empathy, and lack of moral and ethical values cause it to act rationally in the decision-making process. In other words, since there are no problems such as subjectivity and prejudice in the algorithm structure in blockchain applications, the findings have an objective quality. Therefore, all information obtained is open, accountable, transparent and reliable. This shows that ethical and moral values are successfully applied in the decision making process in blockchain implementation.

13.3 Research Objective and Questions

This part of the study explores the effects of ethical judgments and good governance practices in blockchain applications. The researchers prepared research questions by taking into account the studies carried out in the literature. In this context, two research questions guiding the process of conducting the research are proposed below:

- RQ 1: What are the ethical implications of applying blockchain applications?
- RQ 2: Are the users of blockchain applications applying good governance practices to mitigate ethical implications?

In answering the above-mentioned research questions, the Qualitative Evidence Systematic Review method (QES) has been adopted, and the next section provides more details on the methodology and techniques followed.

13.4 Methods, Techniques and Data Analysis

In this part of the study, data analysis, method and empirical findings will be discussed.

13.4.1 Determination of Criteria in Data Analysis

Certain criteria were taken into consideration for the evaluation of research questions. These criteria were determined using guidelines for literature review (Onwuegbuzie et al., 2012). In this context, the following criteria were evaluated for inclusion in this study:

- Articles written in English and peer-reviewed were used for evaluation.
- Articles published in a peer-reviewed journals between 2018–2022 were used. Therefore, current studies in the literature on the subject have been considered.

In the process of selecting the studies, journal papers and book chapters were not taken into consideration.

In line with the criteria determined above, articles were obtained from different databases by considering the research questions.

13.4.2 Method

In this study, the QES method is used by researchers. This method systematically combines results from primary qualitative research. In other words, it is the acquisition of qualitative data on the subject within the framework of research questions and the investigation of these data using various methods in the analysis process (Flemming and Noyes, 2021:1). Therefore, it facilitates the quick and easy determination of the studies carried out in the literature on the subject. The QES method allows a detailed interpretation of the findings obtained as a result of the research. It also helps to obtain studies on the subject in different disciplines (Flemming and Jones, 2020; Flemming and Noyes, 2021). In this regard, the QES method first systematically determines the results of the primary sources related to the research question. Secondly, it shows a summary of the literature on the subject within the framework of research questions guiding the conduct of the research. Therefore, it provides clear and transparent information about the implementation process and planning of the study.

Many methods have been developed for the application of the QES method. One of these methods is the Preferred Reporting Items for Systematic Reviews and Meta-Analysis (PRISMA) and Critical Appraisal Skills Program assessment tool (CAPS). The PRISMA method shows the decision flow chart used in the reporting phase of articles obtained from databases related to research questions (Moher et al., 2009; Booth, 2016; Chhillar and Aguilera, 2022). In other words, to reduce the risk of misreporting qualitative research. However, the PRISMA method is not used in the quality evaluation process of articles. For this reason, the CAPS method is used to eliminate this deficiency in the PRISMA method. In the CAPS method, the articles obtained by the PRISMA method are evaluated by considering certain questions. In this context, PRISMA and CAPS methods are used by researchers in this study. Therefore, all articles obtained from different databases related to the research topic were determined. Thus, the use of different methods enables more comprehensive and interpretative results to be determined from the findings obtained from the study.

The protocol used in qualitative studies was first proposed by Noblit and Hare (1988). In this protocol, a seven-stage path is followed in the analysis process. This protocol is shown in Table 13.1. This protocol also forms the basis of the use of the meta-ethnography method in qualitative studies in the literature (Lee et al., 2015). This protocol has been followed by many authors conducting qualitative research on different topics and used in their studies (McKenna-Plumley et al., 2020). In this context, this protocol is followed by the researchers in order to answer the research questions in the study. Therefore, we have followed a step-by-step guide

Table 13.1. Study procedure.

Step	Description
1	*Crafting a specific question(s)*
2	*Deciding on search databases*
3	*Developing serch items and retrieving articles*
4	*Screening articles for dubilicates and relevency*
5	*Quality appraisal for legibity*
6	*Appraisal for purposively selected qualitative studies*
7	*Final synthesis and presentation of findigs*

Source: Noblit and Hare (1988)

to reviewing the relevant literature within the framework of research questions. The guidelines used for this research are detailed below.

Step 1: Researchers need to prepare research questions on the topic to identify the sources for the study. In this context, research questions in our study were previously formulated as follows:

1) "What are the ethical implications of implementing blockchain applications?"
2) "Are users of blockchain applications implementing good governance practices to mitigate ethical outcomes?"

These research questions were determined to guide the investigation of the ethical considerations and governance practices related to the implementation of blockchain investigations.

Step 2: Harzing's Publish or Perish software was used by the researchers to facilitate access to the source data. The main purpose of using this software in the study is to analyze the articles obtained from *"Crossref, Google Scholar, Scopus, Web of Science, PubMed, Semantic Scholar and OenAlex databases"* (Harzing, 2011). In this context, the articles in the research were obtained from peer-reviewed journals and the most reliable and comprehensive databases in the international arena. Therefore, the studies obtained from the most cited databases were used in the study.

Steps 3 and 4: Search terms in databases were created by considering the critical concepts in the research questions. In this context, search terms were used to find articles suitable for the questions of the study.

Step 5: An evaluation of the selected articles is carried out in order to make a quality assessment of the articles obtained from the research and to check their compliance with the specified criteria. The CAPS method was used for this evaluation. In the CAPS method, various questions are asked in order to evaluate whether the articles obtained from different databases are suitable for the research method and structure (Long et al., 2020). The CAPS method research questions are shown in Table 4. Therefore, while the CAPS method is used in the evaluation process of the articles in the study, the PRISMA method is used to determine the articles related to the subject. Therefore, while the CAPS method is used in the evaluation process of the articles in the study, the PRISMA method is used to identify the relevant articles.

Stages 6 and 7 Step: The findings were obtained using PRISMA and CAPS methods, which are qualitative research methods selected in accordance with the purpose of the study.

Researchers use certain methods in the process of evaluating articles. Therefore, the use of these methods enables many researchers from different fields to make rational decisions while working on similar topics. In addition, with the use of this method, the effects of the prejudices of the researchers in the evaluation process are eliminated. In other words, these methods allow reliable and transparent findings to be obtained from research results.

13.4.3 Data Analysis

In our study, studies on the subject are collected from different databases in a logical and organized manner. The PRISMA method to be applied for editing the articles is shown in Figure 13.1 below. This structure requires researchers to complete specific criteria, for example describing how articles are defined, evaluated, and synthesized (Moher et al., 2015).

Within the framework of the research questions in the study, the previously mentioned criteria were used to determine the articles that are suitable for the structure of the study. In this context, articles were identified from different databases. The number of articles identified in the initial identification is 175 (n = 175), and the number of articles identified through other sources is 270 (n = 160+110). Although there are many studies on blockchain in the literature, the first step is determining the number of articles on the subject as 445. The researchers read the abstracts of these 445 articles. It was decided that 407 of these articles were not relevant to the topic. Firstly, the reason for this situation is that the authors did not clearly determine the research approach in the articles. Secondly, the majority of the articles are non-technical articles on blockchain governance. In other words, it has been determined that there are technical studies related to the blockchain. Thirdly, the same articles from different databases were not considered. In this context, articles in different databases related to blockchain but unrelated to the research topic were removed. Fourthly, all of the remaining 38 articles were read by the researchers. It was decided

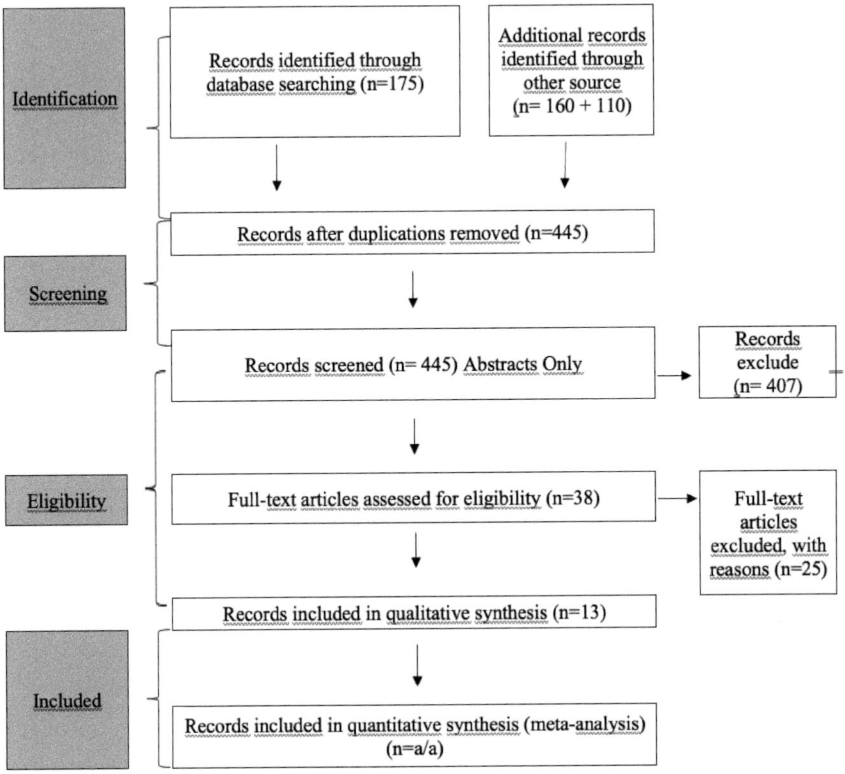

Figure 13.1. PRISMA. Source: Moher et al. (2009).

that 25 of these articles were unrelated to the research questions. Then, the number of articles determined to be suitable for the purpose of the study and included in the qualitative synthesis was determined as 13 (n = 13). These articles were evaluated by the researchers using the CASP method.

The 13 articles obtained by PRISMA were scored according to their ability to answer the CASP scorer's ten (10) critical questions about the quality (Long et al., 2020). These questions are shown in Table 13.2, and the evaluation results of the articles are shown in Table 13.4. In our evaluation, yes = 1, no = 0 and Can not tell = 0.5 were considered.

Considering the findings obtained as a result of the evaluation, four (4) studies were not included in the study because they did not meet the necessary criteria. For this reason, the questions in Table 4 were taken into consideration to evaluate the strengths and weaknesses of the remaining nine (9) articles at the end of the evaluation. In this evaluation phase, all articles with a quality score of less than ten were excluded, while all articles with a quality score of more than ten were included in the final analysis of the study. In other words, the articles that the researchers

Table 13.2. Inclusion/exclusion questions.

Questions	Appraisal Question
Q-1	Clear Research Question
Q-2	Qual - Suitable Method
Q-3	Research Design Suitable
Q-4	Sampling Strategy Suitable/Quality studies
Q-5	Data Collection Strategy Suitable
Q-6	Researcher Role Condideration
Q-7	Ethical Consideration
Q-8	Data Analysis Rigor
Q-9	Clear Statement of Findings
Q-10	Research Value Proposition

Source: Long et al. (2020). Some questions were adapted to suit the purpose of the study.

considered to fulfil all of the above-mentioned questions were taken into consideration. Thus, studies on the subject have been determined in the literature within the framework of research questions. In this context, the researchers evaluation results of 13 articles are shown in Table 13.3.

13.4.4 Empirical Findings

The questions used to evaluate the strengths and weaknesses of the nine (9) articles included in the analysis findings, and the CASP method are shown in Table 13.4 and the evaluation results in Table 13.5.

Evaluation results of 9 articles obtained by the CAPS method were made for each article one by one. Therefore, each article is reported in detail.

When the findings obtained as a result of the CAPS method analysis are taken into consideration, the articles evaluated by the researchers in the studies are clearly stated in the articles with the purpose of the research or the research questions. Secondly, studies on the subject have generally been obtained by researchers from the web of science, Google Scholar, and Semantic Scholar databases. In other words, it can be said that the majority of the articles are obtained from these databases due to a large number of journals in these databases and the ease of access to current articles. Thirdly, the articles obtained from these databases were incorporated into their work by the researchers after a rigorous research process. Fourthly, the researchers used both the method of qualitative synthesis and different methods of analysis in their work. Thus, the qualitative synthesis methods followed in the process of determining the articles allowed the researchers to act rationally. In addition, research questions suitable for the structure of the research and appropriate articles were determined and evaluated

Table 13.3. Inclusion/exclusion report.

Authors	Q-1	Q-2	Q-3	Q-4	Q-5	Q-6	Q-7	Q-8	Q-9	Q-10	Rating	Decision
Tang et al. (2019)	1	1	1	1	1	1	1	1	1	1	10	include
Chang et al. (2020)	1	1	1	1	1	1	1	1	1	1	10	included
Koh et al. (2020)	0	0	1	0	0	1	1	0	1	1	5	not included
De Filippi et al. (2020)	1	1	1	1	1	1	1	1	1	1	10	not included
Daluwathumullagamage and Sims (2020)	1	1	1	1	1	1	1	1	1	1	10	include
Hooper and Holtbrügge (2020)	1	1	1	1	1	1	1	1	1	1	10	include
Srivastava et al. (2021)	1	1	1	1	0	1	1	0	1	1	8	not included
Ronaghi and Mosakhani (2022)	1	1	1	1	1	1	1	1	1	1	10	included
Upadhyay et al. (2021)	1	1	1	1	1	1	1	1	1	1	10	include
Heckler and Kim (2022)	0	0	1	1	0	1	0,5	0	1	1	5,5	not included
"Liu et al. (2022)"	1	1	1	1	1	1	1	1	1	1	10	include
"Tan et al. (2022)"	1	1	1	1	1	1	1	1	1	1	10	include
"Alkhateeb et al. (2022)"	1	1	1	1	1	1	1	1	1	1	10	include

Source: Prepared by the authors.

Table 13.4. CAPS method research questions.

	Appraisal Question
Q-1	*Did the reivew address a clearly focused question?*
Q-2	*Did the autors look at the right type of papers?*
Q-3	*Do you think all the the important, relevent studies were included?*
Q-4	*Did the review authors do enough to assess the quality of the included studies?*
Q-5	*if the results of the review have been comined, ws it reasonable to do so?*
Q-6	*What are the overal results of the review?*
Q-7	*How precise are the results?*
Q-8	*Was the data analysis reported suffiently in a detailed manner?*
Q-9	*Can the results be applied to the local population?*
Q-10	*Where all important outcome considered?*

Source: Long et al. (2020). Some questions were adapted to suit the purpose of the study.

Table 13.5. CASP – included articles appraisal report.

Articles	Q-1	Q-2	Q-3	Q-4	Q-5	Q-6	Q-7	Q-8	Q-9	Q-10
"Chang et al. (2020)"	1	1	1	0,5	1	1	1	1	1	Web of Science
"Tang et al. (2019)"	1	1	1	1	1	1	1	1	1	Google Scholar
"Hooper and Holtbrügge (2020)"	1	1	1	1	1	1	1	1	1	Google Scholar
"Daluwathumullagamage and Sims (2020)"	1	1	1	1	0	1	0	1	0	Semantic Scholar
"Upadhyay et al. (2021)"	1	1	1	1	1	1	1	1	1	Web of Science
"Liu et al. (2022)"	1	1	1	1	1	1	0,5	1	1	Web of Science
"Tan et al. (2022)"	1	1	1	1	1	1	1	1	1	Web of Science
"Alkhateeb et al. (2022)"	1	1	1	1	1	1	1	1	1	Semantic Scholar
"Ronaghi and Mosakhani (2022)"	1	1	1	1	1	1	1	1	1	Web of Science

Source: Prepared by the authors.

with different methods. Fifthly, the findings in these papers have generally been reported in detail by researchers. In this context, it can be said that the articles that are most suitable for the research questions and related to the subject in the literature have been discussed and evaluated. Sixthly, the use of blockchain applications in many different areas causes many problems. For this reason, researchers have made various suggestions to solve the problems.

Considering the studies in the literature, we have discussed the use of blockchain applications in different areas in general. However, no detailed research has been done on how the regulations regarding ethical judgments and governance methods should be considered in the process. Therefore, it can be said that in the evaluation process of ethics and governance methods in blockchain applications, ethical theories and concepts related to governance are generally not taken into account in current research. Therefore, existing research on the governance practices of Blockchain needs to be further developed. In addition, the fact that blockchain technology is changing due to its continuous development means that it needs to be regularly updated in its governance regulations.

13.5 Discussion

In this study, the researchers investigated the concept of ethics and governance practices within the framework of the research questions we created by considering blockchain technology. While conducting this research, the studies conducted between 2018–2022 were examined. During the review, articles on governance and ethical judgments were written with rigorous content analysis. Therefore, it is ensured that the findings obtained within the framework of a systematic review are reported transparently. For this reason, the protocol steps were prepared by the researchers by taking the Noblit and Hare (1988) study into consideration. Thus, the problems encountered in the determination of the data set in qualitative researches have been eliminated. However, there is a problem of poor reporting of the findings of the evaluation process. The researchers used PRISMA and CAPS methods for these problems. The use of the PRISMA method demonstrates the protocol process required for transparent reporting of a systematic review. On the other hand, the use of the CAPS method eliminated the problem of often underreporting important information about this study. Therefore, reliable and transparent results were obtained within the framework of the findings.

Considering the studies on the subject, firstly, there is no common practice for solving the problems related to the governance impact of blockchain applications in commercial activities. Therefore, governance practices in different areas of blockchain application need to be prepared by considering various policies. These policies should take into account the characteristics specific to each area. Secondly, studies should be conducted on the legal validity of smart contracts, which form the basis of global trade. In this context, various regulations need to be made for the digital signatures of individuals and institutions to have legal validity in using smart contracts. The validity of digital signatures in smart contracts will also give these contracts a legal character. Thirdly, the application of blockchain is used by many individuals and institutions on a global scale. In other words, it will be very difficult to implement the rules or legally sanctioned decisions, since blockchain applications are the universal database where global borders disappear. Because the legal rules of each country are different, it will cause many problems in the application of blockchain. For this reason, blockchain legal regulations should provide solutions by taking into account national legislation and global governance regulations. Fourthly, the lack of a centralised structure in blockchain eliminates the existence of an institution to be consulted to solve problems that may arise in the future. Therefore, it causes users to be responsible for everything in the face of problems that may be encountered. For this reason, the blockchain recording of documents approved by an official institution in smart contracts used in global trade will help to create an environment of trust in transactions.

The information entered in the blockchain cannot be changed. In this context, while blockchain is an advantage because it eliminates the problems of reliability and transparency in use, it also causes disadvantages. Because, each transaction in the blockchain can be verified, it is difficult to verify whether the inputs used during the transaction are real (Dey, 2019). For example, false information about a person's or organisation's performance may be entered into the system to discredit them. Therefore, if the registration of the information is correct, the system will recognise it as absolutely correct. Since the information cannot be changed in the blockchain system, it will cause the incorrect information to be continuously registered in the system. In this framework, in order to eliminate these problems in the system, firstly, it is necessary to prepare legal regulations and governance rules that may be problematic from the events that may arise due to the use of blockchain. Secondly, using artificial intelligence, the information entered into the blockchain can be checked for accuracy by comparing it with other information. Therefore, if there are inaccuracies or inconsistencies in the information entered into the system, this node can be indicated as untrustworthy in the blockchain. Thirdly, in a blockchain-based system, features such as company information, product information and transaction time related to sellers can be recorded (Zhou et al., 2021; UTEMIS, 2023). Thus, the information in the system will be checked through many different channels and the reliability of the information content will be ensured.

13.6 Conclusion and Future Research

This study is expected to guide future studies to identify articles on ethical judgements and governance practices in blockchain applications and to summarize them reliably.

In other words, blockchain is becoming important for understanding the state of governance regulations in academic and industrial applications. It therefore helps the study to have information about current studies on the subject for future researchers. In other words, it is important to understand governance arrangements in academic and industrial applications of blockchain technology. For this reason, the study helps future researchers to have information about current studies on the subject.

In future studies on blockchain, researchers are expected to consider the shortcomings of the topics discussed below. Firstly, studies have poorly reported solutions to problems or governance arrangements to be made during blockchain implementations. This situation can be said to cause a lack of research in studies. Hence, governance arrangements in blockchain implementation need to be addressed in more detail. Secondly, it is necessary to determine legal regulations to eliminate the risks arising from the use of blockchain technology. Thus, it will cause individuals and institutions to take responsibility for their unethical and immoral behaviour arising from the use of blockchain. This also provides assurance to organisations and individuals to protect them from risks. Thirdly, there is no consensus on how good governance should be. Fourthly, it can be said that legal responsibilities and practices in the regulation of governance problems in blockchain applications are neglected in the academic literature. Fifthly, different types of blockchain users should be taken into account in studies in general. Because, specifying which type of user the researchers evaluated in the study will eliminate the ambiguity of non-professional readers. Sixthly, empirical studies on ethics and governance issues in blockchain applications can also be conducted using surveys or different data sets.

In this study, the new version of the PRISMA method was not considered in the preparation process. Therefore, studies can be expanded by future researchers using the newly developed version of the PRISMA method, considering current articles. In this context, the results obtained in this study are a guide for future studies.

References

Alkhateeb, A., Catal, C., Kar, G. and Mishra, A. (2022). Hybrid blockchain platforms for the internet of things (IoT): A systematic literature review. A Systematic Literature Review 22: 1–19.

Bassey, R. E. (2009). A Survey of attacks on ethereum smart contracts (SoK). pp. 164–186. In Principles of Security and Trust.

Blohm, I., Antretter, T., Sirén, C., Grichnik, D., Wincent, J. et al. (2022). It's a Peoples Game, Isn't It?! A comparison between the investment returns of business angels and machine learning algorithms. Entrepreneurship: Theory and Practice 46(4): 1054–1091. https://doi.org/10.1177/1042258720945206.

Booth, A. (2016). Searching for qualitative research for inclusion in systematic reviews: A structured methodological review. Systematic Reviews 5(1): 1–23. https://doi.org/10.1186/s13643-016-0249-x.

Brynjolfsson, E., Hui, X. and Liu, M. (2019). Does machine translation affect international trade? Evidence from a large digital platform. In Management Science Ahead of Print (No. 24917).

Chang, V., Baudier, P., Zhang, H., Xu, Q., Zhang, J. et al. (2020). How Blockchain can impact financial services—The overview, challenges and recommendations from expert interviewees. Technological Forecasting and Social Change 158(May): 120166. https://doi.org/10.1016/j.techfore.2020.120166.

Chhillar, D. and Aguilera, R. V. (2022). An Eye for Artificial Intelligence: Insights Into the Governance of Artificial Intelligence and Vision for Future. https://doi.org/10.1177/00076503221080959.

Christopoulos, G. I., Liu, X. X. and Hong, Y. yi. (2016). Toward an understanding of dynamic moral decision making: model-free and model-based learning. Journal of Business Ethics 144(4): 699–715. https://doi.org/10.1007/s10551-016-3058-1.

Daluwathumullagamage, D. J. and Sims, A. (2020). Blockchain-enabled corporate governance and regulation. International Journal of Financial Studies 8(2): 1–41. https://doi.org/10.3390/ijfs8020036.

De Filippi, P., Mannan, M. and Reijers, W. (2020). Blockchain as a confidence machine: The problem of trust & challenges of governance. Technology in Society 62(May): 101284. https://doi.org/10.1016/j.techsoc.2020.101284.

Dey, S. (2019). Securing Majority-Attack in Blockchain Using Machine Learning and Algorithmic Game Theory: A Proof of Work. In 10th Computer Science and Electronic Engineering Conference, CEEC 2018 - Proceedings. IEEE. https://doi.org/10.1109/CEEC.2018.8674185.

Flemming, K. and Jones, L. V. 2020. Using evidence from systematic reviews. pp. 109–125. *In*: Craig, J. V. and Dowding, D. (eds.). Evidence Based Practice in Nursing.

Flemming, K. and Noyes, J. (2021). Qualitative evidence synthesis: where are we at? International Journal of Qualitative Methods 20: 1–13. https://doi.rg/10.1177/1609406921993276.

Harzing, A.-W. (2011). The Publish or Perish Book. In Journal of the American Society for Information Science and Technology (Vol. 62, Issue 7). Melbourne: Tarma Software Research Pty Limited. https://doi.org/10.1002/asi.21535.

Heckler, N. and Kim, Y. (2022). Crypto-governance: the ethical implications of blockchain in public service. Public Integrity 24(1): 66–81. https://doi.org/10.1080/10999922.2020.1848106.

Helliar, C. V., Crawford, L., Rocca, L., Teodori, C., Veneziani, M. et al. (2020). Permissionless and permissioned blockchain diffusion. International Journal of Information Management 54(October 2019): 102136. https://doi.org/10.1016/j.ijinfomgt.2020.102136.

Hileman, G. and Rauchs, M. (2017). Global blockchain benchmarking study. In SSRN Electronic Journal. https://doi.org/10.2139/ssrn.3040224.

Hooper, A. and Holtbrügge, D. (2020). Blockchain technology in international business: changing the agenda for global governance. Review of International Business and Strategy 30(2): 183–200. https://doi.org/10.1108/RIBS-06-2019-0078.

Kim, H. M. and Laskowski, M. (2018). Toward an ontology-driven blockchain design for supply-chain provenance. Intelligent Systems in Accounting, Finance and Management 25(1): 18–27. https://doi.org/10.1002/isaf.1424.

Koh, L., Dolgui, A. and Sarkis, J. (2020). Blockchain in transport and logistics–paradigms and transitions. International Journal of Production Research 58(7): 2054–2062. https://doi.org/10.1080/00207543.2020.1736428.

Kumar, V., Rajan, B., Venkatesan, R. and Lecinski, J. (2019). Understanding the role of artificial intelligence in personalized engagement marketing. California Management Review 61(4): 135–155. https://doi.org/10.1177/0008125619859317.

Lee, R., Hart, R., Watson, R. and Rapley, T. (2015). Qualitative synthesis in practice: some pragmatics of meta-ethnography. Qualitative Research 15(3): 334–350. https://doi.org/10.1177/1468794114524221.

Lehner, O. M., Ittonen, K., Silvola, H., Ström, E., Wührleitner, A. et al. (2022). Artificial intelligence based decision-making in accounting and auditing: ethical challenges and normative thinking. Accounting, Auditing and Accountability Journal 35(9): 109–135. https://doi.org/10.1108/AAAJ-09-2020-4934.

Lin, I. C. and Liao, T. C. (2017). A survey of blockchain security issues and challenges. International Journal of Network Security 19(5): 653–659. https://doi.org/10.6633/IJNS.201709.19(5).01.

Liu, Y., Lu, Q., Yu, G., Paik, H. Y., Zhu, L. et al. (2022). Defining blockchain governance principles: A comprehensive framework. Information Systems 109: 102090. https://doi.org/10.1016/j.is.2022.102090.

Long, H. A., French, D. P. and Brooks, J. M. (2020). Optimising the value of the critical appraisal skills programme (CASP) tool for quality appraisal in qualitative evidence synthesis. Research Methods in Medicine & Health Sciences 1(1): 31–42. https://doi.org/10.1177/2632084320947559.

McKenna-Plumley, P. E., Groarke, J. M., Turner, R. N. and Yang, K. (2020). Experiences of loneliness: a study protocol for a systematic review and thematic synthesis of qualitative literature. Systematic Reviews 9(1): 1–8. https://doi.org/10.1186/s13643-020-01544-x.

McManus, J. (2018). Hubris and unethical decision making: the tragedy of the uncommon. Journal of Business Ethics 149(1): 169–185. https://doi.org/10.1007/s10551-016-3087-9.

Mofokeng, M. J., Nzama, L. L. and Mamaile, L. J. (2020). Risks Caused by Disrupted Forces in Gauteng Information Technology Consulting Firms. The 5th Annual International Conference on Public Administration and Development Alternatives 07–09 October 2020, Virtual Conference.

Moher, D., Liberati, A., Tetzlaff, J. and Altman, D. G. (2009). Preferred reporting ıtems for systematic reviews and meta-analyses: The PRISMA statement. Annals of Internal Medicine 151(4): 264–269.

Moher, D., Shamseer, L., Clarke, M., Ghersi, D., Liberati, A. et al. (2015). Preferred reporting items for systematic review and meta-analysis protocols (prisma-p) 2015 statement. Japanese Pharmacology and Therapeutics 4(1): 1–9.

Nakamoto, S. (2008). Bitcoin: A Peer-to-Peer Electronic Cash System. SSRN Electronic Journal. https://doi.org/10.2139/ssrn.3977007.

Noblit, G. W. and Hare, R. D. (1988). Synthesizing Qualitative Studies. Sage Publications.

Nzama, L. (2021). Enteprise Resource Planning (ERP) upgrades in South African higher education ınstitutions: pros, cons and financial efficacy. Journal of Global Business and Technology 2021 Mar 1; 17(1): 98–109.

Onwuegbuzie, A. J., Leech, N. L. and Collins, K. M. T. (2012). Qualitative analysis techniques for the review of the literature. Qualitative Report 17(28): 1–28. https://doi.org/10.46743/2160-3715/2012.1754.

Ronaghi, M. H. and Mosakhani, M. (2022). The effects of blockchain technology adoption on business ethics and social sustainability: evidence from the Middle East. Environment, Development and Sustainability 24(5): 6834–6859. https://doi.org/10.1007/s10668-021-01729-x.

Srivastava, V., Mahara, T. and Yadav, P. (2021). An analysis of the ethical challenges of blockchain-enabled E-healthcare applications in 6G networks. International Journal of Cognitive Computing in Engineering 2(April): 171–179. https://doi.org/10.1016/j.ijcce.2021.10.002.

Sultanik, E., Remie, A., Manzano, F., Brunson, T., Moelius, S. et al. (2022). Are Blockchains Decentralized?Unintended Centralities in Distributed Ledgers (Issue June). https://www.trailofbits.com.

Tan, E., Mahula, S. and Crompvoets, J. (2022). Blockchain governance in the public sector: A conceptual framework for public management. Government Information Quarterly 39(1): 101625. https://doi.org/10.1016/j.giq.2021.101625.

Tang, Y., Xiong, J., Becerril-Arreola, R. and Iyer, L. (2019). Ethics of blockchain: A framework of technology, applications, impacts, and research directions. Information Technology and People 33(2): 602–632. https://doi.org/10.1108/ITP-10-2018-0491.

Upadhyay, A., Mukhuty, S., Kumar, V. and Kazancoglu, Y. (2021). Blockchain technology and the circular economy: Implications for sustainability and social responsibility. Journal of Cleaner Production 293: 126130. https://doi.org/10.1016/j.jclepro.2021.126130.

UTEMIS. Accessed: Dec. 2023. [Online]. Available: https://www. utemis.com.

Yan, C., Zhang, C., Lu, Z., Wang, Z., Liu, Y. et al. (2022). Blockchain abnormal behavior awareness methods: a survey. Cybersecurity 5: 1–27. https://doi.org/10.1186/s42400-021-00107-4.

Zhao, J. L., Fan, S. and Yan, J. (2016). Overview of business innovations and research opportunities in blockchain and introduction to the special issue. Financial Innovation 2(1): 1–7. https://doi.org/10.1186/s40854-016-0049-2.

Zhou, Z., Wang, M., Yang, C., Fu, Z., Sun, X. et al. (2021). Blockchain-based decentralized reputation system in E-commerce environment. Future Generation Computer Systems 124: 155–167. https://doi.org/10.1016/j.future.2021.05.035.

Zollo, L., Pellegrini, M. M. and Ciappei, C. (2017). What Sparks Ethical Decision Making? The ınterplay between moral ıntuition and moral reasoning: lessons from the scholastic doctrine. Journal of Business Ethics 145(4): 681–700. https://doi.org/10.1007/s10551-016-3221-8.

Chapter 14
Blockchain Application in Government
The Crisis of the State's Legitimacy and the Reproduction of Legitimacy

Derya Aktaş

14.1 Introduction

Technology is critical in the fulfillment of many services such as education, security, health, and many other functions of the state. By influencing the mode of production, technology can shape employment policies and increase welfare. Technology becomes a tool in ensuring the continuity of the state with its "regulatory, supervisory, interventionist" roles, in setting rules within the borders of the state, implementing its regulations and restoring order when the rules are broken (Erat and Arap, 2016; Türkcan, 1981). Ensuring continuity stems from the belief that the rules are legitimate (correct and must be obeyed). The understanding of legitimacy changes according to the transformation in social and economic structure. Technological developments and changes in production-labor relations are effective in the change of social and economic structure, which in turn need to sustain legitimacy in this transformed context. For example, the agricultural revolution, which is one of the three essential revolutions in

Research Assistant, Department of Political Science and Public Administration, İzmir Katip Çelebi University, İzmir, Turkey.
Email: derya.aktas@ikcu.edu.tr

the history of humanity, created radical transformations in the social and economic structure and revealed new forms of administration. In the 18th century, a new social and economic structure was introduced with the Industrial Revolution. In this process, while the capitalist society replaced the feudal society, the feudal state structure was transformed into the formation of nation states. As explained by Schumpeter's concept of "*creative destruction*", the technological developments eliminated existing structures and led to the emergence of new structures. "*Creative destructions*" confront the previous social, political, cultural and economic structure with change (Schumpeter, 2003). There have been developments such as factory production, the separation of home and workplace, migration from rural to urban, intensified division of labor, the growth of cities and sophisticated services in bureaucratic administration. This process has led to the formation of a modern bureaucracy in which centrality and hierarchy come to the fore. Bureaucracy, which is the pure type of legal-rational authority put by Weber that is still valid today, attaches great importance to the continuity of the state and its function of providing order. The organization and management model described is based on predetermined rules, ensuring continuity, and having jurisdictions determined by law. It operates in a hierarchial structure and employs a workfoce with specific skills gained through training. Additionally, this model relies on written records to facilitate its functioning (Weber, 1946). As it can be understood from the specified features, central and restrictive elements are dominant in the continuity and order of the nation-state. In the 21st century, with the technological developments that have come, the central and restrictive bureaucratic elements are desired to be removed. In such a context blockchain technology has emerged that can take the role of the state as an intermediary (De Filippi et al., 2020). This almost revolutionary technology seems to be one of "creative destructive" moments of the 21st century.

Nowadays, technology is developing rapidly and states are in technological competition with each other in order to sustain economic development and take the lead in global competition. For this reason, governments show great interest in technology research. Blockchain technology, which is one of these technologies, is being researched or implemented by many countries. For example, European Blockchain Partnership with 29 members (*Germany, Belgium, France, Bulgaria, Estonia, Austria, Ireland, Spain, Lithuania, Finland, Luxembourg, Portugal, Poland, Czech Republic, Slovakia, Slovenia, Sweden, Latvia, Netherlands, Malta, Norway, Greece, Romania, Denmark, Cyprus, Italy, Liechtenstein, Hungary, Croatia*) was established to develop an EU strategy on blockchain and blockchain infrastructure to be used in public services (europa.eu, 2022). The mentioned countries have made certain strides in blockchain technology in their public administration systems. Estonia, which provides almost all of its public services as e-services (99% and 24 hours a day), has started to use blockchain technology since 2008. The areas of use in Estonia, which is the first to use blockchain technology, are: *"Registry (Healthcare, Property, Business, Succession), Digital Court System, Surveillance/Tracking Information System, Official State Announcements, State Gazette"* (https://e-estonia.com, 2023). Commissioner for the Digital Economy and Society Mariya Gabriel's statement on blockchain points out how blockchain technology will be used extensively in the future (europa.eu, 2022): *"In the future, all public services will use blockchain technology. Blockchain is a great opportunity for Europe and Member States to rethink their information systems."*

Apart from 29 countries, blockchain finds application in all continents. Various blockchain applications are visible in the United States, United Arab Emirates, China and even some African countries (Berryhill et al., 2018; Killmeyer et al., 2017). The Blockchain Government Market Size and Forecast Report also shows the growing interest in blockchain technology. Blockchain Government Market size was valued at USD 153.9 Million in 2021 and is estimated to reach USD 18.15 Billion by 2030, with a growth of 81.12% from 2022 to 2030 (Verified Market Research, 2022).

This study examines how blockchain technology, which has the potential to remove the central and limiting elements of bureaucracy and expressed as *"disruptive technology"* (Atzori, 2017), is and can be used as a tool to ensure the legitimacy of the state. In this direction, the web pages of states that implement blockchain, the Organization for Economic Co-operation and Development's (OECD) and European Union's (EU) blockchain documents are analyzed. The analysis carried out within the scope of this study is on the basis of the declared documents. There may be differences between the declared projects and the realized projects. The extent to which the declared projects have been implemented and the outcomes they have yielded have not been fully revealed yet. The following sections will cover the issues: possible functions of technology in the provision of legitimacy and governmental blockchain applications. The intense interest of states in this technology, which can limit the powers of the nation-state, is explained through blockchain applications and the concept of legitimacy.

14.2 The Role of Technology in Ensuring State Legitimacy and Blockchain

Legitimacy, as a factor that ensures the continuity of the state, is as old as the existence of government and emerges with varying appearances (based on God/based on mind; based on loyalty/based on laws-rational) in different historical epochs. No matter how it arises, the understanding of legitimacy changes with the change of existing structures. With the Enlightenment, the ground of legitimacy of the state shifted to science.

Science and technology have begun to be used as a tool in arranging and explaining both the institutional structure and policies of the state. The success of science in the military and economy has enabled states to use science and technology in the rational policy-making process. Thus, the state is legitimized by rational scientific methods (Erat and Arap, 2016; Poulantzas, 2006). The decisive role of the military, economic and legitimizing functions of technology have led to the widespread use of technology in state policies and institutions (Erat and Arap, 2016). Technology, development, and competition, among other factors are influenced by the accumulation of capital in accordance with the state's adopted understanding of science (Arap and Erat, 2017). This understanding can both shape perspectives and serve as a tool for the state's control and surveillance.

Technology can be used in the regulatory, supervisory and intervening roles of the state in a structure that increasingly encompasses the individual and society. On the other hand, records of public institutions between citizen-citizen, citizens and the state (public service delivery) are essential in transactions. This strengthens the intermediary role of the "reliable" state. The state provides this trust with the data processing, distribution and reproduction of the bureaucracy (Şat, 2019). However, the central, hierarchical and limiting aspects of bureaucracy are often criticized. Technology is also used to address these problem areas.

While technology has the function of legitimizing the state, on the other hand, it causes economic and political changes with its rapid development. A crisis of legitimacy arises when the state cannot achieve economic and political rationalization (Habermas, 1992). In addition to globalization, developments in information and communication technologies bring economic, social and political transformation (Kaya-Bensghir, 1996). The state is also a part of this change. Along with technological developments, alterations in the capital accumulation regime change the way the state intervenes in the economy. These also lead to changes in the administrative, institutional and legal structure. For example, after the 1929 economic crisis, the fordist accumulation regime and the welfare state understanding began to dominate. By the mid-1970s on the other hand the energy crisis that occurred in the mid-1970s brought the crisis of the fordist accumulation regime. In the 1980s, the minimal state approach gained prominence,and in the 1990s the regulatory state and post-Fordist accumulation regime started to be adopted.

In this restructuring process, the function of the state to provide legitimacy has also changed (Şaylan, 1995). In this process, the concept of governance began to be adopted. Technology has been used as a tool to ensure the legitimacy of the state while arranging legislation and creating policies in line with the principles of state governance (transparency, participation, accountability, efficiency, compliance-Commission Of

The European Communities, 2001). With the internet revolution (It has started a "creative destruction" by eliminating the dependence on a certain place and time), states began to develop projects based on internet and information technologies in public institutions and they started to put forward e-government projects for the provision of public services electronically. E-government has been a technological innovation used to provide public services, collect data, and improve democratic processes (Bretschneider, 2003). While the discourse of transparent and accountable service delivery with the e-government project led to the expectations of "limited state power and transparency", e-government became an element that provides legitimacy.

The Internet revolution has removed the dependence on time and space, but it was necessary this time to create a central authority for the protection of digital data. Therefore, the controls and restrictions of the central authority continue to exist. However, a distributed data chain has been discovered, where the information of each transaction is recorded and shared by the participants in the network, which can remove the central and limiting elements of the state (Nakamoto, 2008). Blockchain technology, introduced by Nakamoto in 2008, is initiating a new "creative destruction". "*Blockchain is a general-purpose distributed ledger technology that threatens to disrupt markets and institutions across the world*" (oecd.org.). The blockchain, which eliminates the centralized intermediary systems, chronologically records the transactions completed in a certain time duration. Confirmed transactions are linked together in blocks, forming a chain of data blocks (Zheng et al., 2017).

With the help of blockchain technology, parties can agree on and permanently record information without the need for a third party authority, even if they do not personally know or trust one another. Blockchain technology has the ability to completely transform how we share information and conduct online transactions by establishing trust in data in ways that were previously impossible (europa.eu, 2022).

Blockchain has been the subject of many research and projects referring to its unique features. Moreover, blockchain technology is being researched almost in a race on all continents. Although there are studies (Özkan, 2021; Swan, 2015), which argue that central authority of the state will be limited by blockchain technology, states seem to adopt this technology that can limit their own control or regulatory power. While political scandals, poor performance of state institutions (such as the emergence of a budget deficit), political failures, crises and fluctuations in the economy create discontent in the society and lack of confidence in the state (Nye, 1997), states strive to achieve economic development and take their place in global competition by means of blockchain. Below, the comparitive blockchain implementation status of countries for the years 2017–2018 is shown.

Researching how blockchain can be used in public institutions, Verma and Sheel revealed the chronological development of this technology. Accordingly, while the blockchain was viewed with suspicion in terms of data security between 2013 and 2016, pilot studies on this technology were started after 2016. In the 2016–2020 period, blockchain started to be used in asset transfer, e-voting, economy and in many other functions. Beginning from 2021, rules and regulations related to blockchain have emerged accompanying its implementation (Verma and Sheel, 2021). At this point, blockchain technology basically goes through the stages of "research, acceptance and reproduction of legitimacy".

Blockchain is also commonly associated with illegal activities such as cybercrime. This has caused states to approach this technology with suspicion. In the framework of some public discussions, blockchain is defined as a historical stage in which the conditions for an idealistic, egalitarian society to be created that adopts unanimity and horizontal governance in the widespread network; considers itself a nation community without a homeland or even a nation whose borders cannot be drawn. In some others, it is defined as the possible cause of the privatization of public in which the agreement between the parties may turn out to be forceful and new oligarchic structures may emerge, and this may lead to weakening of citizens (Atzori, 2017; Beck et al., 2018; Ølnes et al., 2017).

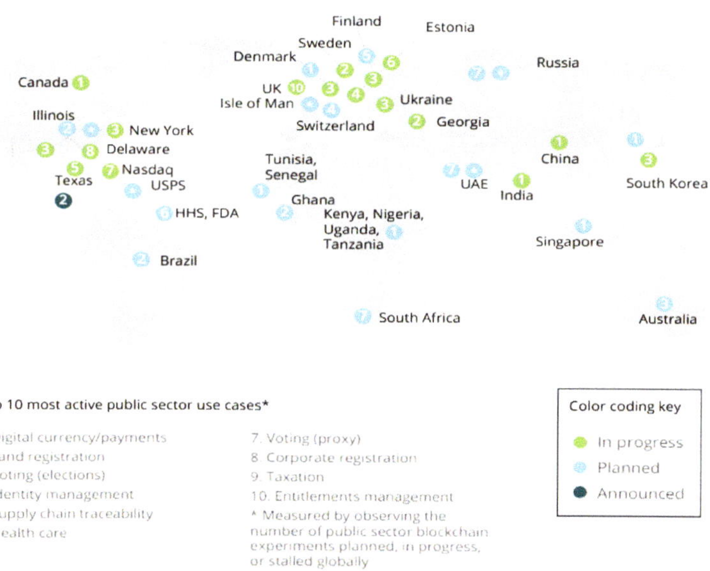

Source: Deloitte analysis in conjunction with the Fletcher School at Tufts University.

Figure 14.1. The year 2017 Blockchain in Government (117 Initiatives in 26 countries). Source: (Killmeyer et al., 2017).

Figure 14.2. The year 2018 Blockchain in Government. Source: (Berryhill et al., 2018).

However, the potential in this technology cannot be overlooked despite all these possible drawbacks. Both government initiatives and academic research on blockchain have gained momentum [see Figure 14.1 and Figure 14.2]. The annual growth rate of the number of academic blockchain studies is 47.16% (Aktaş, 2022a). The bibliometric analysis of blockchain studies in public administration shows the development in the annual scientific production literature. As can be seen in Figure 14.3, there has been a sharp increase in research after 2016. In the following section, examples of states' blockchain research and project applications will be pointed out.

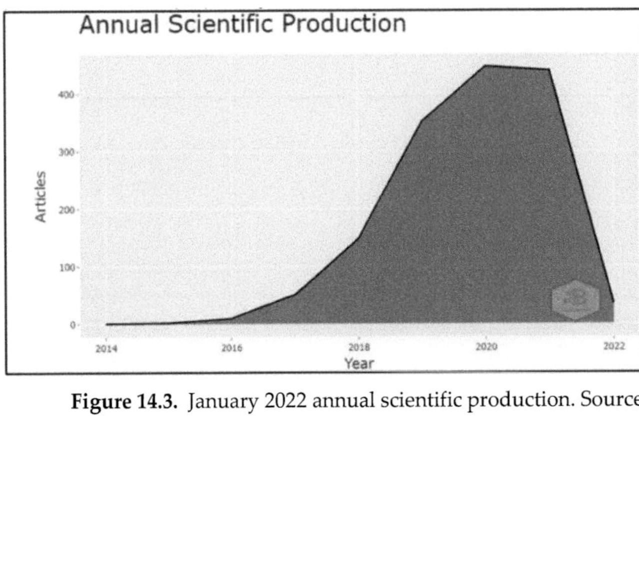

Year	Articles
2014	1
2015	2
2016	10
2017	51
2018	148
2019	352
2020	447
2021	440
2022	35

Figure 14.3. January 2022 annual scientific production. Source: Aktas, 2022a.

14.3 Blockchain Technology Applications in the Reproduction of Legitimacy

States have the potential to create an alternative response with blockchain technology to negative criticisms of traditional bureaucracy such as being "clumsy, overly prescriptive, prone to corruption and error" (Osborne and Gaebler, 1992) or even creating an "iron cage" (Weber, 1993). Increasing hyperconnections and networks in the world are also transforming the functioning and interaction of the economy. The age of the digital economy requires the digitalization of services. This sustains, it is believed, the government's transparency and efficiency. The increasingly digitalized social and economic structure brings with it the change of the traditional bureaucratic structure.

Blockchain comes to the fore despite the problem areas of current administrations, such as inability to provide trust, strict rules of central structures, inability to ensure the security of personal data and high profit rates in intermediation (Şat, 2019). The reasons behind governments's preferences to use blockchain technology, and the aspects that distinguish blockchain technology from other technologies are examined below.

14.3.1 *Benefits and Promises of Blockchain Application in Governmental Services*

The expectations of citizens from the state in the digital age are as follows: (1) Open government: is based on the principles of transparency, integrity, accountability, and stakeholder participation, (2) Better, faster, cheaper services but not privacy breaches, discriminatory practices, or data leakages, (3) Data watchdogs that *are public organisations and agencies that ensure that companies in a particular industry are obeying laws on protection of personal information* (Tan and Crompvoets, 2022).

**Transparency, Accountability and Accessibility*

Today, many governments use electronic services in the delivery of public services. Thus, unlike traditional public service provision, rapid, easy and lower-cost transportation to public services, information and document acquisition, application process and follow-up were ensured, and transparent and accountable service delivery was supported. On the one hand, technology has begun to be used intensively by states in order to find solutions to the problems experienced in public administration and on the other hand, to meet the increasing expectations of citizens. The services provided not only by citizens but also by various public institutions were gathered under a single roof and the negativities of bureaucracy were reduced (Memişoğlu Gökbınar and Aktaş, 2022). However, this system is also subject to the control and restrictions of the

Table 14.1. The potential benefits and promises that blockchain technology can provide in government include:

Benefits and promises of blockchain application in governmental services (Ølnes et al. 2017)	
1. Strategic	Transparency, reducing corruption and avoiding fraud and manipulation.
2. Organizational	Greater trust, Openness and auditability, increased prognostication, better control
3. Economical	Cost savings and improved resistance against spam and DDOS assaults
4. Informational	Improved data quality and data integrity, minimizing human error access to knowledge, Safety and dependability
5. Technological	Flexibility, Safety, Persistence and irreversibility (immutable), Reduced energy consumption.

state (the presumed reliable authority) that plays an intermediary role in the transmission of data and values with centralized computer networks (Mueller, 2013; Mueller, 2017; Özkan, 2021). Blockchain, on the other hand, has enabled the production of data that is both **decentralized** and impossible to copy and manipulate with **distributed** computer networks. Blockchain also ensures that all transactions can be seen since the initial access to the data (Atzori, 2015; Beck et al., 2018; Hughes et al., 2019). This technology weakens the power of central authorities that assume the role of intermediary, reduces supervision and restrictions, and increases the transparency and accountability of transactions. This almost revolutionary technology seems to be one of "creative destructive" moments of the 21st century.

**Reducing Fraud, Manipulation and Corruption*

The use of technology in the public sector has enabled the transfer of data from archives to computers and networks, facilitating data collection and classification, as well as providing effective and efficient public service provision and reduction in bureaucratic processes. However, data piracy, identity theft, fraud and manipulations have also emerged along with the increasing data with the use of technology. Blockchain technology, on the other hand, has entered the field of interest of states with its cryptographic encryption, decentralized with its distributed structure, **immutability** abilities for preventing data corruption, hacking activities and unauthorized changes (Hughes et al., 2019; Swan, 2015).

**Reliability*

Timestamped, immutable structures of transactions made with blockchain increase the reliability of record keeping and data (Hughes et al., 2019). At the same time, a **consensus mechanism** is needed to add a new block to the system. After a block is formed, the data is stored in multiple distributed ledgers. The blocks added with the consent of the users provide both a control mechanism and a consistent archive for the past (Swan, 2015). These control mechanisms can be reliable measures to prevent human errors and corruption in bureaucratic structures. It can provide access to correct information by ensuring **data integrity, quality and security.** The user can be **anonymous** using encryption keys or ensure their **privacy** by preventing other people from viewing the information (Hughes et al., 2019; Tapscott and Tapscot, 2016). For example, in Estonia, KSI (Keyless Signature Interface) is a globally used blockchain technology that maintains 100% data privacy. *"It means that nobody – neither hackers, nor system administrators, nor even the government itself – can manipulate the data and get away with it"* (https://e-estonia.com, 2023).

* *Decrease in Costs*

In a state bureaucratic mechanism, it may be necessary to make transactions with more than one institution in order to access any public service. For example, when you want to buy a house, you find the house with the help of a real estate agent, take a loan from the bank, get the appraisal report, apply to the land registry office to buy it, and pay the relevant taxes to the municipality after completing the purchase process... These steps in different institutions increase the time and cost of the transactions. However, the amount of money to be paid for the house is entered into a block with the "smart contract" that regulates the sales transactions of the house. When the key is delivered, the sale process takes place. If the key is not delivered, the money is returned to the buyer (Ølnes et al., 2017). Thus, since there is no need for an intermediary institution, the cost of performing and verifying a transaction can be reduced. The fact indeed is that automated processes and controls reduce human errors. This will also reduce cost, energy and resource consumption. It is also possible to reduce energy consumption by reducing the transaction mechanisms of the blockchain. In fact, while blockchain was criticized for its "high energy need" (it is still controversial, especially since proof of work requires high energy), it started to be the subject of green technology studies with its development in consensus mechanisms (Aktaş, 2022b).

The decrease in costs is also a positive development for the increasingly digital economy. At the same time, the digital economy accelerates the digitalization of states. For example, according to the World Bank, using a digital signature in Estonia saves five days a year. Thus, as a way to grow e-commerce, blockchain technology is used in the e-identity process. Again in Estonia, since 2014, people from overseas are able to buy a house, make transactions and even establish a company with the e-residence program (e-Residency - e-Estonia, 2023). On the other hand, in an environment where society is increasingly digitalized, citizens demand access to services at any time of the day. Blockchain technology shortens processing times, reduces service access and service delivery costs, reduces paperwork, increases accountability and transparency, increases citizen satisfaction, and uses resources effectively and efficiently (Memişoğlu-Gökbınar and Aktaş, 2022).

14.3.2 Blockchain Application in Government

Blockchain technology finds many applications in public administration. Application areas in public services are gathered under the following headings: (1) National identity management systems (ID cards, driver's license, passport, etc.), (2) Tax collection and monitoring of public revenues, (3) Voting transactions, (4) Secure financial services and banking transactions (5) Health services (6) Distribution and follow-up of social benefits (7) Property records and monitoring of property transfer (Deed Registry System), (8) Food safety, (9) Supply Chain Management (Berryhill et al., 2018; Walport, 2016; Killmeyer et al., 2017). Below are some prominent examples of the state's blockchain applications.

The following figure, organized according to the OECD report, shows the leading project industry areas in the use of blockchain in the public sector.

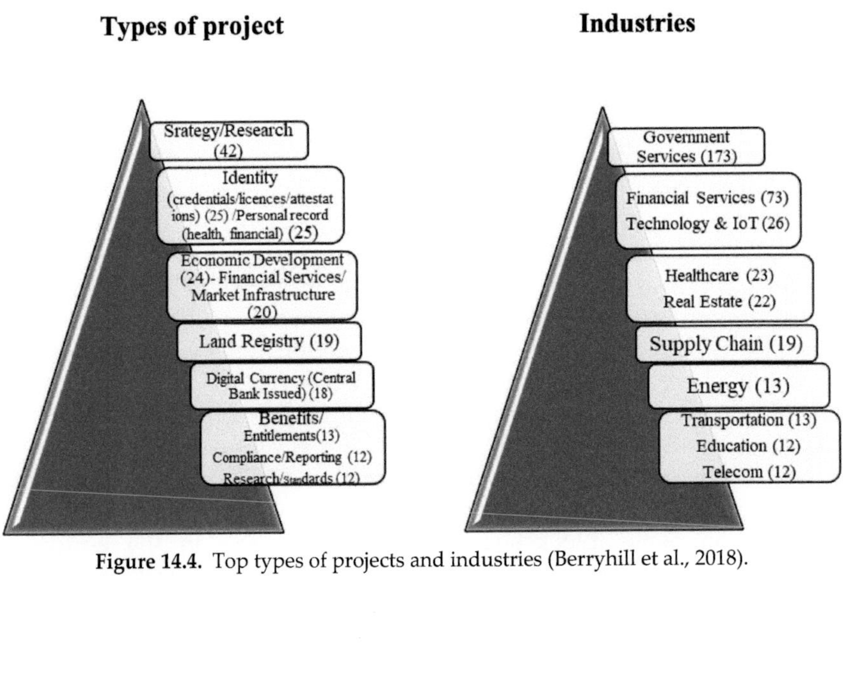

Figure 14.4. Top types of projects and industries (Berryhill et al., 2018).

Accordingly, digital currency, land registration, identity management services, at the top of the list above, will be discussed and examples will be provided in the following section. One of the factors that affect the legitimacy of the state is how it is elected. Therefore, a title is also reserved for voting. Finally, blockchain and smart cities will be emphasized because of its importance for the future of humanity.

14.3.2.1 Central Bank Digital Currency (CBDC)

Digital currencies, which are stated to be low-cost and more functional than traditional currencies, are being researched by many countries due to their advantages such as payment optimization, price stability, secure and flexible payments (Zhang et al., 2021; https://www.bis.org, 2021). In addition to the developments in technology, the reasons such as fading interest in using cash due to the Covid-19 pandemic (Yılmaz Özsoy, 2020), threats to traditional payment methods (corruption, fraud) and the state's unwillingness to lag behind in this technology accelerate research. According to the 2021 Bank for International Settlements (BIS) research, Central Bank Digital Currency (CBDC) is actively researched by central banks at a rate of 86%; technology is tested at a rate of 60%, and pilot projects are implemented at a rate of 14% (https://www.bis.org, 2021).

China started research on digital currencies in 2014 and announced that it would join the project in 2019 to test the use of CBDC in cross-border payments. It also worked with Hong Kong on a technical pilot project for the digital yuan or e-CNY in 2021 (Zhang et al., 2021; https://bctr.org, 2021; https://tr.euronews.com, 2021). Facebook has increased the attention of countries to the issue of digital money by issuing the global sovereign digital currency Libra in 2019 (Taskinsoy, 2019). The Bahamas became the first central bank in the world to use digital currency in 2020, while the Eastern Caribbean became the first currency union to implement digital currency (https://tr.euronews.com, 2021). The UK proposed RSCoin, the world's first central bank digital currency, in 2015 (Danezis and Meiklejohn, 2015; Zhang et al., 2021), accelerating its research on Britcoin (https://tr.euronews.com, 2021). Canada launched the Jasper project to study the digital Canadian dollar in 2017 (Chapman et al., 2017). While the European Central Bank continues its digital euro or e-euro research, it targets 2025 for the e-euro to be launched (Chapman, 2021). In Turkey, the Central Bank of the Republic of Turkey has announced that it has signed a preliminary agreement with ASELSAN, HAVELSAN and TÜBİTAK-BİLGEM in the digital lira trial (https://www.tcmb.gov.tr, 2021) and blockchain-based digital central bank money. It has been announced that the implementation will begin (Presidential Annual Program KP. p249, 2022). As can be seen, the issue of central bank digital currency is developing rapidly with the efforts of governments and private companies to keep up with technological developments and not lag behind other countries.

14.3.2.2 Land Registration

One of the most critical services of the states is land registry. The registration of lost or destroyed property that is not registered in the land registry can consume extended official time. For example, the destruction of state archives, including land records in the 2010 Haiti earthquake or the destruction of state archives during the war may cause the disappearance of the land registry. Even if such disasters and crises do not occur, land registry procedures require many bureaucratic procedures. With the transfer of land registry services to blockchain-based records, the records become immutable and cannot be altered or destroyed. This ensures transparency in the registration process. Thus, corruption such as the illegal transfer of property to more than one person can be prevented. According to Krishnapriya and Greeshma (2020), blockchain ensures the security of land registry records and the effort required to manually keep the records can be reduced by 99% with blockchain. Due to its potential benefits, states on every continent except Antarctica are testing the use of blockchain for land registry (Killmeyer et al., 2017).

In 2016, a project for a blockchain-based land registry started for the storage of land records in Georgia (Pipan, 2017). In 2017, the Georgian Government signed an agreement to use the Bitcoin blockchain to verify property transactions. In Japan, a patented blockchain application has been officially used since 2018 (Southurst, 2018), in line with the goal of combining all land registry records with blockchain and creating a single land registry database (Smolenski, 2017). While using blockchain in the establishment of companies in the US state of Delaware, all deed records are kept on the Ethereum system with the BenBen (2015) project in Ghana. *"70% of court disputes in Ghanaian national courts are land-related."* Average time confirming land entitlement with BenBen's services was reduced from one year to three months (Berryhill et al., 2018). In Turkey, in the 2023 Industry and Technology Strategy, the creation of the National Blockchain Infrastructure and land registry records are targeted as one of the project areas (www.sanayi.gov.tr, 2023).

14.3.2.3 Identity Management

Although there are methodological differences, population services have an important place in each country. In the traditional period, while population services were carried out mostly for the purpose of providing data to the state, the collection of data takes a long time and wide intervals. The up-to-datedness and quality of these data are also hard to sustain. It is also very costly in terms of time and resources. There are problems in collecting population data from citizens and transforming them into service delivery. Besides, with the use of technology in population services, it is seen that censuses are shortened and analysis and classification are easier. Technological developments not only facilitate data collection and classification but also enable citizens to access the service quickly, easily and at a lower cost. Individuals can perform transactions and access services online through their digital identities. In general, in the 2000s, many countries have started using digital technologies in public services. Today, digital identity plans are implemented in more than 60 countries around the world. Some countries are creating blockchain-based digital identities. For example, in digital identity studies conducted in the U.S., there have been attempts to establish a system that allows individuals to have control over the. the use of their identity information. This is achieved by employing blockchain authentication technology to prevent data security problems due to identity fraud (with CIVIC in San Francisco, uPort in New York). A blockchain-based digital identity platform was created in Canada (Memişoğlu-Gökbınar and Aktaş, 2022).

In India, one of the leading countries in creating digital identities, in the 2000s efforts were initiated to register the citizens of the country in a central database and to standardize the database of services. Aadhaar, which was implemented in 2009, is shown as the world's largest biometric identity system. "Face Authentication" has been developed to further strengthen the security of Aadhar, which consists of a 12-digit ID number. Some public subsidies and unemployment benefits, passports, payments, national criminal records, land registers, and more, have all become part of this digital system. In 2015, work was initiated to acquire the Aadhaar connected phone SIM card. Individuals can activate the SIM by sending their Aadhaar number and pressing their fingerprint into a machine (Goel et al., 2022; https://stringfixer.com, 2022). However, there are concerns about the quality and security of the database. The system can be prone to data hacking where so much personal, biometric data is processed. For this reason, there are studies that aim at providing a more severe and transparent blockchain-based Aadhar (Goel et al., 2022).

Estonia stands out in digital identities as well as in many services regarding digital technologies. Blockchain is used to store and manage digital identities, and it can be a secure and convenient tool for government agencies to access services for their citizens. In addition, blockchain can help reduce the cost of authentication and prevent fraud (ID-card - e-Estonia, 2023). Estonians have access to all e-services with their digital identity. The World Bank estimates that Estonians save five days a year using digital signatures (Cyber security - Invest in Estonia, 2023). It applies eIDAS (electronic IDentification, Authentication and trust Services) to audit electronic identification and trust services for electronic transactions in the internal market of the European Union. The European Blockchain Partnership supports compliance with e-signature regulations such as eIDAS and a logical, pragmatic decentralized and self-sovereign digital identity (europa.eu, 2022).

In Turkey, according to the statement made by the Presidency of the Digital Transformation Office, an attempt is made to introduce a blockchain-based login system to the e-Government Gateway. It is stated that with the e-Wallet application, citizens can securely store their digital identities and enter the e-Government Gateway with digital identities created in the blockchain network (cbddo.gov.tr, 2023).

14.3.2.4 Voting

The security of elections have become an important subject matter around the world lately. The healthy functioning of the process, from holding of the elections to the counting and announcement of the votes, is critical. However, disruptions and corruption cast a shadow over the security and reliability of the elections. The negativities experienced cause the elections to lose trustworthiness and legitimacy. One of the alternative methods to solve these problems in elections is the blockchain-based e-voting system.

The anticipated benefits from blockchain technology include its ability to provide a cryptographically secure voting record. Due to the immutable and tamper-resistant nature of the blockchain, votes can be accurately, permanently, securely and transparently recorded (Leary, 2017). With its anonymity, cryptography, immutability, decentralization, transparency and accountability, blockchain can solve the problems of the current voting systems (Jafar et al., 2021). During the testing phase, the voting process was implemented and experimented in various regions including Australia, New York, Texas, Denmark, Estonia, Ukraine and South Korea (Killmeyer et al., 2017). Additionally, in 2017, Russia introduced "The city of Moscow's Active Citizen program" for voting purposes, and the results are publicly auditable. The implementation of blockchain-based voting systems has been observed in various contexts, such as the community projects in the South Korean province of Gyeonggi-do, the annual general meeting of the Estonian tech company LVH Group, and the general elections in Sierra Leone in March 2018 (Kshetri and Voas, 2018). However, in Turkey, the necessary legal, technical and cultural infrastructure to enable e-elections using blockchain technology is not yet in place.

Blockchain not only finds application at the level of central services but also closely concerns local services. As a solution to the problems experienced by local governments, there are smart city applications with blockchain.

14.3.2.5 Smart Cities

Smart cities were developed as a response to the problems posed by rapid urbanization, such as rapid population growth, insufficient infrastructure capacity, pollution and environmental issues. The main objective of snart cities is to offer citizens an improved living environment by integrating technology, innovation and globalization into the urbanization process (Yin et al., 2015). Smart cities and smart municipalities can make the city more livable and sustainable for citizens. For example, smart payment methods can be used in municipal payments, transportation, energy and waste management and automating bureaucratic processes with smart contracts. This, in turn makes processes such as taxation and monitoring the transfer of assets transparent (Quittem, 2018). The demand for a more collaborative, interactive and democratic management approach is increasing in order to combat corruption, efficiency, transparency, security, access to public services and ease of use by national and local governments around the world. Current management understanding and mechanisms cannot solve these problems. Blockchain technology is presented as a solution to these problem areas, as it creates a transparent, non-hierarchical, accessible, immutable (not manipulated), secure platform (Junestrand, 2019).

Blockchain is one of the technologies used in smart city applications with its features such as distributed database, peer-to-peer transmission, transparency and inability to change records. For example, many cities in Australia, Malta, Ghana, China, Estonia, Denmark, Switzerland, United Arab Emirates, Georgia, Honduras, Singapore, United States, United Kingdom, Sweden and other countries are planning, launching or developing blockchain-based initiatives (U4SSC: Blockchain for smart sustainable cities). Estonia has been using blockchain technology in areas such as healthcare, legislative/judicial services, personal data, identity management since 2012 (KSI Blockchain - e-Estonia, 2023). While aiming to be the first blockchain city, Dubai is trying to create a common platform to make the city paperless (U4SSC: Blockchain for smart sustainable cities). Blockchain-based digital certificates called OpenCerts were given to students who graduated from 18 educational institutions in Singapore as of 2019.

In Turkey, it is stated in the 2020–2023 National Smart Cities Strategy and Action Plan (2019) of the Ministry of Environment and Urbanization (2019) that new technologies and approaches such as blockchain are important for smart cities and necessary technical, legal and physical infrastructure works will be carried out.

14.4 Conclusion

With its multidimensional functions (military, economic and legitimizing) technology becomes a tool in the regulation of institutional structures and policies by influencing the management understanding of states. In addition to providing military superiority, technology attracts the attention of states with its benefits in realizing economic development. Technological developments which facilitate the state's security, regulatory, supervisory, interventionist and intermediary roles, have been particularly occupying an important place in public discussions since the late 1990s. Technology increases economic development and social benefits at the national level and enables states to be at the forefront of competition at the international level. For this reason, the interest in technological developments is increasing and high budgets are being allocated. On the one hand, technology can be kept under state control due to its role in state functions and can be used within the framework of state understanding. On the other hand, technological developments affect the economic and political structures and become determinant in institutions and policies. In other words, while technology is used within the framework of the state understanding, technology also triggers changes in public institutions with its development. In particular, technologies that create "creative destruction" are effective in changing existing traditional bureaucratic structures, institutions and policies and are used as a tool by the state to reproduce legitimacy.

States enter into a legitimacy crisis when they cannot achieve economic and social rationalization. Although there is a tendency towards policies that will ensure the legitimacy of the economic and political system, the economic crisis and fluctuations create discontent and the lack of confidence in the state continues. In the transformation process of the economic and social structure, political-legal mechanisms are also undergoing transformation. Today, the ongoing post-Fordist accumulation regime and the implementation of neoliberal policies have been accompanied by attempts to legitimize them with democratic concepts. These concepts include accountable management, transparency, prevention of corruption, citizen participation, transfer of power to civil society, and accountability. However, despite these efforts, various issues persist. Political scandals, ineffeciences in state institutions (such as budget deficits), political failures, economic crises, fluctuations and a decline in employment continue to pose further challenges.

Therefore, the state is questioned. Blockchain, the technology of the 21st century that can create "creative destruction", the evolution of the capitalist, neoliberal systems will be able to change business forms and patterns, and forms of social organization (Herian, 2018). In other words, disruptive blockchain technology has the potential to create new products, services and markets, from new forms of finance, new governance models and social connectivity tools as the next evolution of the digital economy (OECD Global Blockchain Policy Forum, 2022). Therefore, its potential pushes states to compete to be ahead in blockchain technology.

There are over 200 launched or planned blockchain-related initiatives worldwide. Blockchain technology, which has a global application area, seems to be used more intensively in the coming years. Blockchain technology has been actively pursued for full integration into public administration systems in some countries, such as Estonia and Dubai. However, in some countries it finds application in certain public services. Research and projects mostly focus on areas such as digital identity, land registry, digital currencies and voting. Citizens are directly concerned with the processing, storage and security of the information in the identities, where the entire process of the person from birth to death is recorded and the transactions/services should be private. At the same time, land registry services and digital currencies, which directly concern the rights of citizens to acquire property, and elections, which are very important for the operation of democracy and the legitimacy of the state, are factors that can ensure a citizen's trust in the state.

The main condition behind the legitimacy of states is the consent of society. Elimination of corruption and fraud in current administrations and ensuring data security are factors that increase public trust in the state. Shortening the processing times, decreasing the costs of use and provision of services, reducing paperwork, increasing accountability and transparency will increase citizen satisfaction and strengthen the belief in the state. The unique structure of blockchain technology, which can be a solution to such problems, has made it one of the technological tools used to ensure the legitimacy of the state. Blockchain technology, which offers the opportunity to make transactions without intermediaries and the restrictions of time and place promises transparency, immutability and trust. Such a technology may also have direct effects on the state and bureaucratic organization. Moreover, the economy and finance sector is increasingly digitalized. At this point, it is expected that the central, restrictive and excessively normative bureaucratic structures will be eliminated. To what extent blockchain technology can eliminate the negativities of bureaucracy or how it can create a bureaucratic structure is a seperate research topic.

This study discusses the potential to remove the central and limiting elements of bureaucracy. It is taken as one of the creative destructive technologies used as a tool to ensure the legitimacy of the state. In that respect, this study examines the benefits and uses of the "strategic, organizational, economical, informational and technological" features of blockchain technology. Transparency, accountability and accessibility, reducing fraud, manipulation and corruption, reliability and decrease in costs provided by blockchain technology increase its acceptability by citizens and the private sector. Despite the rhetoric about blockchain technology that destroys national communities and borders by means of its independence of borders and limits (Atzori, 2017), intensive research of this technology by states ensures that they attempt to use this technology to reproduce their legitimacy. Some countries include blockchain technology in their legislative and judicial processes (e-law, regulatory frameworks, e-file), as well as in public services. With the legal regulations and the spread of international standards, it will be possible to observe what kind of changes blockchain technology will bring in the existing bureaucratic structures.

References

Aadhaar. (2022). https://stringfixer.com/tr/Unique_Identification_Authority_of_India (23.08.2022).

Aktaş, D. (2022a). Evaluation of the Effects of Blockchain Technology on Public Administrationi/ 25–6 February 2022.

Aktaş, D. (2022b). Environment for technology, technology for the environment: blockchain practices ın the energy industry. DEU Journal of the Institute of Social Sciences 24(special): 267–285.

Atzori, M. (2017). Blockchain technology and decentralized governance: is the state still necessary? Journal of Governance and Regulation 6(1): 45–62.

Arap, İ. and Erat, V. (2017). Science Policy of Turkey: A TUBITAK Based Analysis. Dokuz Eylul University. Journal of the Faculty of Economics and Administrative Sciences. 32(1): 323–339.

Beck, R., Müller-Bloch, C. and King, J. L. (2018). Governance in the blockchain economy: A framework and research agenda. Journal of the Association for Information Systems 19(10): 1020–1034. Doi:10.17705/1jais.00518.

Berryhill, J., Bourgery, T. and ve Hanson, A. (2018). Blockchains Unchained: Blockchain Technology and its Use in the Public Sector. OECD Working Papers on Public Governance, No. 28, OECD Publishing, Paris.

BIS Innovation Hub work on central bank digital currency (CBDC), https://www.bis.org/about/bisih/topics/cbdc.htm (28.02.2022).

Blockchain and competition policy - OECD. Oecd.org (14.02.2023).

Bretschneider, S. (2003). Information technology, e-government and institutional change. Public Administration Review 63(6): 738–741.

Chapman, B. (16.11. 2021). Cryptocurrency warning from the Bank of England: The point at which they will pose a risk is approaching. https://www.indyturk.com/node/436436/ekonomi%CC%87/i%CC%87ngiltere-merkez-bankas%C4%B1ndan-kripto-parauyar%C4%B1s%C4%B1-risk-te%C5%9Fkil-edecekleri-nokta (03.03.2022).

Chapman, J., Garratt, R., Hendry, S., McCormack, A. and ve McMahon, W. (2017). Project Jasper: Are distributed wholesale payment systems feasible yet. Financial System Review 59: 1–11.

China and UAE join cross-border CBDC trials. (24.02.2021), https://bctr.org/cin-ve-bae-sinir-otesi-cbdc-denemelerine-katildi-21190/ (28.02.2022).

Commission Of The European Communities. (2001). European Governance: White Paper.

Danezis, G. and ve Meiklejohn, S. (2015). Centrally banked cryptocurrencies, arXiv:1505.06895.

de Filippi, P., Mannan, M. and Reijers, W. (2020). Blockchain as a confidence machine: The problem of trust & challenges of governance. Technology in Society 62: 101284. https://doi.org/10.1016/j.techsoc.2020.101284.

Erat, V. and Arap, İ. (2016). The significance of science for the state: an analysis of the relationship between the state and the science. Education Science Society 14(53): 0–45.

Estonia-the Digital Republic Secured by Blockchain. estonia-the-digital-republic-secured-by-blockchain.pdf (pwc.com) (24.01.2023).

European Blockchain Partnership I Shaping Europe's digital future (europa.eu) (07.06.2022).

e-Residency - e-Estonia. https://e-estonia.com/solutions/cyber-security/ksi-blockchain/ (14.02.2023).

Goel, V., Aggarwal, M., Gupta, A. K. and Kumar, N. (2022). A blockchain-based Aadhar system: distributed authentication system. TELKOMNIKA Telecommunication Computing Electronics and Control 20(6): 1239–1247.

Habermas, J. (1992). Legitimation Crisis. UK. Polity Press.

Herian, R. (2018). Taking blockchain seriously. Law Critique 29: 163–171 https://doi.org/10.1007/s10978-018-9226-y (11.02.2023).

Hughes, L., Dwivedi, Y., Misra, S., Rana, N., Raghavan, V. et al. (2019). Blockchain research, practice and policy: Applications, benefits, limitations, emerging research themes and research agenda. International Journal of Information Management 49: 114–129. http://dx.doi.org/10.1016/j.ijinfomgt.2019.02.005 (11.02.2023).

Jafar, U., Aziz, M. J. A. and Shukur, Z. (2021). Blockchain for Electronic Voting System-Review and Open-Research Challenges. 1–22.

Japan can switch completely to cryptocurrencies: Central Bank considers "Digital Yen" (05.10.2020), https://tr.euronews.com/2020/02/05/japonya-tamamen-kriptoparayagecebilir-merkez-bankasi-dijital-yen-i-degerlendiriyor (28.02.2022).

Junestrand, S. (2019). Blockchain Revolution in the Governance of Nations and Cities. https://openledger.info/insights/blockchain-public-governance/.

Kaya-Bensghir, T. (1996). Information Technologies and Organizational Change. Ankara: TODAİE.

Killmeyer, J., White, M. and Chew, B. (2017). Will Blockchain Transform the Public Sector? 7, Deloitte University Press.

Krishnapriya, S. and Greeshma Sarath. (2020). Securing Land Registration using Blockchain. Procedia Computer Science 171: 1708–1715

Kshetri, N. and Voas, J. (2018). Blockchain-Enabled E-Voting. IEEE SOFTWARE.

KSI Blockchain, https://e-estonia.com/solutions/cyber-security/ksi-blockchain/ (27.01.2023).

Leary, K. (2017). Blockchain Might Be about to Change the Way We Vote. World Economic Forum, 13 Sept. 2017; https://www.weforum.org /agenda/2017/09/blockchain-could-be-about-to-change-how-you-vote.

Memişoğlu-Gökbınar, D. and ve Aktaş, D. (2022). Digitization of individual and society: population. Digital Man and Digital Society: Past, Present and Future Perspective. Nobel Publishing.

Mueller, M. M. (2013). Networks and States: The Global Politics of Internet Governance. Cambridge: MIT Press

Mueller, M. (2017). Will the Internet Fragment? Sovereignty, Globalization and Cyberspace. Cambridge: Polity.

Nakamoto, S. (2008). Bitcoin: A Peer-To-Peer Electronıc Cash System.

Nye, J. (1997). Introduction. In: Nye, J., Zelikow, P. and King, D. (eds.). Why People Don't Trust Government, Harvard University Press, Cambridge, Massachussetts.

OECD Global Blockchain Policy Forum. (2022). https://www.oecd.org/finance/oecd-blockchain-policy-forum.htm.

Ølnes, S., Ubacht, J. and Janssen, M. (2017). Blockchain in government: Benefits and implications of distributed ledger technology for information sharing. Government Information Quarterly 34(3): 355–364. doi:10.1016/j.giq.2017.09.007.

Osborne, D. and Gaebler, T. (1992). Reinventing Government: How the Entrepreneurial Spirit is Transforming the Public Sector. United States: Addison-Wesley Pub. Co.

Özkan, D. (2021). Liberty possibilities in conditions of diversified data and value sources: blockchain technology and decentralization. Journal of Political Psychology 1(1): 73–89.

Pipan, R. (2017). The Bitfury Group and Government of Republic of Georgia Expand Historic Blockchain Land-Titling Project, Tbilisi.

Poulantzas, N. (2006). Devlet, İktidar Sosyalizm (Ankara: Epos) (Çev. T. Ilgaz).

Press Release on the Central Bank Digital Turkish Lira R&D Project (15.09.2021). https://www.tcmb.gov.tr/wps/wcm/connect/TR/TCMB+TR/Main+Menu/Duyurular/Basin/2021/DUY2021-40 (03.03.2022).

Quittem, B. (2018). 4 Blockchain Projects Leading the Smart City Revolution (investinblockchain.com) (27.01.2023).

Republic of Turkey. Strategy and Budget Department. Presidential Annual Program for 2022. https://www.sbb.gov.tr/yillik-programlar/ (03.03.2022).

Şat, N. (2019). Blockchain's Potential Impact on Public Administration. Amme İdaresi Dergisi. 52(4): 117–147.

Şaylan, Gencay. (1995). Change, globalization and the new function of the state. Ankara: İmge.

Schumpeter, J. A. (2003). Capitalism, Socialism and Democracy. Taylor & Francis e-Library. Routledge: London and New York.

Swan, M. (2015). Blockchain: Blueprint for a New Economy. O'Reilly Media, Inc.

Smolenski, N. (2017). Blockchain in Government Briefing: Q3 2017, Dallas, Texas: Learning Machine 25, 26, 37, 38.

Southurst, J. (2018). Real Estate Tech Firm Zweispace Japan Starts Registering Property Sales on the Blockchain, Bitsonline: https://bitsonline. com/real-estate-zweispace-japan-blockchain/ (Erişim Tarihi: 21.01.2023).

Tan, E. and Crompvoets, J. (2022). Chapter 1: A new era of digital governance. DOI 10.3920/978-90-8686-930-5_1, Wageningen Academic Publishers.

Tapscott, D. and Tapscott, A. (2016). The impact of blockchain goes beyond financial services. Harvard Business Review (Retrieved from https://hbr.org/2016/05/the-impact-of-the-blockchaingoes-beyond-financial-services).

Taskinsoy, J. (20.07.2019). Facebook's Project Libra: Will Libra Sputter Out or Spur Central Banks to Introduce Their Own Unique Cryptocurrency Projects? [Online]. Available: https://ssrn.com/abstract=3423453 (03.03.2022).

TCMB (15.09.2021). Press Release on the Central Bank Digital Turkish Lira R&D Project Hakkında Basın Duyurusu. https://www.tcmb.gov.tr/wps/wcm/connect/TR/TCMB+TR/Main+Menu/Duyurular/Basin/2021/DUY2021-40 (03.03.2022).

To the Digital Transformation Office of the Presidency of the Republic of Turkey-e-Government Gate Work Has Started to Login Using Blockchain Technology.ı (cbddo.gov.tr).

Türkcan, E. (1981). Science policy as a tool of political economy. Economic Approach (Cilt: 2, Sayı: 5): 34–77.

Verma, S. and Sheel, A. (2021). Blockchain for government organizations: past, present and future. Journal of Global Operations and Strategic Sourcing Emerald Publishing Limited 2398-5364, DOI 10.1108/JGOSS-08-2021-0063.

Verified Market Research, Blockchain Government Market Size and Forecast. (2022). Blockchain Government Market Size, Share, Opportunities & Forecast (verifiedmarketresearch.com) (27.01.20223).

Walport, M. (2016). Distributed Ledger Technology: Beyond Blockchain, Londra: UK Government Office for Science.

Weber, M. (1946). From Max Weber: Essays in Sociology. New York: Oxford University Press.

Weber, M. (1993). Essays in Sociology. Trans. Taha Parla, İst: Hürriyet Vakfı Yayınları.

Yılmaz Özsoy, Ç. (2020). Covid-19 Pandemic and Central Bank Digital Currency as the Future of Money. Ekonomi Maliye İşletme Dergisi 3(1): 1–9.

Yin, C., Xiong, Z., Chen, H., Wang, J. Y., Cooper, D., David, B. et al. (2015). A Literature Survey on Smart Cities. Science China Press and Springer-Verlag Berlin Heidelberg.

Zhang, J., Tian, R., Cao, Y., Yuan, X., Yu, Z. et al. (2021). A hybrid model for central bank digital currency based on blockchain. IEEE Access 9: 53589–53601.

Zheng, Z., Xie, S., Dai, H., Chen, X., Wang, H. et al. (2017). An overview of blockchain technology: architecture, consensus, and future trends. Proceedings - 2017 IEEE 6th International Congress on Big Data, BigData Congress 2017: 557–564.

2023 Industry and Technology Strategy. https://www.sanayi.gov.tr/2023-sanayi-ve-teknoloji-stratejisi. (31.08. 2023).

In the 2020–2023 National Smart Cities Strategy and Action Plan, 2019. 2020–2023 National Smart Cities Strategy and Action Plan. (akillisehirler.gov.tr) (09.02.2023).

Chapter 15
Blockchain-Based Systems in the Public Sector

*Razia Abdieva** and *Damira Baigonushova*

15.1 Introduction

Current conditions and challenges and a turbulent environment, require the effective use of innovation and technology in public administration (Frissen et al., 2007). Blockchain technology ensures both public government agencies and citizens with reliable and secure information, it provides all with easier access to critical public-sector data. Blockchains are digital ledgers that are encrypted. A public or private network stores it on multiple computers. A database consists of records, or "blocks". No single actor can alter or delete a chain of blocks once it has been formed. Automation and shared governance protocols are used instead to verify and manage them (Cheng et al., 2017). Blockchain technology is now being accepted as a fundamental infrastructure for visionary and effective governments. It allows governments to streamline processes and improve coordination without compromising transparency, fairness and accountability. This technology ensures transparency, as it records all data and operations in its distributed ledger, which is open to everyone. Once the data is recorded in the block of the ledger, it is virtually impossible to change it. Thus, blockchain technology can significantly increase public

Kyrgyz-Turkish Manas University, Bishkek, Kyrgyzstan.
Email: damira.baigonushova@manas.edu.kg
* Corresponding author: razia.abdieva@manas.edu.kg

welfare by ensuring the accessibility and reliability of information and documents.

This chapter analyses the application of blockchain technology in different government sectors, including voting, taxation, public procurement, social assistance and property registration. It examines all applications of blockchain technology in the public sector, including use cases and challenges, and provides suggestions for improving and successfully implementing blockchain technology, especially in developing countries where improving the quality of governance is a key concern.

15.2 Blockchain and Electronic Voting

Public elections are the main instrument through which citizens can express their opinion and choice. They are a significant element of democracy, social well-being and security. However, in voting, the issue of transparency often arises. Manipulation of ballot boxes, the disappearance of voters from the list, and falsification are not uncommon even today. But such illegal negative events during voting could lead to social tension and instability in the country. Therefore, having non-fraudulent representative elections is critical both for the government and voters.

Elections were conducted using paper ballots, prior to the transition to computerized voting machines. However, these machines are not tamper-proof, despite system checks, security procedures and voting rules. According to critics, the proprietary code that uses the electronic device can be changed. In today's society, online voting is becoming increasingly popular as a method of participating in elections and decision-making processes. It can increase voter turnout as voters will be able to vote from anywhere with an Internet connection. It will lead to minimizing costs for both voters and the government by eliminating the need to print ballots and reducing costs of voters (time and money for transport). At the same time, electronic voting systems are vulnerable to hacking, tampering or manipulation. Electronic voting can be made more secure and reliable using blockchain technology. It can help address issues such as privacy protection, transaction speed, scalability, and end-to-end verification advantages (Jafar et al., 2021). Blockchain provides a foundation for developing more reliable, transparent and more secure e-voting systems in conjunction with smart contracts. Encryption and decentralization make the distributed ledger incorruptible, pseudonymized and verifiable. Any party cannot corrupt or influence the network since it does not exist in a single, centralized location.

Privacy protection and transaction speed are the two topics that are discussed most often in regard to blockchain applications. Scalability and remote participation security must be feasible for an electronic voting system based on blockchain technology to be sustainable and successful. As a result of these concerns, it has been determined that improvements must be made to existing frameworks for use in voting systems (Jafar et al., 2021).

Estonia has been experimenting with blockchain technology since 2008, and in 2014, Estonia became a pioneer in offering electronic residency to people who are living both inside and outside of the country. Korea used blockchain for local community voting, deploying a voting solution for community funding. Through the voting platform, based on blockchains and smart contracts, members of the community could propose and vote on community-supporting initiatives. The provincial government selected 527 projects from more than 9,000 votes. According to the provincial government, the blockchain-based solution provided the opportunity to implement direct democracy (Ojo and Adebayo, 2017). In Denmark, a blockchain-based e-voting system is being used by the Liberal Alliance party. The system provided a verifiable and reliable platform to conduct elections at the national level. It promotes public welfare by making voting more accessible to all citizens (cointelegraph.com, 2023).

15.3 Blockchain and Taxation

Blockchain technology enables peer-to-peer transactions without middlemen. It allows simultaneous verification and maintenance of a continuous public record of all transactions (Koulizakis and Loukis, 2020). Blockchain technology is a secure system, which can be accessed by anyone via the internet. This allows many transactions to be stored electronically. Due to this technology, many transactions no longer have to be kept in the form of printed documents and reduce the administrative cost of tax authorities.

There is great potential for the use of blockchain in taxation. It enhances the trust of citizens in government by providing transparency of tax information. At the same time, blockchain technology can be used by tax authorities for broadening the tax base and combat the shadow economy. Finland has implemented a blockchain system to address real estate taxes. In Sweden, blockchain technology is being tested for the digitalization of receipts, nonresident income taxes, and customs duties. Estonia has developed the Keyless Signature Infrastructure (KSI Blockchain) to facilitate e-commerce and e-Register. This infrastructure enables both citizens and the government to verify the integrity of databases maintained by the government. In Brazil, the federal tax administration has built a blockchain-based system for its taxpayers' registry (Collosa, 2022).

This technology proves to be beneficial in reducing Value Added Tax (VAT) fraud by enabling the of VAT payments and their corresponding locations. For multinational companies, it supports the delivery of consistent data sets to multiple tax authorities, enhancing confidence in the information provided to tax and other regulatory bodies. It also facilitates the verification of judgements and assumptions involved in determining profits for global companies operating in different jurisdictions. Furthermore, it provides greater visibility of micro-transactions, especially those conducted by individuals within the sharing economy (Schofield, 2016).

15.4 Blockchain and Public Procurement

Blockchain technology has the potential to enhance efficiency and transparency in public procurement, another essential government service. By leveraging blockchain, easy access to this market can be provided for all interested firms and citizens. At the same time, it ensures that citizens have transparent information about the goods and services purchased by the government. Consequently, blockchain can serve as an effective instrument in combating corruption.

In the application of blockchain technology and other distributed ledger technologies, procurement authorities should avoid attempting to procure these technologies outright. Instead, they should encourage compliance with the principles established by the international community over decades. By doing so, procurement authorities can leverage the potential benefits of these technologies while ensuring compliance with existing regulations and standards (Michael and Korolevska, 2021).

15.5 Applications of Blockchain in Social Aid

Benefits of Using Blockchain in Humanitarian Aid and First Attempts

To support various social or individual causes, many governments donate large amounts of money every year. The most important of these are in the form of humanitarian aid, social aid, aid for education, the environment, the arts and other areas. Such charity can also take the form of government-to-government aid, which is official assistance provided by donor governments to reduce inequality, eradicate poverty and promote sustainable development. These grant processes are vague, confusing and inefficient in many cases. Economic rents are high and most of the accumulated or pooled funds go to third parties and bank payments.

One hypothesis that has emerged in the literature on distributed ledgers is that this technology can help charities to increase stakeholder trust in their donation distributions. This technology can also reduce corruption and increase public trust by reducing the number of parties involved in authorizing grants and grant management. The result is a modern process that significantly reduces costs and eliminates all opportunities for illegal siphoning of funds. For example, thanks to the first pilot of the Disberse platform, powered by the Ethereum blockchain, in 2017, a Swazi NGO and four local schools that receive funding from donors (i.e., UK NGOs) saved 2.5% on transfer fees, in parallel with real-time end-to-end tracking of funds. The platform accepts donations as fiat money and deposits them in escrow. They are then tokenized and electronic money distributes to all agents that are participating in the project through blockchain wallet.

The World Food Programme (WFP) has developed the Building Blocks platform, which assigns a unique digital identifier to each refugee and connects it to UNHCR's biometric data. This will make aid payments to refugees from Syria in Jordan cheaper, quicker, more secure and traceable. A WFP-authorized recipient can self-identify at participating retailers using an iris scan. The transaction is recorded on the blockchain. The blockchain's audit capabilities allow for real-time accounting and monitoring of all aid funds. Compared to the alternative of transferring funds to individual refugee bank accounts, this saves WFP transfer charges (approximately 3.5% of average aid transferred) and capital costs, as advances to the bank are drastically reduced (GSMA, 2017:20–25).

An Explosion in the Development of Blockchain-Based Charity Programs after 2017

Motivated by the success of Disberse and the WFP, some experts have proposed their own blockchain-based donation systems. Despite the fact that these systems have the same goal, i.e., the support of society in the distribution of humanitarian aid, they are at the same time different in terms of scope. For example, Junfithrana et al. (2018) developed a blockchain and Internet of Things-based rice donation system in response to the large number of orphanages in Indonesia and the complexity of information sharing. Sirisha et al. (2019) and Hande et al. (2020) developed blockchain systems for financial donations. They presented a system based on bidding between organizations for a charity network. Using the Ethereum blockchain with public permission, Farooq et al. (2020) introduced a blockchain-based charity management system designed to provide reliable and verifiable operations for government agencies.

Dajim et al. (2019) and Ranjan et al. (2019), as well as Pradhan and Mishra (2020), designed a blockchain technology for organ donation and organ matching. Pradhan and Mishra (2020) attempted to create an application in Android which connects organ donors and people who require an organ through a sent message request not revealing the details about their identity.

Çağlıyangil et al. (2020) employed a system for blood distribution, and Mostafa et al. (2020) offered a cloud-based and mobile computing structure that connects blood donors and medical institutions to ensure that the right blood type reaches every person in need. To address the issue of trust in supply chains, Malik et al. (2019) have developed blockchain and smart contracts.

To prevent fraud in crowdfunding and to solve the problem of existing online crowdfunding methods that do not allow donors to control the funds they donate, Pandey et al. (2019) suggested a blockchain-based approach and Saleh et al. (2019) proposed a blockchain-based donation platform to address donors' distrust of how donated money is spent. They used smart contracts to track the flow of money and offered a system to prevent fraud in crowdfunding. To advance the transparency and reliability of charity information on the blockchain, Wang et al. (2020) proposed a security control component for managing donations on the blockchain to prevent epidemics.

Badarudin et al. (2020) developed a model for disaster response and post-disaster relief to increase the speed and availability of services during disaster response, proposing a digital asset tokenization scheme using alliance chains and whitelists, as well as using smart contracts to regulate the use of foundation donations to avoid corruption. Based on the background of COVID-19, Marbouh et al. (2020) developed a blockchain-based review, capability and trusted tracking system to make the donation process more transparent and verifiable, and proposed a scheme that uses blockchain technology to eliminate intermediaries, save costs and minimize the cost of donations. Wu et al. (2020) developed a robust charity donation service system to address the practical problems of distributing donated funds and materials faced by charity operators such as COVID-19, and proposed a system using Ethereum to create a donation system to implement grant and distribute funds and materials during an epidemic. Singh et al. (2020) developed a blockchain aid and donation tracking system, proposing a blockchain-based scheme to replace the original centralized donation system, using Proof of Authority (POA) consensus mechanisms for donations and fund transfers. To save time, reduce the cost of donations, and reduce the risk of suspicious donations ending up in campaigns or terrorist projects, Shaheen et al. (2021) initiated a donation blockchain tracker system. The team has also created a web site that can be used as an assistant for users to make the proposed system as easy to use as possible. Li et al. (2021, 2022, 2022a) implemented blockchain-based demand issuance, material donation, demand prioritization, material distribution, and protection of material information during transportation.

Shortcomings, Recommendations and Suggestions

The fact that most of the systems developed above have not yet been tested is a major shortcoming of these systems. Tough it looks promising at this stage; the results of piloting have only begun to reveal the strengths and weaknesses of the systems. For example, in the implementation of Baharmand et al. (2021), in addition to the benefits mentioned above, some interviewees described the pilot as 'an over-engineered solution for targeted goals'. This study proves that there are still some obstacles to the effective application of blockchain in humanitarian supply chains. Therefore, the authors argue that traditional centralized data exchange systems are likely to be more effective and more acceptable IT solutions today than comparatively sophisticated individual permissioned blockchain systems for humanitarian supply chains. But only a few years ago, most blockchain-based donation systems have used cryptocurrency for personal charitable support (Jeong et al., 2020). The success of Disberse and the WFP platform has elevated the role of operators in the delivery of humanitarian aid in a very short time and today's platforms have overcome these inconveniences. Notably, blockchain-enabled platforms capable of leveraging mobile payment systems are a more appropriate, cost-efficient and transparent means for organizations to transfer humanitarian funds across borders, said the GSMA in 2017. Today's platforms can also provide such opportunities. It is a sign that some limitations have been overcome in a short span of time.

The quantity and the difference in the number of systems developed in this area shows that today there is already a sufficient number of systems developed and the next step is not quantity but quality. In other words, based on the results of the ongoing pilot implementations, it is now necessary to simplify and improve the system as much as possible. And after improvements, it would be possible to give donors even more options when choosing the type of charity, they want to give if governments manage to integrate all the above systems into one platform. Such a project would not only help to prevent corruption in the charity sector and increase the confidence of donors, which would stimulate them to contribute without any doubt, but it would also eliminate their hesitation in choosing the type of donation. On the other hand, donors will also be able to find the right person or the right charity with ease.

15.6 Applications of Blockchains in Property Registry

Benefits of Using Blockchain in Property Registry and First Attempts

Researchers believe the entire real estate system could eventually be hosted on blockchains. Transactions could be initiated on smartphones

(Graglia and Mellon, 2018; Golosova, 2018). However, our observations show that many applications in this area today are related to land registration, i.e., real estate. Despite researchers' beliefs in the numerous advantages of blockchain systems, such as eliminating corruption, reducing costs, ensuring transparency, and securing data, the adoption of blockchain in the real estate market has been limited. While there is great potential for its application in the land registration certifications, title transfer, taxation, home loans and mortgages, streamlining land registries in developing countries only a few countries, such as the United Arab Emirates, Georgia, Ukraine, Brazil and the Republic of Honduras (Mutabazi, 2021), have actively implemented blockchain to improve land registration and transaction processes. However, this does not mean that other countries have rejected or are reluctant to implement this alternative. On the contrary, many countries are currently actively developing and piloting various blockchain-based property registration systems, showing growing interest in exploring the benefits of blockchain technology in the real estate sector.

The implementation of any system in this area can take a long time due to certain limitations or obstacles, such as the lack of preparedness of the population and/or civil servants for new technologies (resistance of the local population to change due to their mistrust of the new technology, fear of losing control by senior officials, training a sufficient number of staff to launch the application, sufficient Internet access, implementing smart contracts and electronic signatures).

The implementation of any system in this area can take a long time due to certain limitations or obstacles, such as the lack of preparedness of the population and/or civil servants for new technologies (resistance of the local population to change due to their mistrust in the new technology, fear of losing control in senior officials, training a sufficient number of staff to launch the application, sufficient Internet access, implementing smart contracts and electronic signatures), the lack of local developers or the lack of funds to purchase ready-made software from the private sector and/or to train staff.

The first real attempt in this direction can be seen in the platform BenBen, a Ghana-based landtech company founded in 2015 by Emmanuel Buetey Noah. In an effort to overpass the disagreement between land rights holders and land market actors, BenBen uses distributed ledger technology frameworks to create trusted, transparent and integrated land transaction environments in frontier economies (benben.com.gh, 2022). It provides an Ethereum-based digital registry system for all land registers across Ghana. Previously 70% of legal disputes in Ghana's national jurisdictions were related to land. As of 2017, BenBen has consolidated 10,000 records into its digital registers, many of which have been successfully traded.

Previously, the average time to obtain a land title document was one year. After BenBen's services, it was reduced to three months. The average time to obtain a land report from the Land Commission has been reduced to 3 days with BenBen's services, compared to a month ago (Berryhill et al., 2018).

Implementation Practices, Gained Benefits and Arisen Difficulties

As this blockchain system, built by Noah Raford, is privately owned and developing in what he calls a 'pre-legal phase', businesses and administrations in Dubai have not seen a real strategy and path to develop its use at a systematic level. They were also looking for a centralized platform to share knowledge and best practices. To this end, Dubai has established a large, multi-stakeholder Global Blockchain Council, as it is widely known. According to Berryhill et al. (2018), 15 pilot experimental projects have currently been launched within this new space. Almost all of them are public-private partnerships (PPPs). The Smart Dubai Office has instructed fourteen thousand civil workers in data science and technology literacy as part of this effort. So, it turns out that the Dubai Land Records Authority has become one of the pioneering government agencies to blockchain land records (cointelegraph.com, 2018).

Another country that is actively involved in the realization of the blockchain system in this area is Sweden. In general, transparency and accountability requirements are not met by the centralized data storage system developed in Sweden. In order to ensure a more efficient, faster and more personalized service to citizens, the Swedish Land Registry aims to go ahead with current digital systems to record land transactions and ownership. To achieve this, the Blockchain system is currently being considered as an alternative, and a three-phase project is planned to use it in the Land Registry. Currently, the first phase focuses on the adoption of blockchain technology. The second phase aims to develop a technology that best meets the needs and requirements of asset owners and governments. The final phase is one of experimentation, with the aim of developing an effective proof of concept.

The results of the new system are not yet known, as the project has not yet been adopted on a national scale, despite a successful pilot in 2017–2018 (McMurren et al., 2018). One of the challenges in implementing the project is that the digital signature of smart contracts is not legally recognized. Therefore, even if it functions as a system, it does not have any legal significance: no transaction or deal registered on it may be binding in law. How the governance system around blockchain will work is still unclear. Another major challenge is explaining how the technology works (Snäll, 2017).

Tomicah Tillemann, co-founder of Blockchain Trust Accelerator (BTA), noted in his interview with Berryhill et al. (2018) that currently, when blockchain systems are used in different networks, most systems are developed by a private network and offered to states. For example, the completion of a blockchain trial to enable faster property transactions was recently announced by participants including Barclays, Royal Bank of Scotland (RBS) and blockchain company R3 (coindesk.com, 2019). Every property transaction involves at least eight parties, in addition to the buyer and the seller, and the need to go through a process of information exchange involving a large number of documents, platforms and databases. The result, according to the Instant Property Network (IPN), was transaction delays, errors, cost increases and unpredictability for all participants. Using this new blockchain-based system could save the global real estate market an estimated $160 billion a year, the developers claim, by reducing the process of buying and selling property from more than three months to less than three weeks. For the next phase of the project, the company says it is recruiting "dozens" of private and public sector companies. It plans to release the next version of its platform in September.

BTA has also implemented a number of national government projects around the world, including the successful digitization of the Democratic Republic of Georgia's state land registry, says Tillemann. Georgia announced its plan to realize land registration based on blockchain to increase the reliability of land transaction data in 2016, and by 2017, over 15 million parcels of land had been entered into the blockchain (Shin, 2017). As a result, the time taken to complete a land transaction has been reduced from one day to an average of ten minutes.

The rational development of blockchains in the government sector and for social purposes is hampered by two obvious obstacles, says Tomicah Tillemann. One of them is the secure identification of users participating in technological and blockchain systems. The second is education, which is not enough to make clear to everyone, in simple terms, the possible impact of technology on the daily lives of citizens.

Situation in Developing Countries

One of the most serious problems in developing countries is land registration and data management. For example, among the four main provinces of Pakistan (Sindh, KPK, Balochistan and Punjab), only Punjab has its land data integrated into the country's computer system. In some states or provinces, land records are still not registered, and the data is typically managed in large paper-based records by a central person known as a 'patwari' (Khalid et al., 2022). Despite the magnitude of the problem, attempts to secure property on the basis of blockchain systems have not yet been made by the state, but efforts are being made by private researchers to contribute to the state through the implementation of experimental pilot projects. Khalid et al. (2022), who are working on such a project, highlight that the most challenging barrier will be the 'resistance to change'. This is because many people lack computer skills and may struggle with adopting a new framework that requires significant learning and adaption.

In countries where there is a lack of a secure land registry, the first step is to digitize the property records. This is crucial because having accessible and quality ownership registers and databases is essential (Arruñada, 2012). Only then can the blockchain system become a potential solution to address problems and function as a tool for property management. Currently, many Central Asian countries, namely Kazakhstan, Kyrgyzstan, Tajikistan, Turkmenistan and Uzbekistan, are actively working on digital signatures and identifying and digitizing various types of property to establish a more reliable and efficient land registry system. These studies create the conditions needed to implement the blockchain system in the near future. However, time will be the measure of what these countries will do in the future. Some researchers, such as Bustamante et al. (2022), point out that digitization comes at a cost, and continuing adoption of blockchain technology may not bring many more benefits than such digitization.

The necessity of implementing blockchains in real estate markets may not be clear, given that the majority of economies currently have well-established judicial rights to real estate backed by governments. In most cases where blockchain technologies have been utilized, real estate markets have already been functioning adequately. Therefore, the next steps for Central Asian countries therefore will depend on the effectiveness of blockchain-based property registration systems, which have been increasingly adopted and implemented by many countries worldwide.

15.7 Applications of Blockchain in Public Debt

It is important to understand that the debt incurred today, especially the external public debt, is a burden for the next generation and therefore it is important to approach this situation responsibly. To achieve this,it is essential to gain an understanding of how the borrowed funds are currently being used, assess their effectiveness, and determine whether they are yielding returns or creating a burden for future generations.

One area of government where clear and reliable data are difficult to find today is external debt. In general, information on where and how borrowed funds are spent and who controls them is either absent or scarce and unclear, especially in the social databases of developing countries. This is a sign of corruption in the sector. If the state can use blockchain applications to prevent corruption in other sectors, it should definitely develop applications in this area as well.

In this area, as in others, the state can achieve many other positive results, not only in preventing corruption, but also in reducing bureaucracy, reducing the cost and time of transactions, and increasing efficiency through openness of information.

So far, there has been little interest from blockchain researchers in this area. However, the idea is that an international or global system could also be developed for foreign debt. This would allow countries or international organizations to lend money to other countries through the same system, and at the same time monitor whether the money is being used for its intended purpose.

15.8 Conclusion

The use of blockchain technology could make it more convenient to manage trusted information, allowing governments to access important public data more easily, provided the information remains secure. At the same time, by ensuring public data transparency and access to reliable data for all citizens, it could significantly improve social welfare. The technology also has the potential to be a powerful tool to help fight corruption and for the improvement of public sector efficiency.

The vast majority of the blockchain projects in the public sector that have been launched to date have not yet moved beyond the pilot phase. However, some of the obstacles which were thought to be major barriers to implementation, such as the digital signature requirement for smart contracts, internet access and the ability to connect to the system via smartphones, have been overcome quickly. This reinforces the belief that there will be more examples of successful government implementation in the near future.

Our research has shown that blockchain-based systems in the public sector vary widely from domain to domain. Some areas have been the focus of much research, while others have received little or no attention. But even in areas that have received a lot of attention, implementation tests show that there are still gaps and challenges to be addressed. In this context, the focus should also be on piloting existing projects in areas where a wide range of blockchain-based systems have already been developed, such as taxation, voting, aid and property registration, to overcome the shortcomings and increase their usability and reliability. In areas such as procurement and public debt management, where there are currently existing gaps, it is important to develop and test appropriate systems in the short term.

References

Arruñada, B. (2018). Blockchain's struggle to deliver impersonal exchange. Minn. JL Sci. & Tech. 19: 55.

Badarudin, P. H. A. P., Wan, A. T. and Phon-Amnuaisuk, S. (2020). A Blockchain-based Assistance Digital Model for First Responders and Emergency Volunteers in Disaster Response and Recovery. 2020 8th International Conference on Information and Communication Technology (ICoICT), Yogyakarta, Indonesia, pp. 1–5, doi: 10.1109/ICoICT49345.2020.9166389.

Baharmand, H., Maghsoudi, A. and Coppi, G. (2021). Exploring the application of blockchain to humanitarian supply chains: insights from Humanitarian Supply Blockchain pilot project. International Journal of Operations & Production Management 41(9): 1522–1543. doi: 10.1108/IJOPM-12-2020-088.

benben.com.gh. (2022). http://www.benben.com.gh/about. 14.01.2023.

Berryhill, J., Bourgery, T. and Hanson, A. (2018). Blockchains unchained: Blockchain technology and its use in the public sector. OECD Working Papers on Public Governance, No. 28, OECD Publishing, Paris, https://doi.org/10.1787/3c32c429-en.

Bustamante, P., Cai, M., Gomez, M., Harris, C., Krishnamurthy, P. et al. (2022). Government by code? Blockchain applications to public sector governance. Blockchain Applications to Public Sector Governance (June 21, 2022). Frontiers in Blockchain 5: 1. doi: 10.3389/fbloc.2022.869665.

Çağlıyangil, M., Erdem, S. and Özdağoğlu, G. (2020). A blockchain based framework for blood distribution. *In*: Hacioglu, U. (ed.). Digital Business Strategies in Blockchain Ecosystems. Contributions to Management Science. Springer, Cham. https://doi.org/10.1007/978-3-030-29739-8_4.

Cheng, S., Daub, M., Domeyer, A. and Lundqvist, M. (2017). Using blockchain to improve data management in the public sector. McKinsey Digital. https://www.mckinsey.com/capabilities/mckinsey-digital/our-insights/using-blockchain-to-improve-data-management-in-the-public-sector.

coindesk.com. (2019). Barclays, RBS, R3 Cut Property Transaction Times in Blockchain Trial. Available at: https://www.coindesk.com/markets/2019/04/05/barclays-rbs-r3-cut-property-transaction-times-in-blockchain-trial/. 14.01.2023, 13: 50.

cointelegraph.com. (2018). UAE government launches blockchain strategy 2021—coin telegraph. Available at: https://cointelegraph.com/news/uaegovernment-launches-blockchain-strategy-2021. 15.01.2023.

cointelegraph.com. (2023). How blockchain can transform government sector: E-government, e-voting, e-identities and e-documents. Cointelegraph. https://cointelegraph.com/cryptocurrency-regulation-for-beginners/how-blockchain-can-transform-government-sector.

Collosa, A. (2022). How Global Tax Administrations are Using Blockchain Technology. https://news.bloombergtax.com/daily-tax-report-international/how-global-tax-administrations-are-using-blockchain-technology.

Dajim, L. A., Al-Farras, S. A., Al-Shahrani, B. S., Al-Zuraib, A. A., Merlin Mathew, R. et al. (2019). Organ Donation Decentralized Application Using Blockchain Technology. 2019 2nd International Conference on Computer Applications & Information Security(ICCAIS), pp. 1–4. doi:10.1109/cais.2019.8769459.

Farooq, M. S., Khan, M. and Abid, A. (2020). A framework to make charity collection transparent and auditable using blockchain technology. Computers & Electrical Engineering 83: 106588.

Frissen, V., Millard, J., Huijboom, N., Iversen, J. S., Kool, L. et al. (2007). The future of eGovernment. An Exploration of ICT-driven Models of eGovernment for the EU in 2020. pp 1–15.

Golosova, J. and Romanovs, A. (2018, November). The advantages and disadvantages of the blockchain technology. pp. 1–6. In 2018 IEEE 6th Workshop on Advances in Information, Electronic and Electrical Engineering (AIEEE). IEEE.

Graglia, J. M. and Mellon, C. (2018). Blockchain and property in 2018: At the end of the beginning. Innovations: Technology, Governance, Globalization 12(1-2): 90–116. doi:10.1162/inov_a_00270.

GSMA. (2017). Blockchain for Development: Emerging Opportunities for Mobile, Identity and Aid, London: GSMA, available at https://www.gsma.com/mobilefordevelopment/wp-content/uploads/2017/12/Blockchain-for-Development.pdf (accessed 05 February 2023).

Hande, R., Agarwal, T., Monde, R., Sirisha, N. S., Yadav, R. et al. (2020). CharityChain - donations using blockchain. *In*: Smys, S., Senjyu, T. and Lafata, P. (eds.). Second International Conference on Computer Networks and Communication Technologies. ICCNCT 2019. Lecture Notes on Data Engineering and Communications Technologies, vol 44. Springer, Cham. https://doi.org/10.1007/978-3-030-37051-0_68.

Jafar, U., Aziz, M. J. A. and Shukur, Z. (2021). Blockchain for electronic voting system—review and open research challenges. Sensors 21(17): 5874. https://doi.org/10.3390/s21175874.

Jeong, J. D., Kim, Y. Lee, J. Jung and Son, Y. (2020). A study of private donation system based on blockchain for transparency and privacy. pp. 1–4. 2020 International Conference on Electronics Information and Communication (ICEIC).

Junfithrana, A. P., Liani, E., Suwono, M. Z., Meldiana, D., Suryana, A. et al. (2018). Rice donation system in orphanage based on internet of things, Raspberry-Pi, and blockchain. pp. 235–238. 2018 International Conference on Computing, Engineering, and Design (ICCED), doi:10.1109/icced.2018.00053.

Khalid, M. I., Iqbal, J., Alturki, A., Hussain, S., Alabrah, A. et al. (2022). Blockchain-based land registration system: a conceptual framework. Applied Bionics and Biomechanics 2022. https://doi.org/10.1155/2022/3859629.

Koulizakis, I. and Loukis, E. (2020). A development framework for blockchain technologies in digital government. pp. 129–136. Proceedings of the 13th International Conference on Theory and Practice of Electronic Governance. https://doi.org/10.1145/3428502.3428519.

Li, M., Chen, Y., Zheng, S., Hu, D., Lal, C. et al. (2020). Privacy-preserving navigation supporting similar queries in vehicular networks. IEEE Transactions on Dependable and Secure Computing 19(2): 1133–1148.

Li, M., Chen, Y., Lal, C., Conti, M., Alazab, M. et al. (2021). Eunomia: Anonymous and secure vehicular digital forensics based on blockchain. IEEE Transactions on Dependable and Secure Computing.

Li, M., Zhu, L., Zhang, Z., Lal, C., Conti, M. et al. (2022). User-defined privacy-preserving traffic monitoring against n-by-1 jamming attack. IEEE/ACM Transactions on Networking 30(5): 2060–2073.

Li, T., Hu, D., Li, M., Li, Y., Zheng, S. et al. (2022a). A blockchain-based material donation platform. pp. 246–254. 2022 International Conference on Blockchain Technology and Information Security (ICBCTIS), Huaihua City, China, doi: 10.1109/ICBCTIS55569.2022.00061.

Malik, S., Dedeoglu, V., Salil, S., Kanhere, S., Jurdak, R. et al. (2019). TrustChain: Trust management in blockchain and IoT supported supply chains. pp. 184–193. 2019 IEEE International Conference on Blockchain (Blockchain), Atlanta, GA, USA, doi: 10.1109/Blockchain.2019.00032.

Marbouh, D., Abbasi, T., Maasmi, F., Omar, I. A., Debe, M. S. et al. (2020). Blockchain for COVID-19: Review, opportunities, and a trusted tracking system. Arabian Journal for Science and Engineering, pp. 1–17. doi:10.1007/s13369-020-04950-4.

McMurren, J., Young, A. and Verhulst, S. (2018). Addressing Transaction Costs Through Blockchain and Identity in Swedish Land Transfers GOVLAB. Testo disponibile al sito: https://blockchan. ge/blockchange-land-registry. pdf.

Michael, B. and Korolevska, N. (2021). Some policy issues surrounding the use of FinTech in public procurements. Law and Financial Markets Review 15(1–2): 38–69. https://doi.or g/10.1080/17521440.2022.2063605.

Mostafa, S. A., Mustapha, A., Shamala, P., Obaid, O. I., Khalaf, B. A. et al. (2020). Social networking mobile apps framework for organizing and facilitating charitable and voluntary activities in Malaysia. Bulletin of Electrical Engineering and Informatics 9(2): 827–833.

Mutabazi, P. (2021). Blockchain Based Land Registries - How Technology Can be Used For Land Registration. Available at: https://www.linkedin.com/pulse/blockchain-based-land-registries-how-technology-can-mutabazi. 14.01.2023, 19: 04.

Ojo, A. and Adebayo, S. (2017). Blockchain as a next generation government information infrastructure: a review of initiatives in D5 countries. Ojo, B. A. and Millard, J. (Ред.), Government 3.0 – Next Generation Government Technology Infrastructure and Services (Т. 32, сс. 283–298). Springer International Publishing. https://doi.org/10.1007/978-3-319-63743-3_11.

Pandey, S., Goel, S., Bansla, S. and Pandey, D. (2019). Crowdfunding fraud prevention using blockchain. 1028–1034. 2019 6th International Conference on Computing for Sustainable Global Development (INDIACom).

Pradhan, P. and Mishra, A. (2020). Organ donation—an android application. International Journal of Innovations in Engineering Research and Technology 7(12): 85–89.

Ranjan, P., Srivastava, S., Gupta, V., Tapaswi, S., Kumar, N. et al. (2019). Decentralised and distributed system for organ/tissue donation and transplantation. 2019 IEEE Conference on Information and Communication Technology. doi:10.1109/cict48419.2019.9066225.

Saleh, H., Avdoshin, S. and Dzhonov, A. (2019, November). Platform for tracking donations of charitable foundations based on blockchain technology. pp. 182–187. In 2019 Actual Problems of Systems and Software Engineering (APSSE). IEEE.

Schofield, M. (2016). How blockchain technology could improve the tax system. https://www.pwc.co.uk/issues/futuretax/assets/documents/how-blockchain-could-improve-the-tax-system.pdf.

Shaheen, E., Hamed, M. A., Zaghloul, W., Al Mostafa, E., El Sharkawy, A. et al. (2021, July). A track donation system using blockchain. pp. 1–7. In 2021 international conference on electronic engineering (ICEEM). IEEE. Menouf, Egypt, 2021, doi: 10.1109/ICEEM52022.2021.9480649.

Shin, L. (2017). The First Government to Secure Land Titles on the Bitcoin Blockchain Expands Project. Forbes, February, 7.

Singh, A., Rajak, R., Mistry, H. and Raut, P. (2020). Aid, charity and donation tracking system using blockchain. pp. 457–462. 2020 4th International Conference on Trends in Electronics and Informatics (ICOEI)(48184). doi:10.1109/icoei48184.2020.9143001.

Sirisha, N. S., Agarwal, T., Monde, R., Yadav, R., Hande, R. et al. (2019). Proposed solution for trackable donations using blockchain. 2019 International Conference on Nascent Technologies in Engineering (ICNTE). doi:10.1109/icnte44896.2019.8946019.

Snäll, M. (2017). Blockchain and the Land Register—A New 'Trust Machine'? nd, Submission, (572).

Wang, S., Li, Q., Hou, J. and Jiang, J. (2020). Security control components for epidemic prevention donation management blockchain. pp. 73–84. In Proceedings of the 2nd ACM International Symposium on Blockchain and Secure Critical Infrastructure

(BSCI '20). Association for Computing Machinery, New York, NY, USA. https://doi.org/10.1145/3384943.3409424.

Wu, H. and Zhu, X. (2020). Developing a reliable service system of charity donation during the Covid-19 outbreak. In IEEE Access 8: 154848–154860, doi: 10.1109/ACCESS.2020.3017654.

Chapter 16
Examining Blockchain Applications in Terms of Governance and Ethics
Advantages and Disadvantages

Aysegul Asuman Akdogan[1,*] and *Ceren Aydemir*[2]

16.1 Introduction

With the widespread adoption of digital technologies, society as a whole society has entered a transformative process. Various elements, such as individuals, sectors, institutions, the economy and other technologies, have been impacted by this digital revolution. In this context blockchain stands out as a pioneering technology that has emerged and gained prominence during this digital transformation. Blockchain technology became widely known and gained popularity in 2008 with the publication of an article authored under the pseudonym Satoshi Nakamoto. The author referred to as an anonymous individual or group, introduced the concept of blockchain through this paper (Nakamoto, 2008). Today, blockchain technology has evolved beyond its association with cryptocurrencies and is now applied in numerous domains. Governance is one such are area where blockchain technology that can be leveraged due to the significant advantages it offers. Utilizing blockchain in governance processes provides benefits such as

[1] Erciyes University and, Kyrgyz-Turkish Manas University.
[2] Nuh Naci Yazgan University.
Email: cseyhan@nny.edu.tr
* Corresponding author: akdogana@erciyes.edu.tr, asuman.akdogan@manas.edu.kg

reduced costs, increased liquidity, improved accuracy in record keeping and enhanced transparency in ownership transactions. Demand for individual companies to use blockchain in their operations has increased in some exchanges because they use blockchain technology as a new way for corporate stock trade and track their ownership (Magnier and Barban, 2018). Another issue that needs to be considered with usage of blockchain is ethics. The effects of blockchain technology on society and businesses are revolutionary. This may present ethical challenges today and in the future. The adoption of blockchain and its potential consequences and the emergence of ethical challenges also raise concerns about blockchain applications (Tang et al., 2020). In addition to ethical difficulties, positive aspects can also arise in blockchain technology. The number of studies about this subject should be increased in order to both reveal the positive aspects and overcome the negative situations.

In the literature, there are studies that examine blockchain together with governance (Jayasuriya Daluwathumullagamage and Sims, 2020; De Filippi, 2019; Hooper and Holdbrügge, 2020; Razzaq et al., 2019; Kaal, 2021; Yermack, 2017; Tiwari and Pal, 2022; De Filippi et al., 2020; Akgiray, 2019) and ethics (Sharif and Ghodoosi, 2022; Ronaghi and Mosakhani, 2022; Tang et al., 2020; Tang et al., 2019; Magnier and Barban, 2018). Blockchain is a novel topic, and implementations of blockchain are spreading so fast that in every single case, a new experience arises.

This creates new questions and issues. So, the field is open to development. Therefore, the study is important in this context.

The aim of this study is to examine blockchain technology in terms of governance and ethics and to reveal the advantages and disadvantages in this context. In this chapter, firstly, the conceptual framework related to blockchain technology and governance will be included, and then the relationship of blockchain with governance and ethics will be discussed both in general and within the scope of business applications. Finally, recommendations are made on the subject.

16.2 Blockchain Technology

Blockchain, which is also used as a distributed ledger, was introduced in 2008 by Satoshi Nakamoto to solve the double spending problem (Razzaq et al., 2019). It can basically be described as a data storage approach in which multiple stakeholders reach an agreement among themselves, save transactions on different databases and ensure that they cannot be changed (Deloitte, 2018).

Instead of keeping the records in a table as a database, the blockchain groups the history of the records and the database in a block as a block. Each new block is chained to the previous block using a cryptographic hash, and when they are all added together, the blockchain emerges.

Thanks to this technology, an intermediary institution such as a bank is created and software codes make the records verifiable. Cryptographic hash can be defined as a fingerprint for any digital data. Regardless of the data, the hash is the same when the same data is processed each time (Wüst and Gervais, 2018).

Blockchain technology has some unique characteristics. These features are summarized as decentralization, persistency, anonymity and auditability (Zheng et al., 2018; Ünal and Uluyol, 2020).

- *Decentralization*: In traditional centralized structures, every transaction center needs to be verified by a reliable source. For example, in money transfer transactions, these transactions are verified by banks. This situation creates a bottleneck in terms of performance and financial cost. In structures where blockchains are used, transactions are carried out entirely between sending and receiving peers. Therefore, blockchain applications and servers can significantly reduce costs.
- *Persistency*: Every transaction confirmed on the blockchain and added to the chain is irreversible under normal conditions. This situation has advantages and disadvantages in various aspects. Since transactions are added and controlled by many nodes, the probability of adding incorrect records is very low. However, on the other hand, it is not possible to change or delete the records added to the added blockchain. The immutability of records creates areas of use such as asset representation to blockchains.
- *Anonymity*: In blockchain, users use meaningless addresses consisting of various letters and numbers when interacting with the blockchain network. This is a situation that prevents the disclosure of user information. In this way, no authority can store any personal information belonging to the user who makes the transaction in transactions made on the blockchain. Except for in-depth analyses and some special cases, the information on the blockchain and sensitive information of users cannot be accessed.
- *Auditability*: All records are kept retrospectively in the blockchain, and by virtue of block structure, the previous records of a record can be accessed and its entire history can be extracted. Blockchain records are public. This ensures that the blockchain is auditable and transparent.

The rapid adoption of blockchain technology has initiated a transformation in many sectors, especially in finance. The concept of blockchain, which emerged with cryptocurrencies, has gone beyond cryptocurrencies today and has made asset transfers possible in a wide variety of sectors such as health, insurance and trade (Rennock et al., 2018). Blockchains offer potential advantages over traditional methods in terms of cost, speed, and data integrity. Entrepreneurs are actively exploring the suitability of blockchains to record ownership of various assets such as stocks, bonds, real estate, automobiles and works of art. Apart from these, blockchain also has application areas such as public records such as title deeds, birth certificates, driver's licenses and university degrees. Using blockchains to record ownership in these areas can solve many longstanding problems in this regard (Yermack, 2017).

Blockchain technology changed traditional business processes and the way businesses transact across borders so companies started to operate out of reach of existing laws and governance mechanisms. This accelerated technology change has many implications for companies and corporate environments. This technology potential has the ability to radically change the way firms, employees, shareholders and corporations interact and form relationships (Hooper and Holtbrügge, 2020).

16.3 Governance

Governance is seen as a process that coordinates different network structures, formed by interdependent positions and actors with conflicting and opposing interests (Cope et al., 1997). Because governance looks at the actors in the society as partners it is seen as a pattern of direction and control arising from the interaction of the economic, political and social actors in the society (Tekeli, 1996). Governance can be briefly defined as the act of managing together. It states that governance, management and decision-making processes are carried out with the cooperation and participation of all stakeholders and that managers act with a reconciliatory, transparent, accountable, effective and responsible management approach. In other words, governance is not solely managed by a group elected through elections. It also involves the inclusion of various groups, such as NGOs, chambers, professional groups, private sector organizations, universities in the decision-making processes. Within the concept of governance, it is expected that managers must publicly take their decisions, involve all relevant stakeholders in the process, and exhibit a knowledge-based, conciliatory management approach (Toksöz, 2008). The concept of governance proposes a system that envisages collective management instead of a top-down unilateral management style (Özer, 2006).

The basic principles of governance in terms of public management can be listed as consistency (predictability), responsibility, accountability, fairness, transparency, participation, effectiveness, equality and adherence to the law (Toksöz, 2008; Srivastava, 2009; Firidin and Mazlum, 2022).

- *Consistency*: The compatibility of the decisions made both with each other and over time ensures that the regulations to be made by the state are predictable and that the citizens make future development investments in an environment that they can trust.
- *Responsibility*: The government should have the capacity and flexibility to respond quickly to social changes.
- *Accountability*: Public authorities are responsible for how public resources are used, budgeted and reported, and are accountable when necessary.
- *Fairness*: The fact that the public sector does not favor any part of the society in the decisions taken and that the rules that the citizens are subject to are clearly applied to everyone in the same way ensure citizens' trust in the state.
- *Transparency*: It is the decision-making processes and decisions of public authorities that are open and shared with other stakeholders.
- *Efficiency*: It expresses that decisions should be taken at the appropriate time and in line with the objectives.
- *Equality*: It means that the decisions taken by the management are applied equally and simultaneously to everyone and that there is a reasonable relationship between the expected results and the resources to be used and their effects on the segments that will be adversely affected.
- *Adherence to the law*: It means that the management makes decisions based on objective information while remaining within the rules of law, and that the decisions are audited by legal means.

Governance challenges the notion of manageability as self-governing networks, as it rejects the idea of autonomy and centralized guidance (Cope et al., 1997). From the governance perspective, management is seen as an interactive process because no single actor, whether from the public or private sector, possesses the necessary resource capacity and knowledge to solve complex problems on its own (Stoker, 1998).

Governance is also necessary in businesses because of the differences between ownership and control. Shareholder goals of a business may not always be the same as business goals. There may be differences of opinion between shareholders and managers on issues such as needs and making a profit. In this context, agency theory can be associated with corporate governance. According to the agency theory, because managers prioritize their personal interests, solutions should be found that transform the manager from the position of the agent of the organization to the person who serves the organization (Ronaghi and Mosakhini, 2022; ElGammal et al., 2018). In this context, governance is important. At work, corporate governance ensures that managers' actions are aligned with shareholders' goals through structured policies and processes. When governance is considered within the scope of business and management science, it includes the whole relationships between the right holders of the enterprise and the owners. Governance, which can also be expressed as managing the top management of the enterprise, as a concept intimately related to the activities of the top management and the board of directors, includes the control and direction of the top management of the enterprise and the relationships of the groups that claim rights over the enterprise with the top management (Baraz, 2004). The corporate governance structure and board of directors determines the rights and responsibilities among the different participants of the company such as management, shareholders and other stakeholders, and sets out the rules and practices related to decision-making in company affairs (Ülgen and Mirze, 2013). While the principles of governance for public management are explained with eight principles, four principles stand out for businesses. Transparency, accountability, responsibility and fairness are accepted as corporate governance principles (İşcan and Kayğın, 2009; OECD, 2000):

- *Transparency*: It means the timely, complete, accurate and clear disclosure of information about the company to the public, excluding information that is a trade secret.
- *Accountability*: It is the accountability of the members of the board of directors to the shareholders.
- *Responsibility*: Compliance of the activities carried out by the company management on behalf of the company with the legislation, articles of association, internal regulations and auditing this.
- *Fairness* (Equality): The shareholders and stakeholders are treated fairly in all activities of the management.

16.4 Blockchain and Governance

When it comes to governance, the most important innovation of blockchain technology is that it offers more transparent and less hierarchical structures and distributed governance models. Enables the creation of technology decentralized blockchain-based organizations, allowing people to coordinate themselves peer-to-peer with smart contracts (Wright and De Filippi, 2015). Blockchain technology is a powerful tool for governance, especially for stakeholder engagement (Yermack, 2017; Lafarre and

Van der Elst, 2018). Some of the advantages arising in this context are (Akgiray, 2019):

- *Greater transparency of ownership and changes in ownership*: All users, including the blockchain, can also see the trades of others.
- *Efficient and fair shareholders' meetings*: An annual general meeting designed with blockchain not only accelerates issues such as voting and elections, but also reduces manipulation by providing transparency.
- *Real-time accounting*: Accounting systems structured with blockchain will reduce the need for auditing. At the same time, when smart contracts are implemented correctly, the need for litigation and the expected costs of financial stress will decrease.

The most important effect of blockchain for corporate governance is to attain much more. It achieves this by eliminating intermediaries. The complexity of investment networks can cause inefficiency in governance and poor governance can cause financial crises. Because one of the biggest advantages of blockchain technology is the elimination of some forms of intermediation, it offers an opportunity for better governance (Akgiray, 2019). The fact that information is shared with everyone in the network and is irreversible in blockchain is a very effective mechanism to ensure transparency and accountability in governance. Openness and accessibility in communication channels can help identify and fulfill responsibility. However, smart contracts can be designed to ensure fairness in the decision-making process (Akgiray, 2019).

Trading and tracking the ownership of financial assets make blockchain technology a powerful new method. Exchanges around the world use blockchains as a way to list, trade and vote on company stocks, benefiting from lower trading costs, faster property transfers, more accurate registrations and greater transparency (Yermack, 2017). Issuing and trading company securities on blockchains will create numerous benefits, as well as some costs associated with greater transparency in ownership, greater speed, cheaper trading, and reconciliation. Transparency will significantly impact the profit opportunities available, especially for executives, institutional investors and shareholder activists. Because of the real-time monitoring of transactions offered by blockchain technology, ownership and liquidation incentives can vary significantly. By virtue of technology, changing incentives in trade will provide more secure information about the value of companies, and as a result of these changes, capital suppliers will be able to design securities in different ways by taking advantage of the smart contracting capability of blockchain technology. Firms can hire board members or outside consultants with different skills to deal with these changes, and management incentives will evolve as the blockchain changes (Yermack, 2017).

Both public and private governance could benefit from this technology at the national level (Tiwari and Pal, 2022). Banking, notary public, a title deed, tax tracking, smart contracts, cloud storage, electronic voting, citizen identity records, supply chain management, verification of social assistance payments, health system, patient records, intellectual property, licenses and so on are used in many transactions, which constitute the basis for fast, safe and cheap transactions (Şahin, 2021; Alam et al., 2021; Güven and Şahinöz, 2020). The use of blockchain in public governance will make it easier to perform public services such as tracking the identities and assets of citizens. It is the fundamental duty of the democratic constitutional state to keep the land registry records open and unchangeable to protect the fundamental human right to property. Blockchain technology is the strongest candidate to provide a reliable infrastructure to ensure the right to property in ensuring the unchangeable records, clarity and transparency (Şahin, 2021). One of the most important public usages of the blockchain is "smart contracts". Agreements can be made between stakeholders without the need for a central authority and can be tracked through a series of algorithms. For the time being, it is more reasonable using blockchain in the agreements for automated instructions as self-executing contracts (Werbach, 2021). One of the areas where blockchain will be effective is electronic voting (e-voting). The use of electronic voting in public opinion polls, in various public and private polls, and in general or local elections has the potential to provide a favorable environment for governance by supporting citizens' participation in decisions on a very useful ground in terms of time, space, cost and transparency (Gürfidan and Akçay, 2020).

However, when it comes to private governance, blockchain technology can be applied in many organizations all over the country that provide products and services. In the long run, this will enable blockchain-based corporate governance (Tiwari and Pal, 2022). Many of the practices that have emerged from incorporating blockchain into public governance are also being implemented in private or corporate governance in different ways. In terms of the blockchain and governance relationship, the business can focus on several areas. Documents, policies and procedures are elements that require data management for businesses. It is important that they are both accessible and confidential. At this point, blockchain is one of the most suitable solutions for businesses. All records can be securely placed on the blockchain, keeping confidentiality. All data is publicly stored, but not accessible to everyone. Only the block owner can access it. So blockchain may be a better option than a database. Although databases are also auditable and manageable, they can be compromised by a simple email attack. But blockchains are not like that. One of the basic building blocks of blockchain is immutability. It is not possible to change an entry after putting it in the chain. Therefore, utilizing blockchain in governance procedures for businesses will be safe, secure and immutable (Brown, 2022). This creates a more reliable environment for stakeholders.

16.5 Ethics

It is seen that the concept of ethics, which is a part of social life, has been discussed in many different areas from the past to the present, and it is in a structure that is re-evaluated and handled in every new and/or different conditions in which a community and daily life exist. According to the general view, ethics is a collection of rules containing moral values and principles that guide the behavior of a person or group regarding what is right and wrong. The issue discussed in ethical behavior is questions about what is valuable and what is worthless; what is virtue and what is not; what kinds of actions are right and wrong to do. It has been the case that every person has been torn between different behavioral alternatives at various moments in his life, and has had difficulty deciding what would be the right thing to do at that moment. The question of what would be right for an individual to do in the face of a situation that he or she faces is a question that only the person experiencing that situation can answer. Although ethics deal with human action, they are not considered to be a characteristic theory of action, because the subject of ethics is not about all human activities and actions, but actions that emphasize morality. In other words, ethics asks about the qualitative situation that makes an action a morally good action. Actions that are right and valuable for humanity, society and individuals constitute the subject of ethics (Ülgen and Mirze, 2013).

Business ethics is about what is good or bad, fair or unfair in a particular situation in a business. Questions on this subject are increasing day by day. Business ethics is a set of values and principles that guide employees on these issues (Carroll and Buchholtz, 2003). Most definitions of business ethics relate to rules, principles, and standards about what is right and wrong in specific situations. In simple terms, business ethics encompass the ethical principles and standards that guide our behavior in the business world (Ferrel and Fraedrich, 1994). Although the factors that determine business ethics are basically the organization, society and culture, the use of technology is also important in terms of ethics.

16.6 Blockchain and Ethics

Since the foundation of blockchain is based on data, ethical problems often arise in this area. These issues relate to privacy, accuracy, property, and accessibility (Tang et al., 2020; Zheng et al., 2018). In this context, personal data included in the blockchain can also create ethical problems. Despite the development of various regulations to limit and standardize the use of personal data in electronic media and prevent the unauthorized access by third parties, the inherent structure of blockchain technology poses challenges. The immutability of data storage in blockchain, particularly, when it involves personally identifiable information, is inconsistent with the relevant legislation concerning the protection and storage of personal data (Personal Data Protection Law and Blockchain Technology Report, 2019).

These incompatibilities arise from the nature of data processing in distributed databases using blockchain technology. This technology ensures data integrity, making it imutable and resistant to changes. Moreover, data deletion is not possible in applications using blockchain technology. Additionally, all users in the network have visibility and access to their own copy of the data. In the literature, there are studies (Zyskind et al., 2015; Zheng et al., 2018; Truong et al., 2019) detailing blockchain applications for the control and audit of personal data, and offering suggestions that can provide maximum compatibility with the aforementioned technology within the scope of various legal regulations. Therefore, this deficiency will probably cease to be a problem in the future.

Besides the problems with blockchain, it also creates many ethical advantages. With immutability, being one of the main features of blockchain technology, it aims to prevent various forms of frauds and unauthorized use of personal data. This technology also provides transparency in organizational processes and ethical codes related to the accurate monitoring of managerial activities and valuation of corporate assets. Organizational competition could also be affected by this technology because of the distributed information system in the blockchain network (Ronaghi, 2020; Brav and Mathews, 2011; Tapscott and Tapscott, 2017; Catalini and Tucker, 2018). Thus, unfair competition can be eliminated.

Considering the application of blockchain in business activities (e.g., Human resource management), the issue of ethics primarily manifests itself in the recruitment and placement processes. Through the blockchain technology, it is possible to have an affirmed and transparent recruitment and selection procedure (Sharif and Ghodoosi, 2022). Thus, benefits such as easier organization of candidate information, enlargement of the candidate pool in accordance with the needs and objectives of the business, and a fair area where all candidates have equal conditions are also provided. Applications can be considered very reliable, as blockchain will ensure that the information and documents submitted by candidates with their application are verified. This will make the field fair for all applicants. Recruitments made in this way, especially in crucial sectors such as chemistry and energy, improve the quality of human resources and provide safe operations (Zehir et al., 2022). However, a downside to ethics is that blockchain technology reduces privacy, which can also be associated with personal data. Employees may think that privacy has been violated when they don't have control over the background information that employers have access to.

After selection and placement in enterprises, contracts should be signed to determine the rules of the business relationship and mutual expectations regarding wages and rights. Here, too, blockchain technology comes to the fore with the benefit of smart contracts. Smart contracts are coded deals that self-execute agreements and automate certain decision-making processes. Smart contracts can be used to make employee payments. An automatic payment plan is activated when predetermined conditions are met. Using predefined conditions will also reduce the likelihood of delay or denial of compensation after employees meet them. Thus, a plan in which transparency, speed and accountability is increased and arbitrary practices are reduced is provided (Sharif and Ghodoosi, 2022).

After the organizations complete a recruiting activity, they want to try motivating and retaining recruits. Creating a work atmosphere that fosters employee retention is crucial, considering the substantial costs businesses incur when employees leave. One of the ways businesses keep their existing employees is to ensure justice and to give them the right to participate in organizational processes. Blockchain-based organizations, as in the many technology-oriented businesses, have narrowed their control area and gained a more unlimited structure (Ashkenas, 1995; Devanna and Tichy, 1990). Blockchain-based businesses can foster a managerial process in which leaders' responsibilities are distributed among employees (Pearce and Conger, 2002; Pearce et al., 2008). This shared leadership procedure can make co-decision mechanisms more functional through the blockchain. In this way, employees have the opportunity to access a significant amount of data. However, all users on the blockchain can vote for or against any block attempting to be added to the blockchain. Consequently, blockchain enables an equitable and distributed voting procedure, where employees can voice their opinions.

One of the areas where blockchain can be used to ensure ethical practice is conflict management (Sharif and Ghodoosi, 2022). Here again, smart contracts can be used to resolve the conflict. By coding the probabilities, it is possible for the employee to solve the conflict by evaluating the probabilities over these codes. All of this gives employees a sense of value, as they provide opportunities to voice their opinions and participate in decision-making. It also reduces employee concerns about perceptions of fairness.

Blockchain technology can also be used for performance management. Blockchain provides a distributed and verified performance management, creating transparency, accountability and trust. Thus, prejudice in the evaluation of employees will decrease and healthier decisions can be made in appointments. As all these will make the organization a fairer field, a positive ethical situation will be created. A disadvantage at this point may be that a negative performance appraisal may stick to the person. Since the data recorded in the block will be immutable, this may prevent the employee from getting promoted, especially in cases where performance assessment has not been done fairly. However, blockchain-based performance assessments focus on minimizing such threats for individuals.

Finally, if an employee leaves or is removed from the organization, blockchain can streamline dismissal activities such as verifying and transferring employee documents and build trust. Also, dismissal may present some risks to the organization, including legal risks. Because transparent performance management provides a trackable record of performance to both the organization and employees, the organization and employees better understand the responsibilities and rights associated with leaving. Thus, a more certain evaluation of emerging risks and a more fair and effective determination of debates can be achieved (Sharif and Ghodoosi, 2022).

16.7 Conclusion and Recommendations

Blockchain has the capability to make radical changes in every aspect of society with its innovations. Blockchain, one of the technologies that emerged on the basis of digitalization, increases the participation of everyone who benefits from this technology in all processes, since it is a consensus-based mechanism that eliminates intermediaries. Therefore, since the blockchain includes a transparent management approach, it also overlaps with the governance approach that enables everyone to participate directly in the management processes, thus forming the digital infrastructure of governance. Thanks to the basic features of blockchain, principles such as transparency, efficiency, sustainability, participation and accountability in governance are much better than before (Şahin, 2021). Very successful results are also obtained in terms of durability, security and data transfer criteria. These criteria will bring greater advantages in the future (Ünal and Uluyol, 2020). In this context, it can be said that using blockchain in governance has positive results. In addition to these, blockchain also has some negative aspects. Although transparency from blockchain features is seen as an advantage in terms of governance, it can create major problems in systems with personal privacy such as banking. This situation creates inconsistencies with the regulations within the scope of the personal data protection law. Another disadvantage of the use of blockchain is that the legal infrastructure is not yet clear. Increasing state regulations in this regard will reduce and eliminate the relevant deficiency. Another obstacle facing the blockchain is technical features such as not providing a good user experience, scalability and privacy problems due to being a relatively new technology (Şen and Alnıaçık, 2019). Although blockchain technology allows significant savings in time and transaction costs, the high investment costs in the installation phase of this technology can be a deterrent (Babaoğlu and Karasoy, 2022). In addition, environmental effects such as high energy consumption can also create problems in terms of sustainability principles.

In many blockchain applications, the disappearance of the confidentiality of data can create ethical problems. Apart from this, it provides ethical values such as equality and justice, especially since it has the potential to change human interactions in business practices. Blockchain is also a good solution to control corruption and immorality in the organization such as information distortion and fraud. Thus, using this technology, organizations can enhance their ethical standards and create appropriate business interactive relations. For this, managers need to see blockchain as a versatile application that affects organizational interactions and human behavior rather than just a technical tool. Otherwise, the problems experienced in this regard may reduce the effectiveness of the use of blockchain.

As a result, the positive and negative aspects within the scope of governance and ethics that arise with the use of blockchain may differ according to features such as the purpose of the blockchain, the sector in which it is applied, and the organization. Sometimes what is seen as an advantage for one side can create a disadvantage for the other. In addition, although there are negative aspects, since blockchain is a technology that is open to continuous development by its nature, these problems will decrease and disappear as the technology develops. At the same time, the appropriate environment to be provided with governance and ethics, which are known to be positively related to blockchain applications, will contribute to the more effective work and sustainability of organizations.

References

Akgiray, V. (2019). The potential for blockchain technology in corporate governance. In OECD Corporate Governance Working Papers 21: 1–32. Available at https://doi.org/10.1787/ef4eba4c-en.

Alam, S., Shuaib, M., Khan, W. Z., Garg, S., Kaddoum, G. et al. (2021). Blockchain-based Initiatives: current state and challenges. Computer Networks 198: 1–20.

Ashkenas, R. (1995). The Boundaryless Organization: Breaking the Chains of Organizational Structure. The Jossey-Bass Management Series.

Babaoğlu, C. and Karasoy, H. (2022). Kamu yönetiminde blokzincir: kullanım alanları ve örnek uygulamalar. Sosyoekonomi 30: 283–297.

Baraz, B. (2004). Yönetim kurullarının kurumsal yönetişim açısından kritik önemi: Eskişehir'de bir araştırma. 3.Ulusal Bilgi Ekonomi ve Yönetim Kongresi Bildiriler Kitabı, Osmangazi Üniversitesi İktisadi İdari Bilimler Fakültesi Yayınları, Eskişehir.

Brav, A. and Mathews, R. D. (2011). Empty voting and the efficiency of corporate governance. Journal of Financial Economics 99: 289–307.

Brown, E. (2022, 13 May). Why blockchain technology is important for governance-and why it matters. Available at https://coingeek.com/why-blockchain-technology-is-important-for-governance-and-why-it-matters/.

Carroll, A. B. and Buchholtz, A. K. (2003). Business & Society: Ethics and Stakeholder Management. Thomson South-Western, U.S.A.

Catalini, C. and Tucker, C. E. (2018). Antitrust and Costless Verification: An Optimistic and a Pessimistic View of the Implications of Blockchain Technology (June 19, 2018). MIT Sloan Research Paper No. 5523-18, Available at SSRN: https://ssrn.com/abstract=3199453 or http://dx.doi.org/10.2139/ssrn.

Cope, S. F. and Leishman, P. S. (1997). Globalization, new public management and the enabling state. International Journal of Public Sector Management 10: 444–460.

De Filippi, P. (2019). Blockchain Technology and Decentralized Governance: The Pitfalls of a Trustless Dream. Decentralized Thriving: Governance and Community on the Web 3.0. Available at https://hal.science/hal-02445179/file/66%20-%20(2019)%20DAOstack%20-%20Trustless%20dream.pdf.

De Filippi, P., Mannan, M. and Reijers, W. (2020). Blockchain as a confidence machine: The problem of trust & challenges of governance. Technology in Society 62: 101284.

Deloitte Report. (2018). Deloitte's 2018 global blockchain survey. Available at https://www2.deloitte.com/content/dam/Deloitte/cz/Documents/financial-services/cz-2018-deloitte-global-blockchain-survey.pdf.

Devanna, M. A. and Tichy, N. (1990). Creating the competitive organization of the 21st century: the boundaryless corporation. Human Resource Management 29: 455–471.

ElGammal, W., El-Kassar, A. and Messarra, L. C. (2018). Corporate ethics, governance and social responsibility in MENA countries. Management Decision 56: 273–291.

Ferrel, O. C. and Fraedrich, J. (1994). Business Ethics: Ethical Decision Making and Cases. Haughton Mifflm Comp. New York.

Firidin, E. and Mazlum, S. (2022). The role of the ombudsman in the protection of public value in the context of good governance principles. Ombudsman Akademik 9: 217–236.

Gürfidan, R. and Akçay, Z. (2020). Blok zincir temelli güvenli elektronik oylama modeli. International Journal of Engineering and Innovative Research 2: 148–155.

Güven, V. and Şahinöz, E. (2020). Blokzincir, Kriptoparalar, Bitcoin: Satoshi Dünyayı Değiştiriyor. Kronik Kitap, İstanbul.

Hooper, A. and Holtbrügge, D. (2020). Blockchain technology in international business: changing the agenda for global governance. Review of International Business and Strategy 30: 183–200.

İşcan, Ö. F. and Kayğın, E. (2009). Kurumsal yönetişim sürecinin gelişimi üzerine bir araştırma. Atatürk Üniversitesi Sosyal Bilimler Enstitüsü Dergisi 13: 213–224.

Jayasuriya Daluwathumullagamage, D. and Sims, A. (2020). Blockchain-enabled corporate governance and regulation. International Journal of Financial Studies 8: 1–38.

Kaal, W. A. (2021). Blockchain-based corporate governance. Stanford Journal of Blockchain Law & Policy.

Lafarre, A. and Van der Elst, C. (2018). Blockchain Technology for Corporate Governance and Shareholder Activism (March 2018). European Corporate Governance Institute (ECGI)-Law Working Paper No. 390/2018, Tilburg Law School Research Paper No. 2018-7, Available at SSRN: https://ssrn.com/abstract=3135209 or http://dx.doi.org/10.2139/ssrn.3135209.

Magnier, V. and Barban, P. (2018). The potential impact of blockchains on corporate governance: a survey on shareholders' rights in the digital era. InterEULawEast: Journal for the International and European Law, Economics and Market Integrations 5: 189–226.

Nakamoto, S. (2008). Bitcoin: A peer-to-peer electronic cash system. Available at https://bitcoin.org/bitcoin.pdf.

OECD. (2000, July). Principles of Corporate Governance, Paris. Available at http://www.oecd.org/corporate/principles-corporate-governance.htm.

Özer, M. A. (2006). Yönetişim üzerine notlar. Sayıştay Dergisi 63: 59–89.

Pearce, C. L. and Conger, J. A. (2002). Shared Leadership: Reframing The Hows and Whys of Leadership. SAGE Publications, Inc.

Pearce, C. L., Conger, J. A. and Locke, E. A. (2008). Shared leadership theory. The Leadership Quarterly 19: 622–628.

Personal Data Protection Law and Blockchain Technology Report. (2019, November). Available at https://bctr.org/dokumanlar/KVKK_ve_Blokzincir_Teknolojisi.pdf.

Razzaq, A. K., Talib, M. M., Butt, R., Hanif, A., Afzal, N. et al. (2019). Use of blockchain in governance: a systematic literature review. International Journal of Advanced Computer Science and Applications 10: 685–691.

Rennock, M. J. W., Cohn, A. and Butcher, J. R. (2018). Blockchain technology and regulatory investigations. The Journal Litigation, March: 34–44.

Ronaghi, M. H. (2020). A blockchain maturity model in agricultural supply chain. Information Processing in Agriculture 8: 398–408.

Ronaghi, M. H. and Mosakhani, M. (2022). The effects of blockchain technology adoption on business ethics and social sustainability: evidence from the Middle East. Environ. Dev. Sustain. 24: 6834–6859.

Şahin, D. (2021). Leverage effect in governance: blockchain governance. The Journal of Kesit Academy 7: 94–109.

Şen, E. and Alnıaçık, B. (2019). Blokzincir teknolojisinin yönetim süreçlerine olası etkileri üzerine inceleme. Sosyal Bilimler Dergisi/The Journal of Social Science 34: 660–673.

Sharif, M. M. and Ghodoosi, F. (2022). The ethics of blockchain in organizations. J. Bus Ethics 178: 1009–1025.

Srivastava, M. (2009). Good governance-concept, meaning and features: a detailed study. Available at SSRN: https://ssrn.com/abstract=1528449 or http://dx.doi.org/10.2139/ssrn.1528449.

Stoker, G. (1998). Governance as theory: five positions. International Sociel Science Journal 50: 17–29.

Tang, Y., Xiong, J., Becerril-Arreola, R. and Iyer, L. (2019). Blockchain ethics research: A conceptual model. pp. 43–49. In Proceedings of the 2019 on Computers and People Research Conference, Nashville, USA.

Tang, Y., Xiong, J., Becerril-Arreola, R. and Iyer, L. (2020). Ethics of blockchain: A framework of technology, applications, impacts, and research directions. Information Technology & People 33: 602–632.

Tapscott, D. and Tapscott, A. (2017). How blockchain will change organizations. MIT Sloan Management Review 58: 10–13.

Tekeli, İ. (1996). Yönetim kavramı yanı sıra yönetişim kavramının gelişmesinin nedenleri üzerine. Sosyal Demokrat Değişim 3: 45–54.

Tiwari, C. K. and Pal, A. (2022). Using blockchain for global governance: past, present and future. South Asian Journal of Business Studies (published online ahead of print 23 August 2022). Available at: https://doi.org/10.1108/SAJBS-07-2022-0252.

Toksöz, F. (2008). İyi Yönetişim El Kitabı. Tesev Yayınları, İstanbul.

Truong, N. B. and Lee, G. M. (2019). GDPR-Compliant personal data management: a blockchain-based solution. IEEE Transactions on Information Forensics and Security 15: 1746–1761.

Ülgen, H. and Mirze, S. K. (2013). İşletmelerde Stratejik Yönetim. Beta Yayınları, İstanbul.

Ünal, G. and Uluyol, Ç. (2020). Blokzinciri teknolojisi. Bilişim Teknolojileri Dergisi 13: 167–175.

Werbach, K. (2021). Blokzinciri ve Yeni Güven Mimarisi, Koç Üniversitesi Yayınları, İstanbul.
Wright, A. and De Filippi, P. (2015). Decentralized blockchain technology and the rise of lex cryptographia. Social Science Research Network 34: 41–52.
Wüst, K. and Gervais, A. (2018). Do you need a blockchain? 2018 Crypto Valley Conference on Blockchain Technology (CVCBT), Zug, Switzerland, 45–54.
Yermack, D. (2017). Corporate governance and blockchains. Review of Finance 21: 7–31.
Zehir, C., Zehir, M., Borodin, A., Mamedov, Z. F. and Qurbanov, S. (2022). Tailored blockchain applications for the natural gas industry: the case study of SOCAR. Energies 15: 1–19.
Zheng, X., Mukkamala, R. R., Vatrapu, R. and Meré, J. B. (2018). Blockchain-based personal health data sharing system using cloud storage. pp. 1–6. 2018 IEEE 20th International Conference on e-Health Networking. Applications and Services (Healthcom).
Zheng, Z., Xie, S., Dai, H. N., Chen, X., Wang, H. et al. (2018). Blockchain challenges and opportunities: a survey. Int. J. Web and Grid Services 14: 352–375.
Zyskind, G., Nathan, O. and Pentland, A. S. (2015). Decentralizing privacy: using blockchain to protect personal data. pp. 180–184. 2015 IEEE Security and Privacy Workshops, San Jose, CA, USA.

Chapter 17
Accounting and Auditing Perspective of Blockchain Application

Mehdi Bouchetara

17.1 Introduction

Accounting and auditing professionals are getting increasingly aware of the importance of technology for their industry. Automation, digitization, and data analysis are radically transforming the way accounting professionals work. The majority of professionals surveyed believe that technology is a key element in improving their efficiency, productivity, and quality of work (Deloitte, 2019).

Automation is significantly transforming financial functions. Administrative tasks, such as data entry, account verification, and bank reconciliation, are becoming increasingly automated, allowing professionals to focus on more tasks that are complex. Data analysis and predictive modeling are key areas for the future of accounting and auditing (McKinsey, 2019). Data analysis is becoming an essential skill for accounting and auditing professionals. Data analysis tools, such as data mining techniques and machine learning algorithms, can help identify anomalies and fraud, as well as predict financial trends (PwC, 2020). Block chain can be used to improve transparency and security in financial transactions. Transactions can be stored transparently and immutably, making verification and auditing of accounts easier. In addition, block

Assistant Professor, Higher National School of Management, Algeria.
Email: bouchetara_mehdi2002@yahoo.fr

chain can also help automate account verification processes, which can reduce costs and improve efficiency.

Artificial intelligence (AI) is also transforming the accounting and auditing function. According to a report published by accounting software company Sage (2018); AI can help automate manual tasks, such as data entry and bookkeeping. It can also assist with data analysis, identifying trends and patterns in large datasets.

Furthermore, artificial intelligence (AI) has the capability to detect fraudulent activities and deviations in financial transactions. This can be achieved through the examination of transactional patterns and the identification of atypical behaviors. Additionally, AI can enhance the precision of financial reporting by effectively detecting errors and disparities within data (Forbes, 2021).

Another manner in which artificial intelligence (AI) is revolutionizing the accounting and auditing domain involves the utilization of natural language processing (NLP) and machine learning techniques. NLP can be effectively employed to scrutinize unstructured data sources, such as emails and textual documents, with the aim of extracting valuable insights. Furthermore, machine learning algorithms can be trained to identify patterns and aberrations within financial data. By automating specific tasks like risk assessment and sampling, AI can enhance the audit process, resulting in heightened precision and efficiency. This enables auditors to allocate their efforts towards more intricate endeavors (Deloitte, 2020).

17.2 Definition and Evolution of Blockchain Technology

Block chain technology has been defined in various ways by researchers and experts in recent years. According to Garcia et al. (2021), a blockchain is a secure and decentralized ledger that registers transactions and assets across a network of peers. This ledger offers the capability to generate transparent, tamper-evident, and secure transactions applicable to various domains. The World Economic Forum (2021) defines blockchain as a decentralized and digital ledger that securely records transactions across a computer network while ensuring transparency. Similarly, Harveston and Li (2020) describe blockchain as a decentralized and distributed digital ledger that is employed to record transactions across multiple computers, guaranteeing security and tamper-proof attributes.

The evolution of block chain technology has experienced rapid and constant development since its creation in 2008 with the publication of the Bitcoin whitepaper by Satoshi Nakamoto. Here is an overview of the evolution of block chain:

- 2008–2010: Creation of Bitcoin and initial applications; The first application of block chain was the creation of Bitcoin, a decentralized digital currency, in 2008. The Bitcoin whitepaper describes how block chain technology can be used to create a secure digital currency without the intervention of a central third party (Nakamoto, 2008).
- 2011–2013: Growing adoption and development of decentralized applications; Block chain technology was adopted for many other decentralized applications, such as smart contracts and decentralized data storage applications. The year 2013 saw the creation of many new block chain-based crypto currencies, including Ethereum (Buterin, 2013).
- 2014–2016: Industry maturation and development of new standards; During this period, the block chain industry began to mature and develop new standards for security and performance. Industry consortia such as the Hyperledger Foundation were created to promote adoption and development of block chain technology (Hyperledger, 2016).
- 2017–2021: Massive adoption and development of new commercial applications; The year 2017 saw massive adoption of block chain with the launch of new commercial applications, such as stable coins and decentralized trading platforms. This period also saw accelerated development of block chain technology in many sectors, including finance, health, and supply chains (Garcia et al., 2021).

17.2.1 Advantages of Blockchain

One of the advantages of block chain is that it offers increased transparency and strengthened security due to its decentralized structure and its ability to encrypt data. According to Awan et al. (2019), block chain can offer solutions to problems such as data security, transaction reliability, and privacy protection due to its ability to ensure the integrity and confidentiality of data.

Furthermore, block chain can also improve the efficiency of financial transactions by eliminating the need for intermediaries such as banks and money transfer companies. According to Liu et al. (2020), block chain can accelerate the process of money transfer and decentralized financial contracts, which can reduce costs and delays associated with these processes. Block chain can also be used for identity management by allowing each user to control and manage their own personal data. According to Schwartz et al. (2020), block chain can allow users to securely store and share their data, which can improve privacy protection and online trust.

17.2.2 Limitations of Blockchain

Despite its many benefits, there are also some limitations to block chain technology that must be considered. One of the main limitations of block chain is its scalability. According to Gai et al. (2020), the current block chain architecture can only process a limited number of transactions per second, which may not meet the demands of large-scale applications such as payment systems or stock exchanges. Another limitation of block chain is its energy consumption. According to Wang et al. (2020), the process of validating transactions on a block chain network can consume a significant amount of energy, which is not sustainable in the long term.

Block chain also has privacy and security limitations. According to Liu et al. (2019), block chain is not immune to hacking attacks, and it may raise privacy concerns, as the data stored on the block chain is accessible to all users in the network. Block chain has many advantages; it also has some limitations that need to be addressed, such as scalability, energy consumption, and privacy and security.

17.3 The Functioning of Blockchain in Finance, Auditing, and Accounting

Block chain can be used in various areas of finance, auditing, and accounting to improve the transparency, security, and efficiency of transactions. For example, in finance, block chain can be used for money transfers, decentralized financial contracts, identity management, and payments. According to Böhme et al. (2015), block chain can eliminate intermediaries in international fund transfers, which can result in significant time and cost savings.

In terms of auditing, block chain can help to improve the reliability and transparency of financial data by offering a permanent and unchallenged record of transactions. According to Liu et al. (2019), this can facilitate the verification and auditing of financial data and increase the confidence of investors and users.

In accounting, block chain can be used to automate accounting processes and accelerate the consolidation and production of financial reports. According to Liu et al. (2019), this can also help to reduce errors and accounting frauds by providing reliable evidence of financial transactions. Block chain can be a very useful tool for finance, auditing, and accounting by providing increased transparency, strengthened security, and increased efficiency in financial transactions.

Wang and Chen (2019) explore the implications of block chain for cost accounting and financial statement certification. They concluded that block chain could improve the transparency and reliability of cost accounting by enabling complete traceability of transactions. This can help companies improve the accuracy of their costs and make them more transparent for auditors and investors. Furthermore, block chain can facilitate financial statement certification by enabling auditors to verify accounting transactions. This can reduce audit costs and increase investors' confidence in companies' financial statements.

Abdullah and Mohamed (2020) examine how block chain can improve the reliability and transparency of accounting reporting. They concluded that block chain could improve the reliability of accounting by eliminating manual entry errors and ensuring data integrity. Additionally, block chain can make financial statements more transparent by enabling complete traceability of transactions and providing an immutable record of accounting data.

Block chain has the potential to revolutionize accounting by providing a reliable, secure and transparent record of financial transactions. A lot of scientific research has been conducted on this topic and it is likely that new studies will continue to explore the applications of block chain in this field.

17.3.1 Blockchain and Accounting

The impact of block chain on accounting is changing significantly, as this technology has the potential to replace traditional accounting systems by offering greater transparency, cost reduction, and increased reliability.

According to Lin et al. (2022), block chain can provide a decentralized database that can be used for verifying the integrity of accounting data, which can reduce errors and frauds. Li et al. (2023) examine the potential impacts of block chain on accounting in terms of transparency and efficiency. The authors state that block chain can provide a transparent solution for bookkeeping, which can help reduce errors and costs associated with data verification.

Recent research shows that block chain has the potential to have a significant impact on accounting by offering increased transparency, cost reduction, and increased reliability of accounting data.

In their study, Iqbal and Raza (2022) present a comprehensive analysis of the application of blockchain technology in the field of accounting. The authors explore the potential advantages of utilizing blockchain for financial statement verification, which encompass enhanced transparency and decreased expenses. Additionally, they delve into the potential obstacles, including technical intricacies and security apprehensions. Ultimately, the authors assert that blockchain holds the potential to revolutionize the accounting landscape; however, substantial challenges must be addressed and surmounted before this vision can be actualized.

Nguyen and Tarca (2021) examines the potential benefits of using block chain for financial statement verification. The authors argue that block chain can provide a transparent solution for bookkeeping, which can help reduce errors and costs associated with data verification. The authors also examine potential challenges, such as technical complexity and security concerns. Finally, the authors conclude that block chain can have a significant impact on the way financial statement verification is done, but significant challenges must be overcome before this can become a reality.

Park (2022) examines the potential impacts of block chain on the accounting profession, including the challenges and opportunities for accounting professionals. The authors argue that block chain can transform the way accounting is done, by offering increased transparency, reduced costs, and increased reliability of accounting data. The authors also examine potential challenges for accounting professionals, such as the need to become familiar with new technologies and the need to ensure compliance with accounting standards. Finally, the authors conclude that block chain can have a significant impact on the accounting profession, but significant challenges must be overcome before this can become a reality.

Alkhamisi and Karim (2021) examines the impact of block chain technology on accounting and auditing. The authors perform a systematic review of existing literature on the subject and analyze the advantages and challenges of using block chain in these fields. They find that block chain has the potential to increase transparency, reduce errors, and improve the overall efficiency of accounting and auditing processes. However, they also identify significant challenges, including technical complexity and security concerns, which must be overcome in order for block chain to be fully adopted in these fields. The authors conclude that block chain has the potential to transform accounting and auditing, but further research and development is needed to fully realize its potential.

The research conducted by Arslan and Albayrak (2020) centers on investigating the impact of blockchain technology on the accounting field, specifically within the financial sector. Through the utilization of empirical evidence, the authors analyze the influence of blockchain technology on the financial sector and its prospective impact on accounting practices. The study examines the potential advantages offered by blockchain technology in the financial sector, including heightened transparency and enhanced security. Conversely, it also addresses challenges that must be addressed, such as the necessity for an improved regulatory framework and the establishment of standardized methodologies for the implementation of blockchain technology in financial operations. Ultimately, the authors conclude that the integration of blockchain technology within the financial sector possesses the potential to profoundly affect accounting processes. However, the realization of this potential requires careful consideration, strategic planning, and effective solutions to overcome the challenges encountered along the way.

In their study, Malmi and Ollila (2019) present an extensive overview of the influence of blockchain technology on the accounting domain. The authors meticulously investigate the potential advantages associated with the adoption of blockchain in accounting, such as enhanced transparency, cost reduction, and improved data accuracy. They assert that further empirical research is necessary to assess the practical implications of blockchain on accounting, as well as to gain a deeper understanding of its consequences for accounting professionals and organizations. The authors ultimately conclude that blockchain holds the potential to revolutionize accounting practices, yet significant challenges need to be addressed in order to realize this potential. They emphasize the need for continued research endeavors to enhance comprehension of the impact of blockchain on accounting, thereby aiding organizations and professionals in navigating the intricate intricacies of this emerging technology.

17.3.2 Opportunities and Challenges of Using Blockchain in Audit

The use of block chain in the audit industry is a topic of active debate. While some see the technology as an opportunity to improve transparency, quality, and efficiency of audit, others are concerned about challenges related to security, compatibility, and regulation. In the following, we will examine the opportunities and challenges of using block chain in audit, using scientific articles to support our analysis.

17.3.2.1 Opportunities

According to the article "The Use of Block chain in Auditing: A Review" published in the Journal of Accounting and Taxation in 2021, block chain technology can offer increased transparency by maintaining a permanent and immutable record of all transactions. This can help auditors better understand transactions and better control financial data.

Another article, titled "Block chain in Audit: Opportunities, Challenges and the Future," published by Deloitte in 2021, indicates that block chain can allow auditors to verify financial data more quickly and validate it more easily. This can improve the quality of audit.

According to the report "The Potential of Block chain in the Audit Industry" published by PWC in 2022, block chain can allow for the automation of some audit tasks, reducing errors and speeding up the process.

The automation of some tasks can also reduce the costs associated with audit, according to the same report by PWC.

17.3.2.2 Challenges

According to the Deloitte report, while block chain technology is promising for the audit industry, it may be difficult to achieve wide and effective adoption. Compatibility with existing systems: The Journal of Accounting and Taxation article highlights that block chain systems may not be compatible with existing financial systems, leading to compatibility issues. Security: Security is a major concern for all block chain technologies, and this is true for its use in audit.

Kim and Lee (2022), Rashed and Alqahtani (2021) examines the impact of block chain technology on auditing using data from companies in South Korea and Saudi Arabia. The authors found that block chain could improve the transparency and reliability of financial data, which can assist auditors in performing more efficient and reliable audits. They also found that South Korean companies were positive about the future use of block chain in auditing. However, they also reported challenges such as the high costs associated with technology adoption and the need for adequate standards and regulations.

17.4 The Effects of Block Chain Technology on the Function of Accounting and Auditing

17.4.1 Using of Blockchain in the Accounting Profession

The use of block chain technology can potentially affect the accounting profession in various ways. First, according to Deloitte (2021), block chain can automate certain accounting tasks by allowing for automated verification and validation of transactions. This can reduce potential errors and fraud, which can improve the quality of financial statements.

Second, according to KPMG (2021), block chain can provide increased transparency for financial statements by allowing for real-time verification of transactions and providing a permanent and immutable record of transactions. This can help increase the confidence of investors and stakeholders in financial statements. Finally, according to EY (2021), block chain can also reduce costs for businesses by automating certain tasks and reducing the need for personnel to perform manual activities such as transaction verification.

However, it is important to note that block chain is a relatively new and evolving technology, and there may be challenges to overcome such as ensuring the confidentiality and security of data on the block chain. Accountants must therefore be aware of these challenges and be prepared to work with block chain technology to make the most of their potential to improve accounting activities.

Block chain technology can bring many benefits to the accounting profession, but accountants must also be aware of potential challenges associated with using this technology. The sources mentioned above can be useful in learning more about the impacts of block chain on the accounting profession.

17.4.2 About the Audit Profession!

According to Alqahtani et al. (2020), block chain can have a significant impact on the auditing profession due to its characteristics such as increased transparency, immutability, and data security. The authors of this article concluded that blockchains facilitate the collection and verification of financial data for auditors, which can result in a reduction of errors or fraud risks in the audited financial statements.

Block chain could also offer better collaboration between auditors and companies by allowing real-time access to financial data. The authors also noted that block chain can help improve the quality and speed of the audit by offering verification that is more efficient and increased transparency of financial data (Böhme and Christen, 2019).

Block chain can improve the quality and reliability of the audit by offering increased transparency of financial data, but they also noted that it is important to develop adequate standards and regulations to ensure its effective and ethical use (Alhashmi and Al-Fazari, 2018).

17.4.3 Smart Contracts and Audit Profession: Good Future!

Smart contracts are agreements that automatically execute predefined terms and conditions, as they are directly encoded into lines of code. These contracts, along with their associated agreements, are stored on a blockchain network and are enforced by the network itself.

One of the key benefits of using smart contracts on block chain platforms is that they provide a high level of transparency, as all parties have access to the same information and can see the terms of the agreement and its execution. This eliminates the need for intermediaries and ensures that the terms of the contract are enforced automatically, reducing the risk of disputes and fraudulent behavior.

One additional benefit of smart contracts is their capability to autonomously execute predefined actions when specific conditions are fulfilled. For instance, a smart contract can be programmed to automatically transfer funds from one party to another upon the fulfillment of predetermined conditions, such as the successful delivery of goods or services.

Smart contracts can be used in a variety of industries, including finance, supply chain management, real estate, and more. They can help to streamline processes, reduce costs, and increase efficiency.

Overall, the use of smart contracts on block chain platforms provides a secure, transparent, and efficient way to execute agreements and enforce the terms of a contract.

Block chain can have a significant impact on the auditing profession and audit firms by offering increased transparency, better collaboration between auditors and companies, and a reduction of errors or fraud risks in audited financial statements. However, it is important to develop adequate standards and regulations to ensure effective and ethical use of block chain in the audit sector (blockchainresearchinstitute.org/consulted 11/02/2023).

17.5 Conclusion

From an accounting and auditing perspective, block chain applications have the potential to revolutionize the way financial information is recorded, stored, and verified.

The primary advantage of blockchain technology lies in its capacity to furnish a secure and unalterable record of transactions. This attribute significantly augments the precision and dependability of financial information while concurrently mitigating the risks associated with fraud and errors.

Another benefit is that block chain technology can enable real-time access to financial data, which can greatly improve the efficiency and effectiveness of audits. Auditors would no longer need to spend time gathering and reconciling data from multiple sources, as all transactions are recorded on the block chain in a consistent and transparent manner.

Additionally, the use of smart contracts on block chain platforms can automate many of the manual processes involved in accounting and auditing, such as reconciling accounts and generating financial reports. This can help to reduce errors and increase the speed of the auditing process.

However, it is important to note that while block chain has the potential to greatly improve the accounting and auditing process, it still requires human oversight and interpretation. Auditors will still need to assess the accuracy and completeness of the financial information stored on the block chain, and ensure that it complies with relevant laws, regulations, and accounting standards.

References

Abdullah, A. and Mohamed, B. (2020). How blockchain technology can improve accounting information reliability and transparency. International Journal of Accounting Information Systems 30(2): 87–96.

Alhashmi, H. M. and Al-Fazari, M. S. (2018). The potential impact of blockchain technology on the auditing profession. Auditing: A Journal of Practice & Theory 37(2): 121–140.

Alkhamisi, M. and Karim, A. A. (2021). The impact of blockchain technology on accounting and auditing: a systematic review. Journal of International Technology and Information Management 30(1): 1–22. https://doi.org/10.4018/JITIM.2021070101.

Alqahtani, M., Alrabiah, H. and Alshammari, F. (2020). The impact of blockchain technology on the auditing profession. International Journal of Auditing Technology 5(3): 105–112.

Arslan, M. and Albayrak, S. (2020). The impact of blockchain technology on accounting: Evidence from the financial sector. Journal of International Financial Markets, Institutions and Money 67: 101384. https://doi.org/10.1016/j.intfin.2019.101384.

Awan, M., Moon, J. and Min, G. (2019). Blockchain: A new opportunity for financial institutions? Bank Innovation 3: 12–17.

Böhme, R., Christin, N., Edelman, B. and Moore, T. (2015). Bitcoin: economics, technology, and governance. Journal of Economic Perspectives 29(2): 213–238.

Böhme, R. and Christen, M. (2019). The implications of blockchain technology for the auditing profession: A review. Auditing: A Journal of Practice & Theory 38(3): 1–20.

Buterin, V. (2013). A next-generation smart contract and decentralized application platform.

Deloitte. (2019). Future of finance. https://www2.deloitte.com/content/dam/Deloitte/global/Documents/About-Deloitte/gx-deloitte-future-of-finance.pdf.

Deloitte. (2020). The rise of intelligent automation in accounting and auditing. https://www2.deloitte.com/us/en/insights/focus/cognitive-technologies/intelligent-automation-accounting-auditing.html.

Deloitte. (2021). Blockchain in accounting: Opportunities and challenges. Deloitte Insights. https://www2.deloitte.com/insights/us/en/industry/financial-services/blockchain-in-accounting.html.

EY. (2021). The future of accounting: How blockchain is changing the profession. EY. https://www.ey.com/en_gl/blockchain/the-future-of-accounting-how-blockchain-is-changing-the-profession.

Forbes. (2021). AI and accounting: a powerful combination. https://www.forbes.com/sites/forbestechcouncil/2021/05/06/ai-and-accounting-a-powerful-combination/?sh=6d9d1e7d6b0c.

Gai, K., Li, L., Chen, L. and Sun, Y. (2020). Blockchain scalability: A systematic review of the state-of-the-art solutions. Future Generation Computer Systems 117: 507–521.

Garcia, D., Hurder, A., Serrano, S. and Zohar, A. (2021). On chain governance. arXiv preprint arXiv:2102.12643.

Harveston, P. D. and Li, X. (2020). Blockchain technology: A review and comparison with traditional databases. Information & Management 57(7): 102276.

Hyperledger. (2016). Hyperledger. Retrieved from https://www.hyperledger.org/.

Iqbal, J. and Raza, N. (2022). Blockchain technology in accounting: An overview. International Journal of Accounting Information Systems 27: 56–66.

Kim, D. and Lee, J. (2022). The impact of blockchain technology on auditing: Evidence from South Korean firms. International Journal of Information Management 53: 102173. https://doi.org/10.1016/j.ijinfomgt.2022.102173.

KPMG. (2021). The impact of blockchain on the accounting profession. KPMG. https://home.kpmg/xx/en/home/insights/2021/01/the-impact-of-blockchain-on-the-accounting-profession.html.

Li, Y., Zhang, X. and Du, Y. (2023). Blockchain and its impact on accounting. Journal of Accounting Research 61(2): 153–174.

Lin, J., Gao, J. and Li, Q. (2022). Blockchain for accounting: An exploratory study. Journal of Accounting and Public Policy 41(2): 102–119.

Liu, H., Jia, Y. and Chen, S. (2019). Blockchain privacy and security: A critical review of the state of the art. Future Generation Computer Systems 95: 112–121.

Liu, H., Jia, Y. and Chen, S. (2020). An overview of blockchain technology and its potential applications in finance. Journal of Financial Transformation 51: 93–102.

Malmi, T. and Ollila, S. (2019). Accounting and blockchain: a review and a research agenda. International Journal of Accounting Information Systems 31: 83–97. https://doi.org/10.1016/j.accinf.2019.05.002.

McKinsey. (2019). The future of finance functions. https://www.mckinsey.com/business-functions/strategy-and-corporate-finance/our-insights/the-future-of-finance-functions.

Nakamoto, S. (2008). Bitcoin: A peer-to-peer electronic cash system. Bitcoin.org.

Nguyen, N. T. and Tarca, A. (2021). Exploring the use of blockchain technology in accounting and auditing. The Accounting Review 96(2): 633–651.

Park, H., Lee, J. and Kim, Y. (2022). The potential impact of blockchain on the accounting profession. Current Issues in Auditing 6(2): A24–A30.

PwC. (2020). The future of audit: unlocking the full potential of technology. https://www.pwc.com/gx/en/services/audit-assurance/publications/the-future-of-audit.html.

Rashed, M. A. and Alqahtani, A. A. (2021). The impact of blockchain technology on auditing: Evidence from Saudi Arabia. International Journal of Information Management 51: 102151. https://doi.org/10.1016/j.ijinfomgt.2021.102151.

Sage. (2018). AI and the future of financial services. https://www.sage.com/content/dam/global/Sage_International/AI-and-the-Future-of-Financial-Services-Whitepaper.pdf.

Schwartz, E., Benson, M. and Konstan, J. (2020). The role of blockchain in digital identity management. IEEE Transactions on Engineering Management 67(2): 217–228.

Wang, Q., Li, J., Li, X. and Fang, Y. (2020). Blockchain energy consumption: A critical review of the state of the art. Renewable and Sustainable Energy Reviews 133: 111431.

Wang, X. and Chen, Y. (2019). Implications of blockchain for cost accounting and financial statement certification. Journal of Accounting and Finance 19(1): 1–10.

World Economic Forum. (2021). The Future of Blockchain and Cryptocurrencies. Retrieved from https://www.weforum.org/future-of-blockchain-and-cryptocurrencies.

Index